CORTINA D

D0196024

TRAVELER'S
ITALIAN
DICTIONARY

ENGLISH-ITALIAN / ITALIAN-ENGLISH

by
Dilaver Berberi, Ph.D.
Assoc. Professor of Linguistics and Languages
St. Mary's College, Notre Dame, Indiana

•

SERIES GENERAL EDITORS
Dilaver Berberi, Ph.D.
Edel A. Winje, Ed.D.

CORTINA LEARNING INTERNATIONAL, INC.
Publishers • WESTPORT, CT 06880

Library of Congress Cataloging-in-Publication Data

Berberi, Dilaver.
  Cortina Traveler's Italian dictionary: English-Italian, Italian-
English / by Dilaver Berberi.
    p.   cm.
  Rev. ed. of: Cortina/Grosset basic Italian dictionary. c1975.
  ISBN 0-8327-0724-4 (paper): $6.95
    1. Italian language—Dictionaries—English. 2. English language
—Dictionaries—Italian. I. Berberi, Dilaver. Cortina/Grosset
basic Italian dictionary. II. Title.
PC1640.B434   1993   93-19015
453'.21—dc20   CIP

Printed in the United States of America

HH Editions 9 8 7 6 5 4 3 2 1   9307-16

Contents

How to Use This Dictionary

Here is a handy, pocket-sized Dictionary that will put Italian at your fingertips. Whether you are a beginner or already have a working knowledge of Italian, whether you are a student, a businessperson, or a tourist—this Dictionary will give you what you need to get along in Italian.

The entries are the heart of the Dictionary; they number almost 11,000 (5000-plus in the English-Italian section, 5000-plus in the Italian-English section). On the English side, entries were chosen for their usefulness and applicability to common everyday situations. Italian entries were selected from words that occur most frequently in the course of everyday life in Italian-speaking countries. Thus, you will find here the words you will actually hear and speak when using Italian, whether at home or abroad. In addition, this Dictionary is unique in providing the pronunciation of the Italian words *on both sides,* so that whenever you encounter them you can immediately pronounce them.

Additional Special Features

In addition to the entries themselves, this Dictionary includes the following extra features to enable you to actually use the Italian language in a variety of different situations.

Guide to Pronunciation. The pronunciation of each Italian entry is given in simple English transcriptions. Thus, the user can pronounce a new word immediately, just by following the simple guide which appears with each entry. The "Key to Italian Pronunciation," found on page viii, explains Italian sounds and gives examples of each one, and shows how they compare with English.

Phrases for Use Abroad (page 327). Everyday expressions, requests, statements, questions and answers for specific situations—each with its pronunciation—let you communicate easily.

Menu Reader (page 337). A comprehensive list of food and drink, complete with pronunciation, takes the mystery out of Italian menus.

Concise Italian Grammar (page 343). For the user who wishes a quick overview of Italian grammar, or who wants an explanation of how verbs are conjugated or noun plurals formed, this grammar section is an invaluable aid. It is divided into sections treating nouns, verbs, adjectives, adverbs, sentence formation, etc., for easy reference and use.

Helpful Notes for the Reader

1. *All verbs* are marked *v.*, and irregular verbs are marked *irreg*. Tables of irregular verbs showing their conjugation appear at the end of the "Concise Grammar," which explains the conjugation of regular verbs.

2. *Reflexive verbs* are those that have the suffix *-si*. These are always used with the reflexive pronoun. See the "Concise Grammar" for an explanation of the use of these verbs.

3. *All Italian nouns* have a designated gender. Regularly, nouns ending in *-o* are masculine, and those ending in *-a* are feminine. Exceptions, and all other nouns, are marked *m.* or *f.* in the Dictionary. The formation of plurals of regular nouns is explained in the "Concise Grammar." Irregular plurals are given in the Dictionary along with the singular form.

4. *Adjectives* must agree in gender and number with the nouns they modify. "Gender" adjectives regularly have four forms for masculine and feminine, singular and plural, ending in *-o, -a, -i,* and *-e.* "Neuter" adjectives, ending in *-e* (singular) and *-i* (plural), are the same for both masculine and feminine.

5. *Parts of speech* of entries (except verbs) are not marked unless the translation does not indicate the part of speech or if the word appears more than once as different parts of speech.

6. *Many common or idiomatic expressions* are included in the Dictionary, along with their pronunciation, so that the reader can use them correctly.

Using this Dictionary is sure to make your contact with Italian-speaking people and their language much more pleasurable and satisfying, whether at home or abroad.

Key to Italian Pronunciation

Vowels

Unlike English vowels, Italian vowels are always pronounced the same no matter where they occur in a word. They will be transcribed, however, according to their English pronunciation. There are five vowel sounds in Italian: *i, e, u, o, a*. The following is an approximate English pronunciation of Italian vowels:

Italian spelling	Phonetic symbol	Sound description & examples
i	ee	as *i* in mach*i*ne, or as *ee* in p*ee*l, or *ea* in m*ea*t. *Ex.*: **cabina** [*kah-bee'-nah*] cabin
e	eh	as *e* in n*e*ver, in b*e*t, as the *e* (without *y*) in fate. *Ex.*: **mela** [*meh'-lah*] apple; **fedele** [*feh-deh'-leh*] faithful
u	oo	as *u* in p*u*t or as *oo* in f*oo*t. *Ex.*: **sucursale** [*soo-koor-sah'-leh*] branch
o	oh	as *o* in n*o*rth or z*o*ne. *Ex.*: **poco** [*poh'-koh*] little, few; **solo** [*soh'-loh*] alone
a	ah	as *a* in f*a*ther, b*a*rter, c*a*rbon. *Ex.*: **casa** [*kah'-zah*] house; **cassa** [*kahs'-sah*] case, box

Diphthongs

For diphthongs or two adjacent vowels, each vowel will be transcribed with its phonetic symbol:

ieri [*ee-eh'-ree*] yesterday
maiale [*mah-ee-ah'-leh*] pig
sei [*seh'-ee*] six; you (sing.) are
lui [*loo'-ee*] he
suoi [*soo-oh'-ee*] his, hers, yours (sing.) [polite form]

vii

Consonants

Italian consonants *p*, *b*, *t*, *d*, *g*, *f*, *v*, *m*, and *n* are pronounced approximately like their English counterparts.

Italian spelling	Phonetic symbol	Sound description & examples
h		is never pronounced in Italian. *Ex.*: **ho** [*oh*] I have; **hanno** [*ahn'-noh*] they have; **laghi** [*lah'-gee*] lakes
l	l	is always pronounced like the first *l* in *l*ittle, never as the second one. *Ex.*: **la luna** [*lah loo'-nah*] the moon
r	r	is pronounced with the tip of the tongue touching the upper teeth quickly and vibrating. *Ex.*: **caro** [*kah'*-roh] dear; **rame** [*rah'-meh*] copper; **Roma** [*roh'-mah*] Rome
c	ch	before vowels *i* and *e* as *ch* in *ch*ip or *ch*eat. *Ex.*: **cima** [*chee'-mah*] peak; **cena** [*cheh'-nah*] dinner
c	k	as *k* before consonants (including *h*) and before vowels *a*, *o*, *u*. *Ex.*: **carta** [*kahr'-tah*] paper; **crema** [*kreh'-mah*] cream; **pochi** [*poh'-kee*] few
g		before vowels *i* and *e* as *j* in *j*ello and *j*ust. *Ex.*: **giorno** [*jee-ohr'-noh*] day; **gesso** [*jehs'-soh*] chalk; **giacca** [*jee-ahk'-kah*] jacket
g	g	as *g* in *g*o before a consonant (including *h*) and before vowels *a*, *o*, *u*. *Ex.*: **gara** [*gah'-rah*] race; **grazie** [*grah'-tsee-eh*] thank you; **ghiotto** [*gee-oht'-toh*] greedy
gn	ny	as *ny* in ca*ny*on. *Ex.*: **agnello** [*ah-nyeh'-loh*] lamb; **signore** [*see-nyoh'-reh*] sir
gl	ly	as *lli* in mi*lli*on. *Ex.*: **maglia** [*mah'-lyah*] blouse; **egli** [*eh'-lyee*] he. EXCEPTIONS: **negligenza** [*nehg-lee-jehn'-tsah*] negli-

viii

		gence; **glicerina** [*glee-cheh-ree'-nah*] glycerine
s	s	as in *s*in at the beginning of a word and with a voiceless consonant *p*, *t*, *k*, and *f*. *Ex.*: **sete** [*seh'-teh*] thirst; **sperare** [*speh-rah'-reh*] hope; **psicologia** [*psee-koh-loh-jee'-ah*] psychology
s	z	as in *z*ebra or *z*one between two vowels and before a voiced consonant *b*, *d*, *g*, *v*, *l*, *r*, *m*, *n*. *Ex.*: **casa** [*kah'-zah*] house; **mese** [*meh'-zeh*] month; **sbaglio** [*zbah'-lyoh*] mistake
sc	sh	as in *sh*ip or *sh*ot before vowels *i* and *e*. *Ex.*: **scena** [*sheh'-nah*] scene; **scimmia** [*sheem'-mee-ah*] monkey
sc	sk	as in *sk*irt or *sk*ull before vowels *a*, *o*, *u* and before a consonant. *Ex.*: **scarpa** [*skahr'-pah*] shoe; **scritto** [*skreet'-toh*] written
z	ts	as in ca*ts*. *Ex.*: **lezione** [*leh-tsee-oh'-neh*] lesson; **pezzo** [*pehts'-tsoh*] piece
z	dz	as in be*ds*. *Ex.*: **zio** [*dzee'-oh*] uncle; **mezzo** [*mehdz'-dzoh*] half
qu	koo	as in *qu*est. *Ex.*: **quando** [*koo-ahn'-doh*] when; **quindi** [*koo-een'-dee*] then

Double Consonants

Double consonants are pronounced like single consonants but longer and stronger. The following are contrasts between single and double consonants:

caro [*kah'-roh*] dear	**carro** [*kahr'-roh*] cart
sete [*seh'-teh*] thirsty	**sette** [*seht'-teh*] seven
sano [*sah'-noh*] healthy	**sanno** [*sahn'-noh*] they know
bruto [*broo'-toh*] brute	**brutto** [*broot'-toh*] ugly

Accent or Stress

Accent or stress in Italian words usually falls on the next to the last syllable. Sometimes, however, it falls on the third from the last or on the last syllable. When the stress falls on the last syllable, the vowel is stressed also in Italian spelling with a grave accent: **città,** city; **gioventù,** youth; **finì,** he finished

Accent in this Dictionary is marked in the transcription of the word with a primary stress symbol on the stressed syllable:

matematica [*mah-teh-mah'-tee-kah*] mathematics
prendere [*prehn'-deh-reh*] take
mangiare [*mahn-jee-ah'-reh*] eat

Abbreviations Used in This Dictionary

adj.	adjective	*interr*	interrogative
adv.	adverb	*invar.*	invariable
anat.	anatomy	*irreg.*	irregular
arch.	architecture	*m.*	masculine
art.	article	*naut.*	nautical
Aux.	auxiliary verb	*n.*	noun
bot.	botanical	*obj.*	object
conj.	conjunction	*pers.*	person, personal
dem.	demonstrative	*pl.*	plural
eccl.	ecclesiastic	*prep.*	preposition
Ex.	example	*pron.*	pronoun
f.	feminine	*rel.*	relative
geog.	geographic	*sing.*	singular
indecl.	indeclinable	*subj.*	subject
interj.	interjection	*v.*	verb

English/Italian

A

a, un, uno, una, un' [*oon, oo'-noh, oo'-nah, oon*]
abandon *v.*, abbandonare [*ahb-bahn-doh-nah'-reh*]
abbey, abbazia, badia [*ahb-bah-tsee-ah, bah-dee'-ah*]
abbreviation, abbreviazione (f) [*ahb-breh-vee-ah-tsee-oh'-neh*]
abdomen, addome (m) [*ahd-doh'-meh*]
ability, abilità, capacità (f, indecl) [*ah-bee-lee-tah', kah-pah-chee-tah'*]
able *adj.*, abile, capace [*ah'-bee-leh, kah-pah'-cheh*]
  be able [can, may] *v.*, potere (irreg) [*poh-teh'-reh*]
aboard *adv. & prep.*, a bordo, a bordo di [*ah bohr'-doh, ah bohr'-doh dee*]
abolish *v.*, abolire [*ah-boh-lee'-reh*]
about [approximately] *adv.*, circa, verso [*cheer'-kah, vehr'-soh*]
about [around] *adv.*, intorno [*een-tohr'-noh*]
above *prep.*, su, sopra [*soo, soh'-prah*]
  above all, soprattutto [*soh-praht-toot'-toh*]
above-mentioned *adj.*, suddetto [*soo-deht'-toh*]
abroad *adv.*, all'estero [*ahl-lehs'-teh-roh*]
absence, assenza [*ahs-sehn'-tsah*]
absent *adj.*, assente [*ahs-sehn'-teh*]
absent-minded, distratto [*dees-traht'-toh*]
absolute *adj.*, assoluto [*ahs-soh-loo'-toh*]
absolutely, assolutamente [*ahs-soh-loo-tah-mehn'-teh*]
absorb *v.*, assorbire [*ahs-sohr-bee'-reh*]
abstract *adj.*, astratto [*ahs-traht'-toh*]
absurd, assurdo [*ahs-soor'-doh*]
abundance, abbondanza [*ahb-bohn-dahn'-tsah*]
abundant, abbondante [*ahb-bohn-dahn'-teh*]
abuse *v.*, abusare [*ah-boo-zah'-reh*]
academy, accademia [*ahk-kah-deh'-mee-ah*]
accelerate *v.*, accelerare [*ahch-cheh-leh-rah'-reh*]
accelerator, acceleratore (m) [*ahch-cheh-leh-rah-toh'-reh*]

accent n., accento [*ahch-chehn'-toh*]

accept v., accettare [*ahch-cheht-tah'-reh*]

acceptable, accettabile [*ahch-cheht-tah'-bee-leh*]

access, accesso [*ahch-chehs'-soh*]

accessible, accessibile [*ahch-chehs-see'-bee-leh*]

accident [auto, etc.], incidente (m) [*een-chee-dehn'-teh*]

accidental, accidentale [*ahch-chee-dehn-tah'-leh*]

accommodation, accomodamento [*ahk-koh-moh-dah-mehn'-toh*]

accompany v., accompagnare [*ahk-kohm-pah-nyah'-reh*]

accomplish v., compiere, realizzare [*kohm'-pee-eh-reh, reh-ah-leedz-dzah'-reh*]

accomplishment, compimento [*kohm-pee-mehn'-toh*]

accord n., accordo [*ahk-kohr'-doh*]

accordingly, in/di conseguenza [*een/dee kohn-seh-goo-ehn'-tsah*]

according to, secondo a [*seh-kohn'-doh ah*]

account n., conto, conteggio [*kohn'-toh, kohn-tehj'-jee-oh*]

    bank account, conto in banca [*kohn'-toh een bahn'-kah*]

    on account of, a causa di [*ah kah'-oo-sah dee*]

    settle an account v., regolare un conto [*reh-goh-lah'-reh oon kohn'-toh*]

    statement of account, estratto conto [*ehs-traht'-toh kohn'-toh*]

    withdraw from an account, prelevare da un conto [*preh-leh-vah'-reh dah oon kohn'-toh*]

accountant, contabile (m), ragioniere (m) [*kohn-tah'-bee-leh, rah-jee-oh-nee-eh'-reh*]

accuracy, accuratezza, esattezza [*ahk-koo-rah-tehts'-tsah, eh-zaht-tehts'-tsah*]

accurate, esatto, giusto [*eh-saht'-toh, jee-oos'-toh*]

accusation, accusa [*ahk-koo'-zah*]

accuse v., accusare [*ahk-koo-zah'-reh*]

accustom [oneself] v., abituarsi [*ah-bee-too-ahr'-see*]

    be accustomed to, essere abituato [*ehs'-seh-reh ah-bee-too-ah'-toh*]

ace [card], asso [*ahs'-soh*]

ace [fig.], campione (m) [*kahm-pee-oh'-neh*]

ache *n.*, dolore (m), male (m) [*doh-loh'-reh, mah'-leh*]
  headache, mal di testa [*mahl dee tehs'-tah*]
ache *v.*, far male [*fahr mah'-leh*]
achieve *v.*, compiere [*kohm'-pee-eh-reh*]
acid *n. & adj.*, acido [*ah'-chee-doh*]
acknowledge *v.*, riconoscere, ammettere [*ree-koh-noh'-sheh-reh, ah-meht'-teh-reh*]
acquaint *v.*, informare, far sapere a [*een-fohr-mah'-reh, fahr sah-peh'-reh ah*]
acquaintance, conoscenza [*koh-noh-shehn'-tsah*]
acquire *v.*, acquistare [*ahk-koo-ees-tah'-reh*]
acquisition, acquisizione (f) [*ahk-koo-ee-zee-tsee-oh'-neh*]
acquit *v.*, assolvere [*ahs-sohl'-veh-reh*]
acre *n.*, acro [*ahk'-roh*]
across *adv. & prep.*, attraverso [*aht-trah-vehr'-soh*]
act *n.*, atto [*aht'-toh*]
action, azione (f) [*ahts-ee-oh'-neh*]
act [do] *v.*, agire, fare [*ah-jee'-reh, fah'-reh*]
act [represent] *v.*, recitare [*reh-chee-tah'-reh*]
active, attivo [*aht-tee'-voh*]
activity, attività (f, indecl) [*aht-tee-vee-tah'*]
actor, actress, attore (m), attrice (f) [*aht-toh'-reh, aht-tree'-cheh*]
actual, attuale, reale [*aht-too-ah'-leh, reh-ah'-leh*]
actually, attualmente [*aht-too-ahl-mehn'-teh*]
adapt *v.*, adattare [*ah-daht-tah'-reh*]
add *v.*, aggiungere [*ahj-jee-oon'-jeh-reh*]
  add up [arith.], addizionare, sommare [*ahd-dee-tsee-oh-nah'-reh, sohm-mah'-reh*]
addition, addizione (f) [*ahd-dee-tsee-oh'-neh*]
additional *adj.*, supplementare [*soop-pleh-mehn-tah'-reh*]
address [place] *n.*, indirizzo [*een-dee-reets'-tsoh*]
address [speech] *n.*, discorso [*dees-kohr'-soh*]
address [a letter] *v.*, indirizzare [*een-dee-reets-tsah'-reh*]
address [speak] *v.*, rivolgere la parola a [*ree-vohl'-jeh-reh lah pah-roh'-lah ah*]
adept *adj.*, esperto [*ehs-pehr'-toh*]
adequate, adeguato [*ah-deh-goo-ah'-toh*]

adhesive *adj. & n.*, adesivo [*ah-deh-see'-voh*]
adjacent, adiacente [*ah-dee-ah-chehn'-teh*]
adjective, aggettivo [*ahj-jeht-tee'-voh*]
adjoining, attiguo, contiguo [*aht-tee'-goo-oh, kohn-tee'-goo-oh*]
adjust *v.*, aggiustare [*ahj-jee-oos-tah'-reh*]
adjustment, adattamento [*ah-daht-tah-mehn'-toh*]
administer *v.*, amministrare [*ahm-mee-nees-trah'-reh*]
administration, amministrazione (f) [*ahm-mee-nees-trah-tsee-oh'-neh*]
admirable, ammirabile [*ahm-mee-rah'-bee-leh*]
admiral, ammiraglio [*ahm-mee-rah'-lyoh*]
admiration, ammirazione (f) [*ahm-mee-rah-tsee-oh'-neh*]
admire *v.*, ammirare [*ahm-mee-rah'-reh*]
admirer, ammiratore (m) [*ahm-mee-rah-toh'-reh*]
admission [entry], ammissione (f) [*ahm-mees-see-oh'-neh*]
admit *v.*, ammettere [*ahm-meht'-teh-reh*]
admittance, ammissione (f), ingresso [*ahm-mees-see-oh'-neh, een-grehs'-soh*]
   no admittance, vietato l'ingresso [*vee-eh-tah'-toh leen-grehs'-soh*]
adopt *v.*, adottare [*ah-doht-tah'-reh*]
adoption, adozione (f) [*ah-doh-tsee-oh'-neh*]
adorable, adorabile [*ah-doh-rah'-bee-leh*]
adore *v.*, adorare, venerare [*ah-doh-rah'-reh, veh-neh-rah'-reh*]
adorn *v.*, adornare [*ah-dohr-nah'-reh*]
adult, adulto [*ah-dool'-toh*]
advance [motion] *n.*, avanzamento [*ah-vahn-tsah-mehn'-toh*]
   in advance, in anticipo [*een ahn-tee'-chee-poh*]
advance *v.*, avanzare, progredire [*ah-vahn-tsah'-reh, proh-greh-dee'-reh*]
advantage, vantaggio, beneficio [*vahn-tahj'-jee-oh, beh-neh-fee'-chee-oh*]
adverse, contrario, ostile [*kohn-trah'-ree-oh, ohs-tee'-leh*]
adventure, avventura [*ahv-vehn-too'-rah*]
adverb, avverbio [*ahv-vehr'-bee-oh*]
adversary, avversario [*ahv-vehr-sah'-ree-oh*]

advertise v., reclamizzare, fare pubblicità [*rehk-klah-meedz-dzah'-reh, fah'-reh poob-blee-chee-tah'*]

advertisement, pubblicità (f, indecl), reclame (f) [*poob-blee-chee-tah', reh'-klah-meh*]

advice, consiglio [*kohn-see'-lyoh*]

advise v., consigliare [*kohn-see-lyah'-reh*]

affair, affare (m), faccenda [*ahf-fah'-reh, fahch-chehn'-dah*]

affect v., influenzare, riguardare [*een-floo-ehn-tsah'-reh, ree-goo-ahr-dah'-reh*]

affection, affezione (f), amore (m) [*ahf-feh-tsee-oh'-neh, ah-moh'-reh*]

affectionate, affettuoso [*ahf-feht-too-oh'-zoh*]

affectionately [close of letter], affettuosamente [*ahf-feht-too-oh-zah-mehn'-teh*]

affirm v., affermare [*ahf-fehr-mah'-reh*]

affirmative adj., affermativo [*ahf-fehr-mah-tee'-voh*]

afflict v., affliggere [*ahf-fleej'-jeh-reh*]

affliction, afflizione (f) [*ahf-flee-tsee-oh'-neh*]

afloat adv., a galla [*ah gahl'-lah*]

afford to v., potere permettersi [*poh-teh'-reh pehr-meht-tehr'-see*]

 I can't afford to drink, Non posso permettermi di bere [*nohn pohs'-soh pehr-meht'-tehr-mee dee beh'-reh*]

afraid, impaurito, spaventato [*eem-pah-oo-ree'-toh, spah-vehn-tah'-toh*]

 be afraid v., avere paura [*ah-veh'-reh pah-oo'-rah*]

Africa, Africa [*ah'-free-kah*]

African, africano [*ah-free-kah'-noh*]

after adv., dopo, poi [*doh'-poh, poh'-ee*]

after prep., dopo, in seguito a [*doh'-poh, een seh'-goo-ee-toh ah*]

 after all, dopotutto [*doh-poh-toot'-toh*]

afternoon, pomeriggio [*poh-meh-reej'-jee-oh*]

 Good afternoon, Buon giorno [*boo-ohn' jee-ohr'-noh*]

afterwards, in seguito, dopo, poi [*een seh'-goo-ee-toh, doh'-poh, poh'-ee*]

again adv., ancora, di nuovo [*ahn-koh'-rah, dee noo-oh'-voh*]

 never again, mai più [*mah'-ee pee-oo'*]

once again, ancora una volta [*ahn-koh'-rah oo'-nah vohl'-tah*]

against *prep.*, contro [*kohn'-troh*]

age [era] *n.*, epoca, era [*eh'-poh-kah, eh'-rah*]

age [of a person] *n.*, età (f, indecl) [*eh-tah'*]
  of age, maggiorenne [*mahj-jee-oh-rehn'-neh*]
  under age, minorenne [*mee-noh-rehn'-neh*]

age *v.*, invecchiare [*een-vehk-kee-ah'-reh*]

agency, agenzia [*ah-jehn-tsee'-ah*]
  travel agency, agenzia di viaggi [*ah-jehn-tsee'-ah dee vee-ahj'-jee*]

agent, agente (m) [*ah-jehn'-teh*]

aggressive, aggressivo [*ahg-grehs-see'-voh*]

ago *adv.*, fa, or sono [*fah, ohr soh'-noh*]
  How long ago? Quanto tempo fa? [*koo-ahn'-toh tehm'-poh fah*]
  long ago, molto tempo fa [*mohl'-toh tehm'-poh fah*]
  two weeks ago, due settimane fa [*doo'-eh seht-tee-mah'-neh fah*]

agree *v.*, essere d'accordo [*ehs'-seh-reh dahk-kohr'-doh*]

agreeable, gradevole, piacevole [*grah-deh'-voh-leh, pee-ah-cheh'-voh-leh*]

agreement, accordo [*ahk-kohr'-doh*]

agriculture, agricoltura [*ah-gree-kohl-too'-rah*]

ahead, avanti [*ah-vahn'-tee*]
  get ahead *v.*, farsi avanti, farsi strada [*fahr'-see ah-vahn'-tee, fahr'-see strah'-dah*]

aid *n.*, aiuto, soccorso [*ah-ee-oo'-toh, sohk-kohr'-soh*]
  first aid, pronto soccorso [*prohn'-toh sohk-kohr'-soh*]

aid *v.*, aiutare [*ah-ee-oo-tah'-reh*]

aim [goal] *n.*, scopo [*skoh'-poh*]

aim (at) *v.*, mirare (a), aspirare (a) [*mee-rah'-reh (ah), ahs-pee-rah'-reh (ah)*]

air, aria [*ah'-ree-ah*]

air conditioning, aria condizionata [*ah'-ree-ah kohn-dee-tsee-oh-nah'-tah*]

airline, linea aerea [*lee'-neh-ah ah-eh'-reh-ah*]

airmail, posta aerea, via aerea [*poh'-stah ah-eh'-reh-ah,* *vee'-ah ah-eh'-reh-ah*]

airplane, aereo, aeroplano [*ah-eh'-reh-oh, ah-eh-roh-plah'-noh*]

airport, aeroporto [*ah-eh-roh-pohr'-toh*]

airsickness, mal (m) d'aria [*mahl dah'-ree-ah*]

aisle, navata [*nah-vah'-tah*]

alarm *n.*, allarme (m) [*ahl-lahr'-meh*]

alarm clock, sveglia [*zveh'-lyah*]

Albania, Albania [*ahl-bah-nee'-ah*]

Albanian, albanese [*ahl-bah-neh'-zeh*]

alcohol, alcool (m) [*ahl'-koh-ohl*]

alert *adj.*, sveglio, vigile [*zveh'-lyoh, vee'-jee-leh*]

alike, simile [*see'-mee-leh*]

alive, vivo, vivente [*vee'-voh, vee-vehn'-teh*]

all, tutto [*toot'-toh*]

   all alone, da solo, da se [*dah soh'-loh, dah seh*]

   All right! Va bene! [*vah beh'-neh*]

   not at all, niente affatto [*nee-ehn'-teh ahf-faht'-toh*]

   That's all! Ecco tutto! [*ehk'-koh toot'-toh*]

alley, vicolo [*vee'-koh-loh*]

allow *v.*, permettere [*pehr-meht'-teh-reh*]

   Allow me to . . . , Mi permetta di . . . [*mee pehr-meht'-tah dee*]

almost, quasi [*koo-ah'-zee*]

alone *adj.*, solo [*soh'-loh*]

alone *adv.*, da solo, da se [*dah soh'-loh, dah seh*]

along, lungo [*loon'-goh*]

   get along [together] *v.*, andare d'accordo [*ahn-dah'-reh dahk-kohr'-doh*]

   along with, con [*kohn*]

alongside of, accanto a [*ahk-kahn'-toh ah*]

aloud, ad alta voce [*ahd ahl'-tah voh'-cheh*]

alphabet, alfabeto [*ahl-fah-beh'-toh*]

Alps, (le) Alpi [(*leh*) *ahl'-pee*]

already, già [*jee-ah'*]

also, anche, pure [*ahn'-keh, poo'-reh*]

altar, altare (m) [*ahl-tah'-reh*]

alter *v.*, cambiare, modificare [*kahm-bee-ah'-reh, moh-dee-*

fee-kah'-reh]

alteration [clothing], modifica, ritocco [moh-dee'-fee-kah, ree-tohk'-koh]

although, benchè, sebbene [behn-keh', sehb-beh'-neh]

altitude, altitudine (f) [ahl-tee-too'-dee-neh]

altogether, nell'insieme, in tutto [nehl-leen-see-eh'-meh, een toot'-toh]

always, sempre [sehm'-preh]

am: I am, (Io) sono [(ee'-oh) soh'-noh]

  I am happy, Sono felice [soh'-noh feh-lee'-cheh]

  I am sick, Sto male [stoh mah'-leh]

amazement, meraviglia, stupore (m) [meh-rah-vee'-lyah, stoo-poh'-reh]

ambassador, ambasciatore (m), ambasciatrice (f) [ahm-bah-shee-ah-toh'-reh, ahm-bah-shee-ah-tree'-cheh]

ambiguity, ambiguità (f, indecl) [ahm-bee-goo-ee-tah']

ambition, ambizione (f) [ahm-bee-tsee-oh'-neh]

ambitious, ambizioso [ahm-bee-tsee-oh'-zoh]

ambulance, ambulanza [ahm-boo-lahn'-tsah]

America, America [ah-meh'-ree-kah]

  North America, America del Nord [ah-meh'-ree-kah dehl nohrd]

  South America, America del Sud [ah-meh'-ree-kah dehl sood]

American, americano [ah-meh-ree-kah'-noh]

among, fra, tra [frah, trah]

amount n., quantità (f, indecl) [koo-ahn-tee-tah']

amuse v., divertire [dee-vehr-tee'-reh]

  amuse oneself, divertirsi [dee-vehr-teer'-see]

amusement, divertimento, passatempo [dee-vehr-tee-mehn'-toh, pahs-sah-tehm'-poh]

amusing, divertente [dee-vehr-tehn'-teh]

an, un, uno, una, un' [oon, oo'-noh, oo'-nah, oon]

analysis, analisi (f, pl) [ah-nah'-lee-zee]

analyze v., analizzare [ah-nah-leedz-dzah'-reh]

anarchy, anarchia [ah-nahr-kee'-ah]

ancestor, antenato [ahn-teh-nah'-toh]

anchor n., ancora [ahn'-koh-rah]

ancient, antico [*ahn-tee'-koh*]

and, e, ed [*eh, ehd*]

anecdote, aneddoto [*ah-nehd'-doh-toh*]

angel, angelo [*ahn'-jeh-loh*]

anger *n.*, rabbia, furia [*rahb'-bee-ah, foo'-ree-ah*]

angle, angolo [*ahn'-goh-loh*]

angry, arrabbiato [*ahr-rahb-bee-ah'-toh*]

  get angry *v.*, arrabbiarsi [*ahr-rahb-bee-ahr'-see*]

anguish, angoscia, tormento [*ahn-goh'-shee-ah, tohr-mehn'-toh*]

animal, animale (m) [*ah-nee-mah'-leh*]

ankle, caviglia [*kah-vee'-lyah*]

anniversary, anniversario [*ahn-nee-vehr-sah'-ree-oh*]

announce *v.*, annunciare [*ahn-noon-chee-ah'-reh*]

announcement, annuncio, avviso [*ahn-noon'-chee-oh, ahv-vee'-zoh*]

annoy *v.*, dar fastidio, disturbare [*dahr fahs-tee'-dee-oh, dees-toor-bah'-reh*]

annoying, fastidioso, seccante [*fahs-tee-dee-oh'-zoh, sehk-kahn'-teh*]

annual, annuale [*ahn-noo-ah'-leh*]

anonymous, anonimo [*ah-noh'-nee-moh*]

another, un altro [*oon ahl'-troh*]

answer [reply] *n.*, risposta [*rees-pohs'-tah*]

answer *v.*, rispondere [*rees-pohn'-deh-reh*]

ant, formica [*fohr-mee'-kah*]

anticipate [pay in advance] *v.*, anticipare [*ahn-tee-chee-pah'-reh*]

anticipate [foresee] *v.*, prevedere [*preh-veh-deh'-reh*]

antidote, antidoto [*ahn-tee'-doh-toh*]

antique *adj.*, antico [*ahn-tee'-koh*]

antique *n.*, antichità (f, indecl) [*ahn-tee-kee-tah'*]

antique dealer, antiquario [*ahn-tee-koo-ah'-ree-oh*]

anxious, ansioso, inquieto [*ahn-see-oh'-zoh, een-koo-ee-eh'-toh*]

any, alcuno, qualche [*ahl-koo'-noh, koo-ahl'-keh*]

anybody, chiunque, qualcuno [*kee-oon'-koo-eh, koo-ahl-koo'-noh*]

anyhow, comunque, ad ogni modo [*koh-moon'-koo-eh, ahd oh'-nyee moh'-doh*]

anything, qualunque cosa, qualsiasi cosa [*koo-ah-loon'-koo-eh koh'-zah, koo-ahl-see'-ah-see koh'-zah*]

anyway, ad ogni modo [*ahd oh'-nyee moh'-doh*]

anywhere, dovunque, ovunque [*doh-voon'-koo-eh, oh-voon'-koo-eh*]

apart, separatamente, da parte [*seh-pah-rah-tah-mehn'-teh, dah pahr'-teh*]

apartment, appartamento [*ahp-pahr-tah-mehn'-toh*]

apiece, a testa, al pezzo [*ah tehs'-tah, ahl pehts'-tsoh*]

apologize v., scusarsi, chiedere scusa [*skoo-zahr'-see, kee-eh'-deh-reh skoo'-zah*]

apology, scusa [*skoo'-zah*]

apparatus, apparecchio [*ahp-pah-rehk'-kee-oh*]

apparent, apparente, evidente, manifesto [*ahp-pah-rehn'-teh, eh-vee-dehn'-teh, mah-nee-fehs'-toh*]

appeal n., appello, ricorso [*ahp-pehl'-loh, ree-kohr'-soh*]

appeal v., fare appello, ricorrere [*fah'-reh ahp-pehl'-loh, ree-kohr'-reh-reh*]

appear [show oneself] v., apparire, presentarsi [*ahp-pah-ree'-reh, preh-zehn-tahr'-see*]

appear [seem] v., parere, sembrare [*pah-reh'-reh, sehm-brah'-reh*]

appearance [look] n., aspetto [*ahs-peht'-toh*]

appearance [presence] n., apparizione (f), apparenza [*ahp-pah-ree-tsee-oh'-neh, ahp-pah-rehn'-tsah*]

appendicitis, appendicite (f) [*ahp-pehn-dee-chee'-teh*]

appendix [anat.], appendice (f) [*ahp-pehn-dee'-cheh*]

appetite, appetito [*ahp-peh-tee'-toh*]

appetizer [drink], aperitivo [*ah-peh-ree-tee'-voh*]

appetizer [food], antipasto [*ahn-tee-pahs'-toh*]

applaud v., applaudire [*ahp-plah-oo-dee'-reh*]

applause, applauso [*ahp-plah'-oo-zoh*]

apple, mela [*meh'-lah*]

apple pie, torta di mele [*tohr'-tah dee meh'-leh*]

application, domanda, richiesta [*doh-mahn'-dah, ree-kee-ehs'-tah*]

apply [inquire of] *v.*, rivolgersi [*ree-vohl'-jehr-see*]
  apply for, fare la richiesta [*fah'-reh lah ree-kee-ehs'-tah*]
  apply to [concern], applicare a [*ahp-plee-kah'-reh ah*]
appoint *v.*, nominare [*noh-mee-nah'-reh*]
appointment [meeting], appuntamento [*ahp-poon-tah-mehn'-toh*]
appreciate *v.*, apprezzare [*ahp-prehts-tsah'-reh*]
apprentice, apprendista [*ahp-prehn-dees'-tah*]
approach *v.*, avvicinare [*ahv-vee-chee-nah'-reh*]
appropriate *adj.*, adatto, proprio, appropriato [*ah-daht'-toh, proh'-pree-oh, ahp-proh-pree-ah'-toh*]
approval, approvazione (f) [*ahp-proh-vah-tsee-oh'-neh*]
approve *v.*, approvare [*ahp-proh-vah'-reh*]
approximately, approssimativamente [*ahp-prohs-see-mah-tee-vah-mehn'-teh*]
April, aprile (m) [*ah-pree'-leh*]
apron, grembiule (m) [*grehm-bee-oo'-leh*]
Arab *n.* & *adj.*, arabo [*ah'-rah-boh*]
Arabia, Arabia [*ah-rah'-bee-ah*]
arbitrary, arbitrario [*ahr-bee-trah'-ree-oh*]
arch *n.*, arco [*ahr'-koh*]
archbishop, arcivescovo [*ahr-chee-vehs'-koh-voh*]
architect, architetto [*ahr-kee-teht'-toh*]
architecture, architettura [*ahr-kee-teht-too'-rah*]
are: you are, we are, they are, sei (sing), siete (pl), siamo, sono [*seh'-ee, see-eh'-teh, see-ah'-moh, soh'-noh*]
  How are you? [polite form], Come sta (Lei)? [*koh'-meh stah (leh'-ee)*]
  I am fine, thanks, Sto bene, grazie [*stoh beh'-neh, grah'-tsee-eh*]
  I'm not well, Sto male, Non mi sento bene [*stoh mah'-leh, nohn mee sehn'-toh beh'-neh*]
  there is, there are, c'è, ci sono [*cheh', chee soh'-noh*]
area [measure], area [*ah'-reh-ah*]
Argentina, Argentina [*ahr-jehn-tee'-nah*]
Argentine, argentino [*ahr-jehn-tee'-noh*]
argue *v.*, disputare [*dees-poo-tah'-reh*]
argument, disputa, lite (f) [*dees-poo'-tah, lee'-teh*]

arise _v._, sorgere, alzarsi [_sohr'-jeh-reh, ahl-tsahr'-see_]
aristocracy, aristocrazia [_ah-rees-toh-krah-tsee'-ah_]
aristocratic, aristocratico [_ah-rees-toh-krah'-tee-koh_]
arithmetic, aritmetica [_ah-reet-meh'-tee-kah_]
arm [anat.] _n._, braccio (m), le braccia (pl) [_brahch'-chee-oh, leh brahch'-chee-ah_]
arms [weapon] _n._, (l') arma, (le) armi (pl) [(_l)ahr'-mah, (leh) ahr'-mee_]
armchair, poltrona [_pohl-troh'-nah_]
army, esercito, armata [_eh-zehr'-chee-toh, ahr-mah'-tah_]
around _adv._, intorno [_een-tohr'-noh_]
around _prep._, intorno a [_een-tohr'-noh ah_]
arrange _v._, sistemare, ordinare [_sees-teh-mah'-reh, ohr-dee-nah'-reh_]
arrangement, sistemazione (f), disposizione (f) [_sees-teh-mah-tsee-oh'-neh, dees-poh-zee-tsee-oh'-neh_]
arrest [legal] _n._, arresto, fermo di polizia [_ahr-rehs'-toh, fehr'-moh dee poh-lee-tsee'-ah_]
arrest _v._, arrestare [_ahr-rehs-tah'-reh_]
arrival, arrivo [_ahr-ree'-voh_]
arrive _v._, arrivare, giungere [_ahr-ree-vah'-reh, jee-oon'-jeh-reh_]
arrogance, arroganza [_ahr-roh-gahn'-tsah_]
art, arte (f) [_ahr'-teh_]
artery [anat.], arteria [_ahr-teh'-ree-ah_]
artichoke, carciofo [_kahr-chee-oh'-foh_]
article, articolo [_ahr-tee'-koh-loh_]
artificial, artificiale [_ahr-tee-fee-chee-ah'-leh_]
artist, artista (m, f) [_ahr-tees'-tah_]
artistic, artistico [_ahr-tees'-tee-koh_]
as _adv._, come [_koh'-meh_]
as [because, while] _conj._, siccome, mentre [_seek-koh'-meh, mehn'-treh_]
   as . . . as, as much as, tanto . . . quanto [_tahn'-toh, koo-ahn'-toh_]
   as for, in quanto a [_een koo-ahn'-toh ah_]
   as long as, as far as _prep._, fino a [_fee'-noh ah_]
   as long as _conj._, finché [_feen-keh'_]

as well, anche, pure [*ahn'-keh, poo'-reh*]
as yet, finora [*fee-noh'-rah*]
ascend *v.,* ascendere, salire [*ah-shehn'-deh-reh, sah-lee'-reh*]
ash, cenere (f) [*cheh'-neh-reh*]
ashamed, vergognoso [*vehr-goh-nyoh'-zoh*]
ashore, a terra [*ah tehr'-rah*]
ashtray, portacenere (m) [*pohr-tah-cheh'-neh-reh*]
Asia, Asia [*ah'-zee-ah*]
Asiatic, asiatico [*ah-zee-ah'-tee-koh*]
aside, da parte [*dah pahr'-teh*]
ask (for) *v.,* chiedere [*kee-eh'-deh-reh*]
  ask a question, domandare [*doh-mahn-dah'-reh*]
  ask [oneself], domandarsi [*doh-mahn-dahr'-see*]
asleep, addormentato [*ahd-dohr-mehn-tah'-toh*]
  fall asleep *v.,* addormentarsi [*ahd-dohr-mehn-tahr'-see*]
asparagus, asparago [*ah-spah'-rah-goh*]
aspirin, aspirina [*ahs-pee-ree'-nah*]
assault *n.,* assalto [*ahs-sahl'-toh*]
assault *v.,* assalire [*ahs-sah-lee'-reh*]
assemble [gather] *v.,* radunare, riunire [*rah-doo-nah'-reh,
  ree-oo-nee'-reh*]
assemble [put together] *v.,* montare [*mohn-tah'-reh*]
assembly, assemblea [*ahs-sehm-bleh'-ah*]
assign *v.,* assegnare [*ahs-seh-nyah'-reh*]
assist *v.,* assistere, aiutare [*ahs-sees'-teh-reh, ah-ee-oo-tah'-
  reh*]
assistance, aiuto, assistenza [*ah-ee-oo'-toh, ahs-sees-tehn'-
  zah*]
assistant, assistente (m) [*ahs-sees-tehn'-teh*]
associate *n.,* socio, collega [*soh'-chee-oh, kohl-leh'-gah*]
associate *v.,* associare [*ahs-soh-chee-ah'-reh*]
association, associazione (f) [*ahs-soh-chee-ah-tsee-oh'-neh*]
assortment, assortimento [*ahs-sohr-tee-mehn'-toh*]
assume *v.,* assumere [*ahs-soo'-meh-reh*]
assumption, supposizione (f) [*soop-poh-zee-tsee-oh'-neh*]
assurance, assicurazione (f) [*ahs-see-koo-rah-tsee-oh'-neh*]
assure *v.,* assicurare [*ahs-see-koo-rah'-reh*]
astonish *v.,* meravigliare [*meh-rah-vee-lyah'-reh*]

be astonished, meravigliarsi [*meh-rah-vee-lyahr'-see*]

astronomy, astronomia [*ahs-troh-noh-mee'-ah*]

at, a, ad (before vowel), da, di, in [*ah, ahd, dah, dee, een*]

    at all, affatto [*ahf-faht'-toh*]

    at first, al principio [*ahl preen-chee'-pee-oh*]

    at last, alla fine [*ahl'-lah fee'-neh*]

    at once, subito [*soo'-bee-toh*]

    at six o'clock, alle sei [*ahl'-leh seh'-ee*]

    at the hotel, all'albergo [*ahl-lahl-behr'-goh*]

    at the same time, allo stresso tempo [*ahl'-loh stehs'-soh tehm'-poh*]

    not at all, niente affatto [*nee-ehn'-teh ahf-faht'-toh*]

athlete, atleta (m, f) [*aht-leh'-tah*]

athletics, atletica [*aht-leh'-tee-kah*]

Atlantic, Atlantico [*aht-lahn'-tee-koh*]

atmosphere, atmosfera [*aht-mohs-feh'-rah*]

attach v., attaccare, legare [*aht-tahk-kah'-reh, leh-gah'-reh*]

attack n., attacco, assalto [*aht-tahk'-koh, ahs-sahl'-toh*]

attack v., attaccare, assalire [*aht-tahk-kah'-reh, ahs-sah-lee'-reh*]

attempt n., tentativo [*tehn-tah-tee'-voh*]

attempt v., tentare, provare [*tehn-tah'-reh, proh-vah'-reh*]

attend v., attendere, intervenire a [*aht-tehn'-deh-reh, een-tehr-veh-nee'-reh ah*]

    attend to, occuparsi, assistere [*ohk-koo-pahr'-see, ahs-sees'-teh-reh*]

attention, attenzione (f) [*aht-tehn-tsee-oh'-neh*]

attire n., abbigliamento, abiti [*ahb-bee-lyah-mehn'-toh, ah'-bee-tee*]

attitude, atteggiamento [*aht-tehj-jee-ah-mehn'-toh*]

attorney, avvocato [*ahv-voh-kah'-toh*]

attract v., attrarre (irreg) [*aht-trahr'-reh*]

attraction, attrazione (f) [*aht-trah-tsee-oh'-neh*]

attractive, attraente, piacevole [*aht-trah-ehn'-teh, pee-ah-cheh'-voh-leh*]

auction, asta [*ahs'-tah*]

audience, pubblico, udienza [*poob'-blee-koh, oo-dee-ehn'-tsah*]

August, agosto [*ah-gohs'-toh*]
aunt, zia [*dzee'-ah*]
Australia, Australia [*ah-oos-trah'-lee-ah*]
Australian, australiano [*ah-oos-trah-lee-ah'-noh*]
Austria, Austria [*ah'-oos-tree-ah*]
Austrian, austriaco [*ah-oos-tree'-ah-koh*]
authentic, autentico [*ah-oo-tehn'-tee-koh*]
author, autore (m), autrice (f) [*ah-oo-toh'-reh, ah-oo-tree'-cheh*]
authority, autorità (f, indecl) [*ah-oo-toh-ree-tah'*]
authorize v., autorizzare [*ah-oo-toh-reedz-dzah'-reh*]
automatic, automatico [*ah-oo-toh-mah'-tee-koh*]
automobile, automobile (f), macchina [*ah-oo-toh-moh'-bee-leh, mahk'-kee-nah*]
autonomy, autonomia [*ah-oo-toh-noh-mee'-ah*]
autumn, autunno [*ah-oo-toon'-noh*]
available, disponibile [*dees-poh-nee'-bee-leh*]
avalanche, valanga [*vah-lahn'-gah*]
avenue, viale (m) [*vee-ah'-leh*]
average n., media [*meh'-dee-ah*]
  on the average, in media [*een meh'-dee-ah*]
avoid v., evitare [*eh-vee-tah'-reh*]
awake adj., sveglio [*zveh'-lyoh*]
awake v., svegliare [*zveh-lyah'-reh*]
award n., premio [*preh'-mee-oh*]
aware, conscio, consapevole [*kohn'-shee-oh, kohn-sah-peh'-voh-leh*]
away, via, lontano [*vee'-ah, lohn-tah'-noh*]
  Go away! Vada via! [*vah'-dah vee'-ah*]
awful, terribile [*tehr-ree'-bee-leh*]
awkward, scomodo [*skoh'-moh-doh*]
ax, ascia [*ah'-shee-ah*]
axle, asse (m) [*ahs'-seh*]

B

baby, bimbo, bambino [*beem'-boh, bahm-bee'-noh*]
babysitter, bambinaia [*bahm-bee-nah'-ee-ah*]
bachelor, scapolo, celibe (m) [*skah'-poh-loh, cheh'-lee-beh*]
back [anat.] *n.*, schiena, dorso [*skee-eh'-nah, dohr'-soh*]
back [of a seat] *n.*, spalliera [*spahl-lee-eh'-rah*]
back [support] *v.*, appoggiare, sostenere [*ahp-pohj-jee-ah'-reh, sohs-teh-neh'-reh*]
back *adj.*, posteriore [*pohs-teh-ree-oh'-reh*]
back *adv.*, indietro [*een-dee-eh'-troh*]
  come back *v.*, ritornare [*ree-tohr-nah'-reh*]
  in back of, dietro a [*dee-eh'-troh ah*]
background, sfondo [*sfohn'-doh*]
backward *adv.*, indietro [*een-dee-eh'-troh*]
bad, cattivo [*kaht-tee'-voh*]
  Too bad! Che peccato! [*keh pehk-kah'-toh*]
badge, distintivo, insegna [*dees-teen-tee'-voh, een-seh'-nyah*]
badly, male, malamente [*mah'-leh, mah-lah-mehn'-teh*]
bad-tempered, di cattivo carattere, di malumore [*dee kaht-tee'-voh kah-raht'-teh-reh, dee mahl-oo-moh'-reh*]
bag, borsa, sacco [*bohr'-sah, sahk'-koh*]
baggage, bagaglio [*bah-gah'-lyoh*]
bake *v.*, cuocere [*koo-oh'-cheh-reh*]
bakery, panificio, forno [*pah-nee-fee'-chee-oh, fohr'-noh*]
balance *n.*, equilibrio [*eh-koo-ee-leeb'-ree-oh*]
balance *v.*, bilanciare, equilibrare [*bee-lahn-chee-ah'-reh, eh-koo-ee-lee-brah'-reh*]
balcony, balcone (m) [*bahl-koh'-neh*]
bald, calvo, pelato [*kahl'-voh, peh-lah'-toh*]
ball [dance], ballo [*bahl'-loh*]
ball [sports], palla, pallone (m) [*pahl'-lah, pahl-loh'-neh*]
ballet, balletto [*bahl-leht'-toh*]
band [music], banda [*bahn'-dah*]

bandage *n.*, benda, fascia [*behn'-dah, fah'-shee-ah*]

bank [finance], banca [*bahn'-kah*]

bank [of river], riva, ripa [*ree'-vah, ree'-pah*]

banker, banchiere (m) [*bahn-kee-eh'-reh*]

banknote, banconota [*bahn-koh-noh'-tah*]

baptism, battesimo [*baht-teh'-zee-moh*]

bar [barrier], sbarra [*zbahr'-rah*]

bar [for drinks], bar (m), taverna [*bahr, tah-vehr'-nah*]

barber, barbiere (m) [*bahr-bee-eh'-reh*]

bare *adj.*, nudo [*noo'-doh*]

barefoot, scalzo [*skahl'-tsoh*]

barely [scarcely], appena [*ahp-peh'-nah*]

bargain [merchandise] *n.*, buon affare (m) [*boo'-ohn ahf-fah'-reh*]

bark *v.*, abbaiare [*ahb-bah-ee-ah'-reh*]

barrel, barile (m) [*bah-ree'-leh*]

base *n.*, base (f) [*bah'-zeh*]

basement, seminterrato [*seh-meen-tehr-rah'-toh*]

basic, fondamentale [*fohn-dah-mehn-tah'-leh*]

basket, cesta, cestino [*chehs'-tah, chehs-tee'-noh*]

basketball, pallacanestro [*pahl-lah-kah-nehs'-troh*]

bath, bagno [*bah'-nyoh*]

   take a bath *v.*, fare il bagno [*fah'-reh eel bah'-nyoh*]

bathe, bagnare, fare il bagno [*bah-nyah'-reh, fah'-reh eel bah'-nyoh*]

bathing suit, costume da bagno (m) [*kohs-too'-meh dah bah'-nyoh*]

bathrobe, accappatoio [*ahk-kahp-pah-toh'-ee-oh*]

bathroom, stanza da bagno [*stahn'-tsah dah bah'-nyoh*]

bathtub, vasca da bagno [*vahs'-kah da bah'-nyoh*]

battery, batteria [*baht-teh-ree'-ah*]

battle, battaglia [*baht-tah'-lyah*]

bay [geog.], baia [*bah'-ee-ah*]

be *v.*, essere (irreg), stare [*ehs'-seh-reh, stah'-reh*]

   How are you? come sta? [*koh'-meh stah*]

   I am fine, thank you, Sto bene, grazie [*stoh beh'-neh, grah'-tsee-eh*]

   I don't feel well, I am sick, Non sto bene, sono malato

[*nohn stoh beh'-neh, soh'-noh mah-lah'-toh*]

be afraid, avere paura [*ah-veh'-reh pah-oo'-rah*]
be ashamed, avere vergogna [*ah-veh'-reh vehr-goh'-nyah*]
be cold, avere freddo [*ah-veh'-reh frehd'-doh*]
be hungry, avere fame [*ah-veh'-reh fah'-meh*]
be right, avere ragione [*ah-veh'-reh rah-jee-oh'-neh*]
be sleepy, avere sonno [*ah-veh'-reh sohn'-noh*]
be thirsty, avere sete [*ah-veh'-reh seh'-teh*]
be warm, avere caldo [*ah-veh'-reh kahl'-doh*]
be wrong, avere torto [*ah-veh'-reh tohr'-toh*]
beach, spiaggia [*spee-ahj'-jee-ah*]
bean, faggiolo [*fahj-jee-oh'-loh*]
bear [endure] *v.*, sopportare [*sohp-pohr-tah'-reh*]
bear [produce] *v.*, produrre [*proh-door'-reh*]
beard, barba [*bahr'-bah*]
beat [strike] *v.*, battere (irreg) [*baht'-teh-reh*]
beat [win] *v.*, vincere (irreg) [*veen'-cheh-reh*]
beautiful, bello [*behl'-loh*]
beauty, bellezza [*behl-lehts'-tsah*]
beauty parlor, salone (m) di bellezza [*sah-loh'-neh dee behl-lehts'-tsah*]
because, perchè [*pehr-keh'*]
  because of, a causa di [*ah kah'-oo-zah dee*]
become *v.*, diventare, divenire (irreg) [*dee-vehn-tah'-reh, dee-veh-nee'-reh*]
bed, letto [*leht'-toh*]
bedroom, camera da letto [*kah'-meh-rah dah leht'-toh*]
bedsheet, lenzuolo, (le) lenzuola (pl) [*lehn-tsoo-oh'-loh, (leh) lehn-tsoo-oh'-lah*]
beef, manzo [*mahn'-tsoh*]
beefsteak, bistecca [*bees-tehk'-kah*]
beer, birra [*beer'-rah*]
before [place] *adv. & prep.*, davanti [*dah-vahn'-tee*]
before [time] *adv. & prep.*, prima (di) [*pree'-mah (dee)*]
  before four o'clock, prima delle quattro [*pree'-mah dehl'-leh koo-aht'-troh*]
before *conj.*, prima che [*pree'-mah keh*]
beforehand, in anticipo [*een ahn-tee'-chee-poh*]

beg *v.*, pregare [*preh-gah'-reh*]

begin *v.*, cominciare, iniziare [*koh-meen-chee-ah'-reh, ee-nee-tsee-ah'-reh*]

behave *v.*, comportarsi [*kohm-pohr-tahr'-see*]
   Behave yourself! Comportati bene! [*kohm-pohr'-tah-tee beh'-neh*]

behavior, condotta, comportamento [*kohn-doht'-tah, kohm-pohr-tah-mehn'-toh*]

behind *adv.* & *prep.*, dietro (a) [*dee-eh'-troh (ah)*]

being *n.*, essere (m) [*ehs'-seh-reh*]

Belgian, belga (m & f) [*behl'-gah*]

Belgium, Belgio [*behl'-jee-oh*]

belief, credenza, fede (f) [*kreh-dehn'-tsah, feh'-deh*]

believe *v.*, credere [*kreh'-deh-reh*]

bell, campana [*kahm-pah'-nah*]

bellboy, facchino, fattorino [*fahk-kee'-noh, faht-toh-ree'-noh*]

belong (to) *v.*, appartenere [*ahp-pahr-teh-neh'-reh*]

belongings [personal], effetti personali [*ehf-feht'-tee pehr-soh-nah'-lee*]

below *adv.*, (di) sotto, giù [(*dee*) *soht'-toh, jee-oo'*]

below *prep.*, sotto (a) [*soht'-toh (ah)*]

belt, cintura [*cheen-too'-rah*]

bench, banco [*bahn'-koh*]

bend *v.*, piegare [*pee-eh-gah'-reh*]
   bend down, chinarsi [*kee-nahr'-see*]

benefit *n.*, vantaggio [*vahn-tahj'-jee-oh*]

beside *prep.*, accanto a, al lato di [*ahk-kahn'-toh ah, ahl lah'-toh dee*]

besides *adv.*, inoltre [*ee-nohl'-treh*]

besides *prep.*, oltre a [*ohl'-treh ah*]

best *adj.*, (il, la) migliore [(*eel, lah*) *mee-lyoh'-reh*]

best *adv.*, meglio [*meh'-lyoh*]

bet *n.*, scommessa [*skohm-mehs'-sah*]

betray *v.*, tradire [*trah-dee'-reh*]

better *adj.*, migliore, meglio [*mee-lyoh'-reh, meh'-lyoh*]

between, fra, tra [*frah, trah*]

beware [watch out] *v.*, (fare) attenzione [(*fah'-reh*) *aht-tehn-*

tsee-oh'-neh]

Beware! Guai! [*goo-ah'-ee*]
beyond, al di là, oltre [*ahl dee lah', ohl'-treh*]
Bible, bibbia [*beeb'-bee-ah*]
bicycle, bicicletta [*bee-chee-kleht'-tah*]
big, grande [*grahn'-deh*]
  very big, grandissimo [*grahn-dees'-see-moh*]
bigger, più grande [*pee-oo' grahn'-deh*]
biggest, (il, la) più grande [(*eel, lah*) *pee-oo' grahn'-deh*]
bill, conto [*kohn'-toh*]
  bill of fare, lista delle vivande [*lees'-tah dehl'-leh vee-vahn'-deh*]
bind *v.*, legare [*leh-gah'-reh*]
bird, uccello [*ooch-chehl'-loh*]
birth, nascita [*nah'-shee-tah*]
  childbirth, parto [*pahr'-toh*]
birthday, compleanno [*kohm-pleh-ahn'-noh*]
  Happy birthday! Buon compleanno! [*boo-ohn' kohm-pleh-ahn'-noh*]
bit, little bit, pezzetto, poco [*pehts-tseht'-toh, poh'-koh*]
bite *n.*, morso [*mohr'-soh*]
bite *v.*, mordere (irreg) [*mohr'-deh-reh*]
bitter, amaro [*ah-mah'-roh*]
black, nero [*neh'-roh*]
blame *n.*, colpa [*kohl'-pah*]
blame *v.*, dare la colpa (a) [*dah'-reh lah kohl'-pah* (*ah*)]
blank *adj.*, in bianco [*een bee-ahn'-koh*]
blanket, coperta [*koh-pehr'-tah*]
bless *v.*, benedire [*beh-neh-dee'-reh*]
blessing, benedizione (f) [*beh-neh-dee-tsee-oh'-neh*]
blind, cieco [*chee-eh'-koh*]
blister, bolla [*bohl'-lah*]
blonde, biondo [*bee-ohn'-doh*]
blood, sangue (m) [*sahn'-goo-eh*]
blossom *n.*, fioritura [*fee-oh-ree-too'-rah*]
blouse, blusa, camicetta [*bloo'-za, kah-mee-cheht'-tah*]
blow *n.*, colpo [*kohl'-poh*]
blow *v.*, soffiare [*sohf-fee-ah'-reh*]

blue, azzurro, blu [*ahdz-dzoor'-roh, bloo'*]

blush *v.,* arrossire [*ahr-rohs-see'-reh*]

board [lumber] *n.,* asse (f), tavola [*ahs'-seh, tah'-voh-lah*]

board [ship, train] *v.,* salire su [*sah-lee'-reh soo*]

boardinghouse, pensione (f) [*pehn-see-oh'-neh*]

boarding school, collegio, convitto [*kohl-leh'-jee-oh, kohn-veet'-toh*]

boat, barca, battello [*bahr'-kah, baht-teh'-loh*]

body, corpo [*kohr'-poh*]

boil *v.,* bollire [*bohl-lee'-reh*]

bold, coraggioso [*koh-rahj-jee-oh'-zoh*]

bomb *n.,* bomba [*bohm'-bah*]

bone, osso, le ossa (pl) [*ohs'-soh, leh ohs'-sah*]

book *n.,* libro [*lee'-broh*]

bookkeeper, contabile (m, f), ragioniere (m) [*kohn-tah'-bee-leh, rah-gee-oh-nee-eh'-reh*]

bookstore, libreria [*lee-breh-ree'-ah*]

boot, stivale (m) [*stee-vah'-leh*]

booth, cabina, [*kah-bee'-nah*]

border *n.,* confine (m), frontiera [*kohn-fee'-neh, frohn-tee-eh'-rah*]

bore *v.,* annoiare [*ahn-noh-ee-ah'-reh*]

boring, seccante, noioso [*sehk-kahn'-teh, noh-ee-oh'-zoh*]

born: be born, nascere (irreg) [*nah'-sheh-reh*]

borrow *v.,* prendere in prestito [*prehn'-deh-reh een prehs'-tee-toh*]

bosom, petto, seno [*peht'-toh, seh'-noh*]

boss *n.,* capo, padrone (m) [*kah'-poh, pah-droh'-neh*]

both, ambedue, entrambi [*ahm-beh-doo'-eh, ehn-trahm'-bee*]

   both . . . and, sia . . . sia [*see'-ah . . . see'-ah*]

bother *v.,* infastidire, seccare [*een-fahs-tee-dee'-reh, sehk-kah'-reh*]

   Don't bother! Non si preoccupi! [*nohn see preh-ohk'-koo-pee*]

   Don't bother me! Non mi disturbi [*nohn mee dees-toor'-bee*]

bottle, bottiglia [*boht-tee'-lyah*]

bottle opener, cavatappi (m) [*kah-vah-tahp'-pee*]

bottom, fondo [*fohn'-doh*]
boundary, limite (m) [*lee'-mee-teh*]
bow [salutation] *n.,* inchino [*een-kee'-noh*]
bow [of ship] *n.,* prora [*proh'-rah*]
bowels, intestini, visceri (m, pl) [*een-tehs-tee'-nee, vee'-
    sheh-ree*]
bowl, scodella [*skoh-dehl'-lah*]
box, scatola [*skah'-toh-lah*]
boxing [sport], pugilato [*poo-jee-lah'-toh*]
box office, biglietteria, botteghino [*bee-lyeht-teh-ree'-ah,
    boht-teh-gee'-noh*]
boy, ragazzo [*rah-gahts'-tsoh*]
bracelet, braccialetto [*brahch-chee-ah-leht'-toh*]
brag *v.,* vantarsi [*vahn-tahr'-see*]
brain, cervello [*chehr-vehl'-loh*]
brake *n.,* freno [*freh'-noh*]
brand [trade name] *n.,* marca [*mahr'-kah*]
brand-new, nuovo fiammante [*noo-oh'-voh fee-ahm-man'-teh*]
brandy, cognac, brandy [*koh'-nyahk, brahn'-dee*]
brass, ottone (m) [*oht-toh'-neh*]
brassiere, reggiseno [*rehj-jee-seh'-noh*]
brave, coraggioso [*koh-rahj-jee-oh'-zoh*]
Brazil, Brasile (m) [*brah-zee'-leh*]
Brazilian, brasiliano [*brah-zee-lee-ah'-noh*]
bread, pane (m) [*pah'-neh*]
break *v.,* rompere [*rohm'-peh-reh*]
breakfast, prima colazione [*pree'-mah koh-lah-tsee-oh'-neh*]
breast, petto [*peht'-toh*]
breath, respiro, fiato [*rehs-pee'-roh, fee-ah'-toh*]
breathe *v.,* respirare [*rehs-pee-rah'-reh*]
breathing, respirazione (f) [*rehs-pee-rah-tsee-oh'-neh*]
breeze, brezza [*brehts'-tsah*]
bribe *v.,* corrompere [*kohr-rohm'-peh-reh*]
brick, mattone (m) [*maht-toh'-neh*]
bride, sposa [*spoh'-zah*]
bridegroom, sposo [*spoh'-zoh*]
bridesmaid, damigella d'onore [*dah-mee-jehl'-lah doh-noh'-
    reh*]

bridge [structure], ponte (m) [*pohn'-teh*]
brief *adj.*, breve [*breh'-veh*]
bright, luminoso, chiaro [*loo-mee-noh'-zoh, kee-ah'-roh*]
bring *v.*, portare [*pohr-tah'-reh*]
   bring in, introdurre (irreg) [*een-troh-door'-reh*]
   bring together, riunire (irreg) [*ree-oo-nee'-reh*]
   bring up [rear], educare [*eh-doo-kah'-reh*]
British, britannico, inglese [*bree-tahn'-nee-koh, een-gleh'-zeh*]
broad, largo [*lahr'-goh*]
broadcast *n.*, trasmissione (f) [*trahz-mees-see-oh'-neh*]
broadcast *v.*, trasmettere [*traz-meht'-teh-reh*]
broken *adj.*, rotto, guasto [*roht'-toh, goo-ahs'-toh*]
broil *v.*, arrostire [*ahr-rohs-tee'-reh*]
bronze, bronzo [*brohn'-tsoh*]
broom, scopa [*skoh'-pah*]
broth, brodo [*broh'-doh*]
brother, fratello [*frah-tehl'-loh*]
brother-in-law, cognato [*koh-nyah'-toh*]
brown, marrone, bruno [*mahr-roh'-neh, broo'-noh*]
bruise *n.*, contusione (f) [*kohn-too-zee-oh'-neh*]
brunette, brunetta [*broo-neht'-tah*]
brush *n.*, spazzola [*spahts'-tsoh-lah*]
   clothes brush, spazzola per abiti [*spahts'-tsoh-lah pehr ah'-bee-tee*]
   paintbrush, pennello [*pehn-nehl'-loh*]
   toothbrush, spazzolino da denti [*spahts-tsoh-lee'-noh dah dehn'-tee*]
brush *v.*, spazzolare [*spahts-tsoh-lah'-reh*]
brutal, brutale [*broo-tah'-leh*]
bucket, secchia, secchio [*sehk'-kee-ah, sehk'-kee-oh*]
budget *n.*, bilancio [*bee-lahn'-chee-oh*]
bug, insetto [*een-seht'-toh*]
bulb [light], lampadina [*lahm-pah-dee'-nah*]
build *v.*, costruire [*kohs-troo-ee'-reh*]
building, edificio [*eh-dee-fee'-chee-oh*]
Bulgaria, Bulgaria [*bool-gah-ree'-ah*]
Bulgarian, bulgaro [*bool'-gah-roh*]

bulky, voluminoso [*voh-loo-mee-noh'-zoh*]
bull, toro [*toh'-roh*]
bulletin, bollettino [*bohl-leht-tee'-noh*]
bundle *n.*, fascio, pacco [*fah'-shee-oh, pahk'-koh*]
burden *n.*, carico, peso [*kah'-ree-koh, peh'-zoh*]
bureau [office], ufficio [*oof-fee'-chee-oh*]
burglar, ladro, scassinatore [*lah'-droh, skahs-see-nah-toh'-reh*]
burial, sepoltura [*seh-pohl-too'-rah*]
burn *n.*, bruciatura [*broo-chee-ah-too'-rah*]
burn *v.*, bruciare [*broo-chee-ah'-reh*]
bury *v.*, seppellire [*sehp-pehl-lee'-reh*]
bus, autobus (m) [*ah'-oo-toh-boos*]
bus line, autolinea [*ah-oo-toh-lee'-neh-ah*]
bush, cespuglio [*chehs-poo'-lyoh*]
business, affare (m), commercio [*ahf-fah'-reh, kohm-mehr'-chee-oh*]
businessman, uomo d'affari, commerciante (m, f) [*oo-oh'-moh dahf-fah'-ree, kohm-mehr-chee-ahn'-teh*]
busy, occupato [*ohk-koo-pah'-toh*]
but, ma, peró [*mah, peh-roh'*]
butcher, macellaio [*mah-chehl-lah'-ee-oh*]
butcher shop, macelleria [*mah-chehl-leh-ree'-ah*]
butter, burro [*boor'-roh*]
button, bottone (m) [*boht-toh'-neh*]
buy *v.*, comprare [*kohm-prah'-reh*]
by *prep.*, da, con, per, vicino [*dah, kohn, pehr, vee-chee'-noh*]
  by chance, per caso [*pehr kah'-zoh*]
  by hand, a mano [*ah mah'-noh*]
  by the way, a proposito [*ah proh-poh'-zee-toh*]

C

cab, tassì (m), taxi (m) [*tahs-see', tahk'-see*]
cabin, cabina, capanna [*kah-bee'-nah, kah-pahn'-nah*]

cabinet [government], gabinetto [*gah-bee-neht'-toh*]
cable v., mandare un cablogramma [*mahn-dah'-reh oon kahb-loh-grahm'-mah*]
cablegram, cablogramma (m) [*kah-bloh-grahm'-mah*]
café, caffè (m) [*kahf-feh'*]
cage, gabbia [*gahb'-bee-ah*]
cake, dolce (m), torta [*dohl'-cheh, tohr'-tah*]
calendar, calendario [*kah-lehn-dah'-ree-oh*]
call n., chiamata [*kee-ah-mah'-tah*]
   telephone call, chiamata telefonica, telefonata [*kee-ah-mah'-tah teh-leh-foh'-nee-kah, teh-leh-foh-nah'-tah*]
call v., chiamare [*kee-ah-mah'-reh*]
   call off, sospendere [*sohs-pehn'-deh-reh*]
   call on, fare una visita [*fah'-reh oo'-nah vee'-zee-tah*]
   call out, gridare [*gree-dah'-reh*]
   call up, call together, convocare [*kohn-voh-kah'-reh*]
calm adj., calmo, tranquillo [*kahl'-moh, trahn-koo-eel'-loh*]
calm v., calmare [*kahl-mah'-reh*]
   Calm down! Si calmi! [*see kahl'-mee*]
camera, macchina fotografica [*mahk'-kee-nah foh-toh-grah'-fee-kah*]
camp n., campo, campeggio [*kahm'-poh, kahm-pehj'-jee-oh*]
can n., scatola [*skah'-toh-lah*]
can [be able] v., potere (irreg) [*poh-teh'-reh*]
Canada, (il) Canada [(*eel*) *kah'-nah-dah*]
Canadian n. & adj., canadese [*kah-nah-deh'-zeh*]
canal, canale (m) [*kah-nah'-leh*]
cancel v., cancellare [*kahn-chehl-lah'-reh*]
candle, candela [*kahn-deh'-lah*]
candy, caramella [*kah-rah-mehl'-lah*]
cane, bastone (m) [*bahs-toh'-neh*]
can opener, apriscatole (m) [*ah-pree-skah'-toh-leh*]
cap n., berretto [*behr-reht'-toh*]
capable, capace [*kah-pah'-cheh*]
capacity, capacità (f, indecl) [*kah-pah-chee-tah'*]
capital [city], capitale (f) [*kah-pee-tah'-leh*]
capital [money], capitale (m) [*kah-pee-tah'-leh*]
car, automobile (f), macchina [*ah-oo-toh-moh'-bee-leh,*

mahk'-kee-nah]

  streetcar, tram (m) [*trahm*]

carbon paper, carta carbone [*kahr'-tah kahr-boh'-neh*]

card, carta, cartolina, tessera [*kahr'-tah, kahr-toh-lee'-nah, tehs'-seh-rah*]

  calling card, biglietto da visita [*bee-lyeht'-toh dah vee'-zee-tah*]

  Christmas card, cartolina di natale [*kahr-toh-lee'-nah dee nah-tah'-leh*]

  playing card, carta da gioco [*kahr'-tah dah jee-oh'-koh*]

  postcard, cartolina postale [*kahr-toh-lee'-nah pohs-tah'-leh*]

care *v.,* curarsi, importare [*koo-rahr'-see, eem-pohr-tah'-reh*]

  care for, interessarsi [*een-teh-rehs-sahr'-see*]

  I don't care, Non m'importa [*nohn meem-pohr'-tah*]

  in care of, presso [*prehs'-soh*]

  take care of, preoccuparsi, curare [*preh-ohk-koo-pahr'-see, koor-ah'-reh*]

career, carriera [*kahr-ree-eh'-rah*]

careful, attento, prudente [*aht-tehn'-toh, proo-dehn'-teh*]

  Be careful! (Faccia) Attenzione! [(*fahch'-chee-ah*) *aht-tehn-tsee-oh'-neh*]

carefully, attentamente [*aht-tehn-tah-mehn'-teh*]

careless, imprudente, trascurato [*eem-proo-dehn'-teh, trah-skoo-rah'-toh*]

cargo, carico [*kah'-ree-koh*]

carnival, carnevale (m) [*kahr-neh-vah'-leh*]

carpenter, carpentiere (m), falegname (m) [*kahr-pehn-tee-eh'-reh, fah-leh-nyah'-meh*]

carpet, tappeto [*tahp-peh'-toh*]

carriage, carrozza, vettura [*kahr-rohts'-tsah, veht-too'-rah*]

carry *v.,* portare [*pohr-tah'-reh*]

carve *v.,* scolpire, intagliare [*skohl-pee'-reh, een-tah-lyah'-reh*]

case [situation], caso [*kah'-zoh*]

  in any case, ad ogni modo [*ahd oh'-nyee moh'-doh*]

  in that case, in tal caso [*een tahl kah'-zoh*]

cash *n.,* denaro, contanti (pl) [*deh-nah'-roh, kohn-tahn'-tee*]

pay cash v., pagare in contanti [*pah-gah'-reh een kohn-tahn'-tee*]

cashier, cassiere (m) [*kahs-see-eh'-reh*]

castle, castello [*kahs-tehl'-loh*]

casually, casualmente, per caso [*kah-zoo-ahl-mehn'-teh, pehr kah'-zoh*]

cat, gatto [*gaht'-toh*]

catalog, catalogo [*kah-tah'-loh-goh*]

catch v., afferrare, prendere [*ahf-fehr-rah'-reh, prehn'-deh-reh*]

    catch cold, prendere un raffreddore [*prehn'-deh-reh oon rahf-frehd-doh'-reh*]

    catch up, raggiungere [*raj-jee-oon'-jeh-reh*]

cathedral, cattedrale (f) [*kaht-teh-drah'-leh*]

Catholic, cattolico [*kaht-toh'-lee-koh*]

cause n., causa [*kah'-oo-zah*]

cause v., causare [*kah-oo-zah'-reh*]

caution, cauzione (f), prudenza [*kah-oo-tsee-oh'-neh, proo-dehn'-tsah*]

    Caution! Attenzione! [*aht-tehn-tsee-oh'-neh*]

cave, caverna, grotta [*kah-vehr'-nah, groht'-tah*]

cease v., cessare, fermarsi [*ches-sah'-reh, fehr-mahr'-see*]

celebrate v., celebrare, festeggiare [*cheh-leh-brah'-reh, fehs-tehj-jee-ah'-reh*]

cellar, cantina [*kahn-tee'-nah*]

cement n., cemento [*cheh-mehn'-toh*]

cemetery, cimitero [*chee-mee-teh'-roh*]

censorship, censura [*chehn-soo'-rah*]

cent, centesimo [*chehn-teh'-zee-moh*]

center, centro [*chehn'-troh*]

century, secolo [*seh'-koh-loh*]

cereal, cereale (m) [*cheh-reh-ah'-leh*]

ceremony, cerimonia [*cheh-ree-moh'-nee-ah*]

certain, certo, sicuro [*chehr'-toh, see-koo'-roh*]

certainly, certamente, sicuramente [*chehr-tah-mehn'-teh, see-koo-rah-mehn'-teh*]

certificate, certificato [*chehr-tee-fee-kah'-toh*]

certify v., certificare, attestare [*chehr-tee-fee-kah'-reh, aht-*

tehs-tah'-reh]
chain, catena [*kah-teh'-nah*]
chair, sedia [*seh'-dee-ah*]
chairman, presidente (m) [*preh-see-dehn'-teh*]
challenge *n.*, sfida [*sfee'-dah*]
champagne, sciampagna [*shee-ahm-pah'-nyah*]
champion, campione (m) [*kahm-pee-oh'-neh*]
chance *n.*, caso [*kah'-zoh*]
   by chance, per caso, forse [*pehr kah'-zoh, fohr'-seh*]
   take a chance *v.*, rischiare [*rees-kee-ah'-reh*]
change [money] *n.*, resto [*rehs'-toh*]
   Keep the change, Tenga il resto [*tehn'-gah eel rehs'-toh*]
change *v.*, cambiare [*kahm-bee-ah'-reh*]
chapel, cappella [*kahp-pehl'-lah*]
chapter, capitolo [*kah-pee'-toh-loh*]
character, carattere (m) [*kah-raht'-teh-reh*]
characteristic, caratteristico [*kah-raht-teh-rees'-tee-koh*]
charge *n.*, accusa, carica [*ahk-koo'-zah, kah'-ree-kah*]
charge [a battery] *v.*, caricare [*kah-ree-kah'-reh*]
charge [a customer] *v.*, addebitare [*ahd-deh-bee-tah'-reh*]
charity, beneficenza [*beh-neh-fee-chehn'-tsah*]
charming, affascinante, attraente [*ahf-fah-shee-nahn'-teh, aht-trah-ehn'-teh*]
chart *n.*, carta, cartella [*kahr'-tah, kahr-tehl'-lah*]
charter [lease] *v.*, noleggiare [*noh-lehj-jee-ah'-reh*]
chase *v.*, cacciare [*kahch-chee-ah'-reh*]
chauffeur, autista [*ah-oo-tees'-tah*]
cheap, a buon mercato [*ah boo-ohn' mehr-kah'-toh*]
cheat *v.*, truffare [*troof-fah'-reh*]
check [bill] *n.*, conto [*kohn'-toh*]
check [receipt] *n.*, scontrino [*skohn-tree'-noh*]
check [bank] *n.*, assegno [*ahs-seh'-nyoh*]
check *v.*, controllare, verificare [*kohn-troh-lah'-reh, veh-ree-fee-kah'-reh*]
checking account, conto corrente [*kohn'-toh kohr-rehn'-teh*]
checkroom, guardaroba [*goo-ahr-dah-roh'-bah*]
cheek, guancia [*goo-ahn'-chee-ah*]
cheer *v.*, incoraggiare [*een-koh-rahj-jee-ah'-reh*]

cheerful, allegro [*ahl-leh'-groh*]
cheese, formaggio [*fohr-mahj'-jee-oh*]
cherry, ciliegia [*chee-lee-eh'-jee-ah*]
chest [anat.], torace (m), petto [*toh-rah'-cheh, peht'-toh*]
chest of drawers, cassettone (m) [*kahs-seht-toh'-neh*]
chew *v.,* masticare [*mahs-tee-kah'-reh*]
chicken, pollo [*pohl'-loh*]
chief *n. & adj.,* principale, capo [*preen-chee-pah'-leh, kah'-poh*]
chiefly, principalmente [*preen-chee-pahl-mehn'-teh*]
child, bambino [*bahm-bee'-noh*]
Chile, Cile [*chee'-leh*]
Chilean *n. & adj.,* cileno [*chee-leh'-noh*]
chilly, freddo, fresco [*frehd'-doh, frehs'-koh*]
chin, mento [*mehn'-toh*]
China, Cina [*chee'-nah*]
chinaware, stoviglie (f, pl) di porcellana [*stoh-vee'-lyeh dee pohr-chehl-lah'-nah*]
Chinese *n. & adj.,* cinese [*chee-neh'-zeh*]
chocolate, cioccolata [*chee-oh-koh-lah'-tah*]
choice, scelta [*shehl'-tah*]
choose *v.,* scegliere [*sheh'-lyeh-reh*]
chop [cut of meat] *n.,* costoletta [*kohs-toh-leht'-tah*]
   lamb chop, costoletta d'agnello [*kohs-toh-leht'-tah dah-nyehl'-loh*]
   porkchop, costoletta di maiale [*kohs-toh-leht'-tah dee mah-ee-ah'-leh*]
Christian, cristiano [*krees-tee-ah'-noh*]
Christmas, Natale (m) [*nah-tah'-leh*]
   Merry Christmas! Buon Natale! [*boo-ohn' nah-tah'-leh*]
church, chiesa [*kee-eh'-zah*]
cigar, sigaro [*see'-gah-roh*]
cigarette, sigaretta [*see-gah-reht'-tah*]
circle *n.,* circolo [*cheer'-koh-loh*]
circulation, circolazione (f) [*cheer-koh-lah-tsee-oh'-neh*]
circumstance, circostanza [*cheer-kohs-tahn'-tsah*]
circus, circo [*cheer'-koh*]
citizen, cittadino [*cheet-tah-dee'-noh*]

citizenship, cittadinanza [*cheet-tah-dee-nahn'-tsah*]

city, città (f, indecl) [*cheet-tah'*]

city hall, palazzo del municipio [*pah-lats'-tsoh dehl moo-nee-chee'-pee-oh*]

civilian, borghese [*bohr-geh'-zeh*]

civilization, civilizzazione (f) [*chee-vee-leedz-dza-tsee-oh'-neh*]

claim *n.,* pretesa [*preh-teh'-zah*]

claim *v.,* reclamare [*reh-klah-mah'-reh*]

class, classe (f) [*klahs'-seh*]

classic *n. & adj.,* classico [*klahs'-see-koh*]

classmate, compagno di scuola [*kohm-pah'-nyoh dee skoo-oh'-lah*]

classroom, aula [*ah'-oo-lah*]

clean *adj.,* pulito [*poo-lee'-toh*]

clean *v.,* pulire [*poo-lee'-reh*]

cleaner's (shop), lavanderia a secco, tintoria [*lah-vahn-deh-ree'-ah ah sehk'-koh, teen-toh-ree'-ah*]

cleaning *n.,* pulizia [*poo-lee-tsee'-ah*]

cleaning woman, donna di servizio [*dohn'-nah dee sehr-vee'-tsee-oh*]

clear *adj.,* chiaro [*kee-ah'-roh*]

clergy, clero [*kleh'-roh*]

clerk, impiegato [*eem-pee-eh-gah'-toh*]

clever, abile, astuto [*ah'-bee-leh, ahs-too'-toh*]

client, cliente (m) [*klee-ehn'-teh*]

climate, clima (m) [*klee'-mah*]

climb *v.,* scalare [*skah-lah'-reh*]

clock, orologio [*oh-roh-loh'-jee-oh*]
   at seven o'clock, alle sette [*ahl'-leh seht'-teh*]
   It is three o'clock, Sono le tre [*soh'-noh leh treh*]

close [near] *adj.,* vicino [*vee-chee'-noh*]

close *v.,* chiudere [*kee-oo'-deh-reh*]

closed *adj.,* chiuso [*kee-oo'-zoh*]

closet, armadio [*ahr-mah'-dee-oh*]

cloth, panno [*pahn'-noh*]

clothes, vestiti, abiti [*vehs-tee'-tee, ah'-bee-tee*]
   put on clothes *v.,* vestirsi [*vehs-teer'-see*]
   take off clothes *v.,* spogliarsi [*spoh-lyahr'-see*]

cloud, nuvola [*noo'-voh-lah*]
cloudy, nuvoloso [*noo-voh-loh'-zoh*]
club [association] *n.*, circolo, club (m) [*cheer'-koh-loh, cloob*]
coarse, rude, ruvido [*roo'-deh, roo'-vee-doh*]
coast, costa [*kohs'-tah*]
coat, giacca, giacche (pl) [*jee-ahk'-kah, jee-ahk'-keh*]
  overcoat, cappotto [*kahp-poht'-toh*]
coffee, caffè (m) [*kahf-feh'*]
coffeehouse, caffè (m) [*kahf-feh'*]
coin *n.*, moneta [*moh-neh'-tah*]
coincidence, coincidenza [*koh-een-chee-dehn'-tsah*]
cold, freddo [*frehd'-doh*]
  be cold *v.*, avere freddo [*ah-veh'-reh frehd'-doh*]
  catch a cold *v.*, raffreddarsi [*rahf-frehd-dahr'-see*]
  Are you cold? Ha freddo? [*ah frehd'-doh*]
collar, colletto [*kohl-leht'-toh*]
colleague, collega (m, f) [*kohl-leh'-gah*]
collect *v.*, raccogliere [*rahk-koh'-lyeh-reh*]
collection, raccolta [*rahk-kohl'-tah*]
college, università (f, indecl) [*oo-nee-vehr-see-tah'*]
collide *v.*, urtare [*oor-tah'-reh*]
colloquial, lingua popolare [*leen'-goo-ah poh-poh-lah'-reh*]
color, colore (m) [*koh-loh'-reh*]
Colosseum, Colosseo [*koh-lohs-seh'-oh*]
column, colonna [*koh-lohn'-nah*]
comb *n.*, pettine (m) [*peht'-tee-neh*]
combination, combinazione (f) [*kohm-bee-nah-tsee-oh'-neh*]
combustible, combustibile [*kohm-boos-tee'-bee-leh*]
come *v.*, venire (irreg) [*veh-nee'-reh*]
  come about, accadere [*ahk-kah-deh'-reh*]
  come after, seguire [*seh-goo-ee'-reh*]
  come again, come back, ritornare [*ree-tohr-nah'-reh*]
  come by, passare [*pahs-sah'-reh*]
  come down, discendere [*dee-shehn'-deh-reh*]
  come forward, presentarsi [*preh-zehn-tahr'-see*]
  come in, entrare [*ehn-trah'-reh*]
  Come in! Avanti! [*ah-vahn'-tee*]
  Come on! Via!, Andiamo! [*vee'-ah ahn-dee-ah'-moh*]

comfort, comodità (f, indecl) [*koh-moh-dee-tah'*]
comfortable, comodo [*koh'-moh-doh*]
  Are you comfortable? Sta comodo? [*stah koh'-moh-doh*]
command *n.*, ordine (m) [*ohr'-dee-neh*]
command *v.*, comandare, controllare [*koh-mahn-dah'-reh, kohn-troh-lah'-reh*]
comment *n.*, commento [*kohm-mehn'-toh*]
commentary, commentario [*kohm-mehn-tah'-ree-oh*]
commercial, commerciale [*kohm-mehr-chee-ah'-leh*]
commission, commissione (f) [*kohm-mees-see-oh'-neh*]
commit *v.*, commettere [*kohm-meht'-teh-reh*]
common, comune [*koh-moo'-neh*]
commotion, commozione (f) [*kohm-moh-tsee-oh'-neh*]
communicate *v.*, comunicare [*koh-moo-nee-kah'-reh*]
communication, comunicazione (f) [*koh-moo-nee-kah-tsee-oh'-neh*]
communist, comunista (m, f) [*koh-moo-nees'-tah*]
community, comunità (undecl) [*koh-moo-nee-tah'*]
companion, compagno [*kohm-pah'-nyoh*]
compare *v.*, comparare, paragonare [*kohm-pah-rah'-reh, pah-rah-goh-nah'-reh*]
comparison, comparazione (f), paragone (m) [*kohm-pah-rah-tsee-oh'-neh, pah-rah-goh'-neh*]
compartment, scompartimento [*skohm-pahr-tee-mehn'-toh*]
compass, bussola [*boos'-soh-lah*]
compassion, compassione (f) [*kohm-pahs-see-oh'-neh*]
compel *v.*, costringere [*kohs-treen'-jeh-reh*]
compensation, compensazione (f) [*kohm-pehn-sah-tsee-oh'-neh*]
competent, competente [*kohm-peh-tehn'-teh*]
competition, concorrenza, competizione (f) [*kohn-kohr-rehn'-tsah, kohm-peh-tee-tsee-oh'-neh*]
compile *v.*, compilare [*kohm-pee-lah'-reh*]
complain *v.*, lagnarsi [*lah-nyahr'-see*]
complaint, protesto, lagnanza [*proh-tehs'-toh, lah-nyahn'-tsah*]
complete, completo [*kohm-pleh'-toh*]
completely, completamente [*kohm-pleh-tah-mehn'-teh*]

complex, complesso [*kohm-plehs'-soh*]
complexion [of skin], carnagione (f) [*kahr-nah-jee-oh'-neh*]
complicated, complicato [*kohm-plee-kah'-toh*]
compliment, complimento [*kohm-plee-mehn'-toh*]
compose v., comporre (irreg) [*kohm-pohr'-reh*]
composer, compositore (m) [*kohm-poh-zee-toh'-reh*]
composure, compostezza [*kohm-pohs-tehts'-tsa*]
comprehend v., comprendere [*kohm-prehn'-deh-reh*]
compromise, compromesso [*kohm-proh-mehs'-soh*]
conceal v., nascondere [*nahs-kohn'-deh-reh*]
conceited, vanitoso [*vah-nee-toh'-zoh*]
conceive v., concepire [*kohn-cheh-pee'-reh*]
concentrate v., concentrare [*kohn-chehn-trah'-reh*]
concept, concetto [*kohn-cheht'-toh*]
concerning, riguardo a [*ree-goo-ahr'-doh ah*]
concert, concerto [*kohn-chehr'-toh*]
concise, conciso [*kohn-chee'-zoh*]
conclusion, conclusione (f) [*kohn-kloo-zee-oh'-neh*]
condemn v., condannare [*kohn-dahn-nah'-reh*]
condense v., condensare [*kohn-dehn-sah'-reh*]
condition, condizione (f) [*kohn-dee-tsee-oh'-neh*]
  in good condition, in buono stato [*een boo-oh'-noh stah'-toh*]
conduct n., condotta [*kohn-doht'-tah*]
conduct v., condurre (irreg) [*kohn-door'-reh*]
conductor [of orchestra], direttore (m) [*dee-reht-toh'-reh*]
conductor [of train], conduttore (m) [*kohn-doot-toh'-reh*]
conference, conferenza [*kohn-feh-rehn'-tsah*]
confess v., confessare [*kohn-fehs-sah'-reh*]
confession, confessione (f) [*kohn-fehs-see-oh'-neh*]
confident, fiducioso [*fee-doo-chee-oh'-zoh*]
confidential, confidenziale [*kohn-fee-dehn-tsee-ah'-leh*]
confirm v., confermare [*kohn-fehr-mah'-reh*]
conflict n., conflitto [*kohn-fleet'-toh*]
conflict v., contrastare [*kohn-trahs-tah'-reh*]
confusion, confusione (f) [*kohn-foo-zee-oh'-neh*]
congratulate v., congratularsi [*kohn-grah-too-lahr'-see*]
  Congratulations! Congratulazioni! [*kohn-grah-too-lah-*

  tsee-oh'-nee]
connection, connessione (f) [*kohn-nehs-see-oh'-neh*]
conquer *v.*, conquistare [*kohn-koo-ees-tah'-reh*]
conscientious, coscienzioso [*kohn-shee-ehn-tsee-oh'-zoh*]
conscious, conscio [*kohn'-shee-oh*]
consecutive, consecutivo [*kohn-seh-koo-tee'-voh*]
consent *n.*, consenso [*kohn-sehn'-soh*]
consent *v.*, acconsentire [*ahk-kohn-sehn-tee'-reh*]
consequence, conseguenza [*kohn-seh-goo-ehn'-tsah*]
conservative, conservativo [*kohn-sehr-vah-tee'-voh*]
consider *v.*, considerare [*kohn-see-deh-rah'-reh*]
consideration, considerazione (f) [*kohn-see-deh-rah-tsee-oh'-neh*]
consist *v.*, consistere [*kohn-sees'-teh-reh*]
consistent, compatibile [*kohm-pah-tee'-bee-leh*]
constant, costante [*kohs-tahn'-teh*]
constitute *v.*, costituire [*kohs-tee-too-ee'-reh*]
constitution, costituzione (f) [*kohs-tee-too-tsee-oh'-neh*]
construction, costruzione (f) [*kohs-troo-tsee-oh'-neh*]
consul, console (m) [*kohn'-soh-leh*]
consulate, consolato [*kohn-soh-lah'-toh*]
consult *v.*, consultare [*kohn-sool-tah'-reh*]
consume *v.*, consumare [*kohn-soo-mah'-reh*]
consumer, consumatore (m) [*kohn-soo-mah-toh'-reh*]
contagious, contagioso [*kohn-tah-jee-oh'-zoh*]
contain *v.*, contenere [*kohn-teh-neh'-reh*]
container, recipiente (m) [*reh-chee-pee-ehn'-teh*]
contemporary, contemporaneo [*kohn-tehm-poh-rah'-neh-oh*]
contempt, disprezzo [*dees-prehts'-tsoh*]
content *adj.*, contento [*kohn-tehn'-toh*]
contents, contenuto [*kohn-teh-noo'-toh*]
contest *n.*, concorso [*kohn-kohr'-soh*]
continent, continente (m) [*kohn-tee-nehn'-teh*]
continuation, continuazione (f) [*kohn-tee-noo-ah-tsee-oh'-neh*]
continue *v.*, continuare [*kohn-tee-noo-ah'-reh*]
contract *n.*, contratto [*kohn-traht'-toh*]
contradiction, contradizione (f) [*kohn-trah-dee-tsee-oh'-neh*]

contrary, contrario [*kohn-trah'-ree-oh*]
  on the contrary, al contrario [*ahl kohn-trah'-ree-oh*]
contrast *n.,* contrasto [*kohn-trahs'-toh*]
contribute *v.,* contribuire [*kohn-tree-boo-ee'-reh*]
contribution, contribuzione (f) [*kohn-tree-boo-tsee-oh'-neh*]
control *n.,* controllo [*kohn-trohl'-loh*]
control *v.,* controllare [*kohn-trohl-lah'-reh*]
controversy, controversia, disputa [*kohn-troh-vehr'-see-ah, dees'-poo-tah*]
convenient, conveniente [*kohn-veh-nee-ehn'-teh*]
convent, convento [*kohn-vehn'-toh*]
conversation, conversazione (f) [*kohn-vehr-sah-tsee-oh'-neh*]
convert *v.,* convertire [*kohn-vehr-tee'-reh*]
convict *n.,* condannato [*kohn-dah-nah'-toh*]
convince *v.,* convincere [*kohn-veen'-cheh-reh*]
cook *n.,* cuoco [*koo-oh'-koh*]
cook *v.,* cucinare [*koo-chee-nah'-reh*]
cool *adj.,* fresco [*frehs'-koh*]
cool *v.,* raffreddare [*rahf-frehd-dah'-reh*]
cooperation, cooperazione (f) [*koh-oh-peh-rah-tsee-oh'-neh*]
copper *n.,* rame (m) [*rah'-meh*]
copy *n.,* copia [*koh'-pee-ah*]
copy *v.,* copiare [*koh-pee-ah'-reh*]
cord, corda [*kohr'-dah*]
cordial, cordiale [*kohr-dee-ah'-leh*]
cork, tappo [*tahp'-poh*]
corkscrew, cavatappi (m, sing) [*kah-vah-tahp'-pee*]
corn, granoturco [*grah-noh-toor'-koh*]
corner, angolo [*ahn'-goh-loh*]
corporation, corporazione (f) [*kohr-poh-rah-tsee-oh'-neh*]
correct *adj.,* corretto [*kohr-reht'-toh*]
correction, correzione (f) [*kohr-reh-tsee-oh'-neh*]
correspondence, corrispondenza [*kohr-rees-pohn-dehn'-tsah*]
corridor, corridoio [*kohr-ree-doh'-ee-oh*]
corrupt *adj.,* corrotto [*kohr-roht'-toh*]
cosmetics, cosmetici [*kohz-meh'-tee-chee*]
cost *n.,* costo, spesa [*kohs'-toh, speh'-zah*]
cost of living, costo della vita [*kohs'-toh dehl'-lah vee'-tah*]

cost v., costare [*kohs-tah'-reh*]
  How much does this cost? Quanto costa questo? [*koo-ahn'-toh kohs'-tah koo-ehs'-toh*]
cot, branda [*brahn'-dah*]
cottage, casa di campagna [*kah'-zah dee kahm-pah'-nyah*]
cotton, cotone (m) [*koh-toh'-neh*]
couch, divano [*dee-vah'-noh*]
cough n., tosse (f) [*tohs'-seh*]
cough v., tossire [*tohs-see'-reh*]
counsel v., concigliare [*kohn-chee-lyah'-reh*]
count v., contare [*kohn-tah'-reh*]
  count on, contare su [*kohn-tah'-reh soo*]
country, nazione (f), paese (m) [*nah-tsee-oh'-neh, pah-eh'-zeh*]
country house, casa di campagna [*kah'-zah dee kahm-pah'-nyah*]
countryman, compatriota [*kohm-pah-tree-oh'-tah*]
countryside, campagna [*kahm-pah'-nyah*]
couple n., coppia [*kohp'-pee-ah*]
coupon, scontrino [*skohn-tree'-noh*]
courage, coraggio [*koh-rahj'-jee-oh*]
courageous, coraggioso [*koh-rahj-jee-oh'-zoh*]
course [way], corso [*kohr'-soh*]
  of course, naturalmente [*nah-too-rahl-mehn'-teh*]
  a matter of course, una cosa ovvia [*oo'-nah koh'-zah ohv'-vee-ah*]
course [of a meal], portata [*pohr-tah'-tah*]
court, corte (f), tribunale (m) [*kohr'-teh, tree-boo-nah'-leh*]
courteous, cortese [*kohr-teh'-zeh*]
courtyard, cortile (m) [*kohr-tee'-leh*]
cousin [female], cugina [*koo-jee'-nah*]
cousin [male], cugino [*koo-jee'-noh*]
cover n., copertura [*koh-pehr-too'-rah*]
cover v., coprire [*koh-pree'-reh*]
coward, vigliacco [*vee-lyahk'-koh*]
cracker, biscotto [*bees-koht'-toh*]
cradle, culla [*kool'-lah*]
craftsman, artigiano [*ahr-tee-jee-ah'-noh*]

crash *n.*, fracasso [*frah-kahs'-soh*]
crawl *v.*, strisciarsi [*stree-shee-ahr'-see*]
crazy, pazzo [*pahts'-tsoh*]
cream, crema [*kreh'-mah*]
create *v.*, creare [*kreh-ah'-reh*]
creation, creazione (f) [*kreh-ah-tsee-oh'-neh*]
creature, creatura [*kreh-ah-too'-rah*]
credit *n.*, credito [*kreh'-dee-toh*]
creditor, creditore (m) [*kreh-dee-toh'-reh*]
crew, equipaggio [*eh-koo-ee-pahj'-jee-oh*]
crib, letto da bambino [*leht'-toh dah bahm-bee'-noh*]
crime, crimine (m) [*kree'-mee-neh*]
criminal, criminale [*kree-mee-nah'-leh*]
crisis, crisi (f) [*kree'-zee*]
critical, critico [*kree'-tee-koh*]
criticize *v.*, criticare [*kree-tee-kah'-reh*]
crook [cheat], imbroglione (m) [*eem-broh-lyoh'-neh*]
crop *n.*, raccolto [*rahk-kohl'-toh*]
cross *n.*, croce (f) [*kroh'-cheh*]
cross *v.*, attraversare [*aht-trah-vehr-sah'-reh*]
crossing, traversata [*trah-vehr-sah'-tah*]
crossroad, incrocio [*een-kroh'-chee-oh*]
crowd, folla [*fohl'-lah*]
crowded, affollato [*ahf-fohl-lah'-toh*]
crown *n.*, corona [*koh-roh'-nah*]
cruel, crudele [*kroo-deh'-leh*]
cruelty, crudeltà (f, indecl) [*kroo-dehl-tah'*]
cruise *n.*, crociera [*kroh-chee-eh'-rah*]
crumb, briciola [*bree'-chee-oh-lah*]
crush *v.*, schiacciare [*skee-ahch-chee-ah'-reh*]
cry *n.*, grido [*gree'-doh*]
cry [weep] *v.*, piangere [*pee-ahn'-jeh-reh*]
cry [shout] *v.*, gridare [*gree-dah'-reh*]
crystal, cristallo [*krees-tahl'-loh*]
cube, cubo [*koo'-boh*]
culture [intellectual], cultura [*kool-too'-rah*]
cunning, astuto [*ahs-too'-toh*]
cup, tazza [*tahts'-tsah*]

cupboard, credenza [*kreh-dehn'-tsah*]
cure *v.,* curare [*koo-rah'-reh*]
curiosity, curiosità (f, indecl) [*koo-ree-oh-zee-tah'*]
curious, curioso [*koo-ree-oh'-zoh*]
currency, moneta corrente [*moh-neh'-tah kohr-rehn'-teh*]
current *n.* & *adj.,* corrente (f) [*kohr-rehn'-teh*]
curse *n.,* maledizione (f) [*mah-leh-dee-tsee-oh'-neh*]
curtain, tenda, cortina [*tehn'-dah, kohr-tee'-nah*]
curve, curva [*koor'-vah*]
  dangerous curve, curva pericolosa [*koor'-vah peh-ree-koh-loh'-zah*]
cushion, cuscino [*koo-shee'-noh*]
custody, custodia [*koos-toh'-dee-ah*]
custom, costume (m), usanza [*kohs-too'-meh, oo-zahn'-tsah*]
customary, abituale [*ah-bee-too-ah'-leh*]
customer, cliente (m) [*klee-ehn'-teh*]
customs, customshouse, dogana [*doh-gah'-nah*]
customs duty, dazio di dogana [*dah'-tsee-oh dee doh-gah'-nah*]
customs officer, agente di dogana [*ah-jehn'-teh dee doh-gah'-nah*]
cut [wound] *n.,* ferita [*feh-ree'-tah*]
cut [pattern] *n.,* taglio [*tah'-lyoh*]
cut *v.,* tagliare [*tah-lyah'-reh*]
cylinder, cilindro [*chee-leen'-droh*]
Czechoslovak *n.* & *adj.,* ceco-slovacco [*cheh-koh-sloh-vahk'-koh*]
Czechoslovakia, Ceco-slovacchia [*cheh-kohs-loh-vahk-kee'-ah*]

D

dad, daddy, papà, babbo [*pah-pah', bahb'-boh*]
daily, quotidiano, giornalmente [*koo-oh-tee-dee-ah'-noh, jee-ohr-nahl-mehn'-teh*]

dairy, latteria [*laht-teh-ree'-ah*]

dam *n.*, diga [*dee'-gah*]

damage *v.*, danneggiare [*dahn-nehj-jee-ah'-reh*]

damaged, danneggiato [*dahn-nej-jee-ah'-toh*]

damp, umido [*oo'-mee-doh*]

dance *n.*, danza [*dahn'-tsah*]

dance *v.*, ballare [*bahl-lah'-reh*]

dancer, ballerino, ballerina [*bahl-leh-ree'-noh, bahl-leh-ree'-nah*]

danger, pericolo [*peh-ree'-koh-loh*]

dangerous, pericoloso [*peh-ree-koh-loh'-zoh*]

dare [attempt] *v.*, osare [*oh-zah'-reh*]

daring, intrepido [*een-treh'-pee-doh*]

dark, buio [*boo'-ee-oh*]

   dark complexion, bruno [*broo'-noh*]

darkness, oscurità (f, indecl) [*ohs-koo-ree-tah'*]

darling *adj.*, caro [*kah'-roh*]

date [day] *n.*, data [*dah'-tah*]

date [appointment] *n.*, appuntamento [*ahp-poon-tah-mehn'-toh*]

daughter, figlia [*fee'-lyah*]

daughter-in-law, nuora [*noo-oh'-rah*]

dawn, alba, aurora [*ahl'-bah, ah-oo-roh'-rah*]

day, giorno [*jee-ohr'-noh*]

   all day, tutto il giorno [*toot'-toh eel jee-ohr'-noh*]

   day after tomorrow, dopodomani [*doh-poh-doh-mah'-nee*]

   day before yesterday, l'altro ieri [*lahl-troh ee-eh'-ree*]

   every day, ogni giorno [*oh'-nyee jee-ohr'-noh*]

   the next day, il giorno prossimo [*eel jee-ohr'-noh prohs'-see-moh*]

   twice a day, due volte al giorno [*doo'-eh vohl'-teh ahl jee-ohr'-noh*]

daydream, sogno ad occhi aperti [*soh'-nyoh ahd ohk'-kee ah-pehr'-tee*]

dead, morto [*mohr'-toh*]

deadly, mortale [*mohr-tah'-leh*]

deaf, sordo [*sohr'-doh*]

deal *n.*, affare (m) [*ahf-fah'-reh*]

a great deal, molto [*mohl'-toh*]

deal *v.*, trattare [*traht-tah'-reh*]

dealer, negoziante (m) [*neh-goh-tsee-ahn'-teh*]

dear *adj.*, caro [*kah'-roh*]

dearly, caramente [*kah-rah-mehn'-teh*]

death, morte (f) [*mohr'-teh*]

debt, debito [*deh'-bee-toh*]

decade, decennio [*deh-chehn'-nee-oh*]

decay *n.*, decadenza, rovina [*deh-kah-dehn'-tsah, roh-vee'-nah*]

deceased, defunto [*deh-foon'-toh*]

deceit, inganno [*een-gahn'-noh*]

deceive *v.*, ingannare [*een-gahn-nah'-reh*]

December, dicembre (m) [*dee-chehm'-breh*]

decency, correttezza [*kohr-reht-tehts'-tsah*]

decent, decente [*deh-chehn'-teh*]

deception, illusione (f) [*eel-loo-zee-oh'-neh*]

deck [of ship], ponte (m) [*pohn'-teh*]

deck [of cards], mazzo [*mahts'-tsoh*]

decide *v.*, decidere [*deh-chee'-deh-reh*]

decision, decisione (f) [*deh-chee-zee-oh'-neh*]

declare *v.*, dichiarare [*dee-kee-ah-rah'-reh*]

decline [refuse] *v.*, declinare [*deh-klee-nah'-reh*]

decorate *v.*, decorare [*deh-koh-rah'-reh*]

decoration, decorazione (f) [*deh-koh-rah-tsee-oh'-neh*]

decrease *v.*, diminuire [*dee-mee-noo-ee'-reh*]

decree, decreto [*deh-kreh'-toh*]

dedicate *v.*, consacrare, dedicare [*kohn-sah-krah'-reh, deh-dee-kah'-reh*]

deed [act], fatto, azione (f) [*faht'-toh, ah-tsee-oh'-neh*]

deep, profondo [*proh-fohn'-doh*]

defeat *n.*, sconfitta [*skohn-feet'-tah*]

defeat *v.*, sconfiggere [*skohn-feej'-jeh-reh*]

defective, difettoso [*dee-feht-toh'-zoh*]

defend *v.*, difendere [*dee-fehn'-deh-reh*]

deficient, deficiente [*deh-fee-chee-ehn'-teh*]

define *v.*, definire [*deh-fee-nee'-reh*]

definite, definito [*deh-fee-nee'-toh*]

definition, definizione (f) [*deh-fee-nee-tsee-oh'-neh*]
degree, grado, laurea [*grah'-doh, lah'-oo-reh-ah*]
delay v., ritardare [*ree-tahr-dah'-reh*]
deliberate v., deliberare [*deh-lee-beh-rah'-reh*]
delicate, delicato [*deh-lee-kah'-toh*]
delicious, delizioso [*deh-lee-tsee-oh'-zoh*]
delight n., diletto [*dee-leht'-toh*]
delight v., dilettare [*dee-leht-tah'-reh*]
deliver v., consegnare [*kohn-seh-nyah'-reh*]
demand n., richiesta [*ree-kee-ehs'-tah*]
demand v., richiedere [*ree-kee-eh'-deh-reh*]
democracy, democrazia [*deh-moh-krah-tsee'-ah*]
demonstrate v., dimostrare [*dee-mohs-trah'-reh*]
demonstration, dimostrazione (f) [*dee-mohs-trah-tsee-oh'-neh*]
denial, rifiuto [*ree-fee-oo'-toh*]
dentist, dentista (m) [*dehn-tees'-tah*]
deny v., negare [*neh-gah'-reh*]
depart v., partire [*pahr-tee'-reh*]
department, dipartimento [*dee-pahr-tee-mehn'-toh*]
departure, partenza [*pahr-tehn'-tsah*]
depend on v., dipendere da [*dee-pehn'-deh-reh dah*]
   That depends, Dipende [*dee-pehn'-deh*]
dependent, dipendente [*dee-pehn-dehn'-teh*]
deposit v., depositare [*deh-poh-zee-tah'-reh*]
depot, magazzino [*mah-gahdz-dzee'-noh*]
deprive v., privare [*pree-vah'-reh*]
depth, profondità (f, indecl) [*proh-fohn-dee-tah'*]
deputy, deputato [*deh-poo-tah'-toh*]
descend v., discendere [*dee-shehn'-deh-reh*]
describe v., descrivere [*dehs-kree'-veh-reh*]
description, descrizione (f) [*dehs-kree-tsee-oh'-neh*]
desert n., deserto [*deh-zehr'-toh*]
desert v., disertare [*dee-zehr-tah'-reh*]
deserve v., meritare [*meh-ree-tah'-reh*]
design n., disegno [*dee-zeh'-nyoh*]
desirable, desiderabile [*deh-zee-deh-rah'-bee-leh*]
desire n., desiderio [*deh-zee-deh'-ree-oh*]
desire v., desiderare [*deh-zee-deh-rah'-reh*]

desk, scrivania [*skree-vah-nee'-ah*]

despair *n.*, disperazione (f) [*dees-peh-rah-tsee-oh'-neh*]

desperate, disperato [*dees-peh-rah'-toh*]

despite, malgrado [*mahl-grah'-doh*]

dessert, dolce [*dohl'-cheh*]

destiny, destino [*dehs-tee'-noh*]

destroy *v.*, distruggere [*dees-trooj'-jeh-reh*]

destruction, distruzione (f) [*dees-troo-tsee-oh'-neh*]

detail, dettaglio [*deht-tah'-lyoh*]

detain *v.*, trattenere [*traht-teh-neh'-reh*]

detective, agente (investigativo) (m) [*ah-jehn'-teh (een-vehs-tee-gah-tee'-voh)*]

determine *v.*, determinare [*deh-tehr-mee-nah'-reh*]

detour *n.*, deviazione (f) [*deh-vee-ah-tsee-oh'-neh*]

develop *v.*, sviluppare [*zvee-loop-pah'-reh*]

development, sviluppo [*zvee-loop'-poh*]

device, meccanismo [*mehk-kah-neez'-moh*]

devil, diavolo [*dee-ah'-voh-loh*]

devoted, devoto [*deh-voh'-toh*]

devotion, devozione (f) [*deh-voh-tsee-oh'-neh*]

diagnosis, diagnosi (f, sing) [*dee-ahg-noh'-zee*]

dialect, dialetto [*dee-ah-leht'-toh*]

dialogue, dialogo [*dee-ah'-loh-goh*]

diameter, diametro [*dee-ah'-meh-troh*]

diamond, diamante (m) [*dee-ah-mahn'-teh*]

diary, diario [*dee-ah'-ree-oh*]

dice [gambling] *n. pl.*, dadi (pl) [*dah'-dee*]

dictate *v.*, dettare [*deht-tah'-reh*]

dictation, dettato [*deht-tah'-toh*]

dictionary, dizionario [*dee-tsee-oh-nah'-ree-oh*]

die *v.*, morire (irreg) [*moh-ree'-reh*]

diet *n.*, dieta [*dee-eh'-tah*]

difference, differenza [*deef-feh-rehn'-tsah*]

  It does not make any difference, É la stessa cosa [*eh' lah stehs'-sah koh'-zah*]

  What difference does it make? Che importa? [*keh eem-pohr'-tah*]

different, differente [*deef-feh-rehn'-teh*]

difficult, difficile [*deef-fee'-chee-leh*]

difficulty, difficoltà (f, indecl) [*deef-fee-kohl-tah'*]

dig *v.*, scavare [*skah-vah'-reh*]

digestion, digestione (f) [*dee-jehs-tee-oh'-neh*]

dignity, dignità (f, indecl) [*dee-nyee-tah'*]

dim *adj.*, oscuro [*ohs-koo'-roh*]

diminish *v.*, diminuire [*dee-mee-noo-ee'-reh*]

dine *v.*, cenare [*cheh-nah'-reh*]

dining car, vagone ristorante (m) [*vah-goh'-neh rees-toh-rahn'-teh*]

dining room, sala da pranzo [*sah'-lah dah prahn'-tsoh*]

dinner, cena [*cheh'-nah*]

  Dinner is ready! La cena è pronto! [*lah cheh'-nah eh' prohn'-toh*]

diploma, diploma (m) [*dee-ploh'-mah*]

diplomat, diplomatic, diplomatico [*dee-ploh-mah'-tee-koh*]

direct *adj.*, diretto [*dee-reht'-toh*]

direct *v.*, dirigere [*dee-ree'-jeh-reh*]

direction, direzione (f) [*dee-reh-tsee-oh'-neh*]

director, direttore (m), direttrice (f) [*dee-reht-toh'-reh, dee-reht-tree'-cheh*]

dirt, sporcizia [*spohr-chee'-tsee-ah*]

dirty, sporco [*spohr'-koh*]

disability, incapacità (f, indecl) [*een-kah-pah-chee-tah'*]

disabled, incapace [*een-kah-pah'-cheh*]

disadvantage, svantaggio [*zvahn-tahj'-jee-oh*]

disagree *v.*, non essere d'accordo [*nohn ehs'-seh-reh dahk-kohr'-doh*]

disagreeable, sgradevole [*zgrah-deh'-voh-leh*]

disagreement, disaccordo [*deez-ahk-kohr'-doh*]

disappear *v.*, scomparire [*skohm-pah-ree'-reh*]

disappoint *v.*, deludere [*deh-loo'-deh-reh*]

disappointed, deluso [*deh-loo'-zoh*]

disapprove *v.*, disapprovare [*deez-ahp-proh-vah'-reh*]

disaster, disastro [*dee-zahs'-troh*]

discharge [an employee] *v.*, congedare [*kohn-jeh-dah'-reh*]

discipline *n.*, disciplina [*dee-shee-plee'-nah*]

disclose *v.*, rivelare [*ree-veh-lah'-reh*]

discomfort, disagio [*dee-zah'-jee-oh*]
disconnect *v.*, staccare [*stahk-kah'-reh*]
discontinue *v.*, interrompere [*een-tehr-rohm'-peh-reh*]
discount *n.*, sconto [*skohn'-toh*]
discourage *v.*, scoraggiare [*skoh-rahj-jee-ah'-reh*]
discouraged, demoralizzato [*deh-moh-rah-leedz-dzah'-toh*]
discouraging, demoralizzante [*deh-moh-rah-leedz-dzahn'-teh*]
discover *v.*, scoprire [*skoh-pree'-reh*]
discovery, scoperta [*skoh-pehr'-tah*]
discuss *v.*, discutere [*dees-koo'-teh-reh*]
discussion, discussione (f) [*dees-koos-see-oh'-neh*]
disease, malattia [*mah-laht-tee'-ah*]
disgrace *n.*, disgrazia, disonore (m) [*deez-grah'-tsee-ah, deez-oh-noh'-reh*]
disguise *n.*, travestimento [*trah-vehs-tee-mehn'-toh*]
disgusted, disgustato [*deez-goos-tah'-toh*]
dish, piatto [*pee-aht'-toh*]
dishonest, disonesto [*deez-oh-nehs'-toh*]
dislike *v.*, non amare [*nohn ah-mah'-reh*]
  I dislike it, Non mi piace [*nohn mee pee-ah'-cheh*]
dismiss *v.*, congedare [*kohn-jeh-dah'-reh*]
disobey *v.*, disobbedire [*deez-ohb-beh-dee'-reh*]
disorder, disordine (m) [*deez-ohr'-dee-neh*]
display *v.*, esporre (irreg) [*ehs-pohr'-reh*]
dispose *v.*, disporre (irreg) [*dees-pohr'-reh*]
dispute *n.*, disputa [*dees'-poo-tah*]
dissolve *v.*, dissolvere [*dees-sohl'-veh-reh*]
distance, distanza [*dees-tahn'-tsah*]
distant, distante [*dees-tahn'-teh*]
distinct, distinto [*dees-teen'-toh*]
distinguish *v.*, distinguere [*dees-teen'-goo-eh-reh*]
distinguished, distinto, illustre [*dees-teen'-toh, eel-loos'-treh*]
distress *n.*, difficoltà, pena [*deef-fee-kohl-tah', peh'-nah*]
distress *v.*, affliggere [*ahf-fleej'-jeh-reh*]
distribute *v.*, distribuire [*dees-tree-boo-ee'-reh*]
district, distretto [*dees-treht'-toh*]
distrust *v.*, diffidare [*deef-fee-dah'-reh*]
disturb *v.*, disturbare [*dees-toor-bah'-reh*]

disturbance, disturbo [*dees-toor'-boh*]

ditch *n.*, fossa [*fohs'-sah*]

dive *v.*, tuffarsi (refl) [*toof-fahr'-see*]

divide *v.*, dividere [*dee-vee'-deh-reh*]

divine *adj.*, divino [*dee-vee'-noh*]

division, divisione (f) [*dee-vee-zee-oh'-neh*]

divorce *n.*, divorzio [*dee-vohr'-tsee-oh*]

dizzy, stordito [*stohr-dee'-toh*]

   feel dizzy *v.*, avere le vertigini [*ah-veh'-reh leh vehr-tee'-jee-nee*]

do *v.*, fare (irreg) [*fah'-reh*]

   Do you like it? Vi piace? [*vee pee-ah'-cheh*]

   Don't leave, Non partire [*nohn pahr-tee'-reh*]

   Do me a favor, Mi faccia un favore [*mee fahch'-chee-ah oon fah-voh'-reh*]

   do without, fare a meno di [*fah'-reh ah meh'-noh dee*]

   How do you do? Come sta? [*koh'-meh stah*]

   I do not know her, Non la conosco [*nohn lah koh-nohs'-koh*]

   What can I do for you? Cosa posso servirla? [*koh'-zah pohs'-soh sehr-veer'-lah*]

dock *n.*, molo [*moh'-loh*]

doctor, dottore (m), dottoressa (f) [*doht-toh'-reh, doht-toh-rehs'-sah*]

document, documento [*doh-koo-mehn'-toh*]

dog, cane (m) [*kah'-neh*]

doll, bambola [*bahm'-boh-lah*]

dollar, dollaro [*dohl'-lah-roh*]

domestic, domestico [*doh-mehs'-tee-koh*]

door, porta [*pohr'-tah*]

   Close the door! Chiuda la porta! [*kee-oo'-dah lah pohr'-tah*]

   Open the door! [Apra la porta! [*ah'-prah lah pohr'-tah*]

dormitory, dormitorio [*dohr-mee-toh'-ree-oh*]

double, doppio [*dohp'-pee-oh*]

doubt, dubbio [*doob'-bee-oh*]

doubt *v.*, dubitare [*doo-bee-tah'-reh*]

doubtful, dubbioso [*doob-bee-oh'-zoh*]

doubtless, senza dubbi [*sehn'-tsah doob'-bee*]
down, giù, in basso [*jee-oo', een bahs'-soh*]
   Down with . . . ! Abbasso con . . . ! [*ahb-bahs'-soh kohn*]
   fall down v., cadere [*kah-deh'-reh*]
   go down v., scendere [*shehn'-deh-reh*]
   lie down v., sdraiarsi [*zdrah-ee-ahr'-see*]
   sit down v., sedersi [*seh-dehr'-see*]
   take down v., annotare, demolire [*ahn-noh-tah'-reh, deh-moh-lee'-reh*]
downfall, caduta [*kah-doo'-tah*]
downstairs, al piano inferiore [*ahl pee-ah'-noh een-feh-ree-oh'-reh*]
doze v., sonnecchiare [*sohn-nehk-kee-ah'-reh*]
dozen, dozzina [*dohdz-dzee'-nah*]
draft [bank], tratta di pagamento [*traht'-tah dee pah-gah-mehn'-toh*]
draft [air], corrente (f) d'aria [*kohr-rehn'-teh dahr'-ee-ah*]
drag v., trascinare [*trah-shee-nah'-reh*]
drain, fogna [*foh'-nyah*]
drama, dramma (m) [*drahm'-mah*]
dramatic, drammatico [*drahm-mah'-tee-koh*]
draw [picture], disegnare [*dee-zeh-nyah'-reh*]
drawer, cassetto [*kahs-seht'-toh*]
dreadful, spaventoso [*spah-vehn-toh'-zoh*]
dream n., sogno [*soh'-nyoh*]
dream v., sognare [*soh-nyah'-reh*]
dress n., abito [*ah'-bee-toh*]
   evening dress, abito da sera [*ah'-bee-toh dah seh'-rah*]
dress v., vestire [*vehs-tee'-reh*]
   get dressed, vestirsi (refl) [*vehs-teer'-see*]
dresser, guardarobiere (m) [*goo-ahr-dah-roh-bee-eh'-reh*]
dressing table, toletta [*toh-leht'-tah*]
dressmaker, sarta [*sahr'-tah*]
drink n., bevanda [*beh-vahn'-dah*]
drink v., bere (irreg) [*beh'-reh*]
drive [a car] v., guidare [*goo-ee-dah'-reh*]
driver, autista (m) [*ah-oo-tees'-tah*]
driving license, patente automobilistica (f) [*pah-tehn'-teh*

ah-oo-toh-moh-bee-lees'-tee-kah]
drop *v.*, lasciar cadere [*lah-shee-ahr' kah-deh'-reh*]
drown *v.*, annegarsi [*ahn-neh-gahr'-see*]
drug, droga, narcotico [*droh'-gah, nahr-koh'-tee-koh*]
drugstore, farmacia [*fahr-mah-chee'-ah*]
drum, tamburo [*tahm-boo'-roh*]
drunk, ubriaco [*oo-bree-ah'-koh*]
dry *adj.*, asciutto [*ah-shee-oot'-toh*]
dry *v.*, asciugare [*ah-shee-oo-gah'-reh*]
dry-clean *v.*, pulire a secco [*poo-lee'-reh ah sehk'-koh*]
due (to), a causa di [*ah kah'-oo-zah dee*]
dues *n.*, *pl.*, tributo, debito [*tree-boo'-to, deh'-bee-toh*]
dull, noioso [*noh-ee-oh'-zoh*]
dumb, muto [*moo'-toh*]
durable, durevole [*doo-reh'-voh-leh*]
during, durante [*doo-rahn'-teh*]
dusk, crepuscolo [*kreh-poos'-koh-loh*]
dust *n.*, polvere (f) [*pohl'-veh-reh*]
dusty, polveroso [*pohl-veh-roh'-zoh*]
Dutch *n. & adj.*, olandese [*oh-lahn-deh'-zeh*]
duty, dovere (m) [*doh-veh'-reh*]
  be on duty *v.*, essere di servizio [*ehs'-seh-reh dee sehr-vee'-tsee-oh*]
duty-free, esente da tassa [*eh-zehn'-teh dah tahs'-sah*]
dwell *v.*, abitare [*ah-bee-tah'-reh*]
dye *n.*, tinta, tintura [*teen'-tah, teen-too'-rah*]
dye *v.*, tingere [*teen'-jeh-reh*]
dysentery, dissenteria [*dees-sehn-teh-ree'-ah*]

E

each, ogni, ciascuno [*oh'-nyee, chee-ahs-koo'-noh*]
  each one, ciascuno [*chee-ahs-koo'-noh*]
  each other, l'un l'altro, a vicenda [*loon lahl'-troh, ah vee-chehn'-dah*]

each time, ogni volta [*oh'-nyee vohl'-tah*]

eager, avido [*ah'-vee-doh*]

ear, orecchio, le orecchie (pl) [*oh-rehk'-kee-oh, leh oh-rehk'-kee-eh*]

earring, orecchino [*oh-rehk-kee'-noh*]

early, presto, di buon'ora [*prehs'-toh, dee boo-ohn-oh'-rah*]

earn *v.,* guadagnare [*goo-ah-dah-nyah'-reh*]

earth, terra [*tehr'-rah*]

earthquake, terremoto [*tehr-reh-moh'-toh*]

ease, facilità (f, indecl) [*fah-chee-lee-tah'*]

easily, facilmente [*fah-cheel-mehn'-teh*]

east, est (m) [*ehst*]

    Far East, Oriente (m) [*oh-ree-ehn'-teh*]

    Middle East, Medio Oriente [*meh'-dee-oh oh-ree-ehn'-teh*]

    Near East, Levante (m) [*leh-vahn'-teh*]

easy, facile [*fah'-chee-leh*]

    Take it easy! Con calma! [*kohn kahl'-mah*]

eat *v.,* mangiare [*mahn-jee-ah'-reh*]

echo, eco [*eh'-koh*]

economical, economico [*eh-koh-noh'-mee-koh*]

edge, orlo [*ohr'-loh*]

edition, edizione (f) [*eh-dee-tsee-oh'-neh*]

editor, redattore [*reh-daht-toh'-reh*]

education, istruzione (f) [*ees-troo-tsee-oh'-neh*]

effective, effettivo [*ehf-feht-tee'-voh*]

efficient, efficiente [*ehf-fee-chee-ehn'-teh*]

effort, sforzo [*sfohr'-tsoh*]

egg, uovo, le uova (pl) [*oo-oh'-voh, leh oo-oh'-vah*]

    fried eggs, uova fritte [*oo-oh'-vah freet'-teh*]

    hard-boiled eggs, uova sode [*oo-oh'-vah soh'-deh*]

    scrambled eggs, uova strapazzate [*oo-oh'-vah strah-pahts-tsah'-teh*]

    soft-boiled eggs, uova a la coque [*oo-oh'-vah ah lah kohk*]

Egypt, Egitto [*eh-jeet'-toh*]

Egyptian *n. & adj.,* egiziano [*eh-jee-tsee-ah'-noh*]

eight, otto [*oht'-toh*]

eighteen, diciotto [*dee-chee-oht'-toh*]

eighth, ottavo [*oht-tah'-voh*]

eighty, ottanta [*oht-tahn'-tah*]
either, l'uno o l'altro [*loo'-noh oh lahl'-troh*]
elaborate, accurato [*ahk-koo-rah'-toh*]
elastic n. & adj., elastico [*eh-lahs'-tee-koh*]
elbow, gomito [*goh'-mee-toh*]
elderly, anziano [*ahn-tsee-ah'-noh*]
election, elezione (f) [*eh-leh-tsee-oh'-neh*]
electricity, elettricità (f, indecl) [*eh-leht-tree-chee-tah'*]
elegant, elegante [*eh-leh-gahn'-teh*]
elementary, elementare [*eh-leh-mehn-tah'-reh*]
elevator, ascensore (m) [*ah-shehn-soh'-reh*]
eleven, undici [*oon'-dee-chee*]
eliminate v., eliminare [*eh-lee-mee-nah'-reh*]
else, altro [*ahl'-troh*]
   Anything else? Qualche altra cosa? [*koo-al'-keh ahl'-trah koh'-zah*]
   nobody else, nessun altro [*nehs-soon' ahl'-troh*]
   Nothing else? Nient' altro? [*nee-ehnt-ahl'-troh*]
   somebody else, qualcun altro [*koo-ahl-koon' ahl'-troh*]
   someone else, un altra persona [*oon ahl'-trah pehr-soh'-nah*]
   somewhere else, in un altro posto [*een oon ahl'-troh pohs'-toh*]
embarrassed, imbarazzato [*eem-bah-rahts-tsah'-toh*]
embassy, ambasciata [*ahm-bah-shee-ah'-tah*]
embrace v., abbracciare [*ahb-brahch-chee-ah'-reh*]
emerald, smeraldo [*smeh-rahl'-doh*]
emergency, emergenza [*eh-mehr-jehn'-tsah*]
   in case of emergency, in caso di emergenza [*een kah'-zoh dee eh-mehr-jehn'-tsah*]
emigrant, emigrante [*eh-mee-grahn'-teh*]
emotion, emozione (f) [*eh-moh-tsee-oh'-neh*]
emotional, emotivo [*eh-moh-tee'-voh*]
emperor, imperatore (m) [*eem-peh-rah-toh'-reh*]
emphasize v., mettere in rilievo [*meht'-teh-reh een ree-lee-eh'-voh*]
employ v., impiegare [*eem-pee-eh-gah'-reh*]
employee, impiegato [*eem-pee-eh-gah'-toh*]

employer, datore di lavoro [*dah-toh'-reh dee lah-voh'-roh*]

employment, impiego [*eem-pee-eh'-goh*]

employment agency, agenzia di collocamento [*ah-jehn-tsee'-ah dee kohl-loh-kah-mehn'-toh*]

empty, vuoto [*voo-oh'-toh*]

enclose [surround] *v.*, rinchiudere [*reen-kee-oo'-deh-reh*]

encounter *v.*, incontrare [*een-kohn-trah'-reh*]

encourage *v.*, incoraggiare [*een-koh-rahj-jee-ah'-reh*]

encouragement, incoraggiamento [*een-koh-rahj-jee-ah-mehn'-toh*]

end, ending *n.*, fine (f) [*fee'-neh*]

end *v.*, finire [*fee-nee'-reh*]

endless, infinito [*een-fee-nee'-toh*]

endorse *v.*, girare [*jee-rah'-reh*]

endure *v.*, sopportare [*sohp-pohr-tah'-reh*]

enemy, nemico [*neh-mee'-koh*]

energy, energia [*eh-nehr-jee'-ah*]

engaged, fidanzato [*fee-dahn-tsah'-toh*]

engagement [betrothal], fidanzamento [*fee-dahn-tsah-mehn'-toh*]

engagement [appointment], appuntamento [*ahp-poon-tah-mehn'-toh*]

engine, motore (m), macchina [*moh-toh'-reh, mahk'-kee-nah*]

engineer, ingegnere (m) [*een-jeh-nyeh'-reh*]

England, Inghilterra [*een-geel-tehr'-rah*]

English, inglese [*een-gleh'-zeh*]

enjoy *v.*, godere [*goh-deh'-reh*]

    enjoy life, godere la vita [*goh-deh'-reh lah vee'-tah*]

enjoy (oneself), divertirsi [*dee-vehr-teer'-see*]

    Enjoy yourself! Si diverta! [*see dee-vehr'-tah*]

enjoyment, piacere (m), gioia [*pee-ah-cheh'-reh, jee-oh'-ee-ah*]

enormous, enorme [*eh-nohr'-meh*]

enough, abbastanza [*ahb-bahs-tahn'-tsah*]

    more than enough, più che abbastanza [*pee-oo' keh ahb-bahs-tahn'-tsah*]

    That's enough! Basta! [*bahs'-tah*]

enroll *v.*, arruolare [*ahr-roo-oh-lah'-reh*]

enter *v.*, entrare [*ehn-trah'-reh*]
   Do not enter! Non entri! [*nohn ehn'-tree*]
enterprise, impresa [*eem-preh'-zah*]
entertain *v.*, intrattenere [*een-traht-teh-neh'-reh*]
entertaining, divertente [*dee-vehr-tehn'-teh*]
entertainment, divertimento [*dee-vehr-tee-mehn'-toh*]
enthusiasm, entusiasmo [*ehn-too-zee-ahz'-moh*]
entire, intero [*een-teh'-roh*]
entirely, interamente [*een-teh-rah-mehn'-teh*]
entrance, entrata, ingresso [*ehn-trah'-tah, een-grehs'-soh*]
envelope, busta [*boos'-tah*]
environment, ambiente (m) [*ahm-bee-ehn'-teh*]
envy *n.*, invidia [*een-vee'-dee-ah*]
envy *v.*, invidiare [*een-vee-dee-ah'-reh*]
equal *adj.*, uguale [*oo-goo-ah'-leh*]
equality, uguaglianza [*oo-goo-ah-lyahn'-tsah*]
equipment, equipaggiamento [*eh-koo-ee-pahj-jee-ah-mehn'-toh*]
equivalent, equivalente [*eh-koo-ee-vah-lehn'-teh*]
erase *v.*, cancellare [*kahn-chehl-lah'-reh*]
eraser, gomma da cancellare [*gohm'-mah dah kahn-chehl-lah'-reh*]
err *v.*, sbagliare [*zbah-lyah'-reh*]
errand, commissione (f) [*kohm-mees-see-oh'-neh*]
error, errore (m) [*ehr-roh'-reh*]
escape *v.*, scappare [*skahp-pah'-reh*]
especially, specialmente [*speh-chee-ahl-mehn'-teh*]
essential, essenziale [*ehs-sehn-tsee-ah'-leh*]
establish *v.*, stabilire, fondare [*stah-bee-lee'-reh, fohn-dah'-reh*]
establishment, fondazione, istituto [*fohn-dah-tsee-oh'-neh, ees-tee-too'-toh*]
estate, proprietà (f, indecl) immobiliare [*proh-pree-eh-tah' eem-moh-bee-lee-ah'-reh*]
esteem *v.*, stimare [*stee-mah'-reh*]
estimate *n.*, valutazione (f) [*vah-loo-tah-tsee-oh'-neh*]
estimate *v.*, valutare [*vah-loo-tah'-reh*]
eternal, eterno [*eh-tehr'-noh*]

Europe, Europa [eh-oo-roh'-pah]
European n. & adj., europeo [eh-oo-roh-peh'-oh]
eve, vigilia [vee-jee'-lee-ah]
  Christmas Eve, Vigilia di Natale [vee-jee'-lee-ah dee
    nah-tah'-leh]
even adv., anche [ahn'-keh]
  even him, anche lui [ahn'-keh loo'-ee]
  even so, eppure, ció nonostante [ehp-poo'-reh, chee-oh'
    noh-nohs-tahn'-teh]
  even then, anche allora [ahn'-keh ahl-loh'-rah]
  even though, anche se [ahn'-keh seh]
  not even, neppure, nemmeno [nehp-poo'-reh, nehm-meh'-
    noh]
even adj., pari, uguale, liscio [pah'-ree, oo-goo-ah'-leh, lee'-
  shee-oh]
  even number, numero pari [noo'-meh-roh pah'-ree]
evening, sera [seh'-rah]
  Good evening! Buona sera! [boo-oh'-nah seh'-rah]
  in the evening, durante la sera [doo-rahn'-teh lah seh'-rah]
  tomorrow evening, domani sera [doh-mah'-nee seh'-rah]
  yesterday evening, ieri sera [ee-eh'-ree seh'-rah]
event, avvenimento [ahv-veh-nee-mehn'-toh]
  in the event of, nel caso che [nehl kah'-zoh keh]
eventually, eventualmente [eh-vehn-too-ahl-mehn'-teh]
ever, qualche volta, mai [koo-ahl'-keh vohl'-ta, mah'-ee]
  as ever, come sempre [koh'-meh sehm'-preh]
every, ogni, ciascuno [oh'-nyee, chee-ahs-koo'-noh]
  every day, ogni giorno [oh'-nyee jee-ohr'-noh]
  every other day, ogni altro giorno [oh'-nyee ahl'-troh
    jee-ohr'-noh]
  every time, ogni volta [oh'-nyee vohl'-tah]
everybody, ognuno [oh-nyoo'-noh]
everyone, ciascuno [chee-ahs-koo'-noh]
everything, ogni cosa [oh-nyee koh'-zah]
everywhere, ovunque [oh-voon'-koo-eh]
evidence, evidenza [eh-vee-dehn'-tsah]
evidently, evidentemente [eh-vee-dehn-teh-mehn'-teh]
evil, male, maligno, cattivo [mah'-leh, mah-lee'-nyoh, kaht-

tee'-voh]
exact, esatto [*eh-zaht'-toh*]
exactly, esattamente [*eh-zaht-tah-mehn'-teh*]
exaggerate *v.*, esagerare [*eh-zah-jeh-rah'-reh*]
examination, esame (m) [*eh-zah'-meh*]
examine *v.*, esaminare [*eh-zah-mee-nah'-reh*]
example, esempio [*eh-zehm'-pee-oh*]
exceed *v.*, eccedere [*ehch-cheh'-deh-reh*]
excellent, eccellente [*ehch-chehl-lehn'-teh*]
except, eccetto [*ehch-cheht'-toh*]
exception, eccezione (f) [*ehch-cheh-tsee-oh'-neh*]
exceptional, eccezionale [*ehch-cheh-tsee-oh-nah'-leh*]
excess, eccesso [*ehch-chehs'-soh*]
exchange *n.*, cambio [*kahm'-bee-oh*]
  in exchange for, in cambio di [*een kahm'-bee-oh dee*]
exchange *v.*, scambiare [*skahm-bee-ah'-reh*]
excited, eccitato, agitato [*ehch-chee-tah'-toh, ah-jee-tah'-toh*]
  Don't get excited! Non si agiti! [*nohn see ah'-jee-tee*]
exclusive, esclusivo [*ehs-kloo-zee'-voh*]
excursion, escursione (f) [*ehs-koor-see-oh'-neh*]
excuse *n.*, scusa [*skoo'-zah*]
excuse *v.*, scusare [*skoo-zah'-reh*]
  Excuse me! Mi scusi! [*mee skoo'-zee*]
exercise *n.*, esercizio [*eh-zehr-chee'-tsee-oh*]
exercise *v.*, esercitare [*eh-zehr-chee-tah'-reh*]
exhausted, esaurito [*eh-zah-oo-ree'-toh*]
exhibit *v.*, esibire [*eh-zee-bee'-reh*]
exhibition, esibizione (f) [*eh-zee-bee-tsee-oh'-neh*]
exist *v.*, esistere [*eh-zees'-teh-reh*]
existence, esistenza [*eh-zees-tehn'-tsah*]
exit, uscita [*oo-shee'-tah*]
expect *v.*, aspettare [*ahs-peht-tah'-reh*]
expedition, spedizione (f) [*speh-dee-tsee-oh'-neh*]
expense, spesa [*speh'-zah*]
expensive, caro [*kah'-roh*]
experience *n.*, esperienza [*ehs-peh-ree-ehn'-tsah*]
experiment *n.*, esperimento [*ehs-peh-ree-mehn'-toh*]
expert *adj.*, esperto [*ehs-pehr'-toh*]

explain *v.*, spiegare [*spee-eh-gah'-reh*]
explanation, spiegazione (f) [*spee-eh-gah-tsee-oh'-neh*]
explore *v.*, esplorare [*ehs-ploh-rah'-reh*]
explosion, esplosione (f) [*ehs-ploh-zee-oh'-neh*]
export *n.*, esportazione (f) [*ehs-pohr-tah-tsee-oh'-neh*]
export *v.*, esportare [*ehs-pohr-tah'-reh*]
express *adj.*, espresso [*ehs-prehs'-soh*]
express *v.*, esprimere [*ehs-pree'-meh-reh*]
exquisite, squisito [*skoo-ee-zee'-toh*]
extend *v.*, estendere [*ehs-tehn'-deh-reh*]
extent, extension, estensione (f) [*ehs-tehn-see-oh'-neh*]
   to a certain extent, sino ad un certo punto [*see'-noh ahd oon chehr'-to poon'-toh*]
exterior, esteriore [*ehs-teh-ree-oh'-reh*]
external, esterno [*ehs-tehr'-noh*]
extinguish *v.*, estinguere [*ehs-teen'-goo-eh-reh*]
extra *adj.*, supplementare, straordinario [*soop-pleh-mehn-tah'-reh, strah-ohr-dee-nah'-ree-oh*]
extravagant, stravagante [*strah-vah-gahn'-teh*]
extrarodinary, straordinario [*strah-ohr-dee-nah'-ree-oh*]
extreme, estremo [*ehs-treh'-moh*]
extremely, estremamente [*ehs-treh-mah-mehn'-teh*]
eye, occhio, occhi (pl) [*ohk'-kee-oh, ohk'-kee*]
eyeball, bulbo [*bool'-boh*]
eyebrow, sopracciglio [*soh-prah-chee'-lyoh*]
eye doctor, oculista (m) [*oh-koo-lees'-tah*]
eyeglasses, occhiali (m, pl) [*ohk-kee-ah'-lee*]
eyelashes, ciglia (f, pl) [*chee'-lyah*]
eyelid, palpebra [*pahl'-peh-brah*]
eyesight, vista [*vees'-tah*]
eyewitness, testimone oculare (m) [*tehs-tee-moh'-neh oh-koo-lah'-reh*]

F

fabric, tessuto, stoffa [*tehs-soo'-toh, stohf'-fah*]

face *n.,* faccia, viso [*fahch'-chee-ah, vee'-zoh*]

face *v.,* affrontare [*ahf-frohn-tah'-reh*]

fact, fatto [*faht'-toh*]

  in fact, infatti [*een-faht'-tee*]

factory, fabbrica [*fahb'-bree-kah*]

faculty, facoltà (f, indecl) [*fah-kohl-tah'*]

fad, mania [*mah-nee'-ah*]

fade *v.,* svanire [*zvah-nee'-reh*]

fail *v.,* fallire [*fahl-lee'-reh*]

failure, fallimento [*fahl-lee-mehn'-toh*]

faint *v.,* svenire [*zveh-nee'-reh*]

fairness, giustezza [*jee-oos-tehts'-tsah*]

faith, fede (f) [*feh'-deh*]

faithful, fedele [*feh-deh'-leh*]

fall [descent] *n.,* caduta [*kah-doo'-tah*]

fall [season] *n.,* autunno [*ah-oo-toon'-noh*]

fall *v.,* cadere [*kah-deh'-reh*]

  fall asleep, addormentarsi [*ahd-dohr-mehn-tahr'-see*]

  fall back, retrocedere [*reh-troh-cheh'-deh-reh*]

  fall in love, innamorarsi [*een-nah-moh-rahr'-see*]

fallen, caduto, degradato [*kah-doo'-toh, deh-grah-dah'-toh*]

false, falso [*fahl'-soh*]

fame, fama [*fah'-mah*]

familiar, familiare [*fah-mee-lee-ah'-reh*]

family, famiglia [*fah-mee'-lyah*]

famous, famoso [*fah-moh'-zoh*]

fan [mechanical] *n.,* ventilatore (m) [*vehn-tee-lah-toh'-reh*]

fan [hand] *n.,* ventaglio [*vehn-tah'-lyoh*]

fan [enthusiast] *n.,* ammiratore (m), tifoso [*ahm-mee-rah-toh'-reh, tee-foh'-zoh*]

fancy *n.,* fantasia, capriccio [*fahn-tah-zee'-ah, kah-preech'-*

chee-oh]

fantastic, fantastico [*fahn-tahs'-tee-koh*]

far, lontano, distante [*lohn-tah'-noh, dees-tahn'-teh*]

   far away, molto lontano [*mohl'-toh lohn-tah'-noh*]

   How far? Quanto lontano? [*koo-ahn'-toh lohn-tah'-noh*]

fare [transportation] *n.*, prezzo del viaggio [*prehts'-tsoh dehl vee-ahj'-jee-oh*]

   bill of fare, lista delle vivande, menù (m) [*lees'-tah dehl'-leh vee-vahn'-deh, meh'-noo*]

farewell *n.*, addio [*ahd-dee'-oh*]

farm *n.*, fattoria [*faht-toh-ree'-ah*]

farther, più lontano [*pee-oo' lohn-tah'-noh*]

fascinating, affascinante [*ahf-fah-shee-nahn'-teh*]

fashion, moda [*moh'-dah*]

fashionable, di moda, elegante [*dee moh'-dah, eh-leh-gahn'-teh*]

fast *adj.*, rapido, veloce [*rah'-pee-doh, veh-loh'-cheh*]

fast *v.*, digiunare [*dee-jee-oo-nah'-reh*]

fasten *v.*, fissare, stringere [*fees-sah'-reh, streen'-jeh-reh*]

fat, grasso [*grahs'-soh*]

fatal, fatale [*fah-tah'-leh*]

fate, destino [*dehs-tee'-noh*]

father, padre (m) [*pah'-dreh*]

father-in-law, suocero [*soo-oh'-cheh-roh*]

fatigue *n.*, fatica, stanchezza [*fah-tee'-kah, stahn-kehts'-tsah*]

faucet, rubinetto [*roo-bee-neht'-toh*]

fault *n.*, colpa [*kohl'-pah*]

   It's my fault, È colpa mia [*eh' kohl'-pah mee'-ah*]

favor *n.*, favore (m), piacere (m) [*fah-voh'-reh, pee-ah-cheh'-reh*]

favorite, preferito [*preh-feh-ree'-toh*]

fear *n.*, paura [*pah-oo'-rah*]

fear *v.*, temere [*teh-meh'-reh*]

fearless, intrepido [*een-treh'-pee-doh*]

feast *n.*, festa [*fehs'-tah*]

feather, piuma [*pee-oo'-mah*]

features, lineamenti (m, pl) [*lee-neh-ah-mehn'-tee*]

February, febbraio [*fehb-brah'-ee-oh*]
federal, federale [*feh-deh-rah'-leh*]
fee, onorario [*oh-noh-rah'-ree-oh*]
feed *v.,* nutrire [*noo-tree'-reh*]
feel *v.,* sentire [*sehn-tee'-reh*]
feeling, sentimento [*sehn-tee-mehn'-toh*]
female, femmina [*fehm'-mee-nah*]
feminine, femminile [*fehm-mee-nee'-leh*]
fence, recinto [*reh-cheen'-toh*]
fencing, scherma [*skehr'-mah*]
fender [of car], paracarro [*pah-rah-kahr'-roh*]
ferryboat, nave traghetto [*nah'-veh trah-geht'-toh*]
festival, festival [*fehs'-tee-vahl*]
fever, febbre (f) [*fehb'-breh*]
feverish, febbrile [*fehb-bree'-leh*]
few, pochi (m), poche (f) [*poh'-kee, poh'-keh*]
fewer, di meno [*dee meh'-noh*]
fiancé, fidanzato [*fee-dahn-tsah'-toh*]
fiancée, fidanzata [*fee-dahn-tsah'-tah*]
fiction, narrativa [*nahr-rah-tee'-vah*]
field, campo [*kahm'-poh*]
field glasses, cannocchiali [*kahn-nohk-kee-ah'-lee*]
fifteen, quindici [*koo-een'-dee-chee*]
fifth, quinto [*koo-een'-toh*]
fifty, cinquanta [*cheen-koo-ahn'-tah*]
fight *n.,* lotta [*loht'-tah*]
fight *v.,* lottare [*loht-tah'-reh*]
fill *v.,* riempire [*ree-ehm-pee'-reh*]
filling [tooth], otturazione (f) [*oht-too-rah-tsee-oh'-neh*]
film *n.,* pellicola, film [*pehl-lee'-koh-lah, feelm*]
filter *n.,* filtro [*feel'-troh*]
final, finale [*fee-nah'-leh*]
finally, finalmente [*fee-nahl-mehn'-teh*]
financial, finanziario [*fee-nahn-tsee-ah'-ree-oh*]
find *v.,* trovare [*troh-vah'-reh*]
fine [penalty] *n.,* multa [*mool'-tah*]
fine *adj.,* fine, eccellente [*fee'-neh, ehch-chehl-lehn'-teh*]
finger, dito, le dita (pl) [*dee'-toh, leh dee'-tah*]

fingerprint, impronta digitale [*eem-prohn'-tah dee-jee-tah'-leh*]

finish *v.,* finire [*fee-nee'-reh*]

fire, fuoco [*foo-oh'-koh*]

fireman, pompiere (m) [*pohm-pee-eh'-reh*]

fireplace, focolare (m) [*foh-koh-lah'-reh*]

fireproof, incombustibile [*een-kohm-boos-tee'-bee-leh*]

firm *adj.,* fermo [*fehr'-moh*]

first, primo [*pree'-moh*]

first aid, pronto soccorso [*prohn'-toh sohk-kohr'-soh*]

first class, prima classe [*pree'-mah klahs'-seh*]

first name, nome [*noh'-meh*]

fish *n.,* pesce (m) [*peh'-sheh*]

fish *v.,* pescare [*pehs-kah'-reh*]

fisherman, pescatore (m) [*pehs-kah-toh'-reh*]

fishing, pesca [*pehs'-kah*]

fishing boat, barca da pesca [*bahr'-kah dah pehs'-kah*]

fist, pugno [*poo'-nyoh*]

fit [try on] *v.,* provare [*proh-vah'-reh*]

fit [adjust] *v.,* adattare [*ah-daht-tah'-reh*]

five, cinque [*cheen'-koo-eh*]

fix [fasten] *v.,* fissare [*fees-sah'-reh*]

fix [repair] *v.,* riparare [*ree-pah-rah'-reh*]

fixed price, prezzo fisso [*prehts'-tsoh fees'-soh*]

flag *n.,* bandiera [*bahn-dee-eh'-rah*]

flame, fiamma [*fee-ahm'-mah*]

flannel, flanella [*flah-nehl'-lah*]

flash *n.,* lampo [*lahm'-poh*]

flask, fiaschetta [*fee-ahs-keht'-tah*]

flat *adj.,* piatto [*pee-aht'-toh*]

flatter *v.,* lusingare, adulare [*loo-zeen-gah'-reh, ah-doo-lah'-reh*]

flavor *n.,* sapore (m), aroma [*sah-poh'-reh, ah-roh'-mah*]

flee *v.,* fuggire [*fooj-jee'-reh*]

fleet *n.,* flotta [*floht'-tah*]

flesh, carne (f) [*kahr'-neh*]

flexible, flessibile [*flehs-see'-bee-leh*]

flight [escape], fuga [*foo'-gah*]

flight [flying], volo [*voh'-loh*]

float v., galleggiare [*gahl-lehj-jee-ah'-reh*]

flood n., inondazione (f) [*ee-nohn-dah-tsee-oh'-neh*]

floor, pavimento, piano [*pah-vee-mehn'-toh, pee-ah'-noh*]

Florence, Firenze [*fee-rehn'-tseh*]

flour, farina [*fah-ree'-nah*]

flow v., scorrere [*skohr-reh'-reh*]

flower, fiore (m) [*fee-oh'-reh*]

flower shop, fioraio [*fee-oh-rah'-ee-oh*]

fluent, fluente [*floo-ehn'-teh*]

fluid n. & adj., fluido [*floo'-ee-doh*]

flute, flauto [*flah'-oo-toh*]

fly n., mosca [*mohs'-kah*]

fly v., volare [*voh-lah'-reh*]

foggy, nebbioso [*nehb-bee-oh'-zoh*]

fold v., piegare [*pee-eh-gah'-reh*]

follow v., seguire [*seh-goo-ee'-reh*]

following, seguito [*seh'-goo-ee-toh*]

fond, appassionato, amante di [*ahp-pahs-see-oh-nah'-toh, ah-mahn'-teh dee*]

food, cibo [*chee'-boh*]

fool n., stupido [*stoo'-pee-doh*]

foolish, sciocco [*shee-ohk'-koh*]

foot, piede [*pee-eh'-deh*]

football, (gioco del) calcio [(*jee-oh'-koh dehl*) *kahl'-chee-oh*]

for, per [*pehr*]

  for example, per esempio [*pehr eh-zehm'-pee-oh*]

  for us, for them, per noi, per loro [*pehr noh'-ee, pehr loh'-roh*]

  What for? Perchè? [*pehr-keh'*]

forbid v., proibire [*proh-ee-bee'-reh*]

forbidden, proibito [*proh-ee-bee'-toh*]

forehead, fronte (f) [*frohn'-teh*]

foreign, straniero [*strah-nee-eh'-roh*]

foreigner, straniero [*strah-nee-eh'-roh*]

foreign minister, ministro degli esteri [*mee-nees'-troh deh'-lyee ehs'-teh-ree*]

foreign office, ministero degli affari esteri [*mee-nees-teh'-*

roh deh'-lyee ahf-fah'-ree ehs'-teh-ree]

foreign policy, politica straniera [*poh-lee'-tee-kah strah-nee-eh'-rah*]

foreign trade, commercio con l'estero [*kohm-mehr'-chee-oh kohn lehs'-teh-roh*]

forest, foresta [*foh-rehs'-tah*]

forever, per sempre [*pehr sehm'-preh*]

forget *v.,* dimenticare [*dee-mehn-tee-kah'-reh*]

forgive *v.,* perdonare [*pehr-doh-nah'-reh*]

fork, forchetta [*fohr-keht'-tah*]

formal, formale [*fohr-mah'-leh*]

formality, formalità (f, indecl) [*fohr-mah-lee-tah'*]

former *pron.,* primo [*pree'-moh*]

fortunate, fortunato [*fohr-too-nah'-toh*]

fortunately, fortunatamente [*fohr-too-nah-tah-mehn'-teh*]

fortune, fortuna [*fohr-too'-nah*]

forty, quaranta [*koo-ah-rahn'-tah*]

forward *adv.,* in avanti [*een ah-vahn'-tee*]

foundation, fondazione (f) [*fohn-dah-tsee-oh'-neh*]

fountain, fontana [*fohn-tah'-nah*]

fountain pen, penna stilografica [*pehn'-nah stee-loh-grah'-fee-kah*]

four, quattro [*koo-aht'-troh*]

fourteen, quattordici [*koo-aht-tohr'-dee-chee*]

fourth, quarto [*koo-ahr'-toh*]

fracture *n.,* rottura, frattura [*roht-too'-rah, fraht-too'-rah*]

fragile, fragile [*frah'-jee-leh*]

fragrance, fragranza [*frah-grahn'-tsah*]

frail, fragile [*frah'-jee-leh*]

frame *n.,* forma, struttura [*fohr'-mah, stroot-too'-rah*]

France, Francia [*frahn'-chee-ah*]

frank, franco [*frahn'-koh*]

frantic, frenetico [*freh-neh'-tee-koh*]

fraud, frode (f) [*froh'-deh*]

free [not bound] *adj.,* libero [*lee'-beh-roh*]

free [at no cost] *adj.,* gratuito [*grah-too'-ee-toh*]

free *v.,* liberare [*lee-beh-rah'-reh*]

freedom, libertà (f, indecl) [*lee-behr-tah'*]

freeze v., congelare [*kohn-jeh-lah'-reh*]

freight, carico, trasporto [*kah'-ree-koh, trah-spohr'-toh*]

French adj., francese [*frahn-cheh'-zeh*]

Frenchman, -woman n., francese (m, f) [*frahn-cheh'-zeh*]

frequently, frequentemente [*freh-koo-ehn-teh-mehn'-teh*]

fresh, fresco [*frehs'-koh*]

Friday, venerdì [*veh-nehr-dee'*]

fried, fritto [*freet'-toh*]

friend, amico, amici (pl) [*ah-mee'-koh, ah-mee'-chee*]

frighten v., spaventare [*spah-vehn-tah'-reh*]

from, da, per [*dah, pehr*]

  come from v., venire da [*veh-nee-reh dah*]

  Where do you come from? Da dove viene? [*dah doh'-veh vee-eh'-neh*]

  from far, da lontano [*dah lohn-tah'-noh*]

  from now on, da ora in poi [*dah oh'-rah een poh'-ee*]

front, fronte (m) [*frohn'-teh*]

  in front of, davanti a [*dah-vahn'-tee ah*]

frozen, gelato [*jeh-lah'-toh*]

fruit, frutta [*froot'-tah*]

fruit salad, insalata di frutta [*een-sah-lah'-tah dee froot'-tah*]

fruit store, fruttivendolo [*froot-tee-vehn'-doh-loh*]

fry v., friggere [*freej'-jeh-reh*]

frying pan, padella [*pah-dehl'-lah*]

fuel n., combustibile [*kohm-boos-tee'-bee-leh*]

full, pieno [*pee-eh'-noh*]

fun, divertimento [*dee-vehr-tee-mehn'-toh*]

function n., funzione (f) [*foon-tsee-oh'-neh*]

funds, fondi (m, pl) [*fohn'-dee*]

funeral, funerale (m) [*foo-neh-rah'-leh*]

fur, pellicia [*pehl-lee'-chee-ah*]

funny, comico, scherzoso [*koh'-mee-koh, skehrts-tsoh'-zoh*]

furious, furioso [*foo-ree-oh'-zoh*]

furnish [provide] v., fornire [*fohr-nee'-reh*]

furnish [put furniture into] v., mobiliare [*moh-bee-lee-ah'-reh*]

furnished room, camera da affittare [*kah'-meh-rah dah ahf-fee-tah'-reh*]

furniture, mobili (m, pl) [*moh'-bee-lee*]
further *adj.*, ulteriore [*ool-teh-ree-oh'-reh*]
furthermore, inoltre [*een-ohl'-treh*]
future *n.*, futuro, avvenire (m) [*foo-too'-roh ahv-veh-nee'-reh*]

G

gadget, meccanismo [*mehk-kah-neez'-moh*]
gaiety, allegria [*ahl-leh-gree'-ah*]
gain *v.*, guadagnare [*goo-ah-dah-nyah'-reh*]
gallon, gallone (m) [*gahl-loh'-neh*]
gamble *v.*, giocare d'azzardo [*jee-oh-kah'-reh dahdz-dzahr'-doh*]
game, gioco, partita [*jee-oh'-koh, pahr-tee'-tah*]
garage, autorimessa [*ah-oo-toh-ree-mehs'-sah*]
garbage, immondizia, rifiuti (m, pl) [*eem-mohn-dee'-tsee-ah, ree-fee-oo'-tee*]
garden, giardino [*jee-ahr-dee'-noh*]
gardener, giardiniere (m) [*jee-ahr-dee-nee-eh'-reh*]
garlic, aglio [*ah'-lyoh*]
garment, indumento [*een-doo-mehn'-toh*]
garret, soffitta [*sohf-feet'-tah*]
gasoline, benzina [*behn-dzee'-nah*]
gasoline station, pompa di benzina [*pohm'-pah dee behn-dzee'-nah*]
gate, cancello, porta [*kahn-chehl'-loh, pohr'-tah*]
gather *v.*, raccogliere [*rahk-koh'-lyeh-reh*]
gauge, indicatore (m) [*een-dee-kah-toh'-reh*]
gear [auto] *n.*, ingranaggio [*een-grah-nahj'-jee-oh*]
gem, gemma [*jehm'-mah*]
gender, genere (m) [*jeh'-neh-reh*]
general *n. & adj.*, generale [*jeh-neh-rah'-leh*]
  in general, in generale [*een jeh-neh-rah'-leh*]
general delivery, fermo posta [*fer'-moh pohs'-tah*]
generally, generalmente [*jeh-neh-rahl-mehn'-teh*]

generation, generazione (f) [*jeh-neh-rah-tsee-oh'-neh*]
generator, generatore (m) [*jeh-neh-rah-toh'-reh*]
generous, generoso [*jeh-neh-roh'-zoh*]
genius, genio [*jeh'-nee-oh*]
Genoa, Genova [*jeh'-noh-vah*]
gentle, soave, dolce [*soh-ah'-veh, dohl'-cheh*]
genuine, genuino [*jeh-noo-ee'-noh*]
germ, germe (m) [*jehr'-meh*]
German *n. & adj.,* tedesco [*teh-dehs'-koh*]
Germany, Germania [*jehr-mah'-nee-ah*]
get [obtain] *v.,* ottenere [*oht-teh-neh'-reh*]
get [receive] *v.,* ricevere [*ree-cheh'-veh-reh*]
get [become] *v.,* divenire [*dee-veh-nee'-reh*]
  get back, ritornare [*ree-tohr-nah'-reh*]
  get down, scendere [*shehn'-deh-reh*]
  get in, entrare [*ehn-trah'-reh*]
  get married, sposarsi [*spoh-zahr'-see*]
  get off, scendere [*shehn'-deh-reh*]
  get on, salire [*sah-lee'-reh*]
  get up, alzarsi [*ahl-tsahr'-see*]
gift, regalo [*reh-gah'-loh*]
gifted, dotato [*doh-tah'-toh*]
gin, liquore di ginepro [*lee-koo-oh'-reh dee jee-neh'-proh*]
girdle, reggicalze (f, pl) [*rehj-jee-kahl'-tseh*]
girl, ragazza [*rah-gahts'-tsah*]
give *v.,* dare (irreg) [*dah'-reh*]
  give him, give her, gli dia, le dia [*lyee dee'-ah, leh dee'-ah*]
  give me, mi dia [*mee dee'-ah*]
  give them, dia loro [*dee'-ah loh'-roh*]
  give us, ci dia [*chee dee'-ah*]
  give back, restituire [*rehs-tee-too-ee'-reh*]
  give in, cedere [*cheh'-deh-reh*]
  give up, rinunciare, arrendersi [*ree-noon-chee-ah'-reh, ahr-rehn'-dehr-see*]
glad, contento [*kohn-tehn'-toh*]
glance *n.,* occhiata [*ohk-kee-ah'-tah*]
glance *v.,* dare un'occhiata [*dah'-reh oon-ohk-kee-ah'-tah*]
gland, glandola [*glahn'-doh-lah*]

glare *v.*, splendere [*splehn'-deh-reh*]

glass [container], bicchiere (m) [*beek-kee-eh'-reh*]

glass [material], vetro [*veh'-troh*]

glasses, occhiali (m, pl) [*ohk-kee-ah'-lee*]

glimpse *n.*, sguardo [*zgoo-ahr'-doh*]

gloomy, oscuro, triste [*ohs-koo'-roh, trees'-teh*]

glove, guanto [*goo-ahn'-toh*]

glue *n.*, colla [*kohl'-lah*]

go *v.*, andare (irreg) [*ahn-dah'-reh*]

> **go across,** attraversare, incontrare [*aht-trah-vehr-sah'-reh, een-kohn-trah'-reh*]
>
> **go away,** andare via [*ahn-dah'-reh vee'-ah*]
>
> **Go away!** Vada via! [*vah'-dah vee'-ah*]
>
> **go back,** ritornare [*ree-tohr-nah'-reh*]
>
> **go by,** passare [*pahs-sah'-reh*]
>
> **go down,** scendere [*shehn'-deh-reh*]
>
> **go in,** entrare [*ehn-trah'-reh*]
>
> **go on,** continuare [*kohn-tee-noo-ah'-reh*]
>
> **Go on!** Continui! [*kohn-tee'-noo-ee*]
>
> **go out,** uscire [*oo-shee'-reh*]
>
> **go to bed,** coricarsi [*koh-ree-kahr'-see*]
>
> **go up,** salire (irreg) [*sah-lee'-reh*]

goal, meta [*meh'-tah*]

God, Dio [*dee'-oh*]

gold, oro [*oh'-roh*]

golf, golf (m) [*gohlf*]

good, buono [*boo-oh'-noh*]

> **Good afternoon!** Buon pomeriggio! [*boo-ohn' poh-meh-reej'-jee-oh*]
>
> **Good-bye!** Arrivederla!, Ciao!, Addio! [*ahr-ree-veh-dehr'-lah, chee-ah'-oh, ahd-dee'-oh*]
>
> **Good day!** Buon giorno! [*boo-ohn' jee-ohr'-noh*]
>
> **Good evening!** Buona sera! [*boo-oh'-nah seh'-rah*]
>
> **Good luck!** Buona fortuna! [*boo-oh'-nah fohr-too'-nah*]
>
> **Good morning!** Buon giorno! [*boo-ohn' jee-ohr'-noh*]
>
> **Good night!** Buona notte! [*boo-oh'-nah noht'-teh*]

good-looking, bello [*behl'-loh*]

goodness, bontà (f, indecl) [*bohn-tah'*]

goods, merce (f) [*mehr'-cheh*]
gorgeous, splendido [*splehn'-dee-doh*]
gossip [person], pettegolo (m), pettegola (f) [*peht-teh'-goh-loh, peht-teh'-goh-lah*]
govern *v.,* governare [*goh-vehr-nah'-reh*]
government, governo [*goh-vehr'-noh*]
governor, governatore (m) [*goh-vehr-nah-toh'-reh*]
graceful, grazioso [*grah-tsee-oh'-zoh*]
gradually, gradualmente [*grah-doo-ahl-mehn'-teh*]
graduate *n.,* laureato [*lah-oo-reh-ah'-toh*]
graduate *v.,* laurearsi [*lah-oo-reh-ahr'-see*]
grain, grano, chicco [*grah'-noh, keek'-koh*]
grammar, grammatica [*grahm-mah'-tee-kah*]
grandchild, nipotino (m), nipotina (f) [*nee-poh-tee'-noh, nee-poh-tee'-nah*]
grandfather, nonno [*nohn'-noh*]
grandmother, nonna [*nohn'-nah*]
grant *v.,* accordare [*ahk-kohr-dah'-reh*]
  granted that, ammesso che [*ahm-mehs'-soh keh*]
grape, uva [*oo'-vah*]
grass, erba [*ehr'-bah*]
grateful, riconoscente [*ree-koh-noh-shehn'-teh*]
gratitude, gratitudine (f) [*grah-tee-too'-dee-neh*]
grave *adj.,* grave [*grah'-veh*]
grave *n.,* tomba [*tohm'-bah*]
gravity, gravità (f, indecl) [*grah-vee-tah'*]
grease *n.,* grasso, unto [*grahs'-soh, oon'-toh*]
great, grande [*grahn'-deh*]
greatness, grandezza [*grahn-dehts'-tsah*]
Great Britain, Gran Bretagna [*grahn breh-tah'-nyah*]
Greece, Grecia [*greh'-chee-ah*]
greedy, avido [*ah'-vee-doh*]
Greek, greco [*greh'-koh*]
green, verde [*vehr'-deh*]
greet *v.,* salutare [*sah-loo-tah'-reh*]
greetings, saluti (m, pl) [*sah-loo'-tee*]
grey, grigio [*gree'-jee-oh*]
grief, dolore (m) [*doh-loh'-reh*]

grieve v., affliggere [ahf-fleej'-jeh-reh]

grin n., smorfia [zmohr'-fee-ah]

grind v., macinare [mah-chee-nah'-reh]

grip, stretta [streht'-tah]

groan n., gemito, lamento [jeh'-mee-toh, lah-mehn'-toh]

groan v., gemere [jeh'-meh-reh]

grocery, drogheria [droh-geh-ree'-ah]

ground, terra, suolo [tehr'-rah, soo-oh'-loh]

ground floor, pianterreno [pee-ahn-tehr-reh'-noh]

group, gruppo [groop'-poh]

grow [cultivate] v., coltivare [kohl-tee-vah'-reh]

grow [increase] v., aumentare [ah-oo-mehn-tah'-reh]

grow [become] v., diventare [dee-vehn-tah'-reh]

grow old v., invecchiare [een-vehk-kee-ah'-reh]

guarantee n., garanzia [gah-rahn-tsee'-ah]

guarantee v., garantire [gah-rahn-tee'-reh]

guard n., guardia [goo-ahr'-dee-ah]

guard v., sorvegliare [sohr-veh-lyah'-reh]

guardian, guardiano [goo-ahr-dee-ah'-noh]

guess n., supposizione (f) [soop-poh-zee-tsee-oh'-neh]

guess v., indovinare [een-doh-vee-nah'-reh]

guest, ospite (m, f) [ohs'-pee-teh]

guide n., guida [goo-ee'-dah]

guide v., guidare [goo-ee-dah'-reh]

guilt, colpa [kohl'-pah]

guilty, colpevole [kohl-peh'-voh-leh]

guitar, chitarra [kee-tahr'-rah]

gum [teeth], gengiva [jehn-jee'-vah]

gum [chewing], gomma americana [gohm'-mah ah-meh-ree-
  kah'-nah]

gun, fucile (m), cannone (m) [foo-chee'-leh, kahn-noh'-neh]

gutter, bassifondi (m, pl) [bahs-see-fohn'-dee]

gymnasium [sports], palestra [pah-lehs'-trah]

gypsy, zingaro [dzeen'-gah-roh]

H

habit, abitudine (f) [*ah-bee-too'-dee-neh*]

hair, capello, pelo [*kah-pehl'-loh, peh'-loh*]

hairbrush, spazzola per capelli [*spahts'-tsoh-lah pehr kah-pehl'-lee*]

haircut, taglio di capelli [*tah'-lyoh dee kah-pehl'-lee*]

hairdresser, parrucchiere (m) [*pahr-rook-kee-eh'-reh*]

hair tonic, tonico per capelli [*toh'-nee-koh pehr kah-pehl'-lee*]

half *n.*, metà (f, indecl) [*meh-tah'*]

half *adj.*, mezzo [*mehdz'-dzo*]
  half past two, le due e mezzo [*leh doo'-eh eh mehdz'-dzo*]

halfway, a metà strada [*ah meh-tah' strah'-dah*]

hall, corridoio, vestibolo, sala [*kohr-ree-doh'-ee-oh, vehs-tee'-boh-loh, sah'-lah*]

halt *v.*, fermare [*fehr-mah'-reh*]

Halt! Alt! [*ahlt*]

ham, prosciutto [*proh-shee-oot'-toh*]

hammer, martello [*mahr-tehl'-loh*]

hand, mano, le mani (pl) [*mah'-noh, leh mah'-nee*]
  on the other hand, d'altro canto [*dahl'-troh kahn'-toh*]

handbag, borsa [*bohr'-sah*]

handkerchief, fazzoletto [*fahts-tsoh-leht'-toh*]

handmade, fatto a mano [*faht'-toh ah mah'-noh*]

handsome, bello [*behl'-loh*]

hang [an object] *v.*, appendere [*ahp-pehn'-deh-reh*]

hanger [clothes], attaccapanni (m, pl) [*aht-tahk-kah-pahn'-nee*]

happen *v.*, accadere [*ahk-kah-deh'-reh*]
  What happened? Cosa è successo?, Che è accaduto? [*koh'-zah eh' sooch-chehs'-soh, keh eh' ahk-kah-doo'-toh*]

happiness, felicità (f, indecl) [*feh-lee-chee-tah'*]

happy, felice [*feh-lee'-cheh*]
   Happy Birthday! Buon compleanno! [*boo-ohn' kohm-pleh-ahn'-noh*]
   Happy New Year! Buon Capodanno! [*boo-ohn' kah-poh-dahn'-noh*]
harbor *n.*, porto [*pohr'-toh*]
hard, duro [*doo'-roh*]
hardhearted, inumano [*een-oo-mah'-noh*]
harm *v.*, nuocere [*noo-oh'-cheh-reh*]
harmful, dannoso [*dahn-noh'-zoh*]
harvest *n.*, raccolta [*rahk-kohl'-tah*]
hat, cappello [*kahp-pehl'-loh*]
hate *n.*, odio [*oh'-dee-oh*]
hate *v.*, odiare [*oh-dee-ah'-reh*]
have *v.*, avere (irreg) [*ah-veh'-reh*]
   have to [must], dovere [*doh-veh'-reh*]
   Do you have to study so late? Deve studiare cosi tardi? [*deh'-veh stoo-dee-ah'-reh coh-see' tahr'-dee*]
   I have to study a lot, Devo studiare molto [*deh'-voh stoo-dee-ah'-reh mohl'-toh*]
he, lui, egli [*loo'-ee, eh'-lyee*]
head [body], testa [*tehs'-tah*]
head [chief], capo [*kah'-poh*]
headache, mal di testa [*mahl dee tehs'-tah*]
headlight, fanale (m) [*fah-nah'-leh*]
heal *v.*, guarire [*goo-ah-ree'-reh*]
health, salute (f) [*sah-loo'-teh*]
   To your health! Alla sua salute! [*ahl'-lah soo'-ah sah-loo'-teh*]
   in good health, in buona salute [*een boo-oh'-nah sah-loo'-teh*]
healthy, sano [*sah'-noh*]
hear *v.*, sentire, udire (irreg) [*sehn-tee'-reh, oo-dee'-reh*]
heart, cuore (m) [*koo-oh'-reh*]
   by heart, a memoria [*ah meh-moh'-ree-ah*]
heart disease, malattia del cuore [*mah-laht-tee'-ah dehl koo-oh'-reh*]
heat *n.*, calore (m), caldo [*kah-loh'-reh, kahl'-doh*]

heat *v.*, riscaldare [*rees-kahl-dah'-reh*]

heaven, cielo [*chee-eh'-loh*]

   Heavens! Per l'amor del cielo! [*pehr lah-mohr' dehl chee-eh'-loh*]

heavy, pesante [*peh-zahn'-teh*]

Hebrew, ebreo [*eh-breh'-oh*]

heel [foot], calcagno [*kahl-kah'-nyoh*]

heel [shoe], tacco [*tahk'-koh*]

height, altezza [*ahl-tehts'-tsah*]

heir, heiress, erede [*eh-reh'-deh*]

hell, inferno [*een-fehr'-noh*]

Hello! Ciao!, Salve! [*chee-ah'-oh, sahl'-veh*]

help *n.*, aiuto [*ah-ee-oo'-toh*]

help *v.*, aiutare [*ah-ee-oo-tah'-reh*]

her *pron.*, la, lei [*lah, leh'-ee*]

her *poss. adj.*, suo [*soo'-oh*]

here, quì, quà [*koo-ee', koo-ah'*]

   Come here! Venga quì! [*vehn'-gah koo-ee'*]

   Here it is Eccolo quì [*ehk'-koh-loh koo-ee'*]

hero, eroe (m) [*eh-roh'-eh*]

hers, il suo, la sua (sing), i suoi, le sue (pl) [*eel soo'-oh, lah soo'-ah, ee soo-oh'-ee, leh soo'-eh*]

herself, lei stessa [*leh'-ee stehs'-sah*]

hide *v.*, nascondere [*nahs-kohn'-deh-reh*]

high, alto, elevato [*ahl'-toh, eh-leh-vah'-toh*]

higher, più alto [*pee-oo' ahl'-toh*]

high school, scuola media [*skoo-oh'-lah meh'-dee-ah*]

highway, autostrada [*ah-oo-toh-strah'-dah*]

hill, collina [*kohl-lee'-nah*]

him *pron.*, lo, lui [*loh, loo'-ee*]

himself, lui stesso [*loo'-ee stehs'-soh*]

hint *n.*, accenno [*ahch-chehn'-noh*]

hip, fianco [*fee-ahn'-koh*]

hire [rent] *v.*, affittare [*ahf-feet-tah'-reh*]

history, storia [*stoh'-ree-ah*]

hit *v.*, colpire [*kohl-pee'-reh*]

hitchhiking, autostop [*ah'-oo-toh-stohp*]

hold *v.*, tenere [*teh-neh'-reh*]

hole, buco, cavità (f, indecl) [*boo'-koh, kah-vee-tah'*]
holiday, festa [*fehs'-tah*]
Holland, Olanda [*oh-lahn'-dah*]
holy, santo [*sahn'-toh*]
home, casa [*kah'-zah*]
  at home, a casa [*ah kah'-zah*]
  Make yourself at home! Si faccia comodo! [*see fahch'-chee-ah koh'-moh-doh*]
homeland, patria [*pah'-tree-ah*]
homesick, nostalgico [*nohs-tahl'-jee-koh*]
honest, onesto [*oh-nehs'-toh*]
honey, miele (m) [*mee-eh'-leh*]
honeymoon, luna di miele [*loo'-nah dee mee-eh'-leh*]
honor *n.,* onore (m) [*oh-noh'-reh*]
hook, gancio [*gahn'-chee-oh*]
hope *n.,* speranza [*speh-rahn'-tsah*]
hope *v.,* sperare [*speh-rah'-reh*]
hopeful, promettente [*proh-meht-tehn'-teh*]
hopeless, disperato [*dees-peh-rah'-toh*]
horizon, orizzonte (m) [*oh-reedz-dzohn'-teh*]
horn [animal or shape], corno [*kohr'-noh*]
horn [auto], tromba [*trohm'-bah*]
horrible, orribile [*ohr-ree'-bee-leh*]
horse, cavallo [*kah-vahl'-loh*]
hospital, ospedale (m) [*ohs-peh-dah'-leh*]
hospitality, ospitalità (f, indecl) [*ohs-pee-tah-lee-tah'*]
host, ospite (che òspita) [*ohs'-pee-teh*]
hostess, ostessa, hostess [*ohs-tehs'-sah, ohs'-tehs*]
hostile, ostile [*ohs-tee'-leh*]
hot, caldo [*kahl'-doh*]
hotel, albergo [*ahl-behr'-goh*]
hotel room, camera d'albergo [*kah'-meh-rah dahl-behr'-goh*]
hour, ora [*oh'-rah*]
house, casa [*kah'-zah*]
housekeeper, governante di casa [*goh-vehr-nahn'-teh dee kah'-zah*]
housewife, massaia [*mahs-sah'-ee-ah*]
how, come [*koh'-meh*]

How do you do? Come sta? [*koh'-meh stah*]

How far is it? Quanto è lontano? [*koo-ahn'-toh eh' lohn-tah'-noh*]

How long [time]? Per quanto tempo? [*pehr koo-ahn'-toh tehm'-poh*]

How many? Quanti? Quante? [*koo-ahn'-tee, koo-ahn'-teh*]

How much? Quanto? [*koo-ahn'-toh*]

however, comunque [*koh-moon'-koo-eh*]

hug *n*., abbraccio [*ahb-brach'-chee-oh*]

human, umano [*oo-mah'-noh*]

humanity, umanità (f, indecl) [*oo-mah-nee-tah'*]

humid, umido [*oo'-mee-doh*]

humility, umiltà (f, indecl) [*oo-meel-tah'*]

humorous, umoristico [*oo-moh-rees'-tee-koh*]

hundred, cento (invar.) [*chen'-toh*]

   one hundred, cento [*chen'-toh*]

   two hundred, due cento [*doo'-eh chehn'-toh*]

Hungarian, ungherese [*oon-geh-reh'-zeh*]

Hungary, Ungheria [*oon-geh-ree'-ah*]

hunger *n*., fame (f) [*fah'-meh*]

hungry: be hungry, avere fame [*ah-veh'-reh fah'-meh*]

hunt *v*., cacciare [*kahch-chee-ah'-reh*]

hunting, caccia [*kahch'-chee-ah*]

hurricane, uragano [*oo-rah-gah'-noh*]

hurry *n*., fretta [*freht'-tah*]

   be in a hurry, avere fretta [*ah-veh'-reh freht'-tah*]

   Hurry up! Presto, presto! [*prehs'-toh, prehs'-toh*]

hurt [ache] *v*., sentire dolore [*sehn-tee'-reh doh-loh'-reh*]

hurt [somebody] *v*., fare male a [*fah'-reh mah'-leh ah*]

   hurt one's feelings, offendere [*ohf-fehn'-deh-reh*]

husband, marito [*mah-ree'-toh*]

hypocrisy, ipocrisia [*ee-poh-kree-zee'-ah*]

hysterical, isterico [*ees-teh'-ree-koh*]

I

I, io [*ee'-oh*]
ice, ghiaccio [*gee-ahch'-chee-oh*]
ice cream, gelato [*jeh-lah'-toh*]
idea, idea [*ee-deh'-ah*]
ideal, ideale [*ee-deh-ah'-leh*]
identical, identico [*ee-dehn'-tee-koh*]
identification card, carta d'identità [*kahr'-tah dee-dehn-tee-tah'*]
identify *v.,* identificare [*ee-dehn-tee-fee-kah'-reh*]
identity, identità (f, indecl) [*ee-dehn-tee-tah'*]
idle *adj.,* ozioso [*oh-tsee'-oh-zoh*]
if, se, in caso che [*seh, een kah'-zoh keh*]
   even if, anche se [*ahn'-keh seh*]
ignition, accensione [*ahch-chehn'-see-oh-neh*]
ignorant, ignorante [*ee-nyoh-rahn'-teh*]
ill, ammalato [*ahm-mah-lah'-toh*]
illegal, illegale [*eel-leh-gah'-leh*]
illegible, illegibile [*eel-leh-jee'-bee-leh*]
illiterate *n.,* analfabeta [*ah-nahl-fah-beh'-tah*]
illness, malattia [*mah-laht-tee'-ah*]
image, immagine (f) [*eem-mah'-jee-neh*]
imagination, immaginazione (f) [*eem-mah-jee-nah-tsee-oh'-neh*]
imagine *v.,* immaginare [*eem-mah-jee-nah'-reh*]
   Just imagine! Figurati!, Si figuri! [*fee-goo'-rah-tee, see fee-goo'-ree*]
imitate *v.,* imitare [*ee-mee-tah'-reh*]
imitation, imitazione (f) [*ee-mee-tah-tsee-oh'-neh*]
immaterial, immateriale [*eem-mah-teh-ree-ah'-leh*]
immature, immaturo [*eem-mah-too'-roh*]
immediately, immediatamente [*eem-meh-dee-ah-tah-mehn'-teh*]

immense, immenso [*eem-mehn'-soh*]
immigration, immigrazione (f) [*eem-mee-grah-tsee-oh'-neh*]
immoral, immorale [*eem-moh-rah'-leh*]
immunity, immunità (f, indecl) [*eem-moo-nee-tah'*]
impartial, imparziale [*eem-pah-tsee-ah'-leh*]
impatient, impaziente [*eem-pah-tsee-ehn'-teh*]
imperfect, imperfetto [*eem-pehr-feht'-toh*]
impolite, scortese [*skohr-teh'-zeh*]
import *v.,* importare [*eem-por-tah'-reh*]
importance, importanza [*eem-pohr-tahn'-tsa*]
important, importante [*eem-pohr-tahn'-teh*]
imported, importato [*eem-pohr-tah'-toh*]
impossible, impossibile [*eem-pohs-see'-bee-leh*]
impression, impressione (f) [*eem-prehs-see-oh'-neh*]
impressive, impressionante [*eem-prehs-see-oh-nahn'-teh*]
improbable, improbabile [*eem-proh-bah'-bee-leh*]
improve *v.,* migliorare [*mee-lyoh-rah'-reh*]
improvement, miglioramento [*mee-lyoh-rah-mehn'-toh*]
in, in [*een*]
  in no way, in nessun modo [*een nehs-soon' moh'-doh*]
  in spite of, a dispetto di [*ah dees-peht'-toh dee*]
  in the afternoon, al pomeriggio [*ahl poh-meh-reej'-jee-oh*]
  Is Mr. Cicco in? È in casa il Signor Cicco? [*eh' een kah'-zah eel see-nyohr' cheek'-koh*]
inaccurate, inesatto [*een-eh-zat'-toh*]
inch, pollice (m) [*pohl'-lee-cheh*]
incident, incidente [*een-chee-dehn'-teh*]
incidentally, incidentalmente [*een-chee-dehn-tahl-mehn'-teh*]
inclination, inclinazione (f) [*een-klee-nah-tsee-oh'-neh*]
include *v.,* includere [*een-kloo'-deh-reh*]
included, incluso [*een-kloo'-zoh*]
income, reddito [*rehd'-dee-toh*]
income tax, imposta sul reddito [*eem-pohs'-tah sool rehd'-dee-toh*]
incomparable, incomparabile [*een-kohm-pah-rah'-bee-leh*]
incomplete, incompleto [*een-kohm-pleh'-toh*]
inconvenience, sconvenienza [*skohn-veh-nee-ehn'-tsah*]

incorrect, inesatto [*een-eh-zaht'-toh*]
increase *n.*, aumento [*ah-oo-mehn'-toh*]
increase *v.*, aumentare [*ah-oo-mehn-tah'-reh*]
indeed, in verità [*een veh-ree-tah'*]
   Yes, indeed! Davvero! [*dahv-veh'-roh*]
indefinite, indefinito [*een-deh-fee-nee'-toh*]
independent, indipendente [*een-dee-pehn-dehn'-teh*]
India, India [*een'-dee-ah*]
Indian, indiano [*een-dee-ah'-noh*]
indicate *v.*, indicare [*een-dee-kah'-reh*]
indifferent, indifferente [*een-deef-feh-rehn'-teh*]
indigestion, indigestione (f) [*een-dee-jehs-tee-oh'-neh*]
indignant, indignato [*een-dee-nyah'-toh*]
indirect, indiretto [*een-dee-reht'-toh*]
indiscreet, indiscreto [*een-dees-kreh'-toh*]
individual *adj.*, individuale [*een-dee-vee-doo-ah'-leh*]
indoors, dentro [*dehn'-troh*]
industrial, industriale [*een-doos-tree-ah'-leh*]
industry, industria [*een-doos'-tree-ah*]
inefficient, inefficiente [*een-ehf-fee-chee-ehn'-teh*]
inexpensive, economico [*eh-koh-noh'-mee-koh*]
infant, infante (m) [*een-fahn'-teh*]
infection, infezione (f) [*een-feh-tsee-oh'-neh*]
inferior, inferiore [*een-feh-ree-oh'-reh*]
infinite, infinito [*een-fee-nee'-toh*]
infinitive, infinito [*een-fee-nee'-toh*]
influence *n.*, influenza [*een-floo-ehn'-tsah*]
influence *v.*, influenzare [*een-floo-ehn-zah'-reh*]
inform *v.*, informare [*een-fohr-mah'-reh*]
information, informazione (f) [*een-fohr-mah-tsee-oh'-neh*]
infrequent, infrequente [*een-freh-koo-ehn'-teh*]
inhabitant, abitante [*ah-bee-tahn'-teh*]
inherit *v.*, ereditare [*eh-reh-dee-tah'-reh*]
inheritance, eredità (f, indecl) [*eh-reh-dee-tah'*]
initial *n. & adj.*, iniziale (f) [*ee-nee-tsee-ah'-leh*]
injection, iniezione (f) [*ee-nee-eh-tsee-oh'-neh*]
injure *v.*, ferire [*feh-ree'-reh*]
injury, ferita [*feh-ree'-tah*]

injustice, ingiustizia [*een-jee-oos-tee'-tsee-ah*]
ink, inchiostro [*een-kee-ohs'-troh*]
inn, locanda [*loh-kahn'-dah*]
inner, interiore [*een-teh-ree-oh'-reh*]
innkeeper, oste (m) [*ohs'-teh*]
innocent, innocente [*een-noh-chehn'-teh*]
inquire v., informarsi [*een-fohr-mahr'-see*]
insane, pazzo [*pahts'-tsoh*]
insect, insetto [*een-seht'-toh*]
inside, dentro [*dehn'-troh*]
   inside out, rivoltato [*ree-vohl-tah'-toh*]
insight, intuizione (f) [*een-too-ee-tsee-oh'-neh*]
insist v., insistere [*een-sees'-teh-reh*]
inspect v., ispezionare [*ees-peh-tsee-oh-nah'-reh*]
inspection, ispezione (f) [*ees-peh-tsee-oh'-neh*]
inspector, ispettore (m) [*ees-peht-toh'-reh*]
inspiration, ispirazione (f) [*ees-pee-rah-tsee-oh'-neh*]
install v., installare [*een-stahl-lah'-reh*]
instance, istanza [*ees-tahn'-tsah*]
   for instance, per esempio [*pehr eh-zehm'-pee-oh*]
instead, anziché [*ahn-tsee-keh'*]
   instead of, invece di [*een-veh'-cheh dee*]
instinct, istinto [*ees-teen'-toh*]
institution, istituzione (f) [*ees-tee-too-tsee-oh'-neh*]
instruct v., instruire [*een-stroo-ee'-reh*]
instruction, istruzione (f) [*ees-troo-tsee-oh'-neh*]
instructor, istruttore (m) [*ees-troot-toh'-reh*]
instrument, strumento [*stroo-mehn'-toh*]
insufficient, insufficiente [*een-soof-fee-chee-ehn'-teh*]
insult n., insulto [*een-sool'-toh*]
insult v., insultare [*een-sool-tah'-reh*]
insurance, assicurazione (f) [*ahs-see-koo-rah-tsee-oh'-neh*]
insurance policy, polizza di assicurazione [*poh-leets'-tsah
   dee ahs-see-koo-rah-tsee-oh'-neh*]
insure v., assicurare [*ahs-see-koo-rah'-reh*]
intact, intatto [*een-taht'-toh*]
intellectual, intellettuale [*een-teh-leht-too-ah'-leh*]
intelligent, intelligente [*een-tehl-lee-jehn'-teh*]

intend v., intendere [*een-tehn'-deh-reh*]
intense, intenso [*een-tehn'-soh*]
intention, intenzione (f) [*een-tehn-tsee-oh'-neh*]
interest [concern] n., interesse (m) [*een-teh-rehs'-seh*]
interest [financial] n., profitto [*proh-feet'-toh*]
interest v., interessare [*een-teh-rehs-sah'-reh*]
  be interested in, interessarsi di [*een-teh-rehs-sahr'-see dee*]
interesting, interessante [*een-teh-rehs-sahn'-teh*]
interfere v., interferire [*een-tehr-feh-ree'-reh*]
interior, interiore [*een-teh-ree-oh'-reh*]
intermission, intervallo [*een-tehr-vahl'-loh*]
internal, interno [*een-tehr'-noh*]
international, internazionale [*een-tehr-nah-tsee-oh-nah'-leh*]
interpreter, interprete [*een-tehr'-preh-teh*]
intersection, intersezione (f) [*een-tehr-seh-tsee-oh'-neh*]
interview n., intervista [*een-tehr-vees'-tah*]
intimate adj., intimo [*een'-tee-moh*]
into, nel, nello, nella, nell' [*nehl, nehl'-loh, nehl'-lah, nehl*]
introduce v., presentare, introdurre (irreg) [*preh-zehn-tah'-reh, een-troh-door'-reh*]
introduction, presentazione (f) [*preh-zehn-tah-tsee-oh'-neh*]
intuition, intuizione, intuito [*een-too-ee-tsee-oh'-neh, een-too'-ee-toh*]
invalid, invalido [*een-vah'-lee-doh*]
invaluable, inestimabile [*een-ehs-tee-mah'-bee-leh*]
invasion, invasione (f) [*een-vah-zee-oh'-neh*]
invention, invenzione (f) [*een-vehn-tsee-oh'-neh*]
inventor, inventore (m) [*een-vehn-toh'-reh*]
invest v., investire [*een-vehs-tee'-reh*]
investigate v., investigare [*een-vehs-tee-gah'-reh*]
invisible, invisibile [*een-vee-zee'-bee-leh*]
invitation, invito [*een-vee'-toh*]
invite v., invitare [*een-vee-tah'-reh*]
invoice n., fattura [*faht-too'-rah*]
involuntary, involontario [*een-voh-lohn-tah'-ree-oh*]
Ireland, Irlanda [*eer-lahn'-dah*]
Irish, irlandese [*eer-lahn-deh'-zeh*]
iron [metal] n., ferro [*fehr'-roh*]

iron [for ironing] *n.*, ferro da stiro [*fer'-roh dah stee'-roh*]
iron [clothes] *v.*, stirare [*stee-rah'-reh*]
irrational, illogico [*eel-loh'-jee-koh*]
irregular, irregolare [*eer-reh-goh-lah'-reh*]
irresistible, irresistibile [*eer-reh-zees-tee'-bee-leh*]
irritate *v.*, irritare [*eer-ree-tah'-reh*]
irritation, irritazione (f) [*eer-ree-tah-tsee-oh'-neh*]
is, è, sta [*eh', stah*]
   How is he! Come sta?, Com'è? [*koh'-meh stah, koh'-meh*]
island, isola [*ee'-zoh-lah*]
issue [magazine], numero [*noo'-meh-roh*]
it [obj. of verb], lo, la [*loh, lah*]
Italian *n. & adj.*, italiano [*ee-tah-lee-ah'-noh*]
Italy, Italia [*ee-tah'-lee-ah*]
itch *v.*, prudere [*proo'-deh-reh*]
item [thing], articolo [*ahr-tee'-koh-loh*]
itinerary, itinerario [*ee-tee-neh-rah'-ree-oh*]
its, suo, sua; suoi, sue (pl) [*soo'-oh, soo'-ah; soo-oh'-ee, soo'-eh*]
itself, stesso [*stehs'-soh*]
ivory, avorio [*ah-voh'-ree-oh*]

J

jack [auto], cric [*kreek*]
jacket, giacca, giacche (pl) [*jee-ahk'-kah, jee-ahk'-keh*]
jail, carcere (m, f) [*kahr'-cheh-reh*]
jam, marmellata [*mahr-mehl-lah'-tah*]
janitor, portiere (m) [*pohr-tee-eh'-reh*]
January, gennaio [*jehn-nah'-ee-oh*]
Japan, Giappone (m) [*jee-ahp-poh'-neh*]
Japanese, giapponese [*jee-ahp-poh-neh'-zeh*]
jar [container], giara [*jee-ah'-rah*]
jaw, mascella [*mah-shehl'-lah*]
jazz, giaz [*jee-ahts'*]

jealous, geloso [*jeh-loh'-zoh*]

jelly, gelatina [*jeh-lah-tee'-nah*]

Jew, ebreo [*eh-breh'-oh*]

jewel, gioiello [*jee-oh-ee-ehl'-loh*]

jeweler, gioielliere (m) [*jee-oh-ee-ehl-lee'-eh-reh*]

jeweler's shop, gioielleria [*jee-oh-ee-ehl-leh-ree'-ah*]

Jewish, Giudeo [*jee-oo-deh'-oh*]

job, impiego, lavoro [*eem-pee-eh'-goh, lah-voh'-roh*]

join *v.,* unire [*oo-nee'-reh*]

jointly, unitamente [*oo-nee-tah-mehn'-teh*]

joke *n.,* scherzo [*skehr'-tsoh*]

joker, burlone [*boor-loh'-neh*]

journal, giornale (m) [*jee-ohr-nah'-leh*]

journalism, giornalismo [*jee-ohr-nah-leez'-moh*]

journalist, giornalista (m, f) [*jee-ohr-nah-lees'-tah*]

journey *n.,* viaggio, gita [*vee-ahj'-jee-oh, jee'-tah*]

jovial, gioviale [*jee-oh-vee-ah'-leh*]

joy, gioia, allegria [*jee-oh'-ee-ah, ahl-leh-gree'-ah*]

joyful, gioioso [*jee-oh-ee-oh'-zoh*]

jubilant, giubilante [*jee-oo-bee-lahn'-teh*]

judge *n.,* giudice (m) [*jee-oo'-dee-cheh*]

judge *v.,* giudicare [*jee-oo-dee-kah'-reh*]

judgment, giudizio, sentenza [*jee-oo-dee'-tsee-oh, sehn-tehn'-tsah*]

jug, brocca [*brohk'-kah*]

juice, succo [*sook'-koh*]

  fruit juice, succo di frutta, spremuta [*sook'-koh dee froot'-tah, spreh-moo'-tah*]

July, luglio [*loo'-lyoh*]

jump *n.,* salto [*sahl'-toh*]

jump *v.,* saltare [*sahl-tah'-reh*]

June, giugno [*jee-oo'-nyoh*]

junior, più giovane [*pee-oo' jee-oh'-vah-neh*]

jurisdiction, giurisdizione (f) [*jee-oo-reez-dee-tsee-oh'-neh*]

jury, giuria [*jee-oo-ree'-ah*]

just *adj.,* giusto, equo [*jee-oos'-toh, eh'-koo-oh*]

just *adv.,* proprio, appena [*proh'-pree-oh, ahp-peh'-nah*]

  just as, proprio come [*proh'-pree-oh koh'-meh*]

I just arrived, Sono giusto arrivato [*soh'-noh jee-oos'-toh ahr-ree-vah'-toh*]
  just now, poco fa [*poh'-koh fah*]
justice, giustizia [*jee-oos-tee'-tsee-ah*]

K

keep *v.*, tenere (irreg) [*teh-neh'-reh*]
  keep from, astenersi [*ahs-teh-nehr'-see*]
  keep out, tenersi al di fuori [*teh-nehr'-see ahl dee foo-oh'-ree*]
  Keep out! Vietato l'ingresso! [*vee-eh-tah'-toh leen-grehs'-soh*]
  keep quiet, stare zitto [*stah'-reh dzeet'-toh*]
  Keep quiet! Stia zitto! [*stee'-ah dzeet'-toh*]
kettle, pentolino [*pehn-toh-lee'-noh*]
key *n.*, chiave (f) [*kee-ah'-veh*]
kick *n.*, pedata, colpo [*peh-dah'-tah, kohl'-poh*]
kick *v.*, tirar calci a [*tee-rahr' kahl'-chee ah*]
kid [animal] *n.*, capretto [*kah-preht'-toh*]
kid [child] *n.*, ragazzetto [*rah-gahts-tseht'-toh*]
kid *v.*, scherzare [*skehr-tsah'-reh*]
  No kidding, Senza scherzi [*sehn'-tsah skehr'-tsee*]
kidnap *v.*, rapire [*rah-pee'-reh*]
kidney [food], rognone (m) [*roh-nyoh'-neh*]
kidney [anat.], rene (m) [*reh'-neh*]
kill *v.*, uccidere [*ooch-chee'-deh-reh*]
kilogram, chilo [*kee'-loh*]
kilometer, chilometro [*kee-loh'-meh-troh*]
kind *n.*, genere (m), specie (f) [*jeh'-neh-reh, speh'-chee-eh*]
kind *adj.*, gentile [*jehn-tee'-leh*]
kindness, gentilezza [*jehn-tee-lehts'-tsah*]
king, re (m) [*reh*]
kiss *n.*, bacio [*bah'-chee-oh*]
kiss *v.*, baciare [*bah-chee-ah'-reh*]

kitchen, cucina [*koo-chee'-nah*]

knee, ginocchio [*jee-nohk'-kee-oh*]

kneel v., inginocchiarsi [*een-jee-nohk-kee-ahr'-see*]

knife, coltello [*kohl-tehl'-loh*]

knock n., colpo, bussata [*kohl'-poh, boos-sah'-tah*]

knock v., bussare, colpire [*boos-sah'-reh, kohl-pee'-reh*]

knot n., nodo [*noh'-doh*]

know [be acquainted with] v., conoscere [*koh-noh'-sheh-reh*]

know [general sense] v., sapere (irreg) [*sah-peh'-reh*]

   Do you know? Sa lei? [*sah leh'-ee*]

   I don't know, Non so [*nohn soh*]

   Who knows? Chi sa? [*kee sah*]

knowledge, sapere (m), conoscenza [*sah-peh'-reh, koh-noh-shehn'-tsa*]

L

label, etichetta [*eh-tee-keht'-tah*]

labor n., lavoro, mano d'opera [*lah-voh'-roh, mah'-noh doh'-peh-rah*]

laboratory, laboratorio [*lah-boh-rah-toh'-ree-oh*]

laborer, operaio [*oh-peh-rah'-ee-oh*]

laces [shoe], lacci (m, pl) [*lahch'-chee*]

lack n., mancanza [*mahn-kahn'-tsah*]

lack: be lacking v., mancare [*mahn-kah'-reh*]

   lacking in, privo di [*pree'-voh dee*]

ladder, scala [*skah'-lah*]

ladies' room, per signore (f, pl) [*pehr see-nyoh'-reh*]

lady, signora [*see-nyoh'-rah*]

lake, lago, laghi (pl) [*lah'-goh, lah'-gee*]

lamb, agnello [*ah-nyeh'-loh*]

lame adj., zoppo [*dzohp'-poh*]

lamp, lampada [*lahm'-pah-dah*]

land n., terra [*tehr'-rah*]

land [airplane] v., atterrare [*aht-tehr-rah'-reh*]

land [ship] *v.*, sbarcare [*zbahr-kah'-reh*]
landing [airplane], atterraggio [*aht-tehr-rahj'-jee-oh*]
landing [ship], approdo [*ahp-proh'-doh*]
landlady, padrona di casa [*pah-droh'-nah dee kah'-zah*]
landlord, padrone di casa [*pah-droh'-neh dee kah'-zah*]
landmark, punto di riferimento [*poon'-toh dee ree-feh-ree-mehn'-toh*]
landowner, proprietario di terre [*proh-pree-eh-tah'-ree-oh dee tehr'-reh*]
landscape, paesaggio [*pah-eh-zahj'-jee-oh*]
language, lingua [*leen'-goo-ah*]
large, largo, grande [*lahr'-goh, grahn'-deh*]
last *adj.*, ultimo [*ool'-tee-moh*]
   at last, finalmente [*fee-nahl-mehn'-teh*]
   last night, la notte scorsa [*lah noht'-teh skohr'-sah*]
   last week, la settimana scorsa [*lah seht-tee-mah'-nah skohr'-sah*]
   last year, l'ultimo anno [*lool'-tee-moh ahn'-noh*]
last *v.*, durare [*doo-rah'-reh*]
late *adv.*, tardi [*tahr'-dee*]
   be late *v.*, essere in ritardo [*ehs'-seh-reh een ree-tahr'-doh*]
lately, recentemente [*reh-chehn-teh-mehn'-teh*]
later, più tardi [*pee-oo' tahr'-dee*]
latest, recentissimo [*reh-chehn-tees'-see-moh*]
Latin, latino [*lah-tee'-noh*]
latter, ultimo, secondo [*ool'-tee-moh, seh-kohn'-doh*]
laugh *n.*, riso [*ree'-zoh*]
laugh *v.*, ridere [*ree'-deh-reh*]
laughter, risata [*ree-zah'-tah*]
laundry, lavanderia [*lah-vahn-deh-ree'-ah*]
law, legge (f) [*lehj'-jeh*]
lawful, legittimo [*leh-jeet'-tee-moh*]
lawn, prato [*prah'-toh*]
lawyer, avvocato [*ahv-voh-kah'-toh*]
lay *v.*, mettere [*meht'-teh-reh*]
lazy, pigro [*pee'-groh*]
lead [metal] *n.*, piombo [*pee-ohm'-boh*]
lead *v.*, guidare [*goo-ee-dah'-reh*]

leader, capo [*kah'-poh*]

lean *v.*, appoggiare [*ahp-pohj-jee-ah'-reh*]

leaning *adj.*, pendente [*pehn-dehn'-teh*]

learn *v.*, imparare [*eem-pah-rah'-reh*]

learned *adj.*, istruito [*ees-troo-ee'-toh*]

lease *n.*, contratto d'affitto [*kohn-traht'-toh dahf-feet'-toh*]

lease *v.*, affittare [*ahf-feet-tah'-reh*]

least, minimo [*mee'-nee-moh*]

   at least, al meno [*ahl meh'-noh*]

leather, cuoio [*koo-oh'-ee-oh*]

leave [abandon] *v.*, abbandonare [*ahb-bahn-doh-nah'-reh*]

leave [allow] *v.*, permettere [*pehr-meht'-teh-reh*]

leave [depart] *v.*, partire [*pahr-tee'-reh*]

lecture *n.*, conferenza [*kohn-feh-rehn'-tsah*]

left [direction], sinistro [*see-nees'-troh*]

   to the left, a sinistra [*ah see-nees'-trah*]

leg, gamba [*gahm'-bah*]

legal, legale [*leh-gah'-leh*]

legible, leggibile [*lehj-jee'-bee-leh*]

legitimate, legittimo [*leh-jeet'-tee-moh*]

leisure, agio [*ah'-jee-oh*]

lemon, limone (m) [*lee-moh'-neh*]

lemonade, limonata [*lee-moh-nah'-tah*]

lend *v.*, prestare [*prehs-tah'-reh*]

length, lunghezza [*loon-gehts'-tsah*]

lens, lente (f) [*lehn'-teh*]

less, meno [*meh'-noh*]

   more or less, più o meno [*pee-oo' oh meh'-noh*]

lesson, lezione (f) [*leh-tsee-oh'-neh*]

let [permit] *v.*, permettere [*pehr-meht'-teh-reh*]

let [rent] *v.*, affittare [*ahf-fee-tah'-reh*]

   Room to let, Stanza d'affittare [*stahn'-tsah dahf-feet-tah'-reh*]

let [leave] *v.*, lasciare [*lah-shee-ah'-reh*]

   let alone *v.*, lasciar stare [*lah-shee-ahr' stah'-reh*]

   Let him go, Lo lasci andare [*loh lah'-shee ahn-dah'-reh*]

letter, lettera [*leht'-teh-rah*]

   letter of introduction, lettera di presentazione [*leht'-teh-*

    rah dee preh-zehn-tah-tsee-oh'-neh]

letter box, cassetta da lettere [kahs-seht'-tah dah leht'-teh-reh]

level n., livello [lee-vehl'-loh]

liability, obbligo [ohb'-blee-goh]

liar, bugiardo [boo-jee-ahr'-doh]

liberal, liberale [lee-beh-rah'-leh]

liberty, libertà (f, indecl) [lee-behr-tah']

library, biblioteca [bee-blee-oh-teh'-kah]

license n., licenza [lee-chehn'-tsah]

lid, coperchio [koh-pehr'-kee-oh]

    eyelid, palpebra [pahl'-peh-brah]

lie [untruth] n., bugia [boo-jee'-ah]

lie [tell an untruth] v., mentire [mehn-tee'-reh]

lie down, sdraiarsi [zdrah-ee-ahr'-see]

life, vita [vee'-tah]

lifeboat, scialuppa [shee-ah-loop'-pah]

lifeguard, bagnino [bah-nyee'-noh]

life insurance, assicurazione sulla vita [ahs-see-koo-rah-tsee-oh'-neh sool'-lah vee'-tah]

life jacket, salvagente (m) [sahl-vah-jehn'-teh]

lift v., sollevare [sohl-leh-vah'-reh]

light n., luce (f) [loo'-cheh]

light v., accendere [ahch-chehn'-deh-reh]

light adj., leggero, chiaro [lehj-jeh'-roh, kee-ah'-roh]

lighter [cigarette] n., accendi-sigaro [ahch-chehn'-dee-see'-gah-roh]

lighthouse, faro [fah'-roh]

lightning, fulmine (f), lampo [fool'-mee-neh, lahm'-poh]

lights [car], fari [fah'-ree]

likable, piacevole [pee-ah-cheh'-voh-leh]

like adv. & prep., simile, come [see'-mee-leh, koh'-meh]

like v., piacere, amare [pee-ah-cheh'-reh, ah-mah'-reh]

    I don't like it, Non mi piace [nohn mee pee-ah'-cheh]

    I like it very much, Mi piace moltissimo [mee pee-ah'-cheh mohl-tees'-see-moh]

    Would you like . . .? Le piacerebbe . . .? [leh pee-ah-cheh-rehb'-beh]

limit *n.*, limite (m) [*lee'-mee-teh*]
limit *v.*, limitare [*lee-mee-tah'-reh*]
line, linea [*lee'-neh-ah*]
linen [clothing], biancheria [*bee-ahn-keh-ree'-ah*]
lip, labbro, le labbra (pl) [*lahb'-broh, leh lahb'-brah*]
lipstick, rossetto [*rohs-seht'-toh*]
liquid, liquido [*lee'-koo-ee-doh*]
liquor, liquore (m) [*lee-koo-oh'-reh*]
list *n.*, lista [*lees'-tah*]
listen *v.*, ascoltare, sentire [*ahs-kohl-tah'-reh, sehn-tee'-reh*]
literally, letteralmente [*leht-teh-rahl-mehn'-teh*]
literature, letteratura [*leht-teh-rah-too'-rah*]
little *adj.*, piccolo [*peek'-koh-loh*]
little *adv.*, poco [*poh'-koh*]
   a little bit, proprio un poco [*proh'-pree-oh oon poh'-koh*]
   little by little, poco a poco [*poh'-koh ah poh'-koh*]
live [be alive] *v.*, vivere [*vee'-veh-reh*]
live [reside] *v.*, abitare [*ah-bee-tah'-reh*]
live *adv.*, vivo [*vee'-voh*]
lively, vivace [*vee-vah'-cheh*]
liver, fegato [*feh'-gah-toh*]
living room, stanza soggiorno [*stahn'-tsah sohj-jee-ohr'-noh*]
load *n.*, carico [*kah'-ree-koh*]
load *v.*, caricare [*kah-ree-kah'-reh*]
loaf [of bread], panino [*pah-nee'-noh*]
loan *n.*, prestito [*prehs'-tee-toh*]
lobby, vestibolo [*vehs-tee'-boh-loh*]
local, locale [*loh-kah'-leh*]
locate *v.*, collocare [*kohl-loh-kah'-reh*]
located, situato [*see-too-ah'-toh*]
location, località (f, indecl) [*loh-kah-lee-tah'*]
lock *v.*, chiudere a chiave [*kee-oo'-deh-reh ah kee-ah'-veh*]
lodging, alloggio [*ahl-lohj'-jee-oh*]
logical, logico [*loh'-jee-koh*]
lonely, solitario [*soh-lee-tah'-ree-oh*]
long *adj.*, lungo [*loon'-goh*]
long for *v.*, desiderare [*deh-zee-deh-rah'-reh*]
longer [distance], più lungo [*pee-oo' loon'-goh*]

longer [time], più a lungo [*pee-oo' ah loon'-goh*]
longing, desiderio [*deh-zee-deh'-ree-oh*]
look *n.*, sguardo [*zgoo-ahr'-doh*]
look *v.*, guardare [*goo-ahr-dah'-reh*]
    Look! Guardi! [*goo-ahr'-dee*]
   look for, cercare [*chehr-kah'-reh*]
    Look out! Attenzione! [*aht-tehn-tsee-oh'-neh*]
looks [appearance], aspetto [*ahs-peht'-toh*]
loose, sciolto, libero [*shee-ohl'-toh, lee'-beh-roh*]
loosen *v.*, allentare [*ahl-lehn-tah'-reh*]
lose *v.*, perdere [*pehr'-deh-reh*]
loss, perdita [*pehr'-dee-tah*]
lost, perduto [*pehr-doo'-toh*]
lot [quantity], molto [*mohl'-toh*]
loud, aloud alta voce [*ahl'-tah voh'-cheh*]
loudspeaker, altoparlante [*ahl-toh-pahr-lahn'-teh*]
love *n.*, amore (m) [*ah-moh'-reh*]
love *v.*, amare [*ah-mah'-reh*]
lovely, grazioso [*grah-tsee-oh'-zoh*]
lover, amante (m, f) [*ah-mahn'-teh*]
low *adj.*, basso [*bahs'-soh*]
loyal, leale [*leh-ah'-leh*]
lubricate *v.*, lubrificare [*loo-bree-fee-kah'-reh*]
lubrication, lubrificazione (f) [*loo-bree-fee-kah-tsee-oh'-neh*]
luck, fortuna [*fohr-too'-nah*]
    Good luck! Buona fortuna! [*boo-oh'-nah fohr-too'-nah*]
lucky, fortunato [*fohr-too-nah'-toh*]
luggage, bagaglio [*bah-gah'-lyoh*]
lunch *n.*, pranzo, seconda colazione [*prahn'-tsoh, seh-kohn'-dah koh-lah-tsee-oh'-neh*]
   have lunch *v.*, pranzare [*prahn-tsah'-reh*]
lung, polmone (m) [*pohl-moh'-neh*]
luxurious, lussuoso [*loos-soo-oh'-zoh*]
luxury, lusso [*loos'-soh*]

M

machine, macchina [*mahk'-kee-nah*]

madam, signora [*see-nyoh'-rah*]

made, fatto [*faht'-toh*]

  made of cotton, di cotone [*dee koh-toh'-neh*]

magazine, rivista [*ree-vees'-tah*]

maid, domestica, cameriera [*doh-mehs'-tee-kah, kah-meh-ree-eh'-rah*]

mail *n.,* posta [*pohs'-tah*]

mail *v.,* spedire, imbucare [*speh-dee'-reh, eem-boo-kah'-reh*]

mailbox, cassetta delle lettere [*kahs-seht'-tah dehl'-leh leht'-teh-reh*]

mailman, postino [*pohs-tee'-noh*]

main, principale [*preen-chee-pah'-leh*]

  main office, ufficio centrale [*oof-fee'-chee-oh chehn-trah'-leh*]

  main street, via principale [*vee'-ah preen-chee-pah'-leh*]

mainly, principalmente [*preen-chee-pahl-mehn'-teh*]

majority, maggioranza [*mahj-jee-oh-rahn'-tsah*]

make *v.,* fare (irreg) [*fah'-reh*]

  make a mistake, sbagliarsi (refl) [*zbah-lyahr'-see*]

  make a speech, fare un discorso [*fah'-reh oon dees-kohr'-soh*]

  make fun of, prendere in giro [*prehn'-deh-reh een jee'-roh*]

  make up for, compensare per [*kohm-pehn-sah'-reh pehr*]

male, maschio [*mahs'-kee-oh*]

man, uomo, uomini (pl) [*oo-oh'-mo, oo-oh'-mee-nee*]

  young man, giovanotto [*jee-oh-vah-noht'-toh*]

manage *v.,* amministrare [*ahm-mee-nees-trah'-reh*]

manager, direttore (m), direttrice (f) [*dee-reht-toh'-reh, dee-reht-tree'-chee*]

manicure, manicure (f) [*mah-nee-koo'-reh*]
manner, maniera [*mah-nee-eh'-rah*]
manual, manuale [*mah-noo-ah'-leh*]
manufacture *v.*, fabbricare [*fahb-bree-kah'-reh*]
manufacturer, fabbricante [*fahb-bree-kahn'-teh*]
manuscript, manoscritto [*mah-noh-skreet'-toh*]
many, molti [*mohl'-tee*]
   How many? Quanti? [*koo-ahn'-tee*]
   too many, troppi [*trohp'-pee*]
   very many, moltissimi [*mohl-tees'-see-mee*]
map, carta geografica [*kahr'-tah jeh-oh-grah'-fee-kah*]
   road map, carta stradale [*kahr'-tah strah-dah'-leh*]
mar *v.*, sfigurare [*sfee-goo-rah'-reh*]
marble, marmo [*mahr'-moh*]
March, marzo [*mahr'-tsoh*]
march *n.*, marcia [*mahr'-chee-ah*]
march *v.*, marciare [*mahr-chee-ah'-reh*]
mark *n.*, segno [*seh'-nyoh*]
mark *v.*, segnare [*seh-nyah'-reh*]
market, mercato [*mehr-kah'-toh*]
marriage, matrimonio [*mah-tree-moh'-nee-oh*]
married, sposato [*spoh-zah'-toh*]
   get married *v.*, sposarsi [*spoh-zahr'-see*]
Mass [eccles.], messa [*mehs'-sah*]
mass [quantity], massa [*mahs'-sah*]
mass production, produzione (f) in serie [*proh-doo-tsee-oh'-neh een seh'-ree-eh*]
massage *n.*, massaggio [*mahs-sahj'-jee-oh*]
master *n.*, padrone (m) [*pah-droh'-neh*]
master *v.*, dominare [*doh-mee-nah'-reh*]
masterpiece, capolavoro [*kah-poh-lah-voh'-roh*]
match [for igniting], fiammifero [*fee-ahm-mee'-feh-roh*]
material [matter], materiale (m) [*mah-teh-ree-ah'-leh*]
material [cloth], stoffa [*stohf'-fah*]
maternal, materno [*mah-tehr'-noh*]
maternity, maternità (f, indecl) [*mah-tehr-nee-tah'*]
mathematics, matematica [*mah-teh-mah'-tee-kah*]
matter *n.*, materia, argomento [*mah-teh'-ree-ah, ahr-goh-*

mehn'-toh]

What's the matter? Che cosa c'è? [*keh koh'-zah cheh'*]
matter *v.*, importare [*eem-pohr-tah'-reh*]
  It doesn't matter, Non importa [*nohn eem-pohr'-tah*]
  matter of fact, positivo [*poh-zee-tee'-voh*]
mattress, materasso [*mah-teh-rahs'-soh*]
mature, maturo [*mah-too'-roh*]
May, maggio [*mahj'-jee-oh*]
may *v.*, posso, puoi, può [*pohs'-soh, poo-oh'-ee, poo-oh'*]
  It may be, Può essere, Può darsi [*poo-oh' ehs'-seh-reh, poo-oh' dahr'-see*]
  It may be that . . . Può darsi che . . . [*poo-oh' dahr'-see keh*]
maybe, forse [*fohr'-seh*]
mayor, sindaco [*seen'-dah-koh*]
me, me [*meh*]
meal, pasto [*pahs'-toh*]
mean *adj.*, meschino [*mehs-kee'-noh*]
mean *v.*, significare [*see-nyee-fee-kah'-reh*]
  What does it mean? Che cosa significa? [*keh koh'-zah see-nyee'-fee-kah*]
  What do you mean? Che cosa vuol dire! [*keh koh'-zah voo-ohl' dee'-reh*]
means, mezzi, rendite (pl) [*mehdz'-dzee, rehn'-dee-teh*]
  by all means, certamente [*chehr-tah-mehn'-teh*]
  by means of, per mezzo di [*pehr mehdz'-dzoh dee*]
  by no means, niente affatto [*nee-ehn'-teh ahf-faht'-toh*]
meantime, meanwhile, frattanto, intanto [*fraht-tahn'-toh, een-tahn'-toh*]
measles, morbillo [*mohr-beel'-loh*]
measure *n.*, misura [*mee-zoo'-rah*]
measure *v.*, misurare [*mee-zoo-rah'-reh*]
meat, carne (f) [*kahr'-neh*]
mechanic, mechanical, meccanico [*mehk-kah'-nee-koh*]
medical, medico [*meh'-dee-koh*]
medicine, medicina [*meh-dee-chee'-nah*]
Mediterranean, Mediterraneo [*meh-dee-tehr-rah'-neh-oh*]
medium *adj.*, medio [*meh'-dee-oh*]

meet v., incontrare [een-kohn-trah'-reh]
  Delighted to meet you! Piacere di conoscerla! [pee-ah-
    cheh'-reh dee koh-noh'-shehr-lah]
  I meet him every Sunday, L'incontro ogni domenica
    [leen-kohn'-troh oh'-nyee doh-mehn'-ee-kah]
meeting [group], riunione (f) [ree-oo-nee-oh'-neh]
meeting [encounter], incontro [een-kohn'-troh]
melon, melone (m) [meh-loh'-neh]
melt v., sciogliere [shee-oh'-lyeh-reh]
member, membro [mehm'-broh]
memory, memoria [meh-moh'-ree-ah]
mend v., rammendare [rahm-mehn-dah'-reh]
mental, mentale [mehn-tah'-leh]
mention v., menzionare [mehn-tsee-oh-nah'-reh]
merchandise, merce (f) [mehr'-cheh]
merchant, mercante (m) [mehr-kahn'-teh]
mercy, misericordia, pietà (f, indecl) [mee-zeh-ree-kohr'-dee-
    ah, pee-eh-tah']
  at the mercy of, alla mercè di [ahl'-lah mehr-cheh' dee]
merely, semplicemente [sehm-plee-cheh-mehn'-teh]
merit n., merito [meh'-ree-toh]
merit v., meritare [meh-ree-tah'-reh]
message, messaggio [mehs-sahj'-jee-oh]
messenger, messaggero [mehs-sahj-jeh'-roh]
metal, metallo [meh-tahl'-loh]
meter [measure] n., metro [meh'-troh]
meter [counter] n., contatore (m) [kohn-tah-toh'-reh]
method, metodo [meh'-toh-doh]
metric system, sistema (m) metrico [sees-teh'-mah meh'-tree-
    koh]
Mexican, messicano [mehs-see-kah'-noh]
Mexico, Messico [mehs'-see-koh]
middle n., mezzo, centro [mehdz-dzoh, chehn'-troh]
midnight, mezzanotte (f) [mehdz-dzah-noht'-teh]
midway, a metà strada [ah meh-tah' strah'-dah]
Milan, Milano [mee-lah'-noh]
mild, mite [mee'-teh]
mile, miglio, miglia (pl) [mee'-lyoh, mee'-lyah]

military, militare [*mee-lee-tah'-reh*]
  military service, servizio militare [*sehr-vee'-tsee-oh mee-lee-tah'-reh*]
milk, latte (m) [*laht'-teh*]
million, milione (m) [*mee-lee-oh'-neh*]
  two million, due milioni, [*doo'-eh mee-lee-oh'-nee*]
mind *n.,* mente (f) [*mehn'-teh*]
mind *v.,* badare a [*bah-dah'-reh ah*]
  Do you mind if I sit here? Le dispiace se mi siedo qui?
  [*leh dees-pee-ah'-cheh seh mee see-eh'-doh koo-ee'*]
mine *pron.,* mio, mia; miei, mie (pl) [*mee'-oh, mee'-ah; mee-eh'-ee, mee'-eh*]
mine *n.,* miniera [*mee-nee-eh'-rah*]
miner, minatore (m) [*mee-nah-toh'-reh*]
mineral, minerale (m) [*mee-neh-rah'-leh*]
minimum, minimo [*mee'-nee-moh*]
minister [government] *n.,* ministro [*mee-nees'-troh*]
minister [religious] *n.,* sacerdote (m) [*sah-chehr-doh'-teh*]
minister *v.,* somministrare [*sohm-mee-nees-trah'-reh*]
minor [age], minorenne [*mee-noh-rehn'-neh*]
minority, minoranza [*mee-noh-rahn'-tsah*]
minus, meno [*meh'-noh*]
minute, minuto [*mee-noo'-toh*]
  Wait a minute! Aspetti un minuto! [*ahs-peht'-tee oon mee-noo'-toh*]
mirror *n.,* specchio [*spehk'-kee-oh*]
mischief, cattiveria [*kaht-tee-veh'-ree-ah*]
miserable, miserabile [*mee-zeh-rah'-bee-leh*]
misery, miseria [*mee-zeh'-ree-ah*]
misfortune, sfortuna [*sfohr-too'-nah*]
Miss, Signorina [*see-nyoh-ree'-na*]
miss [someone] *v.,* sentire la mancanza [*sehn-tee'-reh lah mahn-kahn'-tsah*]
miss [lose, fail] *v.,* perdere [*pehr'-deh-reh*]
  I missed the train, Ho perduto il treno [*oh pehr-doo'-toh eel treh'-noh*]
missing, scomparso, sparito [*skohm-pahr'-soh, spah-ree'-toh*]
missionary, missionario [*mees-see-oh-nah'-ree-oh*]

mistake *n.*, errore (m) [*ehr-roh'-reh*]
mistaken, sbagliato [*zbah-lyah'-toh*]
  be mistaken *v.*, sbagliarsi [*zbah-lyahr'-see*]
mistrust *v.*, diffidarsi di [*deef-fee-dahr'-see dee*]
misunderstanding, malinteso [*mahl-een-teh'-zoh*]
mix *v.*, mescolare [*mehs-koh-lah'-reh*]
mixture, mescuglio [*mehs-koo'-lyoh*]
model *n.*, modello [*moh-dehl'-loh*]
modern, moderno [*moh-dehr'-noh*]
modest, modesto [*moh-dehs'-toh*]
modesty, modestia [*moh-dehs'-tee-ah*]
moisture, umidità (f, indecl) [*oo-mee-dee-tah'*]
moment, momento [*moh-mehn'-toh*]
monarchy, monarchia [*moh-nahr-kee'-ah*]
monastery, monastero [*moh-nahs-teh'-roh*]
Monday, lunedì (m) [*loo-neh-dee'*]
money, denaro, soldi, quattrini [*deh-nah'-roh, sohl'-dee, koo-aht-tree'-nee*]
monotonous, monotono [*moh-noh'-toh-noh*]
month, mese (m) [*meh'-zeh*]
monthly, mensile [*mehn-see'-leh*]
monument, monumento [*moh-noo-mehn'-toh*]
mood [feeling], umore (m) [*oo-moh'-reh*]
  be in a bad mood *v.*, essere di malumore [*ehs'-seh-reh dee mahl-oo-moh'-reh*]
  be in a good mood *v.*, essere di buonumore [*ehs'-seh-reh dee boo-ohn-oo-moh'-reh*]
moon, luna [*loo'-nah*]
moonlight, chiaro di luna [*kee-ah'-roh dee loo'-nah*]
moral, morale, morale [*moh-rah'-leh*]
morality, moralità (f, indecl) [*moh-rah-lee-tah'*]
more, più [*pee-oo'*]
  all the more, tanto più [*tahn'-toh pee-oo'*]
  more or less, più o meno [*pee-oo' oh meh'-noh*]
  no more, non più [*nohn pee-oo'*]
  once more, ancora una volta [*ahn-koh'-rah oon'-ah vohl'-tah*]
moreover, inoltre [*een-ohl'-treh*]

morning, mattina [*maht-tee'-nah*]
   Good morning! Buon giorno! [*boo-ohn' jee-ohr'-noh*]
mortgage, ipoteca [*ee-poh'-teh-kah*]
most, il più, la maggior parte [*eel pee-oo', lah mahj-jee-ohr' pahr'-teh*]
mother, madre (f) [*mah'-dreh*]
mother-in-law, suocera [*soo-oh'-cheh-rah*]
motion, movimento [*moh-vee-mehn'-toh*]
motive, motivo [*moh-tee'-voh*]
motor, motore (m) [*moh-toh'-reh*]
motorcycle, motocicletta [*moh-toh-chee-kleht'-tah*]
mountain, montagna [*mohn-tah'-nyah*]
mourning, lutto [*loot'-toh*]
mouth, bocca [*bohk'-kah*]
move [change position of] *v.,* muovere [*moo-oh'-veh-reh*]
move [emotionally] *v.,* commuoversi [*kohm-moo-oh'-vehr-see*]
movies, cinema [*chee'-neh-mah*]
Mr., Sig. (signore) [*see-nyoh'-reh*]
Mrs., Sigra. (signora) [*see-nyoh'-rah*]
much, molto [*mohl'-toh*]
   as much as, tanto quanto [*tahn'-toh koo-ahn'-toh*]
   How much? Quanto? [*koo-ahn'-toh*]
   too much, troppo [*trohp'-poh*]
   very much, moltissimo [*mohl-tees'-see-moh*]
mud, fango [*fahn'-goh*]
murder *v.,* assassinare [*ahs-sahs-see-nah'-reh*]
murderer, assassino [*ahs-sahs-see'-noh*]
muscle, muscolo [*moos'-koh-loh*]
museum, museo [*moo-zeh'-oh*]
music, musica [*moo'-zee-kah*]
musical, musicale [*moo-zee-kah'-leh*]
musician, musicista (m, f) [*moo-zee-chees'-tah*]
must *v.,* dovere (irreg) [*doh-veh'-reh*]
   I must go home, Devo andare a casa [*deh'-voh ahn-dah'-reh ah kah'-zah*]
mustache, baffo [*bahf'-foh*]
mustard, mostarda [*mohs-tahr'-dah*]

mutual, reciproco [*reh-chee'-proh-koh*]
my, mio, mia; miei, mie (pl) [*mee'-oh, mee'-ah; mee-eh'-ee, mee'-eh*]
myself, io stesso [*ee'-oh stehs'-soh*]
mystery, mistero [*mees-teh'-roh*]
mystic, mistico [*mees'-tee-koh*]

N

nail [fingernail], unghia [*oon'-gee-ah*]
nail [carpentry], chiodo [*kee-oh'-doh*]
naive, ingenuo [*een-jeh'-noo-oh*]
naked, nudo [*noo'-doh*]
name *n.*, nome (m) [*noh'-meh*]
   first name, nome [*noh'-meh*]
   last name, cognome (m) [*koh-nyoh'-meh*]
   What is your name? Quale è il suo nome? [*koo-ah'-leh eh' eel soo'-oh noh'-meh*]
   My name is . . ., Mi chiamo . . . [*mee kee-ah'-moh*]
nap, sonnellino [*sohn-nehl-lee'-noh*]
napkin, tovagliolo [*toh-vah-lyoh'-loh*]
   sanitary napkin, tovagliolo igienico [*toh-vah-lyoh'-loh ee-jee-eh'-nee-koh*]
Naples, Napoli [*nah'-poh-lee*]
narrate *v.*, narrare [*nahr-rah'-reh*]
narrative, storia [*stoh'-ree-ah*]
narrow *adj.*, stretto [*streht'-toh*]
nasty, cattivo [*kaht-tee'-voh*]
nation, nazione (f) [*nah-tsee-oh'-neh*]
national, nazionale [*nah-tsee-oh-nah'-leh*]
nationality, nazionalità (f, indecl) [*nah-tsee-oh-nah-lee-tah'*]
native, nativo [*nah-tee'-voh*]
natural, naturale [*nah-too-rah'-leh*]
naturally, naturalmente [*nah-too-rahl-mehn'-teh*]
nature, natura [*nah-too'-rah*]

naughty, birichino [*bee-ree-kee'-noh*]

naval, navale [*nah-vah'-leh*]

navy, marina [*mah-ree'-nah*]

near, nearby, vicino [*vee-chee'-noh*]

nearly, quasi [*koo-ah'-zee*]

neat, lindo [*leen'-doh*]

necessary, necessario [*neh-chehs-sah'-ree-oh*]

neck, collo [*kohl'-loh*]

necklace, collana [*kohl-lah'-nah*]

necktie, cravatta [*krah-vaht'-tah*]

need *n.*, bisogno [*bee-zoh'-nyoh*]

need *v.*, aver bisogno [*ah-vehr' bee-zoh'-nyoh*]

needle, ago, aghi (pl) [*ah'-goh, ah'-gee*]

negative *adj.*, negativo [*neh-gah-tee'-voh*]

negative [film] *n.*, negativa [*neh-gah-tee'-vah*]

neglect *v.*, trascurare [*trahs-koo-rah'-reh*]

Negro, negro [*neh'-groh*]

neighbor, vicino [*vee-chee'-noh*]

neighborhood, quartiere (m) [*koo-ahr-tee-eh'-reh*]

neither, neanche, nessuno [*neh-ahn'-keh, nehs-soo'-noh*]

neither . . . nor, nè . . . nè [*neh' . . . neh'*]

nephew, nipote (m) [*nee-poh'-teh*]

nerves, nervi [*nehr'-vee*]

    What a nerve! Che coraggio! [*keh koh-rahj'-jee-oh*]

nervous, nervoso [*nehr-voh'-zoh*]

net [fishing], rete (f) [*reh'-teh*]

never, mai [*mah'-ee*]

    Never mind! Non fa niente! [*nohn fah nee-ehn'-teh*]

nevermore, mai più [*mah'-ee pee-oo'*]

nevertheless, tuttavia [*toot-tah-vee'-ah*]

new, nuovo [*noo-oh'-voh*]

    What's new? Che c'è di nuovo? [*keh cheh' dee noo-oh'-voh*]

news, notizie (f, pl) [*noh-tee'-tsee-eh*]

newspaper, giornale (m) [*jee-ohr-nah'-leh*]

newsstand, edicola [*eh-dee'-koh-lah*]

next, prossimo [*prohs'-see-moh*]

    next month, il prossimo mese [*eel prohs'-see-moh meh'-zeh*]

next time, la prossima volta [*lah prohs'-see-mah vohl'-tah*]
next week, la settimana prossima [*lah seht-tee-mah'-nah prohs'-see-mah*]
next year, il prossimo anno [*eel prohs'-see-moh ahn'-noh*]
next to, vicino a [*vee-chee'-noh ah*]
nice, buono, simpatico [*boo-oh'-noh, seem-pah'-tee-koh*]
nickname, nomignolo [*noh-mee'-nyoh-loh*]
niece, nipote (f) [*nee-poh'-teh*]
night, notte (f) [*noht'-teh*]
  Good night! Buona notte! [*boo-oh'-nah noht'-teh*]
  last night, la notte scorsa [*lah noht'-teh skohr'-sah*]
nightclub, locale notturno [*loh-kah'-leh noht-toor'-noh*]
nightfall, sera [*seh'-rah*]
nightgown, camicia da notte [*kah-mee'-chee-ah dah noht'-teh*]
nightmare, incubo [*een'-koo-boh*]
nine, nove [*noh'-veh*]
nineteen, dicianove [*dee-chee-ah-noh'-veh*]
ninety, novanta [*noh-vahn'-tah*]
ninth, nono [*noh'-noh*]
nipple, capezzolo, biberon [*kah-pehts'-tsoh-loh, bee-beh-rohn'*]
no *adv.*, no, non [*noh, nohn*]
  No, I'm not going, No, non ci vado [*noh, nohn chee vah'-doh*]
  No fooling! Senza scherzi! [*sehn'-tsah skehr'-tsee*]
  by no means, in nessun modo, per nessun motivo [*een nehs-soon' moh'-doh, pehr nehs-soon' moh-tee'-voh*]
  no longer, non più [*nohn pee-oo'*]
  no more, non più [*nohn pee-oo'*]
noble, nobile [*noh'-bee-leh*]
nobody, nessuno [*nehs-soo'-noh*]
noise, chiasso, rumore (m) [*kee-ahs'-soh, roo-moh'-reh*]
noisy, chiassoso, rumoroso [*kee-ahs-soh'-zoh, roo-moh-roh'-zoh*]
none, nessuno, nulla [*nehs-soo'-noh, nool'-lah*]
nonsense, sciocchezza [*shee-ohk-kehts'-tsah*]
noon, mezzogiorno [*mehdz-dzoh-jee-ohr'-noh*]

nor, nè, neppure [*neh', nehp-poo'-reh*]
normal, normale [*nohr-mah'-leh*]
north, nord [*nohrd*]
North America, America del Nord [*ah-meh'-ree-kah dehl nohrd*]
northeast, nord-est [*nohrd-ehst'*]
Northern, settentrionale [*seht-tehn-tree-oh-nah'-leh*]
northwest, nord-ovest [*nohrd-oh'-vehst*]
Norway, Norvegia [*nohr-veh'-jee-ah*]
Norwegian, norvegese [*nohr-veh-jeh'-zeh*]
nose, naso [*nah'-zoh*]
not, non [*nohn*]
  not even, neanche [*neh-ahn'-keh*]
  not once, non una volta [*nohn oo'-nah vohl'-tah*]
note *n.,* nota [*noh'-tah*]
note *v.,* annotare [*ahn-noh-tah'-reh*]
notebook, taccuino [*tahk-koo-ee'-noh*]
nothing, niente, nulla [*nee-ehn'-teh, nool'-lah*]
notice *n.,* avviso, notifica [*ahv-vee'-zoh, noh-tee'-fee-kah*]
notice *v.,* notare [*noh-tah'-reh*]
notify *v.,* notificare [*noh-tee-fee-kah'-reh*]
notion, nozione (f) [*noh-tsee-oh'-neh*]
noun, nome (m) [*noh'-meh*]
novel *n.,* romanzo [*roh-mahn'-tsoh*]
novelist, romanziere (m) [*roh-mahn-tsee-eh'-reh*]
novelty, novità (f, indecl) [*noh-vee-tah'*]
November, novembre (m) [*noh-vehm'-breh*]
now, ora, adesso [*oh'-rah, ah-dehs'-soh*]
  now and then, di quando in quando [*dee koo-ahn'-doh een koo-ahn'-doh*]
  until now, fino ad ora [*fee'-noh ahd oh'-rah*]
nowhere, in nessun posto [*een nehs-soon' pohs'-toh*]
number *n.,* numero [*noo'-meh-roh*]
number *v.,* numerare [*noo-meh-rah'-reh*]
numerous, numeroso [*noo-meh-roh'-zoh*]
nun, monaca [*moh'-nah-kah*]
nurse [for the sick] *n.,* infermiera [*een-fehr-mee-eh'-rah*]
nurse [children] *n.,* bambinaia [*bahm-bee-nah'-ee-ah*]

nurse *v.*, curare [*koo-rah'-reh*]
nut [food] noce (f) [*noh'-cheh*]
nylon, nylon [*nah'-ee-lohn*]

O

oak, quercia [*koo-ehr'-chee-ah*]
oar, remo [*reh'-moh*]
oath, giuramento [*jee-oo-rah-mehn'-toh*]
obedient, ubbidiente [*oob-bee-dee-ehn'-teh*]
obey *v.*, ubbidire [*oob-bee-dee'-reh*]
object *n.*, oggetto [*ohj-jeht'-toh*]
object *v.*, opporsi [*ohp-pohr'-see*]
objection, obiezione (f) [*oh-bee-eh-tsee-oh'-neh*]
obligation, obbligo [*ohb'-blee-goh*]
obscene, osceno [*oh-sheh'-noh*]
obscure *adj.*, oscuro [*ohs-koo'-roh*]
observe *v.*, osservare [*ohs-sehr-vah'-reh*]
obstacle, ostacolo [*ohs-tah'-koh-loh*]
obvious, ovvio [*ohv'-vee-oh*]
occasion, occasione (f) [*ohk-kah-zee-oh'-neh*]
occasionally, di tanto in tanto [*dee tahn'-toh een tahn'-toh*]
occupation, occupazione (f) [*ohk-koo-pah-tsee-oh'-neh*]
occupied, occupato [*ohk-koo-pah'-toh*]
occupy *v.*, occupare [*ohk-koo-pah'-reh*]
occur *v.*, accadere [*ahk-kah-deh'-reh*]
occurrence, avvenimento [*ahv-veh-nee-mehn'-toh*]
ocean, oceano [*oh-cheh'-ah-noh*]
o'clock, l'ora, le ore (pl) [*loh'-rah, leh oh'-reh*]
   one o'clock, l'una, l'ora una [*loo'-nah, loh'-rah oo'-nah*]
   five o'clock, le cinque, le ore cinque [*leh cheen'-koo-eh,
     leh oh'-reh cheen'-koo-eh*]
October, ottobre [*oht-toh'-breh*]
oculist, oculista (m) [*oh-koo-lees'-tah*]
odd [unusual] strano [*strah'-noh*]

odd [uneven] dispari [*dees'-pah-ree*]
odds probabilità (f, indecl) [*proh-bah-bee-lee-tah'*]
odor, odore (m) [*oh-doh'-reh*]
of, di [*dee*]
   of course, naturalmente [*nah-too-rahl-mehn'-teh*]
off, via, lontano, libero [*vee'-ah, lohn-tah'-noh, lee'-beh-roh*]
offend v., offendere [*ohf-fehn'-deh-reh*]
offer n., offerta [*ohf-fehr'-tah*]
offer v., offrire [*ohf-free'-reh*]
office, ufficio [*oof-fee'-chee-oh*]
officer, ufficiale (m) [*oof-fee-chee-ah'-leh*]
official adj., ufficiale [*oof-fee-chee-ah'-leh*]
often, spesso [*spehs'-soh*]
oil [edible] n., olio [*oh'-lee-oh*]
oil [petroleum] n., petrolio [*peh-troh'-lee-oh*]
oil v., lubrificare [*loo-bree-fee-kah'-reh*]
oil field, campo petrolifero [*kahm'-poh peh-troh-lee'-feh-roh*]
oil painting, pittura ad olio [*peet-too'-rah ahd oh'-lee-oh*]
old, vecchio [*vehk'-kee-oh*]
   How old are you? Quanti anni ha? [*koo-ahn'-tee ahn'-nee ah*]
olive, oliva [*oh-lee'-vah*]
olive oil, olio di oliva [*oh'-lee-oh dee oh-lee'-vah*]
omelet, frittata [*freet-tah'-tah*]
omission, omissione (f) [*oh-mees-see-oh'-neh*]
omit v., omettere [*oh-meht'-teh-reh*]
on, su, sopra [*soo, soh'-prah*]
   and so on, e così via [*eh koh-zee' vee'-ah*]
   on the contrary, al contrario [*ahl kohn-trah'-ree-oh*]
   on duty, di servizio [*dee sehr-vee'-tsee-oh*]
   on foot, a piedi [*ah pee-eh'-dee*]
   on the left, alla sinistra [*ahl'-lah see-nees'-trah*]
   on purpose, di proposito [*dee proh-poh'-zee-toh*]
   on time, a tempo [*ah tehm'-poh*]
once, una volta [*oo'-nah vohl'-tah*]
   at once, subito [*soo'-bee-toh*]
   once more, ancora una volta [*ahn-koh'-rah oo'-nah*

vohl'-tah]

one, un, uno, una [*oon, oo'-noh, oo'-nah*]

one-way street, senso unico [*sehn'-soh oo'-nee-koh*]

onion, cipolla [*chee-pohl'-lah*]

onlooker, spettatore (m) [*speht-tah-toh'-reh*]

only *adv.,* solamente, soltanto [*soh-lah-mehn'-teh, sohl-tahn'-toh*]

only *adj.,* solo, unico [*soh'-loh, oo'-nee-koh*]

open *adj.,* aperto [*ah-pehr'-toh*]

open *v.,* aprire [*ah-pree'-reh*]

opening, apertura [*ah-pehr-too'-rah*]

opera, opera [*oh'-peh-rah*]

operate [a machine] *v.,* maneggiare [*mah-nehj-jee-ah'-reh*]

operate [perform surgery] *v.,* operare [*oh-peh-rah'-reh*]

operation, operazione (f) [*oh-peh-rah-tsee-oh'-neh*]

opinion, opinione (f) [*oh-pee-nee-oh'-neh*]

opportunity, opportunità (f, indecl) [*ohp-pohr-too-nee-tah'*]

oppose *v.,* opporre (irreg) [*ohp-pohr'-reh*]

opposite *n. & adj.,* opposto [*ohp-pohs'-toh*]

optimist, optimistic, ottimista (m & f) [*oht-tee-mees'-tah*]

or, o, oppure [*oh, ohp-poo'-reh*]

oral, orale [*oh-rah'-leh*]

orange, arancia [*ah-rahn'-chee-ah*]

orange juice, succo d'arancia [*sook'-koh dah-rahn'-chee-ah*]

orchard, frutteto [*froot-teh'-toh*]

orchestra, orchestra [*ohr'-kehs-trah*]

order *n.,* ordine (m) [*ohr'-dee-neh*]

order [someone] *v.,* comandare [*koh-mahn-dah'-reh*]

order [something] *v.,* ordinare [*ohr-dee-nah'-reh*]

ordinarily, ordinariamente [*ohr-dee-nah-ree-ah-mehn'-teh*]

ordinary, ordinario [*ohr-dee-nah'-ree-oh*]

organization, organizzazione (f) [*ohr-gah-needz-dzah-tsee-oh'-neh*]

oriental, orientale [*oh-ree-ehn-tah'-leh*]

original, originale [*oh-ree-jee-nah'-leh*]

ornament *n.,* ornamento [*ohr-nah-mehn'-toh*]

other, altro [*ahl'-troh*]

  on the other hand, d'altra parte [*dahl'-trah pahr'-teh*]

otherwise, altrimenti [*ahl-tree-mehn'-tee*]

ought *v.*, dovere [*doh-veh'-reh*]
  I ought to go, Dovrei andare [*doh-vreh'-ee ahn-dah'-reh*]
  You ought to rest, Lei dovrebbe riposare [*leh'-ee doh-vrehb'-beh ree-poh-zah'-reh*]

our, nostro, nostra (sing); nostri, nostre (pl) [*nohs'-troh, nohs'-trah; nohs'-tree, nohs'-treh*]

ours, il nostro, la nostra (sing); i nostri, le nostre (pl) [*eel nohs'-troh, lah nohs'-trah; ee nohs'-tree, leh nohs'-treh*]

out, fuori, via [*foo-oh'-ree, vee'-ah*]
  out of order, fuori uso [*foo-oh'-ree oo'-zoh*]

outdoors, all'aperto [*ahl-lah-pehr'-toh*]

outrageous, atroce [*ah-troh'-cheh*]

outside, fuori, esterno [*foo-oh'-ree, ehs-tehr'-noh*]

outstanding, prominente [*proh-mee-nehn'-teh*]

outward, esterno [*ehs-tehr'-noh*]

oven, forno [*fohr'-noh*]

over [finished], finito [*fee-nee'-toh*]

over [above], sopra, su [*soh'-prah, soo*]

overcoat, soprabito [*soh-prah'-bee-toh*]

overcome *v.*, vincere [*veen'-cheh-reh*]

overdo *v.*, esagerare [*eh-zah-jeh-rah'-reh*]

overflow *n.*, eccedenza [*ehch-cheh-dehn'-tsah*]

overhead *n.*, spese generali (pl) [*speh'-zeh jeh-neh-rah'-lee*]

overnight, per una notte [*pehr oo'-nah noht'-teh*]

overseas, oltremare [*ohl-treh-mah'-reh*]

overtime, straordinario [*strah-ohr-dee-nah'-ree-oh*]

overturn *v.*, capovolgere [*kah-poh-vohl'-jeh-reh*]

owe *v.*, dovere [*doh-veh'-reh*]
  How much do I owe you? Quanto le devo? [*koo-ahn'-toh leh deh'-voh*]

own *adj.*, proprio [*proh'-pree-oh*]

own *v.*, possedere [*pohs-seh-deh'-reh*]

owner, proprietario [*proh-pree-eh-tah'-ree-oh*]

oxygen, ossigeno [*ohs-see'-jeh-noh*]

oyster, ostrica [*ohs'-tree-kah*]

P

pack *n.*, pacco [*pahk'-koh*]
pack [of cards] *n.*, mazzo di carte [*mahts'-tsoh dee kahr'-teh*]
pack (of cigarettes) *n.*, pacchetto (di sigarette) [*pahk-keht'-toh (dee see-gah-reht'-teh)*]
pack *v.*, impaccare [*eem-pahk-kah'-reh*]
package, pacco [*pahk'-koh*]
page *n.*, pagina [*pah'-jee-nah*]
paid, pagato [*pah-gah'-toh*]
pain, dolore (m), pena [*doh-loh'-reh, peh'-nah*]
painful, doloroso [*doh-loh-roh'-zoh*]
paint *n.*, pittura, colore (m) [*peet-too'-rah, koh-loh'-reh*]
paint *v.*, dipingere [*dee-peen'-jeh-reh*]
painter, pittore (m), pittrice (f) [*peet-toh'-reh, peet-tree'-cheh*]
painting, pittura, vernice (f) [*peet-too'-rah, vehr-nee'-cheh*]
pair *n.*, paio, paia (pl) [*pah'-ee-oh, pah'-ee-ah*]
palace, palazzo [*pah-lahts'-tsoh*]
pale *adj.*, pallido [*pahl'-lee-doh*]
palm, palma [*pahl'-mah*]
pan, padella [*pah-dehl'-lah*]
panic *n.*, panico [*pah'-nee-koh*]
pants, calzoni (pl) [*kahl-tsoh'-nee*]
paper, carta [*kahr'-tah*]
    toilet paper, carta igienica [*kahr'-tah ee-jee-eh'-nee-kah*]
    writing paper, carta da scrivere [*kahr'-tah dah skree'-veh-reh*]
parade *n.*, parata [*pah-rah'-tah*]
paragraph, paragrafo [*pah-rah'-grah-foh*]
paralyzed, paralizzato [*pah-rah-leedz-dzah'-toh*]
pardon *n.*, perdono [*pehr-doh'-noh*]
pardon *v.*, perdonare [*pehr-doh-nah'-reh*]
    Pardon me! Mi scusi! [*mee skoo'-zee*]

parents, genitori [*jeh-nee-toh′-ree*]
park *n.*, parco [*pahr′-koh*]
park *v.*, parcheggiare [*pahr-kehj-jee-ah′-reh*]
parking, parcheggio [*pahr-kehj′-jee-oh*]
  No parking! Sosta vietata! [*sohs′-tah vee-eh-tah′-tah*]
parliament, parlamento [*pahr-lah-mehn′-toh*]
parlor, salotto [*sah-loht′-toh*]
part [of whole] *n.*, parte (f) [*pahr′-teh*]
part [of machine] *n.*, pezzo [*pehts′-tsoh*]
participate *v.*, partecipare [*pahr-teh-chee-pah′-reh*]
particular, particolare [*pahr-tee-koh-lah′-reh*]
particularly, particolarmente [*pahr-tee-koh-lahr-mehn′-teh*]
partly, in parte [*een pahr′-teh*]
partner [business], socio [*soh′-chee-oh*]
party [entertainment], ricevimento [*ree-cheh-vee-mehn′-toh*]
party [political], partito [*pahr-tee′-toh*]
pass [permit] *n.*, permesso [*pehr-mehs′-soh*]
pass [mountain] *n.*, passo [*pahs′-soh*]
pass *v.*, passare [*pahs-sah′-reh*]
passage, passaggio [*pahs-sahj′-jee-oh*]
passenger, passeggero [*pahs-sehj-jeh′-roh*]
passenger train, treno passeggeri [*treh′-noh pahs-sehj-jeh′-ree*]
passerby, passante [*pahs-sahn′-teh*]
passionate, appassionato [*ahp-pahs-see-oh-nah′-toh*]
passive, passivo [*pahs-see′-voh*]
passport, passaporto [*pahs-sah-pohr′-toh*]
past, passato [*pahs-sah′-toh*]
paste *n.*, colla, pasta [*kohl′-lah, pahs′-tah*]
pastry, pasta [*pahs′-tah*]
pastry shop, pasticceria [*pahs-tee-cheh-ree′-ah*]
path, sentiero [*sehn-tee-eh′-roh*]
patience, pazienza [*pah-tsee-ehn′-tsah*]
patient *n. & adj.*, paziente [*pah-tsee-ehn′-teh*]
patriotic, patriotico [*pah-tree-oh′-tee-koh*]
pattern *n.*, modello [*moh-dehl′-loh*]
pavement, pavimento [*pah-vee-mehn′-toh*]
pay *v.*, pagare [*pah-gah′-reh*]

pay a compliment, fare un complimento [*fah'-reh oon kohm-plee-mehn'-toh*]

pay a fine, pagare una multa [*pah-gah'-reh oo'-nah mool'-tah*]

pay by installments, pagare mensilmente [*pah-gah'-reh mehn-seel-mehn'-teh*]

pay cash, pagare in contanti [*pah-gah'-reh een kohn-tahn'-tee*]

payment *n.,* pagamento [*pah-gah-mehn'-toh*]

pea, pisello [*pee-zehl'-loh*]

peace, pace (f) [*pah'-cheh*]

peaceful, pacifico [*pah-chee'-fee-koh*]

peach, pesca [*pehs'-kah*]

pear, pera [*peh'-rah*]

pearl, perla [*pehr'-lah*]

peculiar, strano [*strah'-noh*]

pedal *n.,* pedale (m) [*peh-dah'-leh*]

peddler, venditore ambulante (m) [*vehn-dee-toh'-reh ahm-boo-lahn'-teh*]

pedestrian, pedestre [*peh-dehs'-treh*]

peel *v.,* pelare, sbucciare [*peh-lah'-reh, zbooch-chee-ah'-reh*]

pen, penna [*pehn'-nah*]

  fountain pen, penna stilografica [*pehn'-nah stee-loh-grah'-fee-kah*]

pen name, pseudonimo [*pseh-oo-doh'-nee-moh*]

penalty, penalità (f, indecl) [*peh-nah-lee-tah'*]

pencil, matita [*mah-tee'-tah*]

people, gente (f), popolo [*jehn'-teh, poh'-poh-loh*]

pepper, pepe (m) [*peh'-peh*]

perceive *v.,* percepire [*pehr-cheh-pee'-reh*]

percent, percento [*pehr-chehn'-toh*]

perfect *adj.,* perfetto [*pehr-feht'-toh*]

performance [showing], esibizione (f) [*eh-zee-bee-tsee-oh'-neh*]

performance [of machine], funzionamento [*foon-tsee-oh-nah-mehn'-toh*]

perfume, profumo [*proh-foo'-moh*]

perhaps, forse [*fohr'-seh*]
period [punctuation], punto fermo [*poon'-toh fehr'-moh*]
period [time], periodo [*peh-ree-oh'-doh*]
permanent *adj.*, permanente [*pehr-mah-nehn'-teh*]
permanent wave, ondulazione permanente [*ohn-doo-lah-tsee-oh'-neh pehr-mah-nehn'-teh*]
permission, permesso [*pehr-mehs'-soh*]
permit *v.*, permettere [*pehr-meht'-teh-reh*]
Persian, persiano [*pehr-see-ah'-noh*]
persist *v.*, persistere [*pehr-sees'-teh-reh*]
person, persona [*pehr-soh'-nah*]
personal, personale [*pehr-soh-nah'-leh*]
personality, personalità (f, indecl) [*pehr-soh-nah-lee-tah'*]
personnel, personale (m) [*pehr-soh-nah'-leh*]
perspiration, sudore (m) [*soo-doh'-reh*]
perspire *v.*, sudare [*soo-dah'-reh*]
persuade *v.*, persuadere [*pehr-soo-ah-deh'-reh*]
pessimist, pessimistic, pessimista [*pehs-see-mees'-tah*]
pet, animale favorito [*ah-nee-mah'-leh fah-voh-ree'-toh*]
pharmacy, farmacia [*fahr-mah-chee'-ah*]
phase, fase (f) [*fah'-zeh*]
philosopher, filosofo [*fee-loh'-zoh-foh*]
philosophy, filosofia [*fee-loh-zoh-fee'-ah*]
phone *n.*, telefono [*teh-leh'-foh-noh*]
  by phone, per telefono [*pehr teh-leh'-foh-noh*]
phone *v.*, telefonare [*teh-leh-foh-nah'-reh*]
phonograph, fonografo [*foh-noh'-grah-foh*]
photograph *n.*, fotografia [*foh-toh-grah-fee'-ah*]
photograph *v.*, fotografare [*foh-toh-grah-fah'-reh*]
photographer, fotografo [*foh-toh'-grah-foh*]
physical, fisico [*fee'-zee-koh*]
physician, medico [*meh'-dee-koh*]
pianist, pianista (m, f) [*pee-ah-nees'-tah*]
piano, pianoforte (m) [*pee-ah-noh-fohr'-teh*]
pick *v.*, cogliere [*koh'-lyeh-reh*]
  pick up, raccogliere [*rahk-koh'-lyeh-reh*]
pickpocket, borsaiuolo [*bohr-sah-ee-oh'-loh*]
picture, quadro [*koo-ah'-droh*]

piece, pezzo [*pehts'-tsoh*]

pier, molo [*moh'-loh*]

pig, maiale [*mah-ee-ah'-leh*]

pill, pillola [*peel'-loh-lah*]

pillow, cuscino [*koo-shee'-noh*]

pilot *n.*, pilota (m) [*pee-loh'-tah*]

pin *n.*, spilla [*speel'-lah*]

pinch *v.*, pizzicare [*peets-tsee-kah'-reh*]

pipe [smoking], pipa [*pee'-pah*]

pistol, pistola [*pees-toh'-lah*]

pity *n.*, pietà (f, indecl) [*pee-eh-tah'*]

   What a pity! Che peccato! [*keh pehk-kah'-toh*]

place *n.*, luogo [*loo-oh'-goh*]

   in place of, in luogo di [*een loo-oh'-goh dee*]

   take place *v.*, aver luogo [*ah-vehr' loo-oh'-goh*]

place *v.*, collocare [*kohl-loh-kah'-reh*]

plain [simple], semplice [*sehm'-plee-cheh*]

plan *n.*, piano, progetto [*pee-ah'-noh, proh-jeht'-toh*]

plan *v.*, progettare [*proh-jeht-tah'-reh*]

planet, pianeta (m) [*pee-ah-neh'-tah*]

plant *n.*, pianta [*pee-ahn'-tah*]

plant *v.*, piantare [*pee-ahn-tah'-reh*]

plaster *n.*, stucco [*stook'-koh*]

plastic, plastico [*plahs'-tee-koh*]

plate [dish], piatto [*pee-aht'-toh*]

platform, piattaforma [*pee-aht-tah-fohr'-mah*]

play *n.*, dramma (m), gioco [*drahm'-mah, jee-oh'-koh*]

play [a game] *v.*, giocare [*jee-oh-kah'-reh*]

play [an instrument] *v.*, suonare [*soo-oh-nah'-reh*]

playful, scherzoso [*skehr-tsoh'-zoh*]

playground, terreno di gioco [*tehr-reh'-noh dee jee-oh'-koh*]

playmate, compagno di giochi [*kohm-pah'-nyoh dee jee-oh'-kee*]

pleasant, piacevole [*pee-ah-cheh'-voh-leh*]

please *v.*, piacere (irreg) [*pee-ah-cheh'-reh*]

   Please bring me . . . , Per favore, mi porti . . . [*pehr fah-voh'-reh, mee pohr'-tee*]

   Pleased to meet you! Piacere di conoscerla! [*pee-ah-*

cheh'-reh dee koh-noh'-shehr-lah]

Please! Per favore!, Per piacere! [*pehr fah-voh'-reh, pehr
pee-ah-cheh'-reh*]

Please! [not at all], Prego! [*preh'-goh*]
   Please, come in! Prego, entri! [*preh'-goh, ehn'-tree*]

pleasure, piacere (m) [*pee-ah-cheh'-reh*]
   The pleasure is mine, Il piacere è mio [*eel pee-ah-cheh'-
   reh eh' mee'-oh*]
   With pleasure, Con piacere [*kohn pee-ah-cheh'-reh*]
   With much pleasure, Con molto piacere [*kohn mohl'-toh
   pee-ah-cheh'-reh*]

pleasure trip, viaggio di piacere [*vee-ahj'-jee-oh dee pee-ah-
   cheh'-reh*]

plenty, in abbondanza [*een ahb-bohn-dahn'-tsah*]

plow *v.,* arare [*ah-rah'-reh*]

plug [electric] *n.,* presa [*preh'-zah*]

plumber, idraulico [*ee-drah'-oo-lee-koh*]

plural, plurale [*ploo-rah'-leh*]

plus, più [*pee-oo'*]

pneumonia, polmonite (f) [*pohl-moh-nee'-teh*]

pocket, tasca, tasche (pl) [*tahs'-kah, tahs'-keh*]

pocketbook, portafoglio [*pohr-tah-foh'-lyoh*]

poem, poema (m) [*poh-eh'-mah*]

poet, poeta (m), poetessa (f) [*poh-eh'-tah, poh-eh-tehs'-sah*]

poetry, poesia [*poh-eh-zee'-ah*]

point [abstract] *n.,* punto [*poon'-toh*]
   point of view, punto di vista [*poon'-toh dee vees'-tah*]

point [of form] *n.,* punta [*poon'-tah*]

point *v.,* puntare [*poon-tah'-reh*]
   point out, far notare [*fahr noh-tah'-reh*]

poison, veleno [*veh-leh'-noh*]

poisonous, velenoso [*veh-leh-noh'-zoh*]

Poland, Polonia [*poh-loh'-nyah*]

pole [stick], palo [*pah'-loh*]

pole [geographical], polo [*poh'-loh*]

police, polizia [*poh-lee-tsee'-ah*]

policeman, poliziotto [*poh-lee-tsee-oht'-toh*]

police station, stazione di polizia [*stah-tsee-oh'-neh dee*

poh-lee-tsee'-ah]
policy [government] *n.*, politica [*poh-lee'-tee-kah*]
policy [insurance] *n.*, polizza [*poh'-leets-tsah*]
Polish, polacco [*poh-lahk'-koh*]
polish *n.*, lucido [*loo'-chee-doh*]
polish *v.*, lucidare [*loo-chee-dah'-reh*]
polite, educato, gentile [*eh-doo-kah'-toh, jehn-tee'-leh*]
political, politico [*poh-lee'-tee-koh*]
politics, politica [*poh-lee'-tee-kah*]
pool [swimming], piscina [*pee-shee'-nah*]
poor *adj.*, povero [*poh'-veh-roh*]
Pope, papa (m) [*pah'-pah*]
popular, popolare [*poh-poh-lah'-reh*]
population, popolazione (f) [*poh-poh-lah-tsee-oh'-neh*]
porch, portico [*pohr'-tee-koh*]
pork, maiale (m) [*mah-ee-ah'-leh*]
port, porto [*pohr'-toh*]
portable, portabile [*pohr-tah'-bee-leh*]
porter [baggage], facchino [*fahk-kee'-noh*]
portrait, ritratto [*ree-traht'-toh*]
Portugal, Portogallo [*pohr-toh-gahl'-loh*]
Portuguese, portoghese [*pohr-toh-geh'-zeh*]
pose *v.*, posare [*poh-zah'-reh*]
position, posizione [*poh-zee-tsee-oh'-neh*]
positive, positivo [*poh-zee-tee'-voh*]
possession, possesso [*pohs-sehs'-soh*]
possible, possibile [*pohs-see'-bee-leh*]
   as soon as possible, il più presto possibile [*eel pee-oo' prehs'-toh pohs-see'-bee-leh*]
post, posta [*pohs'-tah*]
postage, affrancatura [*ahf-frahn-kah-too'-rah*]
postage stamp, francobollo [*frahn-koh-bohl'-loh*]
post card, cartolina postale [*kahr-toh-lee'-nah pohs-tah-leh*]
poster, affisso, manifesto [*ahf-fees'-soh, mah-nee-fehs'-toh*]
post office, ufficio postale [*oof-fee'-chee-oh pohs-tah'-leh*]
post office box, fermo-posta [*fehr-moh-pohs'-tah*]
postpone *v.*, rimandare [*ree-mahn-dah'-reh*]
potato, patata [*pah-tah'-tah*]

pottery, vasellame [*vah-zehl-lah'-meh*]

pound [money], lira sterlina [*lee'-rah stehr-lee'-nah*]

pound [weight], libbra [*leeb'-brah*]

pour *v.,* versare [*vehr-sah'-reh*]

poverty, povertà (f, indecl) [*poh-vehr-tah'*]

powder [cosmetics], cipria, polvere [*chee'-pree-ah, pohl'-veh-reh*]

power, potere (m), forza [*poh-teh'-reh, fohr'-tsah*]

powerful, potente, possente [*poh-tehn'-teh, pohs-sehn'-teh*]

practical, pratico [*prah'-tee-koh*]

practice *v.,* praticare, esercitare [*prah-tee-kah'-reh, eh-zehr-chee-tah'-reh*]

praise *v.,* lodare [*loh-dah'-reh*]

pray *v.,* pregare [*preh-gah'-reh*]

prayer, preghiera [*preh-gee-eh'-rah*]

precaution, precauzione (f) [*preh-kah-oo-tsee-oh'-neh*]

precede *v.,* precedere [*preh-cheh'-deh-reh*]

precious, prezioso [*preh-tsee-oh'-zoh*]

precious stone, pietra preziosa [*pee-eh'-trah preh-tsee-oh'-zah*]

precise, preciso [*preh-chee'-zoh*]

prefer *v.,* preferire [*preh-feh-ree'-reh*]

preference, preferenza [*preh-feh-rehn'-tsah*]

pregnancy, gravidanza [*grah-vee-dahn'-tsah*]

pregnant, incinta [*een-cheen'-tah*]

prejudice, pregiudizio [*preh-jee-oo-dee'-tsee-oh*]

preliminary, preliminare [*preh-lee-mee-nah'-reh*]

preparation, preparazione (f) [*preh-pah-rah-tsee-oh'-neh*]

prepare *v.,* preparare [*preh-pah-rah'-reh*]

prescription, ricetta [*ree-cheht'-tah*]

presence, presenza [*preh-zehn'-tsah*]

present [time] *n.,* presente (m) [*preh-zehn'-teh*]

  at present, al momento [*ahl moh-mehn'-toh*]

present [gift] *n.,* regalo [*reh-gah'-loh*]

present *v.,* presentare [*preh-zehn-tah'-reh*]

presentable, presentabile [*preh-zehn-tah'-bee-leh*]

preserve *v.* preservare [*preh-zehr-vah'-reh*]

president, presidente (m) [*preh-zee-dehn'-teh*]

press v., pressare [*prehs-sah'-reh*]
press [clothes] v., stirare [*stee-rah'-reh*]
pressing, urgente [*oor-jehn'-teh*]
pressure, pressione (f) [*prehs-see-oh'-neh*]
prestige, prestigio [*prehs-tee'-jee-oh*]
presume v., presupporre (irreg) [*preh-zoop-pohr'-reh*]
pretend v., pretendere [*preh-tehn'-deh-reh*]
pretentious, pretenzioso [*preh-tehn-tsee-oh'-zoh*]
pretty, graziosa, bella [*grah-tsee-oh'-zah, behl'-lah*]
prevent v., prevenire [*preh-veh-nee'-reh*]
previous, precedente [*preh-cheh-dehn'-teh*]
price n., prezzo [*prehts'-tsoh*]
pride, orgoglio [*ohr-goh'-lyoh*]
priest, prete (m) [*preh'-teh*]
primitive, primitivo [*pree-mee-tee'-voh*]
principal adj., principale [*preen-chee-pah'-leh*]
principles [moral], principi (pl) [*preen-chee'-pee*]
print v., stampare, imprimere [*stahm-pah'-reh, eem-pree'-meh-reh*]
printed matter, stampato [*stahm-pah'-toh*]
printer, tipografo [*tee-poh'-grah-foh*]
prison, prigione (f), carcere (m, f) [*pree-jee-oh'-neh, kahr'-cheh-reh*]
  put in prison v., imprigionare [*eem-pree-jee-oh-nah'-reh*]
prisoner, prigioniero [*pree-jee-oh-nee-eh'-roh*]
privacy, intimità (f, indecl) [*een-tee-mee-tah'*]
private, privato [*pree-vah'-toh*]
privilege, privilegio [*pree-vee-leh'-jee-oh*]
prize n., premio [*preh'-mee-oh*]
probable, probabile [*proh-bah'-bee-leh*]
probably, probabilmente [*proh-bah-beel-mehn'-teh*]
problem, problema (m) [*proh-bleh'-mah*]
procedure, procedimento [*proh-cheh-dee-mehn'-toh*]
proceed v., procedere [*proh-cheh'-deh-reh*]
process n., processo [*proh-chehs'-soh*]
produce v., produrre (irreg) [*proh-door'-reh*]
product, prodotto [*proh-doht'-toh*]
production, produzione (f) [*proh-doo-tsee-oh'-neh*]

profession, professione (f) [*proh-fehs-see-oh'-neh*]
professor, professore (m), professoressa (f) [*proh-fehs-soh'-reh, proh-fehs-soh-rehs'-sah*]
profit *n.,* profitto, guadagno [*proh-feet'-toh, goo-ah-dah'-nyoh*]
program *n.,* programma (m) [*proh-grahm'-mah*]
progress *n.,* progresso [*proh-grehs'-soh*]
progressive, progressivo [*proh-grehs-see'-voh*]
prohibit *v.,* proibire [*proh-ee-bee'-reh*]
prohibited, proibito [*proh-ee-bee'-toh*]
project *n.,* progetto [*proh-jeht'-toh*]
project *v.,* progettare [*proh-jeht-tah'-reh*]
prominent, prominente [*proh-mee-nehn'-teh*]
promise *n.,* promessa [*proh-mehs'-sah*]
promise *v.,* promettere [*proh-meht'-teh-reh*]
promotion, promozione (f) [*proh-moh-tsee-oh'-neh*]
prompt, immediato [*eem-meh-dee-ah'-toh*]
pronoun, pronome (m) [*proh-noh'-meh*]
pronounce *v.,* pronunciare [*proh-noon-chee-ah'-reh*]
  How do you pronounce . . . ? Come si pronuncia . . . ?
  [*koh'-meh see proh-noon'-chee-ah*]
pronunciation, pronuncia [*proh-noon'-chee-ah*]
proof, prova [*proh'-vah*]
propaganda, propaganda [*proh-pah-gahn'-dah*]
propeller, elica [*eh'-lee-kah*]
proper, proprio, corretto [*proh'-pree-oh, kohr-reht'-toh*]
property, proprietà (f, indecl) [*proh-pree-eh-tah'*]
prophecy, profezia [*proh-feh-tsee'-ah*]
proportion, proporzione (f) [*proh-pohr-tsee-oh'-neh*]
proposal, proposta [*proh-pohs'-tah*]
propose *v.,* proporre (irreg) [*proh-pohr'-reh*]
proposition, proposizione (f) [*proh-poh-zee-tsee-oh'-neh*]
proprietor, proprietario [*proh-pree-eh-tah'-ree-oh*]
propriety, proprietà (f, indecl) [*proh-pree-eh-tah'*]
prosperity, prosperità (f, indecl) [*prohs-peh-ree-tah'*]
prosperous, prospero [*prohs'-peh-roh*]
protect *v.,* proteggere [*proh-tehj'-jeh-reh*]
protection, protezione (f) [*proh-teh-tsee-oh'-neh*]

protest *n.*, protesta [*proh-tehs'-tah*]
protest *v.*, protestare [*proh-tehs-tah'-reh*]
Protestant, protestante [*proh-tehs-tahn'-teh*]
proud, orgoglioso [*ohr-goh-lyoh'-zoh*]
prove *v.*, provare [*proh-vah'-reh*]
proverb, proverbio [*proh-vehr'-bee-oh*]
provide *v.*, provvedere [*prohv-veh-deh'-reh*]
province, provincia [*proh-veen'-chee-ah*]
provincial, provinciale [*proh-veen-chee-ah'-leh*]
provisions, provviste (pl) [*prohv-vees'-teh*]
psychiatrist, psichiatra (m) [*psee-kee-ah'-trah*]
psychoanalysis, psicoanalisi (f) [*psee-koh-ah-nah'-lee-zee*]
psychological, psicologico [*psee-koh-loh'-jee-koh*]
public *n. &. adj.*, pubblico [*poob'-blee-koh*]
publication, pubblicazione (f) [*poob-blee-kah-tsee-oh'-neh*]
publicity, pubblicità (f, indecl) [*poob-blee-chee-tah'*]
publish *v.*, pubblicare [*poob-blee-kah'-reh*]
pull *v.*, tirare [*tee-rah'-reh*]
   pull out, tirare fuori [*tee-rah'-reh foo-oh'-ree*]
pulse *n.*, polso [*pohl'-soh*]
pump *n.*, pompa [*pohm'-pah*]
punch *n.*, pugno, ponce [*poo'-nyoh, pohn'-cheh*]
punctual, puntuale [*poon-too-ah'-leh*]
punish *v.*, punire [*poo-nee'-reh*]
punishment, punizione (f) [*poo-nee-tsee-oh'-neh*]
pupil, alunno [*ah-loon'-noh*]
puppet, marionetta [*mah-ree-oh-neht'-tah*]
purchase *v.*, acquistare [*ahk-koo-ees-tah'-reh*]
pure, puro [*poo'-roh*]
purple, violetto [*vee-oh-leht'-toh*]
purpose, scopo [*skoh'-poh*]
   on purpose, di proposito [*dee proh-poh'-zee-toh*]
purse, borsa [*bohr'-sah*]
pursue *v.*, perseguire [*pehr-seh-goo-ee'-reh*]
push *v.*, spingere [*speen'-jeh-reh*]
put *v.*, mettere, porre [*meht'-teh-reh, pohr'-reh*]
   put aside, mettere da parte [*meht'-teh-reh dah pahr'-teh*]
   put down, sopprimere [*sohp-pree'-meh-reh*]

put off, rimandare [*ree-mahn-dah'-reh*]
put on [clothes], indossare [*een-dohs-sah'-reh*]
puzzle *n.*, enigma [*eh-neeg'-mah*]

Q

qualification, qualifica [*koo-ah-lee'-fee-kah*]
qualified, qualificato [*koo-ah-lee-fee-kah'-toh*]
qualify *v.*, qualificare [*koo-ah-lee-fee-kah'-reh*]
quality, qualità (f, indecl) [*koo-ah-lee-tah'*]
quantity, quantità (f, indecl) [*koo-ahn-tee-tah'*]
quarrel *n.*, lite (f) [*lee'-teh*]
quarter, quarto, trimestre (m) [*koo-ahr'-toh, tree-mehs'-treh*]
　quarter hour, quarto d'ora [*koo-ahr'-toh doh'-rah*]
queen, regina [*reh-jee'-nah*]
queer, strano [*strah'-noh*]
　How queer! Che strano! [*keh strah'-noh*]
question *n.*, questione (f), domanda [*koo-ehs-tee-oh'-neh, doh-mahn'-dah*]
questionable, incerto, discutibile [*een-cher'-toh, dees-koo-tee'-bee-leh*]
question mark, punto interrogativo [*poon'-toh een-tehr-roh-gah-tee'-voh*]
quick, svelto, presto, rapido [*zvehl'-toh, prehs'-toh, rah'-pee-doh*]
　Quick, quick! Presto, presto! [*prehs'-to, prehs'-toh*]
quickly, rapidamente [*rah-pee-dah-mehn'-teh*]
quiet, tranquillo, quieto [*trahn-koo-eel'-loh, koo-ee-eh'-toh*]
　Be quiet! [to many] Zitto!, Silenzio! [*dzeet'-toh, see-lehn'-tsee-oh*; [to one person] Stia calmo! [*stee'-ah kahl'-moh*]
quite, assai, molto [*ahs-sah'-ee, mohl'-toh*]
　quite so, precisamente, proprio così [*preh-chee-zah-mehn'-teh, proh'-pree-oh koh-zee'*]

quota, aliquota [*ah-lee'-koo-oh-tah*]
quotation [of words], citazione (f) [*chee-tah-tsee-oh'-neh*]
quotation [of price] quotazione (f) [*koo-oh-tah-tsee-oh'-neh*]
quote *v.*, citare [*chee-tah'-reh*]

R

rabbi, rabbino [*rahb-bee'-noh*]
race [human] *n.*, razza [*rahts'-tsah*]
race [contest] *n.*, corsa, gara [*kohr'-sah, gah'-rah*]
  horse race, corsa di cavalli [*kohr'-sah dee kah-vahll'-lee*]
radiator, termosifone (m) [*tehr-moh-see-foh'-neh*]
radical, radicale [*rah-dee-kah'-leh*]
radio, radio (f) [*rah'-dee-oh*]
radio station, stazione radio (f) [*stah-tsee-oh'-neh rah'-dee-oh*]
radish, ravanello [*rah-vah-nehll'-loh*]
rag, straccio [*strach'-chee-oh*]
rage, rabbia, furore (m) [*rahb'-bee-ah, foo-roh'-reh*]
raid *n.*, incursione (f) [*een-koor-see-oh'-neh*]
railroad, railway, ferrovia [*fehr-roh-vee'-ah*]
railroad car, vagone ferroviario (m) [*vah-goh'-neh fehr-roh-vee-ah'-ree-oh*]
railroad crossing, passaggio a livello [*pahs-sahj'-jee-oh ah lee-vehl'-loh*]
railroad station, stazione ferroviaria [*sta-tsee-oh'-neh fehr-roh-vee-ah'-ree-ah*]
rain *n.*, pioggia [*pee-ohj'-jee-ah*]
rain *v.*, piovere [*pee-oh'-veh-reh*]
  It's raining, Piove [*pee-oh'-veh*]
rainbow, arcobaleno [*ahr-koh-bah-leh'-noh*]
raincoat, impermeabile (f) [*eem-pehr-meh-ah'-bee-leh*]
rainproof, impermeabile [*eem-pehr-meh-ah'-bee-leh*]
raise [lift] *v.*, sollevare [*sohl-leh-vah'-reh*]
raise [rear] *v.*, allevare [*ahl-leh-vah'-reh*]

random, a casaccio [*ah kah-zahch'-chee-oh*]

range, fila, catena, estensione (f) [*fee'-lah, kah-teh'-nah, ehs-tehn-see-oh'-neh*]

rank *n.*, ordine (m), fila [*ohr'-dee-neh, fee'-lah*]

rape *n.*, violenza carnale [*vee-oh-lehn-tsah kahr-nah'-leh*]

rapid, rapido [*rah'-pee-doh*]

rapidly, rapidamente [*rah-pee-dah-mehn'-teh*]

rare [unusual], raro [*rah'-roh*]

rare [undercooked], poco cotto [*poh'-koh koht'-toh*]

rarely, raramente [*rah-rah-mehn'-teh*]

rash *n.*, eruzione [*eh-roo-tsee-oh'-neh*]

rash *adj.*, precipitoso, temerario [*preh-chee-pee-toh'-zoh, teh-meh-rah'-ree-oh*]

rate [price] *n.*, prezzo, tariffa [*prehts'-tsoh, tah-reef'-fah*]

rather, piuttosto [*pee-oot-tohs'-toh*]

   Would you rather . . . , Vorrebbe piuttosto . . . [*vohr-rehb'-beh pee-oot-tohs'-toh*]

rave *v.*, delirare [*deh-lee-rah'-reh*]

raw, grezzo, crudo [*grehdz'-dzoh, kroo'-doh*]

raw material, materiale grezzo [*mah-teh-ree-ah'-leh grehdz'-dzoh*]

ray, raggio [*rahj'-jee-oh*]

razor, rasoio [*rah-zoh'-ee-oh*]

   electric razor, rasoio elettrico [*rah-zoh'-ee-oh eh-leht'-tree-koh*]

   safety razor, rasoio di sicurezza [*rah-zoh'-ee-oh dee see-koo-rehts'-tsah*]

razor blade, lametta [*lah-meht'-tah*]

reach *v.*, raggiungere [*rahj-jee-oon'-jeh-reh*]

reaction, reazione (f) [*reh-ah-tsee-oh'-neh*]

read *v.*, leggere (irreg) [*lehj'-jeh-reh*]

reading, lettura [*leht-too'-rah*]

ready, pronto [*prohn'-toh*]

   ready to wear, già fatto [*jee-ah' faht'-toh*]

real, vero, reale [*veh'-roh, reh-ah'-leh*]

real estate, beni immobili [*beh'-nee eem-moh'-bee-lee*]

realize *v.*, realizzare [*reh-ah-leedz-dzah'-reh*]

really, realmente [*reh-ahl-mehn'-teh*]

rear v., allevare [ahl-leh-vah'-reh]
reason n., ragione (f) [rah-jee-oh'-neh]
reason v., ragionare [rah-jee-oh-nah'-reh]
reasonable, ragionevole [rah-jee-oh-neh'-voh-leh]
reassure v., rassicurare [rahs-see-koo-rah'-reh]
rebel n., ribelle (m, f) [ree-behl'-leh]
rebel v., ribellarsi [ree-behl-lahr'-see]
recall v., richiamare (alla memoria) [ree-kee-ah-mah'-reh
    (ahl'-lah meh-moh'-ree-ah)]
receipt, ricevuta [ree-cheh-voo'-tah]
receive v., ricevere [ree-cheh'-veh-reh]
recent, recente [reh-chehn'-teh]
recently, recentemente [reh-chehn-teh-mehn'-teh]
reception, accoglienza [ahk-koh-lyehn'-tsah]
recession, crisi economica (f) [kree'-zee eh-koh-noh'-mee-
    kah]
recipe, ricetta [ree-cheht'-tah]
reciprocate v., contraccambiare [kohn-trahk-kahm-bee-ah'-
    reh]
recite v., recitare [reh-chee-tah'-reh]
reckless, imprudente, avventato [eem-proo-dehn'-teh,
    ahv-vehn-tah'-toh]
recline v., reclinare [reh-klee-nah'-reh]
recognize v., riconoscere [ree-koh-noh'-sheh-reh]
recommend v., raccomandare [rahk-koh-mahn-dah'-reh]
recommendation, raccomandazione (f) [rahk-koh-mahn-dah-
    tsee-oh'-neh]
record [for phonograph] n., disco [dees'-koh]
record [in sports] n., record (m) [reh'-kohrd]
recover [something] v., ritrovare [ree-troh-vah'-reh]
recover [from illness] v., ricuperare [ree-koo-peh-rah'-reh]
recovery, ricupero [ree-koo'-peh-roh]
recreation, ricreazione (f) [ree-kreh-ah-tsee-oh'-neh]
red, rosso [rohs'-soh]
Red Cross, Croce Rossa [kroh'-cheh rohs'-sah]
redeem v., redimere [reh-dee'-meh-reh]
red tape, burocrazia [boo-roh-krah-tsee'-ah]
reduce v., ridurre (irreg) [ree-door'-reh]

reduction, riduzione (f) [*ree-doo-tsee-oh'-neh*]
redundant, superfluo [*soo-pehr'-floo-oh*]
refer v., riferire, indirizzare [*ree-feh-ree'-reh, een-dee-reets-tsah'-reh*]
referee, arbitro [*ahr'-bee-troh*]
reference, riferimento [*ree-feh-ree-mehn'-toh*]
  in reference to, in rapporto a [*een rahp-pohr'-toh ah*]
refill n., ricambio [*ree-kahm'-bee-oh*]
refill v., riempire [*ree-ehm-pee'-reh*]
refined, raffinato [*rahf-fee-nah'-toh*]
reflect [light] v., riflettere [*ree-fleht'-teh-reh*]
reflect [think on] v., meditare [*meh-dee-tah'-reh*]
reflection [thought] riflessione (f) [*ree-flehs-see-oh'-neh*]
reflex, riflesso [*ree-flehs'-soh*]
reform v., riformare [*ree-fohr-mah'-reh*]
refrain v., astenersi [*ahs-teh-nehr'-see*]
refresh v., rinfrescare [*reen-frehs-kah'-reh*]
refreshing, rinfrescante [*reen-frehs-kahn'-teh*]
refreshment, rinfresco [*reen-frehs'-koh*]
refrigerator, frigorifero [*free-goh-ree'-feh-roh*]
refuge, rifugio [*ree-foo'-jee-oh*]
refugee, profugo, profughi (pl) [*proh'-foo-goh, proh'-foo-gee*]
refund n., rimborso [*reem-bohr'-soh*]
refusal, rifiuto [*ree-fee-oo'-toh*]
refuse v., rifiutare [*ree-fee-oo-tah'-reh*]
regain v., riacquistare [*ree-ahk-koo-ees-tah'-reh*]
regard v., riguardo [*ree-goo-ahr'-doh*]
  with regard to, in riguardo a [*een ree-goo-ahr'-doh ah*]
regardless, incurante, nonostante, a malgrado di [*een-koo-rahn'-teh, nohn-ohs-tahn'-teh, ah mahl-grah'-doh dee*]
regards, complimenti, auguri, saluti [*kohm-plee-mehn'-tee, ah-oo-goo'-ree, sah-loo'-tee*]
  kind regards, cordiali saluti, tante belle cose [*kohr-dee-ah'-lee sah-loo'-tee, tahn'-teh behl'-leh koh'-zeh*]
region, regione (f), paese (m) [*reh-jee-oh'-neh, pah-eh-zeh*]
register n., registro [*reh-jees'-troh*]
register v., iscrivere [*ees-kree'-veh-reh*]
registered letter, lettera raccomandata [*leht'-teh-rah rahk-*

koh-mahn-dah'-tah]

regret *n.*, dispiacere [*dees-pee-ah-cheh'-reh*]

regret *v.*, rimpiangere [*reem-pee-ahn'-jeh-reh*]

regular, regolare [*reh-goh-lah'-reh*]

  regular gas, ordinario [*ohr-dee-nah'-ree-oh*]

regulate *v.*, regolare [*reh-goh-lah'-reh*]

regulation, regolamento [*reh-goh-lah-mehn'-toh*]

rehearsal, ripetizione, prova [*ree-peh-tee-tsee-oh'-nee, proh'-vah*]

reign *v.*, regnare [*reh-nyah'-reh*]

rejoin *v.*, raggiungere [*rahj-jee-oon'-jeh-reh*]

relate *v.*, raccontare [*rahk-kohn-tah'-reh*]

related, imparentato, connesso [*eem-pah-rehn-tah'-toh, kohn-nehs'-soh*]

  be related *v.*, essere imparentato [*ehs'-seh-reh eem-pah-rehn-tah'-toh*]

relationship, parentela, rapporto [*pah-rehn-teh'-lah, rahp-pohr'-toh*]

relative *adj.*, relativo [*reh-lah-tee'-voh*]

relative [family] *n.*, parente (m) [*pah-rehn'-teh*]

relatively, relativamente [*reh-lah-tee-vah-mehn'-teh*]

relax *v.*, rilassare, riposare [*ree-lahs-sah'-reh, ree-poh-zah'-reh*]

relaxation, riposo, distensione (f) [*ree-poh'-zoh, dees-tehn-see-oh'-neh*]

release *v.*, liberare [*lee-beh-rah'-reh*]

relevant, pertinente [*pehr-tee-nehn'-teh*]

reliable, degno di fiducia [*deh'-nyoh dee fee-doo'-chee-ah*]

relief [from discomfort], sollievo [*sohl-lee-eh'-voh*]

relief [aid], soccorso [*sohk-kohr'-soh*]

relieve *v.*, alleviare [*ahl-leh-vee-ah'-reh*]

religion, religione (f) [*reh-lee-jee-oh'-neh*]

religious, religioso [*reh-lee-jee-oh'-zoh*]

reluctant, riluttante [*ree-loot-tahn'-teh*]

rely (on) *v.*, fidarsi di [*fee-dahr'-see dee*]

remain *v.*, rimanere [*ree-mah-neh'-reh*]

remainder, residuo [*reh-zee'-doo-oh*]

remark *n.*, osservazione (f) [*ohs-sehr-vah-tsee-oh'-neh*]

remark v., osservare [*ohs-sehr-vah'-reh*]
remarkable, notevole [*noh-teh'-voh-leh*]
remedy n., rimedio [*ree-meh'-dee-oh*]
remember v., ricordarsi [*ree-kohr-dahr'-see*]
   Do you remember me? Si ricorda di me? [*see ree-kohr'-dah dee meh*]
remind v., ricordare a [*ree-kohr-dah'-reh ah*]
remittance, rimessa [*ree-mehs'-sah*]
remorse, rimorso [*ree-mohr'-soh*]
remote, remoto [*reh-moh'-toh*]
remove v., rimuovere [*ree-moo-oh'-veh-reh*]
renew v., rinnovare [*reen-noh-vah'-reh*]
rent n., affitto [*ahf-feet'-toh*]
   for rent, da affittare [*dah ahf-feet-tah'-reh*]
rent v., affittare [*ahf-feet-tah'-reh*]
repair n., riparazione (f) [*ree-pah-rah-tsee-oh'-neh*]
repair v., riparare [*ree-pah-rah'-reh*]
repay v., rimborsare [*reem-bohr-sah'-reh*]
repeat v., ripetere [*ree-peh'-teh-reh*]
   Please repeat! Per favore ripeta? [*pehr fah-voh'-reh ree-peh'-tah*]
repel v., respingere [*rehs-peen'-jeh-reh*]
replace v., sostituire [*sohs-tee-too-ee'-reh*]
reply n., risposta [*rees-pohs'-tah*]
reply v., rispondere [*rees-pohn'-deh-reh*]
report n., resoconto [*reh-zoh-kohn'-toh*]
report v., riferire, riportare [*ree-feh-ree'-reh, ree-pohr-tah'-reh*]
reporter, cronista (m, f) [*kroh-nees'-tah*]
represent v., rappresentare [*rahp-preh-sehn-tah'-reh*]
representative, rappresentante [*rahp-preh-zehn-tahn-teh*]
reproduction, riproduzione (f) [*ree-proh-doo-tsee-oh'-neh*]
republic, republica [*reh-poob'-lee-kah*]
reputation, reputazione (f) [*reh-poo-tah-tsee-oh'-neh*]
request n., richiesta [*ree-kee-ehs'-tah*]
request v., richiedere [*ree-kee-eh'-deh-reh*]
require v., esigere [*eh-zee'-jeh-reh*]
requirement, requisito [*reh-koo-ee-zee'-toh*]

rescue *n*., salvamento, soccorso [*sahl-vah-mehn'-toh, sohk-kohr'-soh*]

rescue *v*., salvare [*sahl-vah'-reh*]

research *n*., ricerca, ricerche (pl) [*ree-chehr'-kah, ree-chehr'-keh*]

research *v*., fare ricerche [*fah'-reh ree-chehr'-keh*]

resemblance, rassomiglianza [*rahs-soh-mee-lyahn'-tsah*]

resemble *v*., rassomigliare [*rahs-soh-mee-lyah'-reh*]

resentment, risentimento [*ree-sehn-tee-mehn'-toh*]

reservation [hotel], prenotazione (f) [*preh-noh-tah-tsee-oh'-neh*]

reserve *v*., riservare, prenotare [*ree-zehr-vah'-reh, preh-noh-tah'-reh*]

residence, residenza [*reh-zee-dehn'-tsah*]

resident, residente [*reh-zee-dehn'-teh*]

resignation, dimissione (f), rinuncia [*dee-mees-see-oh'-neh, ree-noon'-chee-ah*]

resistance, resistenza [*reh-zees-tehn'-tsah*]

resolution, risoluzione (f) [*ree-zoh-loo-tsee-oh'-neh*]

resolve *v*., risolvere [*ree-zohl'-veh-reh*]

resort *n*., stazione climatica [*stah-tsee-oh'-neh klee-mah'-tee-kah*]

resort *v*., ricorrere a [*ree-kohr'-reh-reh ah*]

respect *n*., rispetto [*rees-peht'-toh*]
  with respect to, in riguardo a [*een ree-goo-ahr'-doh ah*]

respect *v*., rispettare [*rees-peht-tah'-reh*]

respectable, rispettabile [*rees-peht-tah'-bee-leh*]

respectful, rispettoso [*rees-peht-toh'-zoh*]

respective, rispettivo [*rees-peht-tee'-voh*]

response, risposta, reazione (f) [*rees-pohs'-tah, reh-ah-tsee-oh'-neh*]

responsibility, responsabilità (f, indecl) [*rehs-pohn-sah-bee-lee-tah'*]

responsible, responsabile [*rehs-pohn-sah'-bee-leh*]

rest *n*., riposo [*ree-poh'-zoh*]

rest *v*., riposare [*ree-poh-zah'-reh*]

restaurant, ristorante (m) [*rees-toh-rahn'-teh*]

restless, irrequieto, inquieto [*eer-reh-koo-ee-eh'-toh,* *een-koo-ee-eh'-toh*]

restore *v.*, restaurare [*rehs-tah-oo-rah'-reh*]

restrain *v.*, trattenere [*traht-teh-neh'-reh*]

restraint, contegno [*kohn-teh'-nyoh*]

result *n.*, risultato [*ree-zool-tah'-toh*]

resume *v.*, riprendere [*ree-prehn'-deh-reh*]

retail, vendita al minuto [*vehn'-dee-tah ahl mee-noo'-toh*]

retain *v.*, ritenere [*ree-teh-neh'-reh*]

retire *v.*, ritirarsi [*ree-tee-rahr'-see*]

return *n.*, ritorno [*ree-tohr'-noh*]

return *v.*, ritornare [*ree-tohr-nah'-reh*]

   When will you return? Quando ritornerà? [*koo-ahn'-doh ree-tohr-neh-rah'*]

reveal *v.*, rivelare [*ree-veh-lah'-reh*]

revenge, vendetta [*vehn-deht'-tah*]

reverence, riverenza [*ree-veh-rehn'-tsah*]

reverse *v.*, rovesciare, invertire [*roh-veh-shee-ah'-reh, een-vehr-tee'-reh*]

review *n.*, rivista [*ree-vees'-tah*]

review *v.*, riesaminare [*ree-eh-zah-mee-nah'-reh*]

revise *v.*, rivedere [*ree-veh-deh'-reh*]

revolution, rivoluzione (f) [*ree-voh-loo-tsee-oh'-neh*]

revolve *v.*, girare [*jee-rah'-reh*]

reward *n.*, ricompensa [*ree-kohm-pehn'-sah*]

reward *v.*, ricompensare [*ree-kohm-pehn-sah'-reh*]

rheumatism, reumatismo [*reh-oo-mah-teez'-moh*]

rhyme, rima [*ree'-mah*]

rhythm *n.*, ritmo [*reet'-moh*]

rib, costola [*kohs'-toh-lah*]

ribbon, nastro [*nahs'-troh*]

rice riso [*ree'-zoh*]

rich, ricco [*reek'-koh*]

rid *v.*, liberare [*lee-beh-rah'-reh*]

   get rid of, sbarazzarsi di [*zbah-rahts-tsahr'-see dee*]

ride *n.*, passeggiata [*pahs-sehj-jee-ah'-tah*]

ride [a bicycle] *v.*, andare in bicicletta [*ahn-dah'-reh een bee-chee-kleht'-tah*]

ride [a horse], cavalcare [*kah-vahl-kah'-reh*]

ridicule *n.*, ridicolo [*ree-dee'-koh-loh*]
ridicule *v.*, deridere [*deh-ree'-deh-reh*]
ridiculous, ridicolo [*ree-dee'-koh-loh*]
right [direction] *n.*, destra [*dehs'-trah*]
  on the right, a destra [*ah dehs'-trah*]
right [correct], giusto [*jee-oos'-toh*]
  all right, va bene [*vah beh'-neh*]
  be right *v.*, avere ragione [*ah-veh'-reh rah-jee-oh'-neh*]
  right away, subito [*soo'-bee-toh*]
  right here, proprio qui [*pro'-pree-oh koo-ee'*]
ring [for finger] *n.*, anello [*ah-nehl'-loh*]
ring *v.*, suonare [*soo-oh-nah'-reh*]
  ring up, chiamare al telefono [*kee-ah-mah'-reh ahl teh-leh'-foh-noh*]
ringing *n.*, suonata [*soo-oh-nah'-tah*]
rinse *v.*, risciacquare [*ree-shee-ahk-koo-ah'-reh*]
riot *n.*, tumulto, rivolta [*too-mool'-toh, ree-vohl'-tah*]
riot *v.*, rivoltarsi [*ree-vohl-tahr'-see*]
rip *n.*, strappo [*strahp'-poh*]
rip *v.*, strappare [*strahp-pah'-reh*]
ripe, maturo [*mah-too'-roh*]
rise *v.*, sorgere [*sohr'-jeh-reh*]
rising *n.*, sorgere (m) [*sohr'-jeh-reh*]
risk *n.*, rischio [*rees'-kee-oh*]
ritual *n.*, rituale [*ree-too-ah'-leh*]
rival *adj. & n.*, rivale [*ree-vah'-leh*]
river, fiume (m) [*fee-oo'-meh*]
road, strada, via [*strah'-dah, vee'-ah*]
roadway, autostrada [*ah-oo-toh-strah'-dah*]
roam *v.*, vagare [*vah-gah'-reh*]
roast *n.*, arrosto [*ahr-rohs'-toh*]
roast *v.*, arrostire [*ahr-rohs-tee'-reh*]
roasted, arrostito [*ahr-rohs-tee'-toh*]
rob *v.*, derubare [*deh-roo-bah'-reh*]
robbery, furto [*foor'-toh*]
rock *n.*, roccia, rocca [*rohch'-chee-ah, rohk'-kah*]
rocking chair, sedia a dondolo [*seh'-dee-ah ah dohn'-doh-loh*]
roll *v.*, avvolgere [*ahv-vohl'-jeh-reh*]

Roman, romano [*roh-mah'-noh*]
romance, romanza [*roh-mahn'-tsah*]
Romanesque, romanico [*roh-mah'-nee-koh*]
romantic, romantico [*roh-mahn'-tee-koh*]
Rome, Roma [*roh'-mah*]
roof, tetto [*teht'-toh*]
room [house] *n.,* stanza, camera [*stahn'-tsah, kah'-meh-rah*]
room [space] *n.,* spazio [*spah'-tsee-oh*]
   There is no room, Non c'è spazio [*nohn cheh' spah'-tsee-oh*]
root *n.,* radice (f) [*rah-dee'-cheh*]
rope *n.,* corda [*kohr'-dah*]
rose *n.,* rosa [*roh'-sah*]
rotten, marcio [*mahr'-chee-oh*]
rouge [*rohs-seht'-toh*]
rough, ruvido, rozzo [*roo'-vee-doh, rohts'-tsoh*]
round *adj.,* rotondo [*roh-tohn'-doh*]
round trip, andata e ritorno [*ahn-dah'-tah eh ree-tohr'-noh*]
route, rotta [*roht'-tah*]
routine, abitudine (f) [*ah-bee-too'-dee-neh*]
row [line] *n.,* fila [*fee'-lah*]
royal, reale [*reh-ah'-leh*]
rub *v.,* fregare, strofinare [*freh-gah'-reh, stroh-fee-nah'-reh*]
   rub out *v.,* cancellare [*kahn-chehl-lah'-reh*]
rubber, gomma [*gohm'-mah*]
ruby, rubino [*roo-bee'-noh*]
rude, rude, ruvido [*roo'-deh, roo'-vee-doh*]
rudeness, scortesia [*skohr-teh-zee'-ah*]
rug, tappeto [*tahp-peh'-toh*]
ruin *n.,* rovina [*roh-vee'-nah*]
rule *n.,* regola [*reh'-goh-lah*]
rule *v.,* regolare, governare [*reh-goh-lah'-reh, goh-vehr-nah'-reh*]
ruler [measure], riga [*ree'-gah*]
ruler [governor], governante, sovrano [*goh-vehr-nahn'-teh, soh-vrah'-noh*]
rumor, rumore (m) [*roo-moh'-reh*]
run *v.,* correre [*kohr'-reh-reh*]

run across, incontrare per caso [*een-kohn-trah'-reh pehr kah'-zoh*]

run after, inseguire [*een-seh-goo-ee'-reh*]

run away, scappare [*skahp-pah'-reh*]

run into, scontrarsi [*skohn-trahr'-see*]

run over, investire [*een-vehs-tee'-reh*]

runaway *n., adj.*, fuggitivo [*fooj-jee-tee'-voh*]

running, corsa [*kohr'-sah*]

runway, pista [*pees'-tah*]

rural, rurale [*roo-rah'-leh*]

rush *n.*, afflusso [*ahf-floos'-soh*]

Russia, Russia [*roos'-see-ah*]

Russian, russo [*roos'-soh*]

rust *n.*, ruggine (f) [*rooj'-jee-neh*]

rustic, rustico [*roos'-tee-koh*]

ruthless, spietato [*spee-eh-tah'-toh*]

S

sabotage *n.*, sabotaggio [*sah-boh-tahj'-jee-oh*]

sack, sacco [*sahk'-koh*]

sacred, sacro [*sah'-kroh*]

sacrifice *n.*, sacrificio [*sah-kree-fee'-chee-oh*]

sad, triste [*trees'-teh*]

saddle, sella [*sehl'-lah*]

sadness, tristezza [*trees-tehz'-zah*]

safe *adj.*, salvo [*sahl'-voh*]

safe and sound, sano e salvo [*sah'-noh eh sahl'-voh*]

safe conduct, salva-condotta (m) [*sahl-vah-kohn-doht'-tah*]

safety, sicurezza [*see-koo-rehts'-tsah*]

safety pin, spilla di sicurezza [*speel'-lah dee see-koo-reht'-tsah*]

safety razor, rasoio di sicurezza [*rah-zoh'-ee-oh dee see-koo-rehts'-tsah*]

sail *n.*, vela [*veh'-lah*]

sail *v.*, navigare [*nah-vee-gah'-reh*]

sailboat, barca a vela [*bahr'-kah ah veh'-lah*]

sailor, marinaio [*mah-ree-nah'-ee-oh*]

saint *n. & adj.*, santo [*sahn'-toh*]

sake, scopo, fine (m), amore (m) [*skoh'-poh, fee'-neh, ah-moh'-reh*]

   For heaven's sake! Per l'amor del cielo! [*pehr lah-mohr' dehl chee-eh'-loh*]

   for your sake, per il suo bene [*pehr eel soo'-oh beh'-neh*]

salad, insalata [*een-sah-lah'-tah*]

salary, salario, stipendio [*sah-lah'-ree-oh, stee-pehn'-dee-oh*]

sale, vendita [*vehn'-dee-tah*]

   for sale, in vendita [*een vehn'-dee-tah*]

salesclerk, commesso [*kohm-mehs'-soh*]

salmon, salmone (m) [*sahl-moh'-neh*]

salt, sale (m) [*sah'-leh*]

salty, salato [*sah-lah'-toh*]

same, stesso, medesimo [*stehs'-soh, meh-deh'-zee-moh*]

   all the same, ciononostante [*chee-oh-noh-nohs-tahn'-teh*]

   at the same time, nello stesso tempo [*nehl'-loh stehs'-soh tehm'-poh*]

   It's all the same to me, È lo stesso per me [*eh' loh stehs'-soh pehr meh*]

sample *n.,* campione (m), esempio [*kahm-pee-oh'-neh, eh-zehm'-pee-oh*]

sand, sabbia [*sahb'-bee-ah*]

sandal, sandalo [*sahn'-dah-loh*]

sandwich, panino [*pah-nee'-noh*]

sandy, sabbioso [*sahb-bee-oh'-zoh*]

sane, sano di mente [*sah'-noh dee mehn'-teh*]

sanitary, igienico [*ee-jee-eh'-nee-koh*]

sanitary napkin, pannino igienico [*pah-nee'-noh ee-jee-eh'-nee-koh*]

sapphire, zaffiro [*dzahf'-fee-roh*]

sarcastic, sarcastico [*sahr-kahs'-tee-koh*]

satin, raso [*rah'-soh*]

satire, satira [*sah'-tee-rah*]

satisfaction, soddisfazione (f) [*sohd-dees-fah-tsee-oh'-neh*]

satisfactory, soddisfacente [*sohd-dees-fah-chehn'-teh*]

satisfied, soddisfatto [*sohd-dees-faht'-toh*]

satisfy *v.*, soddisfare [*sohd-dees-fah'-reh*]

Saturday, sabato [*sah'-bah-toh*]

sauce, salsa [*sahl'-sah*]

saucer, piattino [*pee-aht-tee'-noh*]

sausage, salsiccia [*sahl-seech'-chee-ah*]

save [money] *v.*, risparmiare [*rees-pahr-mee-ah'-reh*]

save [life] *v.*, salvare [*sahl-vah'-reh*]

saving, risparmio [*rees-pahr'-mee-oh*]

savings account, libretto di risparmio [*lee-breht'-toh dee rees-pahr'-mee-oh*]

say *v.*, dire (irreg) [*dee'-reh*]

saying, proverbio [*proh-vehr'-bee-oh*]

scale [music, etc.] scala [*skah'-lah*]

scales, bilancia [*bee-lahn'-chee-ah*]

scandal, scandalo [*skahn'-dah-loh*]

scar *n.*, cicatrice (f) [*chee-kah-tree'-cheh*]

scarce, scarso [*skahr'-soh*]

scare *v.*, spaventare [*spah-vehn-tah'-reh*]

scarf, sciarpa [*shee-ahr'-pah*]

scatter *v.*, disperdere [*dees-pehr'-deh-reh*]

scene, scena [*sheh'-nah*]

scenery, scenario [*sheh-nah'-ree-oh*]

scent *n.*, odore (m) [*oh-doh'-reh*]

schedule *n.*, orario [*oh-rah'-ree-oh*]

scheme *n.*, schema (m), disegno [*skeh'-mah, dee-zeh'-nyoh*]

scholar, studioso, erudito [*stoo-dee-oh'-zoh, eh-roo-dee'-toh*]

school, scuola [*skoo-oh'-lah*]

schoolmate, compagno di scuola [*kohm-pah'-nyoh dee skoo-oh'-lah*]

schoolteacher, maestro [*mah-ehs'-troh*]

science, scienza [*shee-ehn'-tsah*]

scientist, scienziato [*shee-ehn-tsee-ah'-toh*]

scissors, forbici [*fohr'-bee-chee*]

scold *v.*, rimproverare [*reem-proh-veh-rah'-reh*]

score *n.*, punteggio [*poon-tehj'-jee-oh*]

score *v.*, segnare [*seh-nyah'-reh*]

scorn *n.*, disprezzo [*dees-prehts'-tsoh*]

scorn v., disprezzare [dees-prehts-tsah'-reh]

Scot, Scottish n. & adj. scozzese [skohts-tseh'-zeh]

Scotland, Scozia [skoh'-tsee-ah]

scrape v., raschiare [rahs-kee-ah'-reh]

scratch n., graffio [grahf'-fee-oh]

scratch v., graffiare [grahf-fee-ah'-reh]

scream n., grido [gree'-doh]

scream v., gridare [gree-dah'-reh]

screen n., schermo [skehr'-moh]

screw n., vite (f) [vee'-teh]

screwdriver, cacciavite (m) [kahch-chee-ah-vee'-teh]

scrub v., strofinare [stroh-fee-nah'-reh]

sculpture n., scultura [skool-too'-rah]

sea, mare (m) [mah'-reh]

seal [animal] n., foca [foh'-kah]

seal [stamp] n., sigillo [see-jeel'-loh]

seal v., sigillare [see-jeel-lah'-reh]

seam n., cucitura [koo-chee-too'-rah]

seaport, porto [pohr'-toh]

sea shell, conchiglia marina [kohn-kee'-lyah mah-ree'-nah]

search n., ricerca [ree-chehr'-kah]

search for v., cercare [chehr-kah'-reh]

season n., stagione (f) [stah-jee-oh'-neh]

season [flavor] v., condire [kohn-dee'-reh]

seat n., posto [pohs'-toh]

   Have a seat, please! Si sieda, per favore! [see see-eh'-dah, pehr fah-voh'-reh]

seated, seduto [seh-doo'-toh]

second adj., secondo [seh-kohn'-doh]

second [time] n., secondo [seh-kohn'-doh]

secondary, secondario [seh-kohn-dah'-ree-oh]

secret n. & adj., segreto [seh-greh'-toh]

secretary, segretario [seh-greh-tah'-ree-oh]

section, sezione (f) [seh-tsee-oh'-neh]

secular, laico [lah'-ee-koh]

secure adj., sicuro [see-koo'-roh]

secure [make sure] v., assicurare [ahs-see-koo-rah'-reh]

secure [obtain] v., procurarsi [proh-koo-rahr'-see]

security, sicurezza [*see-koo-rehts'-tsah*]

seduce *v.*, sedurre (irreg) [*seh-door'-reh*]

see *v.*, vedere [*veh-deh'-reh*]

   Let me see, Mi faccia vedere [*mee fahch'-chee-ah veh-deh'-reh*]

   Let's see, vediamo un pò [*veh-dee-ah'-moh oon poh'*]

seed, seme (m) [*seh'-meh*]

seek *v.*, cercare [*chehr-kah'-reh*]

seem *v.*, sembrare [*sehm-brah'-reh*]

   How does it seem to you? Come le sembra? [*koh'-meh leh sehm'-brah*]

   It seems to me that . . . , Mi sembra che . . . [*mee sehm'-brah keh*]

seize *v.*, afferrare [*ahf-fehr-rah'-reh*]

seldom, raramente [*rah-rah-mehn'-teh*]

select *v.*, scegliere (irreg) [*sheh'-lyeh-reh*]

self, stesso [*stehs'-soh*]

   myself, me stesso [*meh stehs'-soh*]

   themselves, loro stessi [*loh'-roh stehs'-see*]

self-conscious timido [*tee'-mee-doh*]

selfish, egoista [*eh-goh-ees'-tah*]

sell, vendere [*vehn'-deh-reh*]

senate, senato [*seh-nah'-toh*]

senator, senatore (m) [*seh-nah-toh'-reh*]

send *v.*, mandare [*mahn-dah'-reh*]

   send for, mandare a chiamare [*mahn-dah'-reh ah kee-ah-mah'-reh*]

   send forth, spedire [*speh-dee'-reh*]

sender, speditore (m) [*speh-dee-toh'-reh*]

senior, più anziano [*pee-oo' ahn-tsee-ah'-noh*]

sense *n.*, senso [*sehn'-soh*]

   common sense, buon senso [*boo-ohn' sehn'-soh*]

sensible, sensibile [*sehn-see'-bee-leh*]

sensitive, sensitivo [*sehn-see-tee'-voh*]

sentence [speech] *n.*, frase (f) [*frah'-zeh*]

sentimental, sentimentale [*sehn-tee-mehn-tah'-leh*]

separate *adj.*, separato [*seh-pah-rah'-toh*]

separate *v.*, separare [*seh-pah-rah'-reh*]

separately, separatamente [*seh-pah-rah-tah-mehn'-teh*]

separation, separazione (f) [*seh-pah-rah-tsee-oh'-neh*]

September, settembre (m) [*seht-tehm'-breh*]

serenade *n.*, serenata [*seh-reh-nah'-tah*]

serene, sereno [*seh-reh'-noh*]

series, serie (f, sing & pl) [*seh'-ree-eh*]

serious, serio [*seh'-ree-oh*]

seriously, seriamente [*seh-ree-ah-mehn'-teh*]

sermon, predica [*preh'-dee-kah*]

servant, servitore (m), servitrice (f) [*sehr-vee-toh'-reh, sehr-vee-tree'-cheh*]

serve *v.*, servire [*sehr-vee'-reh*]

service, servizio [*sehr-vee'-tsee-oh*]

  at your service, ai suoi ordini [*ah'-ee soo-oh'-ee ohr'-dee-nee*]

session, sessione (f) [*sehs-see-oh'-neh*]

set *n.*, assortimento [*ahs-sohr-tee-mehn'-toh*]

set *v.*, mettere [*meht'-teh-reh*]

  set aside, mettere da parte [*meht'-teh-reh dah pahr'-teh*]

  set a watch, regolare l'orologio [*reh-goh-lah'-reh loh-roh-loh'-jee-oh*]

  set free, mettere in libertà [*meht'-teh-reh een lee-behr-tah'*]

  set off, mettere in azione [*meht'-teh-reh een ah-tsee-oh'-neh*]

  set up, costruire [*kohs-troo-ee'-reh*]

settle *v.*, regolare [*reh-goh-lah'-reh*]

seven, sette [*seht'-teh*]

seventeen, diciassette [*dee-chee-ah-seht'-teh*]

seventh, settimo [*seht'-tee-moh*]

seventy, settanta [*seht-tahn'-tah*]

sever *v.*, troncare [*trohn-kah'-reh*]

several, parecchi [*pah-rehk'-kee*]

severe, severo [*seh-veh'-roh*]

sew *v.*, cucire [*koo-chee'-reh*]

sewing machine, macchina da cucire [*mahk'-kee-nah dah koo-chee'-reh*]

sex, sesso [*sehs'-soh*]

shade, shadow, ombra [*ohm'-brah*]

shake v., agitare [*ah-jee-tah'-reh*]
  shake hands, darsi la mano [*dahr'-see lah mah'-noh*]
shallow, poco profondo [*poh'-koh proh-fohn'-doh*]
shame, vergogna [*vehr-goh'-nyah*]
shameful, vergognoso [*vehr-goh-nyoh'-zoh*]
shampoo n., shampoo [*shahm'-poo*]
shape n., forma [*fohr'-mah*]
shape v., formare [*fohr-mah'-reh*]
share v., spartire, condividere [*spahr-tee'-reh, kohn-dee-vee'-deh-reh*]
sharp, aguzzo, furbo [*ah-goots'-tsoh, foor'-boh*]
shave n., rasatura [*rah-zah-too'-rah*]
shave v., radere, radersi [*rah-deh'-reh, rah-dehr'-see*]
shaving brush, pennello da barba [*pehn-nehl'-loh dah bahr'-bah*]
shaving cream, crema da barba [*kreh'-mah dah bahr'-bah*]
shaving lotion, lozione (f) da barba [*loh-tsee-oh'-neh dah bahr'-bah*]
shawl, scialle (m) [*shee-ahl'-leh*]
she, essa, ella, lei [*ehs'-sah, ehl'-lah, leh'-ee*]
sheep, pecora [*peh'-koh-rah*]
sheet [bedding], lenzuolo, le lenzuola (pl) [*lehn-tsoo-oh'-loh, leh lehn-tsoo-oh'-lah*]
sheet [paper], foglio [*foh'-lyoh*]
shelf, scaffale (m) [*skahf-fah'-leh*]
shell [eggshell], guscio [*goo'-shee-oh*]
shell [seashell], conchiglia [*kohn-kee'-lyah*]
shelter n., rifugio [*ree-foo'-jee-oh*]
shield v., difendere [*dee-fehn'-deh-reh*]
shift v., cambiare [*kahm-bee-ah'-reh*]
shine v., brillare [*breel-lah'-reh*]
shine [shoes] v., lucidare [*loo-chee-dah'-reh*]
ship n., nave (f) [*nah'-veh*]
ship v., imbarcare, spedire [*eem-bahr-kah'-reh, speh-dee'-reh*]
shipment, imbarco, carico [*eem-bahr'-koh, kah'-ree-koh*]
shirt, camicia [*kah-mee'-chee-ah*]
shiver v., tremare [*treh-mah'-reh*]

shock *n.*, urto, scossa [*oor'-toh, skohs'-sah*]
shoe, scarpa [*skahr'-pah*]
shoe laces, lacci di scarpe [*lahch'-chee dee skahr'-peh*]
shoemaker, calzolaio [*kahl-tsoh-lah'-ee-oh*]
shoeshine boy, lustrascarpe (m) [*loos-trah-skahr'-peh*]
shoe store, calzoleria [*kahl-tsoh-leh-ree'-ah*]
shoot [fire] *v.*, sparare [*spah-rah'-reh*]
shop *n.*, negozio, bottega [*neh-goh'-tsee-oh, boht-teh'-gah*]
shop *v.*, fare le compre [*fah'-reh leh kohm'-preh*]
shopping, spesa, compere (f, pl) [*speh'-zah, kohm'-peh-reh*]
shop window, vetrina [*veh-tree'-na*]
shore, riva [*ree'-vah*]
short, corto, basso [*kohr'-toh, bahs'-soh*]
   in a short time, in poco tempo [*een poh'-koh tehm'-poh*]
   in short, in breve [*een breh'-veh*]
shortcut, scorciatoia [*skohr-chee-ah-toh'-ee-ah*]
shorts, calzoncini (m, pl) [*kahl-tsohn-chee'-nee*]
shorten *v.*, abbreviare [*ahb-breh-vee-ah'-reh*]
shortsighted, miope [*mee'-oh-peh*]
should, dovere [*doh-veh'-reh*]
   We should leave, Dovremmo partire [*doh-vrehm'-moh
     pahr-tee'-reh*]
   You should see it, Lei dovrebbe vederlo [*leh'-ee doh-
     vrehb'-beh veh-dehr'-loh*]
shoulder, spalla [*spahl'-lah*]
shout *n.*, grido [*gree'-doh*]
shout *v.*, gridare [*gree-dah'-reh*]
show [theater] *n.*, spettacolo [*speht-tah'-koh-loh*]
show [exhibition] *n.*, esposizione (f) [*ehs-poh-zee-tsee-oh'-
   neh*]
show *v.*, mostrare [*mohs-trah'-reh*]
   Show me! Mi faccia vedere! [*mee fahch'-chee-ah veh-
     deh'-reh*]
shower [bath], doccia [*dohch'-chee-ah*]
shrewd, astuto, maligno [*ahs-too'-toh, mah-lee'-nyoh*]
shrimp, gamberetto [*gahm-beh-reht'-toh*]
shrine, santuario [*sahn-too-ah'-ree-oh*]
shrink *v.*, contrarsi [*kohn-trahr'-see*]

shut v., chiudere [*kee-oo'-deh-reh*]
  Shut up! Silenzio! [*see-lehn'-tsee-oh*]
shy, timido [*tee'-mee-doh*]
Sicilian, siciliano [*see-chee-lee-ah'-noh*]
Sicily, Sicilia [*see-chee'-lee-ah*]
sick, malato [*mah-lah'-toh*]
sickness, malattia [*mah-laht-tee'-ah*]
side, lato, fianco [*lah'-toh, fee-ahn'-koh*]
sidewalk, marciapiede (m) [*mahr-chee-ah-pee-eh'-deh*]
sideways, lateralmente [*lah-teh-rahl-mehn'-teh*]
siege, assedio [*ahs-seh'-dee-oh*]
sigh n., sospiro [*sohs-pee'-roh*]
sigh v., sospirare [*sohs-pee-rah'-reh*]
sight, vista, veduta [*vees'-tah, veh-doo'-tah*]
sightseeing, giro turistico [*jee'-roh too-rees'-tee-koh*]
sign [mark] n., segno [*seh'-nyoh*]
sign [street] n., cartellone (m) [*kahr-tehl-loh'-neh*]
sign v., firmare [*feer-mah'-reh*]
signal n., segnale (m) [*seh-nyah'-leh*]
signal v., segnalare [*seh-nyah-lah'-reh*]
signature n., firma [*feer'-mah*]
significance, significato [*see-nyee-fee-kah'-toh*]
signpost, palo indicatore [*pah'-loh een-dee-kah-toh'-reh*]
silence n., silenzio [*see-lehn'-tsee-oh*]
silent, silenzioso [*see-lehn-tsee-oh'-zoh*]
silk, seta [*seh'-tah*]
silly, sciocco [*shee-ohk'-koh*]
silver, argento [*ahr-jehn'-toh*]
silverware, argenteria [*ahr-jehn-teh-ree'-ah*]
similar, simile [*see'-mee-leh*]
simple, semplice [*sehm'-plee-cheh*]
simply, semplicemente [*sehm-plee-cheh-mehn'-teh*]
sin n., peccato [*pehk-kah'-toh*]
since conj., poichè [*poh-ee-keh'*]
since prep., da [*dah*]
  Since when? Da quando? [*dah koo-ahn'-doh*]
since adv., dopo, di poi [*doh'-poh, dee poh'-ee*]

sincere, sincero [*seen-cheh'-roh*]

sincerely, sinceramente [*seen-cheh-rah-mehn'-teh*]

sing v., cantare [*kahn-tah'-reh*]

singer, cantante (m, f) [*kahn-tahn'-teh*]

single [sole], solo, uno [*soh'-loh, oo'-noh*]
   not a single one, neanche uno/una [*neh-ahn'-keh oo'-noh/ oo'-nah*]

single [unmarried man], scapolo, celibe (m) [*skah'-poh-loh, cheh'-lee-beh*]

single [unmarried woman], signorina, nubile (f) [*see-nyoh-ree'-nah, noo'-bee-leh*]

sink v., affondare [*ahf-fohn-dah'-reh*]

sir, signore (m) [*see-nyoh'-reh*]

sister, sorella [*soh-rehl'-lah*]

sister [religious], suora [*soo-oh'-rah*]

sister-in-law, cognata [*koh-nyah'-tah*]

sit, sit down v., sedersi [*seh-dehr'-see*]
   Sit down, please! Si sieda, per favore! [*see see-eh'-dah, pehr fah-voh'-reh*]

situated, situato [*see-too-ah'-toh*]

situation, situazione (f) [*see-too-ah-tsee-oh'-neh*]

six, sei [*seh'-ee*]

sixteen, sedici [*seh'-dee-chee*]

sixth, sesto [*sehs'-toh*]

sixty, sessanta [*sehs-sahn'-tah*]

size [general], misura [*mee-zoo'-rah*]

size [of clothing], taglia [*tah'-lyah*]

skate v., pattinare [*paht-tee-nah'-reh*]
   ice skates, pattini (m, pl) [*paht'-tee-nee*]

skeleton, scheletro [*skeh'-leht-roh*]

sketch n., schizzo [*skeets'-tsoh*]

ski n., sci [*shee*]

ski v., sciare [*shee-ah'-reh*]

skid n., scivolare, slittare [*shee-voh-lah'-reh, zleet-tah'-reh*]

skill, abilità (f, indecl) [*ah-bee-lee-tah'*]

skillful, abile [*ah'-bee-leh*]

skin, pelle (f) [*pehl'-leh*]

skinny, magro [*mah'-groh*]

skirt, sottana, gonna, falda [*soht-tah'-nah, gohn'-nah, fahl'-dah*]

skull, cranio [*krah'-nee-oh*]

sky, cielo [*chee-eh'-loh*]

skyscraper, grattacielo [*graht-tah-chee-eh'-loh*]

slander *v.,* calunniare [*kah-loon-nee-ah'-reh*]

slang, gergo [*jehr'-goh*]

slap *n.,* schiaffo [*skee-ahf'-foh*]

slap *v.,* schiaffeggiare [*skee-ahf-fehj-jee-ah'-reh*]

sleep *n.,* sonno [*sohn'-noh*]

sleep *v.,* dormire [*dohr-mee'-reh*]

  (be) asleep, (essere) addormentato [(*ehs'-seh-reh*) *ahd-dohr-mehn-tah'-toh*]

  be sleepy, avere sonno [*ah-veh'-reh sohn'-noh*]

sleeping car, vagone letto (m) [*vah-goh'-neh leht'-toh*]

sleeve, manica [*mah'-nee-kah*]

slender, snello [*znehl'-loh*]

slice *n.,* fetta [*feht'-tah*]

slide *v.,* slittare [*zleet-tah'-reh*]

slight, tenuo, leggero [*teh'-noo-oh, lehj-jeh'-roh*]

slightly, leggermente [*lehj-jehr-mehn'-teh*]

slip [lingerie] *n.,* sottoveste (f) [*soht-toh-vehs'-teh*]

slippers, pantofole [*pahn-toh'-foh-leh*]

slippery, scivoloso [*shee-voh-loh'-zoh*]

slow, lento, piano [*lehn'-toh, pee-ah'-noh*]

slowly, lentamente [*lehn-tah-mehn'-teh*]

small, piccolo [*peek'-koh-loh*]

smaller, più piccolo [*pee-oo' peek'-koh-loh*]

smart, furbo, intelligente [*foor'-boh, een-tehl-lee-jehn'-teh*]

smash *v.,* fracassare [*frah-kahs-sah'-reh*]

smell *n.,* odore (m) [*oh-doh'-reh*]

smell *v.,* odorare [*oh-doh-rah'-reh*]

smile *n.,* sorriso [*sohr-ree'-zoh*]

smile *v.,* sorridere [*sohr-ree'-deh-reh*]

smoke *n.,* fumo [*foo'-moh*]

smoke *v.,* fumare [*foo-mah'-reh*]

smoking car, scompartimento per fumatori [*skohm-pahr-tee-mehn'-toh pehr foo-mah-toh'-ree*]

smooth, liscio [*lee'-shee-oh*]

smother *v.,* soffocare [*sohf-foh-kah'-reh*]

smuggle *v.,* fare contrabando [*fah'-reh kohn-trah-bahn'-doh*]

snack *n.,* spuntino [*spun-tee'-noh*]

snail, lumaca [*loo-mah'-kah*]

sneeze *n.,* starnuto [*stahr-noo'-toh*]

sneeze *v.,* starnutire [*stahr-noo-tee'-reh*]

snore *v.,* russare [*roos-sah'-reh*]

snow *n.,* neve (f) [*neh'-veh*]

snow *v.,* nevicare [*neh-vee-kah'-reh*]

snowstorm *n.,* bufera di neve [*boo-feh'-rah dee neh'-veh*]

so [thus] *adv.,* così, quindi, perciò [*koh-zee', koo-een'-dee, pehr-chee-oh'*]

    and so forth, e così via [*eh koh-zee' vee'-ah*]

    I don't think so, Credo di no [*kreh'-doh dee noh*]

    I hope so, Lo spero [*loh speh'-roh*]

    I think so, Credo di sì [*kreh'-doh dee see'*]

    Is that so? È vero? [*eh' veh'-roh*]

    just so, proprio così [*proh'-pree-oh koh-zee'*]

    so that, di modo che [*dee moh'-doh keh*]

so [much] *adv.,* tanto [*tahn'-toh*]

    so far, sinora [*seen-oh'-rah*]

    so-so, così, così [*koh-zee', koh-zee'*]

    so much the better, tanto meglio [*tahn'-toh meh'-lyoh*]

soap, sapone (m) [*sah-poh'-neh*]

sober, sobrio [*soh'-bree-oh*]

social, sociale [*soh-chee-ah'-leh*]

socialist, socialista [*soh-chee-ah-lees'-tah*]

society, società (f, indecl) [*soh-chee-eh-tah'*]

sock [apparel], calzino [*kahl-tsee'-noh*]

soda [bicarbonate], soda [*soh'-dah*]

soda water, acqua seltz [*ahk'-koo-ah sehlts*]

soft, morbido, tenero [*mohr'-bee-doh, teh'-neh-roh*]

softness, morbidezza [*mohr-bee-dehts'-tsah*]

soiled, sudicio [*soo-dee'-chee-oh*]

sold, venduto [*vehn-doo'-toh*]

soldier, soldato [*sohl-dah'-toh*]

sole [only] *adj.,* unico [*oo'-nee-koh*]

sole [fish] *n.*, sogliola [*soh-lyee-oh'-lah*]

sole [of shoe] *n.*, suola [*soo-oh'-lah*]

solid, solido [*soh'-lee-doh*]

solitary, solitario [*soh-lee-tah'-ree-oh*]

solution (f) [*soh-loo-tsee-oh'-neh*]

solve *v.*, risolvere [*ree-zohl'-veh-reh*]

some [certain], qualche (sing), alcuni (pl) [*koo-ahl'-keh, ahl-koo'-nee*]

some [partitive], del, della, dei [*dehl, dehl'-lah, deh'-ee*]
  some bread, del pane [*dehl pah'-neh*]
  some flowers, dei fiori [*deh'-ee fee-oh'-ree*]

someone, qualcuno [*koo-ahl-koo'-noh*]

something, qualcosa [*koo-ahl-koh'-zah*]

some time, passato, ex [*pahs-sah'-toh, ehks*]

sometimes, qualche volta [*koo-ahl'-keh vohl'-tah*]

somewhat, un poco [*oon poh'-koh*]

somewhere, in qualche luogo [*een koo-ahl'-keh loo-oh'-goh*]

somewhere else, altrove [*ahl-troh'-veh*]

son, figlio [*fee'-lyoh*]

son-in-law, genero [*jeh'-neh-roh*]

song, canzone (f) [*kahn-tsoh'-neh*]

soon, presto [*prehs'-toh*]
  as soon as, non appena [*nohn ahp-peh'-nah*]
  as soon as possible, il più presto possibile [*eel pee-oo' prehs'-toh pohs-see'-bee-leh*]
  How soon? Quando? [*koo-ahn'-doh*]

sooner, più presto [*pee-oo' prehs'-toh*]

sooner or later, presto o tardi [*prehs'-toh oh tahr'-dee*]

sore *adj.*, infiammato [*een-feem-ah-mah'-toh*]

sore *n.*, piaga, ulcera [*pee-ah'-gah, ool'-cheh-rah*]

sore throat, mal di gola [*mahl dee goh'-lah*]

sorrow, dispiacere (m) [*dees-pee-ah-cheh'-reh*]

sorrowful, triste, addolorato [*trees'-teh, ahd-doh-loh-rah'-toh*]

sorry, spiacente [*spee-ah-chehn'-teh*]
  be sorry *v.*, essere spiacente [*ehs'-seh-reh spee-ah-chehn'-teh*]
  I am very sorry, Mi dispiace molto [*mee dees-pee-ah'-cheh mohl'-toh*]

sort *n.*, specie (f) [*speh'-chee-eh*]

soul, anima [*ah'-nee-mah*]

sound [noise] *n.*, suono [*soo-oh'-noh*]

sound *v.*, suonare [*soo-oh-nah'-reh*]

sound proof, antisonoro [*ahn-tee-soh-noh'-roh*]

soup, minestra [*mee-nehs'-trah*]

sour, aspro, acido [*ahs'-proh, ah'-chee-doh*]

south, sud (m) [*sood*]

South America, America del Sud [*ah-meh'-ree-kah dehl sood*]

South American, sudamericano [*sood-ah-meh-ree-kah'-noh*]

southern, meridionale [*meh-ree-dee-oh-nah'-leh*]

souvenir, ricordo [*ree-kohr'-doh*]

sow *v.*, seminare [*seh-mee-nah'-reh*]

space, spazio [*spah'-tsee-oh*]

spacious, spazioso [*spah-tsee-oh'-zoh*]

Spain, Spagna [*spah'-nyah*]

Spaniard, Spanish, spagnolo [*spah-nyoh'-loh*]

spare *adj.*, di ricambio [*di ree-kahm'-bee-oh*]

spare *v.*, risparmiare [*rees-pahr-mee-ah'-reh*]

spare parts, pezzi di ricambio [*pehts'-tsee dee ree-kahm'-bee-oh*]

spare tire, pneumatico di ricambio [*pneh-oo-mah'-tee-koh dee ree-kahm'-bee-oh*]

sparkling, spumeggiante [*spoo-mehj-jee-ahn'-teh*]

sparkplug, candela d'accensione [*kahn-deh'-lah dahch-chehn-see-oh'-neh*]

speak *v.*, parlare [*pahr-lah'-reh*]

   Do you speak English! Parla inglese? [*pahr'-lah een-gleh'-zeh*]

speaker, oratore (m) [*oh-rah-toh'-reh*]

special, speciale [*speh-chee-ah'-leh*]

specialist, specialista [*speh-chee-ah-lees'-tah*]

specially, specialmente [*speh-chee-ahl-mehn'-teh*]

specialty, specialità (f, indecl) [*speh-chee-ah-lee-tah'*]

spectator, spettatore (m), spettatrice (f) [*speht-tah-toh'-reh, speht-tah-tree'-cheh*]

speech, discorso [*dees-kohr'-soh*]

speed, velocità (f, indecl) [*veh-loh-chee-tah'*]
   Full speed ahead, A tutta velocità [*ah toot'-tah veh-loh-chee-tah'*]
speed v., accelerare [*ahch-cheh-leh-rah'-reh*]
speed limit, velocità massima [*veh-loh-chee-tah' mahs'-see-mah*]
spell v., scrivere [*skree'-veh-reh*]
   How do you spell it? Come si scrive? [*koh'-meh see skree'-veh*]
spelling, ortografia [*ohr-toh-grah-fee'-ah*]
spend [money] v., spendere [*spehn'-deh-reh*]
spend [time] v., passare (il tempo) [*pahs-sah'-reh (eel tehm'-poh)*]
spice, spezie (f) [*speh'-tsee-eh*]
spill v., versare [*vehr-sah'-reh*]
spin v., filare [*fee-lah'-reh*]
spinach, spinaci [*spee-nah'-chee*]
spine, spina [*spee'-nah*]
spiral, spirale (f) [*spee-rah'-leh*]
spirit, spirito [*spee'-ree-toh*]
spiritual, spirituale [*spee-ree-too-ah'-leh*]
spit v., sputare [*spoo-tah'-reh*]
spite, dispetto, rancore (m) [*dees-peht'-toh, rahn-koh'-reh*]
   in spite of, a dispetto di, nonostante [*ah dees-peht'-toh dee, noh-nohs-tahn'-teh*]
splendid, splendido [*splehn'-dee-doh*]
split, dividere [*dee-vee'-deh-reh*]
spoil v., guastare [*goo-ahs-tah'-reh*]
spoil [a child] v., viziare [*vee-tsee-ah'-reh*]
sponge, spugna [*spoo'-nyah*]
spontaneous, spontaneo [*spohn-tah'-neh-oh*]
spoon, cucchiaio [*kook-kee-ah'-ee-oh*]
   teaspoon, cucchiaino [*kook-kee-ah-ee'-noh*]
sport, sport (m) [*spohrt*]
spot [place] n., posto [*pohs'-toh*]
spot [stain] n., macchia [*mahk'-kee-ah*]
spotless, immacolato [*eem-mah-koh-lah'-toh*]
spouse, sposo, sposa [*spoh'-zoh, spoh'-zah*]

sprain *n.*, storta [*stohr'-tah*]
spray *v.*, spruzzare [*sproots-tsah'-reh*]
spread *v.*, spargere [*spahr'-jeh-reh*]
   spread on, spalmare [*spahl-mah'-reh*]
spring [season] *n.*, primavera [*pree-mah-veh'-rah*]
spring [machine] *n.*, molla [*mohl'-lah*]
spring [water] *n.*, fonte (f), sorgente (f) [*fohn'-teh, sohr-jehn'-teh*]
spring up *v.*, scattare [*skaht-tah'-reh*]
spy *n.*, spia [*spee'-ah*]
spy *v.*, spiare [*spee-ah'-reh*]
square *adj.*, quadrato [*koo-ah-drah'-toh*]
square [city] *n.*, piazza [*pee-ahts'-tsah*]
squeeze *v.*, spremere [*spreh'-meh-reh*]
stab *v.*, pugnalare [*poo-nyah-lah'-reh*]
stable *adj.*, stabile [*stah'-bee-leh*]
stadium, stadio [*stah'-dee-oh*]
stage [theater] *n.*, palcoscenico [*pahl-koh-sheh'-nee-koh*]
stain *n.*, macchia [*mahk'-kee-ah*]
stain *v.*, macchiare [*mahk-kee-ah'-reh*]
stairs, staircase, scala [*skah'-lah*]
stamp *n.*, francobollo [*frahn-koh-bohl'-loh*]
stamp *v.*, timbrare [*teem-brah'-reh*]
stand [newspaper], edicola (m) [*eh-dee'-koh-lah*]
stand *v.*, stare in piedi [*stah'-reh een pee-eh'-dee*]
   stand out, eccellere [*ehch-chehl'-leh-reh*]
   stand up, alzarsi in piedi [*ahl-tsahr'-see een pee-eh'-dee*]
standard *n.*, norma, modello [*nohr'-mah, moh-dehl'-loh*]
standing *adj.*, in piedi, fermo [*een pee-eh'-dee, fehr'-moh*]
standing *n.*, posizione (f) [*poh-zee-tsee-oh'-neh*]
standpoint, punto di vista [*poon'-toh dee vees'-tah*]
star, stella [*stehl'-lah*]
starch, amido [*ah'-mee-doh*]
start *v.*, iniziare [*ee-nee-tsee-ah'-reh*]
starter [auto], messa in moto [*mehs'-sah een moh'-toh*]
starve *v.*, affamare [*ahf-fah-mah'-reh*]
state *n.*, stato [*stah'-toh*]
state *v.*, dichiarare [*dee-kee-ah-rah'-reh*]

statement, dichiarazione (f) [*dee-kee-ah-rah-tsee-oh'-neh*]

stateroom, cabina riservata [*kah-bee'-nah ree-zehr-vah'-tah*]

statesman, statista (m) [*stah-tees'-tah*]

station, stazione (f) [*stah-tsee-oh'-neh*]
   railway station, stazione ferroviaria [*stah-tsee-oh'-neh fehr-roh-vee-ah'-ree-ah*]

stationary, fermo [*fehr'-moh*]

stationery, cartoleria [*kahr-toh-leh-ree'-ah*]

statue, statua [*stah'-too-ah*]

stay *v.,* stare (irreg) [*stah'-reh*]

steady, costante [*kohs-tahn'-teh*]

steak, bistecca [*bees-tehk'-kah*]

steal *v.,* rubare [*roo-bah'-reh*]

steam *n.,* vapore (m) [*vah-poh'-reh*]

steamship line, compagnia di navigazione [*kohm-pah-nyee'-ah dee nah-vee-gah-tsee-oh'-neh*]

steel, acciaio [*ahch-chee-ah'-ee-oh*]

steering wheel, volante (m) [*voh-lahn'-teh*]

stenographer, stenografo [*steh-noh'-grah-foh*]

step *n.,* passo [*pahs'-soh*]

sterilized, sterilizzato [*steh-ree-leets-tsah'-toh*]

stern *adj.,* severo [*seh-veh'-roh*]

steward, cameriere di bordo (m) [*kah-meh-ree-eh'-reh dee bohr'-doh*]

stewardess, cameriera di bordo [*kah-meh-ree-eh'-rah dee bohr'-doh*]

sting *n.,* pungiglione (m) [*poon-jee-lyee-oh'-neh*]

sting *v.,* pungere [*poon'-geh-reh*]

stir *v.,* agitare [*ah-jee-tah'-reh*]

stitch *n.,* punto [*poon'-toh*]

stitch *v.,* cucire, suturare [*koo-chee'-reh, soo-too-rah'-reh*]

stock [supply] *n.,* provvista [*prohv-vees'-tah*]

stock [shares] *n.,* azioni (f, pl) [*ah-tsee-oh'-nee*]

stockbroker, agente di cambio [*ah-jehn'-teh dee kahm'-bee-oh*]

stock exchange, borsa valori [*bohr'-sah vah-loh'-ree*]

stockings, calze (per donne) [*kahl'-tseh (pehr dohn'-neh)*]

stolen, rubato [*roo-bah'-toh*]

stomach, stomaco [*stoh'-mah-koh*]

stomachache, mal di stomaco [*mahl dee stoh'-mah-koh*]

stone, pietra [*pee-eh'-trah*]

stop *n.,* fermata [*fehr-mah'-tah*]

stop *v.,* fermare, fermarsi [*fehr-mah'-reh, fehr-mahr'-see*]
    Stop! Alt! [*ahlt*]
    Stop here! Si fermi qui! [*see fehr'-mee koo-ee'*]
    Stop that! La smetta! [*lah zmeht'-tah*]

stop sign, fermata [*fehr-mah'-tah*]

stopwatch, cronometro [*kroh-noh'-meh-troh*]

storage, magazzino [*mah-gahdz-dzee'-noh*]

store *n.,* negozio, deposito [*neh-goh'-tsee-oh, deh-poh'-zee-toh*]
    department store, grande negozio [*grahn'-deh neh-goh'-tsee-oh*]

store *v.,* depositare [*deh-poh-zee-tah'-reh*]

storm *n.,* tempesta [*tehm-pehs'-tah*]

story [tale], storia, racconto [*stoh'-ree-ah, rahk-kohn'-toh*]

story [floor], piano [*pee-ah'-noh*]

stove, stufa [*stoo'-fah*]

straight, diritto, onesto [*dee-reet'-toh, oh-nehs'-toh*]
    straight ahead, diritto avanti [*dee-reet'-toh ah-vahn'-tee*]

strain *n.,* sforzo [*sfohr'-tsoh*]

strange, strano [*strah'-noh*]

stranger, estraneo [*ehs-trah'-neh-oh*]

strap, cinghia [*cheen'-gee-ah*]

straw, paglia [*pah'-lyah*]

strawberry, fragola [*frah'-goh-lah*]

stream, corrente (f) [*kohr-rehn'-teh*]

street, strada [*strah'-dah*]

streetcar, tram [*trahm*]

strength, forza [*fohr'-tsah*]

stress *n.,* tensione (f) [*tehn-see-oh'-neh*]

stretch *v.,* stendere [*stehn'-deh-reh*]

strict, rigido [*ree'-jee-doh*]

strictly, precisamente [*preh-chee-zah-mehn'-teh*]

strike [hit] *v.,* colpire [*kohl-pee'-reh*]

strike [cease working] *v.,* scioperare [*shee-oh-peh-rah'-reh*]

strike [by labor] *n.*, sciopero [*shee-oh'-peh-roh*]
string, corda, laccio [*kohr'-dah, lahch'-chee-oh*]
stripe, striscia [*stree'-shee-ah*]
stroll *v.*, passeggiare [*pahs-sehj-jee-ah'-reh*]
strong, forte [*fohr'-teh*]
structure, struttura [*stroot-too'-rah*]
struggle *n.*, lotta [*loht'-tah*]
struggle *v.*, lottare [*loht-tah'-reh*]
stubborn, ostinato [*ohs-tee-nah'-toh*]
student, studente (m), studentessa (f) [*stoo-dehn'-teh, stoo-dehn-tehs'-sah*]
study *v.*, studiare [*stoo-dee-ah'-reh*]
stumble *v.*, inciampare [*een-chee-ahm-pah'-reh*]
stupid, stupido [*stoo'-pee-doh*]
style, stile (m) [*stee'-leh*]
subject *n.*, soggetto [*sohj-jeht'-toh*]
submit *v.*, sottomettere [*soht-toh-meht'-teh-reh*]
substantial *adj.*, sostanziale [*sohs-tahn-tsee-ah'-leh*]
substitute *v.*, sostituire [*sohs-tee-too-ee'-reh*]
subtraction, sottrazione (f) [*soht-trah-tsee-oh'-neh*]
suburb, sobborgo, periferia [*sohb-bohr'-goh, peh-ree-feh-ree'-ah*]
subway, sotterranea, metropolitana [*soht-tehr-rah'-neh-ah, meh-troh-poh-lee-tah'-nah*]
succeed *v.*, riuscire [*ree-oo-shee'-reh*]
success, successo [*sooch-chehs'-soh*]
successive, successivo [*sooch-chehs-see'-voh*]
such, tale [*tah'-leh*]
  such a good man, un uomo tanto buono [*oon oo-oh'-moh tahn'-toh boo-oh'-noh*]
  Such is life, Così è la vita [*koh-zee' eh' lah vee'-tah*]
  There is no such thing, Tale cosa non esiste [*tah'-leh koh'-zah nohn eh-zees-'teh*]
suddenly, improvvisamente, subitamente [*eem-prohv-vee-zah-mehn'-teh, soo-bee-tah-mehn'-teh*]
suffer *v.*, soffrire [*sohf-free'-reh*]
sufficient, sufficiente [*soof-fee-chee-ehn'-teh*]
sugar, zucchero [*dzook'-keh-roh*]

sugar bowl, zuccheriera [*dzook-keh-ree-eh'-rah*]

suggest *v.*, suggerire, proporre (irreg) [*sooj-jeh-ree'-reh, proh-pohr'-reh*]

suggestion, proposta [*proh-pohs'-tah*]

suicide, suicidio [*soo-ee-chee'-dee-oh*]

suit [of clothing] *n.*, abito [*ah'-bee-toh*]

suit [at law] *n.*, petizione (f) [*peh-tee-tsee-oh'-neh*]

suit *v.*, convenire a [*kohn-veh-nee'-reh ah*]

suitable, adatto [*ah-daht'-toh*]

suitcase, valigia [*vah-lee'-jee-ah*]

suitor, corteggiatore (m) [*kohr-tehj-jee-ah-toh'-reh*]

sum *n.*, somma [*sohm'-mah*]

sum up *v.*, sommare [*sohm-mah'-reh*]

summary, sommario [*sohm-mah'-ree-oh*]

summer, estate (f) [*ehs-tah'-teh*]

sun, sole (m) [*soh'-leh*]

sunburn, bruciatura di sole [*broo-chee-ah-too'-rah dee soh'-leh*]

Sunday, domenica [*doh-meh'-nee-kah*]

sunglasses, occhiali da sole (m, pl) [*ohk-kee-ah'-lee dah soh'-leh*]

sunrise, levar del sole (m) [*leh-vahr' dehl soh'-leh*]

sunset, tramonto [*trah-mohn'-toh*]

sunshine, luce del sole (f) [*loo'-cheh dehl soh'-leh*]

suntan, abbronzatura [*ahb-brohn-tsah-too'-rah*]

superficial, superficiale [*soo-pehr-fee-chee-ah'-leh*]

superior, superiore [*soo-peh-ree-oh'-reh*]

superstitious, superstizioso [*soo-pehr-stee'-tsee-oh-zoh*]

supper, cena [*cheh'-nah*]

   have supper *v.*, cenare [*cheh-nah'-reh*]

supply *n.*, provista [*proh-vees'-tah*]

supply *v.*, provvedere [*prohv-veh-deh'-reh*]

support *n.*, appoggio, sostegno [*ahp-pohj'-jee-oh, sohs-teh'-nyoh*]

support *v.*, sostenere [*sohs-teh-neh'-reh*]

suppose *v.*, supporre (irreg) [*soop-pohr'-reh*]

supreme, supremo [*soo-preh'-moh*]

sure, sicuro [*see-koo'-roh*]

Are you sure? È sicuro? [*eh' see-koo'-roh*]
surely, sicuramente [*see-koo-rah-mehn'-teh*]
surface *n.,* superficie (f) [*soo-pehr-fee'-chee-eh*]
surgeon, chirurgo [*kee-roor'-goh*]
surgery, chirurgia [*kee-roor-jee'-ah*]
surprise *n.,* sorpresa [*sohr-preh'-zah*]
surprise *v.,* sorprendere [*sohr-prehn'-deh-reh*]
surrender *v.,* arrendersi [*ahr-rehn'-dehr-see*]
surround *v.,* circondare [*cheer-kohn-dah'-reh*]
surroundings, dintorni [*deen-tohr'-nee*]
survival, sopravvivenza [*soh-prahv-vee-vehn'-tsah*]
survive *v.,* sopravvivere [*soh-prahv-vee'-veh-reh*]
survivor, sopravvivente (m) [*soh-prahv-vee-vehn'-teh*]
suspect *v.,* sospettare [*sohs-peht-tah'-reh*]
suspicious, sospettoso [*sohs-peht-toh'-zoh*]
swallow *v.,* inghiottire [*een-gee-oht-tee'-reh*]
swear *v.,* giurare [*jee-oo-rah'-reh*]
Sweden, Svezia [*zveh'-tsee-ah*]
Swedish, svedese [*zveh-deh'-zeh*]
sweep, *v.,* scopare [*skoh-pah'-reh*]
sweet *adj.,* dolce [*dohl'-cheh*]
sweetheart, innamorato [*een-nah-moh-rah'-toh*]
swell *v.,* gonfiare [*gohn-fee-ah'-reh*]
swim *v.,* nuotare [*noo-oh-tah'-reh*]
swimmer, nuotatore (m) [*noo-oh-tah-toh'-reh*]
swimming pool, piscina [*pee-shee'-nah*]
swimsuit, costume (m) da bagno [*kohs-too'-meh dah bah'-nyoh*]
Swiss, svizzero [*zveets'-tseh-roh*]
switch [electric], interruttore (m) [*een-tehr-root-toh'-reh*]
Switzerland, Svizzera [*zveets'-tseh-rah*]
sympathy, simpatia [*seem-pah-tee'-ah*]
  My deepest sympathy, Con sentite condoglianze [*kohn sehn-tee'-teh kohn-doh-lyahn'-tseh*]
symphony, sinfonia [*seen-foh-nee'-ah*]
synthetic, sintetico [*seen-teh'-tee-koh*]
system, sistema (m) [*sees-teh'-mah*]
systematic, sistematico [*sees-teh-mah'-tee-koh*]

T

table, tavola [*tah'-voh-lah*]
  set the table *v.*, preparare la tavola [*preh-pah-rah'-reh lah tah'-voh-lah*]
tablecloth, tovaglia [*toh-vah'-lyah*]
tablespoon, cucchiaio [*kook-kee-ah'-ee-oh*]
tack *n.*, bulletta [*boo-leht'-tah*]
tact, tatto [*taht'-toh*]
tactless, indelicato [*een-deh-lee-kah'-toh*]
tail, coda [*koh'-dah*]
tailor, sarto [*sahr'-toh*]
tailor's shop, sartoria [*sahr-toh-ree'-ah*]
take *v.*, prendere [*prehn'-deh-reh*]
  take advantage of, approfittare di [*ahp-proh-feet-tah'-reh dee*]
  take a walk, fare una passeggiata [*fah'-reh oo'-nah pahs-sehj-jee-ah'-tah*]
  take care of, avere cura [*ah-veh'-reh koo'-rah*]
  take place, avere luogo [*ah-veh'-reh loo-oh'-goh*]
  take the opportunity, cogliere l'opportunità [*koh'-lyeh-reh lohp-pohr-too-nee-tah'*]
take [carry] *v.*, portare [*pohr-tah'-reh*]
tale, racconto [*rahk-kohn'-toh*]
talent, talento [*tah-lehn'-toh*]
talk, *n.*, conversazione (f), parlare (m) [*kohn-vehr-sah-tsee-oh'-neh, pahr-lah'-reh*]
talk *v.*, parlare [*pahr-lah'-reh*]
tall, alto [*ahl'-toh*]
tame *adj.*, mansueto [*mahn-soo-eh'-toh*]
tan, abbronzatura [*ahb-brohn-tsah-too'-rah*]
tape, nastro [*nahs'-troh*]
tapestry, tappezzeria [*tahp-pehts-tseh-ree'-ah*]
tardy, lento [*lehn'-toh*]

tariff, tariffa [*tah-reef'-fah*]

task, compito [*kohm'-pee-toh*]

taste *n.*, sapore (m) [*sah-poh'-reh*]

  bad taste, cattivo gusto [*kaht-tee'-voh goos'-toh*]

taste *v.*, assaggiare [*ahs-sahj-jee-ah'-reh*]

tasty, saporito [*sah-poh-ree'-toh*]

tax *n.*, tassa [*tahs'-sah*]

tax *v.*, tassare [*tahs-sah'-reh*]

tax-free, esente da imposte [*eh-zehn'-teh dah eem-pohs'-teh*]

taxi, tassì (m) [*tahs-see'*]

tea, tè (m) [*teh'*]

teach *v.*, insegnare [*een-seh-nyah'-reh*]

teacher, insegnante (m) [*een-seh-nyahn'-teh*]

teacup, tazza di tè [*tahts'-tsah dee teh'*]

team, squadra [*skoo-ah'-drah*]

teapot *n.*, teiera [*teh-ee-eh'-rah*]

tear *v.*, strappare [*strahp-pah'-reh*]

teardrop, lacrima, pianto [*lah'-kree-mah, pee-ahn'-toh*]

teaspoon, cucchiaino da tè [*kook-kee-ah-ee'-noh dah teh'*]

technical, tecnico [*tehk'-nee-koh*]

teeth, denti (m, pl) [*dehn'-tee*]

telegram *n.*, telegramma (m) [*teh-leh-grahm'-mah*]

telephone *n.*, telefono [*teh-leh'-foh-noh*]

telephone *v.*, telefonare [*teh-leh-foh-nah'-reh*]

telephone book, elenco telefonico [*eh-lehn'-koh teh-leh-foh'-nee-koh*]

telephone call, chiamata telefonica, telefonata [*kee-ah-mah'-tah teh-leh-foh'-nee-kah, teh-leh-foh-nah'-tah*]

telephone number, numero di telefono [*nooh'-meh-reh dee teh-leh'-foh-noh*]

telephone operator, telefonista [*teh-leh-foh-nees'-tah*]

telescope, telescopo [*teh-lehs'-koh-poh*]

television, televisione (f) [*teh-leh-vee-zee-oh'-neh*]

television set televisore (m) [*teh-leh-vee-zoh'-reh*]

tell *v.*, dire (irreg) [*dee'-reh*]

  Tell me, please, Mi dica, per favore [*mee dee'-kah, pehr fah-voh'-reh*]

  Don't tell me, Non mi dica [*nohn mee dee'-kah*]

temperature, temperatura [*tehm-peh-rah-too'-rah*]
temple, tempio [*tehm'-pee-oh*]
temporary, temporaneo [*tehm-poh-rah'-neh-oh*]
temptation tentazione (f) [*tehn-tah-tsee-oh'-neh*]
ten, dieci [*dee-eh'-chee*]
tenant, inquilino [*een-koo-ee-lee'-noh*]
tendency, tendenza [*tehn-dehn'-tsah*]
tender, tenero [*teh'-neh-roh*]
tenth, decimo [*deh'-chee-moh*]
terminal [railroad] *n.*, (stazione) termini [(*stah-tsee-oh'-neh*) *tehr'-mee-nee*]
terms, condizioni (f, pl) [*kohn-dee-tsee-oh'-nee*]
terrible, terribile [*tehr-ree'-bee-leh*]
terrify *v.*, spaventare [*spah-vehn-tah'-reh*]
territory, territorio [*tehr-ree-toh'-ree-oh*]
terror, terrore (m) [*tehr-roh'-reh*]
test *n.*, prova [*proh'-vah*]
test *v.*, esaminare [*eh-zah-mee-nah'-reh*]
testify *v.*, testimoniare [*tehs-tee-moh-nee-ah'-reh*]
text, testo [*tehs'-toh*]
textile, tessile [*tehs'-see-leh*]
than, che, di [*keh, dee*]
thank *v.*, ringraziare [*reen-grah-tsee-ah'-reh*]
   Thank you, Grazie [*grah'-tsee-eh*]
   Thanks a lot, Grazie tanto [*grah'-tsee-eh tahn'-toh*]
   Thank you very much, Molte grazie [*mohl'-teh grah'-tsee-eh*]
thankful, grato [*grah'-toh*]
that, *demons. adj. & pron.*, quello, quella, quel [*koo-ehl'-loh, koo-ehl'-lah, koo-ehl'*]
that, *rel. pron.*, che; il quale, la quale [*keh; eel koo-ah'-leh, lah koo-ah'-leh*]
that *conj.* che [*keh*]
   that which, quello che [*koo-ehl'-loh keh*]
the, il, lo, l' (m, sing), la, l' (f, sing); i, gli (m, pl), le (f, pl) [*eel, loh, l, la, l, ee, lyee, leh*]
theater, teatro [*teh-ah'-troh*]
theft, furto [*foor'-toh*]

their, loro [*loh'-roh*]

theirs, il loro (m, sing), la loro (f, sing); i loro (m, pl), le loro (f, pl) [*eel loh'-roh, lah loh'-roh; ee loh'-roh, leh loh'-roh*]

them, loro (m or f, pl), essi (m, pl), esse (f, pl) [*loh'-roh, ehs'-see, ehs'-seh*]

  to them, a loro [*ah loh'-roh*]

  for them, per loro [*pehr loh'-roh*]

themselves, se stessi (m), se stesse (f), loro stessi (m), loro stesse (f) [*seh stehs'-see, seh stehs'-seh, loh'-roh stehs'-see, loh'-roh stehs'-seh*]

then [at that time], allora [*ahl-loh'-rah*]

then [afterwards], poi [*poh'-ee*]

  now and then, di tanto in tanto [*dee tahn'-toh een tahn'-toh*]

theory, teoria [*teh-oh-ree'-ah*]

there, là, lì [*lah', lee'*]

  there are, ci sono [*chee soh'-noh*]

  there is, c'è [*cheh'*]

therefore, perciò, quindi [*pehr-chee-oh', koo-een'-dee*]

thermometer, termometro [*tehr-moh'-meh-troh*]

these, questi (m, pl), queste (f, pl) [*koo-ehs'-tee, koo-ehs'-teh*]

they, loro (m & f pl), essi (m, pl), esse (f, pl) [*loh'-roh, ehs'-see, ehs'-seh*]

thick, grosso [*grohs'-soh*]

thief, ladro [*lah'-droh*]

thin, sottile [*soht-tee'-leh*]

thing, cosa [*koh'-zah*]

think *v.*, pensare [*pehn-sah'-reh*]

  Don't you think so? Non ci crede? [*nohn chee kreh'-deh*]

  I don't think so, Non ci credo [*nohn chee kreh'-doh*]

third, terzo [*tehr'-tsoh*]

thirst, sete (f) [*seh'-teh*]

thirsty, assetato [*ahs-seh-tah'-toh*]

  be thirsty *v.*, avere sete [*ah-veh'-reh seh'-teh*]

thirteen, tredici [*treh'-dee-chee*]

thirty, trenta [*trehn'-tah*]

this, questo, questa [*koo-ehs'-toh, koo-ehs'-tah*]
  What is this? Che cosa è questo [*keh koh'-zah eh' koo-ehs'-toh*]

thoroughly, completamente [*kohm-pleh-tah-mehn'-teh*]

those, quelli (m, pl) quelle (f, pl) [*koo-ehl'-lee, koo-ehl'-leh*]

though, sebbene [*sehb-beh'-neh*]

thought, pensiero [*pehn-see-eh'-roh*]
  well-thought, ben pensato [*behn pehn-sah'-toh*]

thoughtful, attento [*aht-tehn'-toh*]

thoughtless, spensierato [*spehn-see-eh-rah'-toh*]

thousand, mille, mila (pl) [*meel'-leh, mee'-lah*]

thread, filo [*fee'-loh*]

threat, minaccia [*mee-nahch'-chee-ah*]

threaten *v.,* minacciare [*mee-nahch-chee-ah'-reh*]

three, tre [*treh*]

thrifty, frugale [*froo-gah'-leh*]

thrilled, emozionato [*eh-moh-tsee-oh-nah'-toh*]

throat, gola [*goh'-lah*]
  sore throat, mal (m) di gola [*mahl dee goh'-lah*]

through *prep.,* tramite, attraverso [*trah'-mee-teh, aht-trah-vehr'-soh*]

throughout, durante [*doo-rahn'-teh*]

throw *v.,* gettare [*jeht-tah'-reh*]
  throw away, buttar via [*boot-tahr' vee'-ah*]

thunder, tuono [*too-oh'-noh*]

thunderstorm, temporale (m) [*tehm-poh-rah'-leh*]

Thursday, giovedì [*jee-oh-veh-dee'*]

thus, così [*koh-zee'*]

Tiber, Tevere (m) [*teh'-veh-reh*]

ticket, biglietto [*bee-lyeht'-toh*]
  round-trip ticket, biglietto di andata e ritorno [*bee-lyeht'-toh dee ahn-dah'-tah eh ree-tohr'-noh*]

ticket office, biglietteria [*bee-lyeht-teh-ree'-ah*]

ticket window, sportello [*spohr-tehl'-loh*]

tie [apparel], cravatta [*krah-vaht'-tah*]

tie *v.,* legare [*leh-gah'-reh*]

tight, stretto [*streht'-toh*]

tighten *v.*, stringere [*streen'-jeh-reh*]

till [until] *prep.*, fino a [*fee'-noh ah*]

till [until] *conj.*, finchè [*feen-keh'*]

time [duration], tempo [*tehm'-poh*]

  a long time, molto tempo [*mohl'-toh tehm'-poh*]

  at the same time, allo stesso tempo [*ahl'-loh stehs'-soh tehm'-poh*]

  At what time? A che ora? [*ah keh oh'-rah*]

  How long? Quanto tempo? [*koo-ahn'-toh tehm'-poh*]

  How long ago? Quanto tempo fa? [*koo-ahn'-toh tehm'-poh fah*]

  for the time being, per il momento [*pehr eel moh-mehn'-toh*]

  long ago, molto tempo fa [*mohl'-toh tehm'-poh fah*]

  Have a good time! Si diverta! [*see dee-vehr'-tah*]

  What time is it? Che ore sono? [*keh oh'-reh soh'-noh*]

time [instance], volta [*vohl'-tah*]

  at times, a volte, a ore [*ah vohl'-teh, ah oh'-reh*]

timetable, orario [*oh-rah'-ree-oh*]

timid, timido [*tee'-mee-doh*]

tip [gratuity], mancia [*mahn'-chee-ah*]

tire [of a car], ruota, gomma [*roo-oh'-tah, gohm'-mah*]

  flat tire, gomma a terra [*gohm'-mah ah tehr'-rah*]

tired, stanco [*stahn'-koh*]

tiresome, faticoso, noioso [*fah-tee-koh'-zoh, noh-ee-oh'-zoh*]

title, titolo [*tee'-toh-loh*]

to a, per [*ah, pehr*]

  to and fro, avanti e dietro [*ah-vahn'-tee eh dee-eh'-troh*]

toast [speech] *n.*, brindisi [*breen'-dee-zee*]

toast [food] *n.*, pane abbrustolito [*pah'-neh ahb-broos-toh-lee'-toh*]

toaster, tostapane (m) [*tohs-tah-pah'-neh*]

tobacco, tabacco [*tah-bahk'-koh*]

today, oggi [*ohj'-jee*]

toe, dito, (le) dita (pl) [*dee'-toh, (leh) dee'-tah*]

together, insieme [*een-see-eh'-meh*]

toilet, toletta [*toh-leht'-tah*]

toilet paper, carta igienica [*kahr'-tah ee-jee-eh'-nee-kah*]
tolerate *v.*, tollerare [*tohl-leh-rah'-reh*]
toll [fee] *n.*, pedaggio, tributo [*peh-dahj'-jee-oh, tree-boo'-toh*]
tomato, pomodoro [*poh-moh-doh'-roh*]
tomato juice, succo di pomodoro [*sook'-koh dee poh-moh-doh'-roh*]
tomb, tomba [*tohm'-bah*]
tomorrow, domani [*doh-mah'-nee*]
  tomorrow morning, domani mattina [*doh-mah'-nee maht-tee'-nah*]
ton, tonnellata [*tohn-neh-lah'-tah*]
tone, tono [*toh'-noh*]
tongue, lingua [*leen'-goo-ah*]
tonight, stasera [*stah-seh'-rah*]
too [also], anche, pure [*ahn'-keh, poo'-reh*]
  too much, too many, troppo, troppi [*trohp'-poh, trohp'-pee*]
tool, strumento [*stroo-mehn'-toh*]
tooth, dente (m) [*dehn'-teh*]
toothache, mal di denti [*mahl dee dehn'-tee*]
toothbrush, spazzolino da denti [*spahts-tsoh-lee'-noh dah dehn'-tee*]
toothpaste, dentifricio [*dehn-tee-free'-chee-oh*]
toothpick, stuzzicadenti [*stoots-tsee-kah-dehn'-tee*]
top [cover] *n.*, coperchio [*koh-pehr'-kee-oh*]
top [high point] *n.*, sommità (f, indecl.) [*sohm-mee-tah'*]
  on top of, in cima a [*een chee'-mah ah*]
topic, soggetto [*sohj-jeht'-toh*]
tornado, burrasca [*boor-rahs'-kah*]
torture *n.*, tortura [*tohr-too'-rah*]
total *n.*, totale [*toh-tah'-leh*]
touch *v.*, toccare [*tohk-kah'-reh*]
touching, commovente [*kohm-moh-vehn'-teh*]
tough, duro [*doo'-roh*]
tour *n.*, giro [*jee'-roh*]
tourist, turista (m, f) [*too-rees'-tah*]
tourist office, agenzia di turismo [*ah-jen-tsee'-ah dee too-*

rees'-moh]

tow *v.*, rimorchiare [*ree-mohr-kee-ah'-reh*]

toward, verso [*vehr'-soh*]

towel [bath], asciugamano [*ah-shee-oo-gah-mah'-noh*]

tower, torre (f) [*tohr'-reh*]

town, città (f, indecl) [*cheet-tah'*]

townhall, palazzo municipale [*pah-lats'-tsoh moo-nee-chee-pah'-leh*]

toy, giocattolo [*jee-oh-kaht'-toh-loh*]

track [train], binario [*bee-nah'-ree-oh*]

track [race], pista [*pees'-tah*]

trade *n.*, commercio [*kohm-mehr'-chee-oh*]

trade [do business] *v.*, negoziare [*neh-goh-tsee-ah'-reh*]

trade [exchange] *v.*, barattare [*bah-raht-tah'-reh*]

trademark, marca di fabbrica [*mahr'-kah dee fahb'-bree-kah*]

tradesman, commerciante (m, f) [*kohm-mehr-chee-ahn'-teh*]

tradition, tradizione (f) [*trah-dee-tsee-oh'-neh*]

traditional, tradizionale [*trah-dee-tsee-oh-nah'-leh*]

traffic, traffico [*trahf'-fee-koh*]

tragedy, tragedia [*trah-jeh'-dee-ah*]

tragic, tragico [*trah'-jee-koh*]

trail *n.*, pista [*pees'-tah*]

train *n.*, treno [*treh'-noh*]

training, addestramento [*ahd-dehs-trah-mehn'-toh*]

trait, caratteristica [*kah-raht-teh-rees'-tee-kah*]

traitor, traditore (m), traditrice (f) [*trah-dee-toh'-reh, trah-dee-three'-cheh*]

tranquil, tranquillo [*trahn-koo-eel'-loh*]

transfer, *n.*, trasferimento [*trahs-feh-ree-mehn'-toh*]

transfer *v.*, trasferire [*trahs-feh-ree'-reh*]

translate *v.*, tradurre (irreg) [*trah-door'-reh*]

translation, traduzione (f) [*trah-doo-tsee-oh'-neh*]

transmission, trasmissione (f) [*trahz-mees-see-oh'-neh*]

transportation, trasporto [*trahs-pohr'-toh*]

trap *n.*, trappola [*trahp'-poh-lah*]

travel *n.*, viaggio [*vee-ahj'-jee-oh*]

travel *v.*, viaggiare [*vee-ahj-jee-ah'-reh*]

travel agency, agenzia di viaggi [ah-jehn-tsee'-ah dee vee-ahj'-jee]

traveler, viaggiatore (m), viaggiatrice (f) [vee-ahj-jee-ah-toh'-reh, vee-ahj-jee-ah-tree'-cheh]

traveler's check, assegno turistico [ahs-seh'-nyoh too-rees'-tee-koh]

tray, vassoio [vahs-soh'-ee-oh]

treason, tradimento [trah-dee-mehn'-toh]

treasure n., tesoro [teh-zoh'-roh]

treasurer, tesoriere (m) [teh-zoh-ree-eh'-reh]

treat [deal with] v., trattare [traht-tah'-reh]

treatment, trattamento [trah-tah-mehn'-toh]

tree, albero [ahl'-beh-roh]

tremendous, tremendo [treh-mehn'-doh]

trespass v., trasgredire [trahz-greh-dee'-reh]

trial [test], prova [proh'-vah]

trial [at law], processo [proh-chehs'-soh]

tribute, tributo, omaggio [tree-boo'-toh, oh-mahj'-jee-oh]

trick n., trucco [trook'-koh]

trim v., guarnire [goo-ahr-nee'-reh]

trip n., viaggio, gita [vee-ahj'-jee-oh, jee'-tah]

trip [stumble] v., inciampare [een-chee-ahm-pah'-reh]

triple, triplice [tree'-plee-cheh]

triumphant, trionfante [tree-ohn-fahn'-teh]

trivial, triviale [tree-vee-ah'-leh]

tropical, tropicale [troh-pee-kah'-leh]

trouble n., disturbo [dees-toor'-boh]

trouble v., disturbare [dees-toor-bah'-reh]

   Don't trouble yourself, Non si disturbi [nohn see dees-toor'-bee]

trousers, pantaloni lunghi (m, pl) [pahn-tah-loh'-nee loon'-gee]

truck, camion (m) [kah-mee-ohn']

true, vero [veh'-roh]

   It is true, È vero [eh' veh'-roh]

   It isn't true, Non è vero [nohn eh' veh'-roh]

trunk [container], baule (m) [bah-oo'-leh]

trust n., fiducia, credito [fee-doo'-chee-ah, kreh'-dee-toh]

trust *v.*, fidarsi [*fee-dahr'-see*]
truth, verità (f, indecl) [*veh-ree-tah'*]
try *v.*, tentare, provare [*tehn-tah'-reh, proh-vah'-reh*]
  try on, provare [*proh-vah'-reh*]
tube, tubo [*too'-boh*]
Tuesday, martedì [*mahr-teh-dee'*]
tugboat, rimorchiatore (m) [*ree-mohr-kee-ah-toh'-reh*]
tune [melody] *n.*, aria [*ah'-ree-ah*]
tunnel, galleria sotterranea [*gahl-leh-ree'-ah soht-tehr-rah'-neh-ah*]
Turkey, Turchia [*toor-kee'-ah*]
Turkish, turco [*toor'-koh*]
turmoil, confusione (f) [*kohn-foo-zee-oh'-neh*]
Turin, Torino [*toh-ree'-noh*]
turn [order] *n.*, turno, giro [*toor'-noh, jee'-roh*]
turn [curve] *n.*, svolta, curva [*zvohl'-tah, koor'-vah*]
turn *v.*, girare [*jee-rah'-reh*]
  turn around, rivoltarsi [*ree-vohl-tahr'-see*]
  turn off, spegnere [*speh'-nyeh-reh*]
  turn on, accendere [*ahch-chehn'-deh-reh*]
twelfth, dodicesimo [*doh-dee-cheh'-zee-moh*]
twelve, dodici [*doh'-dee-chee*]
twenty, venti [*vehn'-tee*]
twice, due volte [*doo'-eh vohl'-teh*]
twilight, crepuscolo [*kreh-poos'-koh-loh*]
twin, gemello [*jeh-mehl'-loh*]
twist *v.*, torcere [*tohr'-cheh-reh*]
two, due [*doo'-eh*]
type *n.*, tipo [*tee'-poh*]
type(write) *v.*, scrivere a macchina [*skree'-veh-reh ah mahk'-kee-nah*]
typewriter, macchina da scrivere [*mahk'-kee-nah dah skree'-veh-reh*]
typical, tipico [*tee'-pee-koh*]
typist, dattilografo [*daht-tee-loh'-grah-foh*]
tyrant, tiranno [*tee-rahn'-noh*]

U

ugly, brutto [*broot'-toh*]
ultimate, ultimo, finale [*ool'-tee-moh, fee-nah'-leh*]
umbrella, ombrello [*ohm-brehl'-loh*]
unable, incapace [*een-kah-pah'-cheh*]
  be unable to . . . , non potere . . . [*nohn poh-teh'-reh*]
  I am unable to come, Non posso venire [*nohn pohs'-soh veh-nee'-reh*]
unanimous, unanime [*oo-nah'-nee-meh*]
unbearable, insopportabile [*een-sohp-pohr-tah'-bee-leh*]
uncertain, incerto [*een-chehr'-toh*]
uncle, zio, zii (pl) [*dzee'-oh, dzee'-ee*]
uncomfortable scomodo [*skoh'-moh-doh*]
unconscious, inconsapevole [*een-kohn-sah-peh'-voh-leh*]
uncover *v.,* scoprire [*skoh-pree'-reh*]
undecided, indeciso [*een-deh-chee'-zoh*]
under, underneath, sotto [*soht'-toh*]
underground, sottosuolo [*soht-toh-soo-oh'-loh*]
understand *v.,* comprendere, capire [*kohm-prehn'-deh-reh, kah-pee'-reh*]
  Do you understand? Comprende lei? [*kohm-prehn'-deh leh'-ee*]
  It is understood, È inteso [*eh' een-teh'-zoh*]
understanding *n.,* intesa [*een-teh'-zah*]
undertake *v.,* intraprendere [*een-trah-prehn'-deh-reh*]
undertaking, impresa [*eem-preh'-zah*]
underwear, biancheria personale [*bee-ahn-keh-ree'-ah pehr-soh-nah'-leh*]
undress *v.,* svestire [*zvehs-tee'-reh*]
  undress oneself, svestirsi, spogliarsi [*zvehs-teer'-see, spoh-lyahr'-see*]
uneasy, inquieto [*een-koo-ee-eh'-toh*]
unemployed, disoccupato [*deez-ohk-koo-pah'-toh*]

unequal, disuguale [*deez-oo-goo-ah'-leh*]
unexpected, inatteso [*een-aht-teh'-zoh*]
unfair, ingiusto [*een-jee-oos'-toh*]
unfaithful, infedele [*een-feh-deh'-leh*]
unfavorable, sfavorevole [*sfah-voh-reh'-voh-leh*]
unforeseen, imprevisto [*eem-preh-vees'-toh*]
unforgettable, indimenticabile [*een-dee-mehn-tee-kah'-bee-leh*]
unforgiving, implacabile [*eem-plah-kah'-bee-leh*]
unforgivable, imperdonabile [*eem-pehr-doh-nah'-bee-leh*]
unfortunate, disgraziato [*deez-grah-tsee-ah'-toh*]
unfortunately, disgraziatamente [*deez-grah-tsee-ah-tah-mehn'-teh*]
ungrateful, ingrato [*een-grah'-toh*]
unhappy, infelice [*een-feh-lee'-cheh*]
unharmed, illeso [*eel-leh'-zoh*]
unhealthy, malsano [*mahl-sah'-noh*]
uniform, uniforme [*oo-nee-fohr'-meh*]
unimportant, insignificante [*een-see-nyee-fee-kahn'-teh*]
uninteresting, non interessante [*nohn een-teh-rehs-sahn'-teh*]
union [labor union], sindicato [*seen-dee-kah'-toh*]
unit, unity, unità (f, indecl) [*oo-nee-tah'*]
unite *v.*, unire [*oo-nee'-reh*]
united, unito [*oo-nee'-toh*]
United States, gli Stati Uniti [*lyee stah'-tee oo-nee'-tee*]
universal, universale [*oo-nee-vehr-sah'-leh*]
universe, universo [*oo-nee-vehr'-soh*]
university, università (f, indecl) [*oo-nee-vehr-see-tah'*]
unjust, ingiusto [*een-jee-oos'-toh*]
unkind, scortese [*skohr-teh'-zeh*]
unknown, sconosciuto [*skoh-noh-shee-oo'-toh*]
unlawful, illegale [*eel-leh-gah'-leh*]
unless, a meno che, eccetto [*ah meh'-noh keh, ehch-cheht'-toh*]
unlike, dissimile, a differenza di [*dees-see'-mee-leh, ah deef-feh-rehn'-tsah dee*]
unlikely, improbabile [*eem-proh-bah'-bee-leh*]
unload *v.*, scaricare [*skah-ree-kah'-reh*]

unlock v., aprire [ah-pree'-reh]
unlucky, sfortunato [sfohr-too-nah'-toh]
unoccupied, disoccupato [deez-ohk-koo-pah'-toh]
unorganized, disorganizzato [deez-ohr-gah-needz-dzah'-toh]
unpack v., disfare [dees-fah'-reh]
unpleasant, sgradevole [zgrah-deh'-voh-leh]
unprepared, impreparato [eem-preh-pah-rah'-toh]
unselfish, disinteressato [deez-een-teh-rehs-sah'-toh]
until, finchè [feen-keh']
untrue, falso, non vero, inesatto [fahl'-soh, nohn veh'-roh, een-eh-zaht'-toh]
unusual, insolito [een-soh'-lee-toh]
unwelcome, sgradito [zgrah-dee'-toh]
unwilling, maldisposto [mahl-dees-pohs'-toh]
unyielding, inflessibile [een-flehs-see'-bee-leh]
up, sopra, su [soh'-prah, soo]
   get up v., alzarsi [ahl-tsahr'-see]
   go up v., salire [sah-lee'-reh]
   up and down, su e giù [soo eh jee-oo']
   up to now, fino ad ora [fee'-noh ahd oh'-rah]
upbringing, educazione (f) [eh-doo-kah-tsee-oh'-neh]
uphill, ripido [ree'-pee-doh]
uphold v., sostenere [sohs-teh-neh'-reh]
upon, su, sopra [soo, soh'-prah]
upper, superiore [soo-peh-ree-oh'-reh]
   upper floor, piano di sopra [pee-ah'-noh dee soh'-prah]
uproar, tumulto [too-mool'-toh]
ups and downs (of life), gli alti e bassi (della vita) [lyee ahl'-tee eh bahs'-see (deh'-lah vee-tah)]
upset adj., preoccupato [preh-ohk-koo-pah'-toh]
upside down, sotto sopra, capovolto [soht-toh-soh'-prah, kah-poh-vohl'-toh]
upstairs, al piano superiore [ahl pee-ah'-noh soo-peh-ree-oh'-reh]
up-to-date, aggiornato [ahj-jee-ohr-nah'-toh]
urban, urbano [oor-bah'-noh]
urgent, urgente [oor-jehn'-teh]
us, noi, ci [noh'-ee, chee]

to us, a noi [*ah noh'-ee*]
They call us, Ci chiamano [*chee kee-ah'-mah-noh*]
use *n.*, uso [*oo'-zoh*]
use *v.*, usare [*oo-zah'-reh*]
  What is this used for! A che cosa serve questo? [*ah keh koh'-zah sehr'-veh koo-ehs'-toh*]
  be used to *v.*, essere abituato [*ehs'-seh-reh ah-bee-too-ah'-toh*]
used, usato [*oo-zah'-to*]
useful, utile [*oo'-tee-leh*]
useless, inutile [*een-oo'-tee-leh*]
usher, usciere (m) [*oo-shee-eh'-reh*]
usual, abituale [*ah-bee-too-ah'-leh*]
usually, di solito, abitualmente [*dee soh'-lee-toh, ah-bee-too-ahl-mehn'-teh*]
utmost, massimo [*mahs'-see-moh*]

V

vacancy, disponibilità (f, indecl), posto vacante [*dees-poh-nee-bee-lee-tah', pohs'-toh vah-kahn'-teh*]
  no vacancy, nessuna camera libera [*nehs-soo'-nah kah'-meh-rah lee'-beh-rah*]
vacant, vacante [*vah-kahn'-teh*]
vacation, vacanza [*vah-kahn'-tsah*]
vaccination, vaccinazione (f) [*vahch-chee-nah-tsee-oh'-neh*]
vacuum cleaner, aspirapolvere (m) [*ahs-pee-rah-pohl'-veh-reh*]
vague, vago [*vah'-goh*]
vain, vano, vanitoso [*vah'-noh, vah-nee-toh'-zoh*]
  in vain, invano [*een-vah'-noh*]
valid, valido [*vah'-lee-doh*]
valley, valle (f) [*vahl'-leh*]
valuable, prezioso [*preh-tsee-oh'-zoh*]
value *n.*, valore (m) [*vah-loh'-reh*]

value v., stimare, apprezzare [*stee-mah'-reh, ahp-prehts-tsah'-reh*]

vanish v., svanire, sparire [*zvah-nee'-reh, spah-ree'-reh*]

vanity, vanità (f, indecl) [*van-nee-tah'*]

variety, varietà (f, indecl) [*vah-ree-eh-tah'*]

various, vari, diversi [*vah'-ree, dee-vehr'-see*]

vast, vasto [*vahs'-toh*]

Vatican, Vaticano [*vah-tee-kah'-noh*]

vault, volta [*vohl'-tah*]

veal, carne (f) di vitello [*kahr'-neh dee vee-tehl'-loh*]

vegetables, legumi [*leh-goo'-mee*]

vehicle, veicolo [*veh-ee'-koh-loh*]

veil n., velo [*veh'-loh*]

vein, vena [*veh'-nah*]

velvet, velluto [*vehl-loo'-toh*]

Venice, Venezia [*veh-neh'-tsee-ah*]

verb, verbo [*vehr'-boh*]

verdict, verdetto, sentenza [*vehr-deht'-toh, sehn-tehn'-tsah*]

verge n., bordo, orlo [*bohr'-doh, ohr'-loh*]

verify v., verificare [*veh-ree-fee-kah'-reh*]

versatile, versatile [*vehr-sah'-tee-leh*]

verse, verso [*vehr'-soh*]

version, versione (f) [*vehr-see-oh'-neh*]

vertical, verticale [*vehr-tee-kah'-leh*]

very, molto, troppo [*mohl'-toh, trohp'-poh*]

   very bad, malissimo [*mah-lees'-see-moh*]

   very much, moltissimo [*mohl-tees'-see-moh*]

   very well, benissimo [*beh-nees'-see-moh*]

veteran, veterano [*veh-teh-rah'-noh*]

veterinary, veterinario [*veh-teh-ree-nah'-ree-oh*]

vibrate v., vibrare [*vee-brah'-reh*]

vice, vizio [*vee'-tsee-oh*]

vicinity, vicinanza [*vee-chee-nahn'-tsah*]

vicious, vizioso, corrotto [*vee-tsee-oh'-zoh, kohr-roht'-toh*]

victim, vittima [*veet'-tee-mah*]

victory, vittoria [*veet-toh'-ree-ah*]

view n., vista, veduta [*vees'-tah, vee-doo'-tah*]

viewpoint, punto di vista [*poon'-toh dee vees'-tah*]

vigorous, vigoroso [*vee-goh-roh'-zoh*]

villa, villa [*veel'-lah*]

village, villaggio [*veel-lahj'-jee-oh*]

villain, furfante (m) [*foor-fahn'-teh*]

vine, vigna [*vee'-nyah*]

vinegar, aceto [*ah-cheh'-toh*]

violate *v.*, violare [*vee-oh-lah'-reh*]

violence, violenza [*vee-oh-lehn'-tsah*]

violin, violino [*vee-oh-lee'-noh*]

virgin, vergine [*vehr'-jee-neh*]

virtue, virtù (f, indecl) [*veer-too'*]

visa, visto [*vees'-toh*]

visible, visibile [*vee-zee'-bee-leh*]

vision, visione (f) [*vee-zee-oh'-neh*]

visit *n.*, visita [*vee'-zee-tah*]

  pay a visit to *v.*, fare una visita [*fah'-reh oo'-nah vee'-zee-tah*]

visit *v.*, visitare [*vee-zee-tah'-reh*]

visiting-card, biglietto da visita [*bee-lyeht'-toh dah vee'-zee-tah*]

visitor, visitatore (m), visitatrice (f) [*vee-zee-tah-toh'-reh, vee-zee-tah-tree'-cheh*]

vocabulary, vocabolario [*voh-kah-boh-lah'-ree-oh*]

vocal, vocale [*voh-kah'-leh*]

vocation, vocazione (f) [*voh-kah-tsee-oh'-neh*]

vocational, professionale [*proh-fehs-see-oh-nah'-leh*]

voice *n.*, voce (f) [*voh'-cheh*]

volcano, vulcano [*vool-kah'-noh*]

volume, volume (m) [*voh-loo'-meh*]

vomit *v.*, vomitare [*voh-mee-tah'-reh*]

vote *n.*, voto [*voh'-toh*]

vote *v.*, votare [*voh-tah'-reh*]

voucher, garante (m) [*gah-rahn'-teh*]

vow *n.*, voto (sacro) [*voh'-toh (sah'-kroh)*]

vowel, vocale (f) [*voh-kah'-leh*]

voyage *n.*, viaggio (per mare) [*vee-ahj'-jee-oh (pehr mah'-reh)*]

vulgar, volgare [*vohl-gah'-reh*]

vulnerable, vulnerabile [*vool-neh-rah'-bee-leh*]

W

wages, salario (m, sing) [*sah-lah'-ree-oh*]
wagon, vagone (m) [*vah-goh'-neh*]
waist, vita [*vee-tah*]
wait v., aspettare [*ahs-peht-tah'-reh*]
    Wait a moment! Aspetti un momento! [*ahs-peht'-tee oon moh-mehn'-toh*]
    Wait for me, Mi aspetti [*mee ahs-peht'-tee*]
waiter, cameriere (m) [*kah-meh-ree-eh'-reh*]
waiting room, sala d'aspetto [*sah'-lah dahs-peht'-toh*]
waitress, cameriera [*kah-meh-ree-eh'-rah*]
wake up v., svegliare [*zveh-lyah'-reh*]
wake up [oneself], svegliarsi [*zveh-lyahr'-see*]
walk n., passeggiata [*pahs-sehj-jee-ah'-tah*]
    take a walk v., fare una passeggiata [*fah'-reh oo'-nah pahs-sehj-jee-ah'-tah*]
walk v., camminare [*kahm-mee-nah'-reh*]
    walk in, entrare [*ehn-trah'-reh*]
    walk out, uscire [*oo-shee'-reh*]
wall, muro, parete (f) [*moo'-roh, pah-reh'-teh*]
wallet, portafoglio [*pohr-tah-foh'-lyoh*]
wander, v. vagare [*vah-gah'-reh*]
want v., volere (irreg) [*voh-leh'-reh*]
war, guerra [*goo-ehr'-rah*]
wardrobe, armadio [*ahr-mah'-dee-oh*]
warehouse, magazzino [*mah-gahdz-dzee'-noh*]
warm adj., caldo [*kahl'-doh*]
warm v., riscaldare [*rees-kahl-dah'-reh*]
warmth, calore (m) [*kah-loh'-reh*]
warn v., avvertire [*ahv-vehr-tee'-reh*]
warning, avvertimento [*ahv-vehr-tee-mehn'-toh*]
warrant n., mandato, autorizzazione (f) [*mahn-dah'-toh, ah-oo-toh-reedz-dzah-tsee-oh'-neh*]

was, ero, era [*eh'-roh, eh'-rah*]
   There was . . . , C'era . . . [*cheh'-rah*]
wash *v.,* lavare [*lah-vah'-reh*]
   wash [oneself], lavarsi [*lah-vahr'-see*]
washbasin, lavabó [*lah-vah-boh'*]
waste *v.,* sciupare, sprecare [*shee-oo-pah'-reh, spreh-kah'-reh*]
wastebasket, cestino [*chehs-tee'-noh*]
watch *n.,* orologio [*oh-roh-loh'-jee-oh*]
   wind a watch *v.,* caricare l'orologio [*kah-ree-kah'-reh loh-roh-loh'-jee-oh*]
   wristwatch, orologio da polso [*oh-roh-loh'-jee-oh dah pohl'-soh*]
watch *v.,* sorvegliare, osservare [*sohr-veh-lyah'-reh, ohs-sehr-vah'-reh*]
   Watch out! Attento! [*aht-tehn'-toh*]
watchmaker, orologiaio [*oh-roh-loh-jee-ah'-ee-oh*]
watchman, guardiano [*goo-ahr-dee-ah'-noh*]
water, acqua [*ahk'-koo-ah*]
   fresh water, acqua fresca [*ahk'-koo-ah frehs'-kah*]
   mineral water, acqua minerale [*ahk'-koo-ah mee-neh-rah'-leh*]
   running water, acqua corrente [*ahk'-koo-ah kohr-rehn'-teh*]
water bottle, borraccia [*bohr-rahch'-chee-ah*]
water closet, latrina [*lah-tree'-nah*]
watercolors, acquarello [*ahk-koo-ah-rehl'-loh*]
waterfall, cascata [*kahs-kah'-tah*]
watermelon, cocomero [*koh-koh'-meh-roh*]
wave *n.,* onda, ondata, cenno [*ohn'-dah, ohn-dah'-tah, chehn'-noh*]
   short wave, onde corte (f, pl) [*ohn'-deh kohr'-teh*]
wave *v.,* ondeggiare, ondulare [*ohn-dehj-jee-ah'-reh, ohn-doo-lah'-reh*]
   wave [one's hand], fare cenno [*fah'-reh chehn'-noh*]
wax *n.,* cera [*cheh'-rah*]
way [route] *n.,* via [*vee'-ah*]
   Is this the right way? È questa la via giusta? [*eh' koo-*

ehs'-tah lah vee'-ah jee-oos'-tah]

way [manner] *n.*, modo, maniera *[moh'-doh, mah-nee-eh'-rah]*

  by the way, a proposito *[ah proh-poh'-zee-toh]*

  in no way, in nessun modo *[een nehs-soon' moh'-doh]*

  in this way, in questa maniera *[een koo-ehs'-tah mah-nee-eh'-rah]*

we, noi *[noh'-ee]*

weak, debole *[deh'-boh-leh]*

weakness, debolezza *[deh-boh-lehts'-tsah]*

wealth, ricchezza *[reek-kehts'-tsah]*

wealthy, ricco *[reek'-koh]*

weapon, arma *[ahr'-mah]*

wear [clothes] *v.*, indossare *[een-dohs-sah'-reh]*

wear [glasses] *v.*, portare *[pohr-tah'-reh]*

  wear out, consumare *[kohn-soo-mah'-reh]*

weary, stanco *[stahn'-koh]*

weather *n.*, tempo *[tehm'-poh]*

  How is the weather? Come è il tempo? *[koh'-meh eh' eel tehm'-poh]*

wedding, nozze (f, pl) *[nohts'-tseh]*

wedding cake, torta nuziale *[tohr'-tah noo-tsee-ah'-leh]*

wedding ring, fede (f) *[feh'-deh]*

Wednesday, mercoledì *[mehr-koh-leh-dee']*

weed *n.*, erbaccia *[ehr-bahch'-chee-ah]*

week, settimana *[seht-tee-mah'-nah]*

  last week, la settimana scorsa *[lah seht-tee-mah'-nah skohr'-sah]*

  next week, la settimana prossima *[lah seht-tee-mah'-nah prohs'-see-mah]*

weekend, fine-settimana *[fee-neh-seht-tee-mah'-nah]*

weekly, settimanale *[seht-tee-mah-nah'-leh]*

weep *v.*, piangere *[pee-ahn'-jeh-reh]*

weigh *v.*, pesare *[peh-zah'-reh]*

weight, peso *[peh'-zoh]*

welcome *n.*, benvenuto *[behn-veh-noo'-toh]*

  You're welcome! Prego! *[preh'-goh]*

welcome *v.*, dare il benvenuto, accogliere *[dah'-reh eel behn-veh-noo'-toh, ahk-koh'-lyeh-reh]*

welfare, benessere (m) *[behn-ehs'-seh-reh]*

well *n.*, pozzo [*pohts'-tsoh*]
well *adv. & adj.*, bene [*beh'-neh*]
  be well *v.*, stare bene [*stah'-reh beh'-neh*]
Well! Bene! [*beh'-neh*]
well-bred, educato [*eh-doo-kah'-toh*]
well-known, molto conosciuto [*mohl'-toh koh-noh-shee-oo'-toh*]
well-off, benestante [*beh-neh-stahn'-teh*]
were, eravamo, eravate, erano (1st, 2nd & 3rd person pl) [*eh-rah-vah'-moh, eh-rah-vah'-teh, eh'-rah-noh*]
  There were . . . C'erano . . . [*cheh'-rah-noh*]
west, ovest (m), occidente (m) [*oh'-vehst, ohch-chee-dehn'-teh*]
western *adj.*, occidentale [*ohch-chee-dehn-tah'-leh*]
wet *adj.*, bagnato [*bah-nyah'-toh*]
  get wet *v.*, bagnarsi [*bah-nyahr'-see*]
what, che, che cosa, quale [*keh, keh koh'-zah, koo-ah'-leh*]
  What a pity! Che peccato! [*keh pehk-kah'-toh*]
  What else? Che altro? [*keh ahl'-troh*]
  What for? Perchè? [*pehr-keh'*]
  What is the matter? Che succede? [*keh sooch-cheh'-deh*]
whatever, qualunque [*koo-ah-loon'-koo-eh*]
  whatever you wish, quello che desidera [*koo-ehl'-loh keh deh-zee'-deh-rah*]
wheel, ruota [*roo-oh'-tah*]
  steering wheel, volante (m) [*voh-lahn'-teh*]
when, quando [*koo-ahn'-doh*]
  since when, da quando [*dah koo-ahn'-doh*]
  When will you (he, she) return? Quando ritornerà? [*koo-ahn'-doh ree-tohr-neh-rah'*]
whenever, ogni volta che [*oh'-nyee vohl'-tah keh*]
where, dove [*doh'-veh*]
  Where is it (he, she)? Dov'è? [*doh-veh'*]
Wherever, dovunque [*doh-voon'-koo-eh*]
whether, se [*seh*]
  Whether he comes or not . . . Se viene oppure non viene . . [*seh vee-eh'-neh ohp-poo'-reh nohn vee-eh'-neh*]
which [of several] *adj. & pron.*, quale [*koo-ah'-leh*]
which *rel. pron.*, chi [*kee*]
while *cons.*, mentre [*mehn'-treh*]

While I was eating, Mentre mangiavo [*mehn'-treh mahn-jee-ah'-voh*]

a while ago, poco tempo fa [*poh'-koh tehm'-poh fah*]

whisper *n.*, mormorio [*mohr-moh-ree'-oh*]

whisper *v.*, sussurrare [*soos-soor-rah'-reh*]

whistle *n.*, fischio [*fees'-kee-oh*]

whistle *v.*, fischiare [*fees-kee-ah'-reh*]

white, bianco [*bee-ahn'-koh*]

who, che [*keh*]

  who? chi? [*kee*]

whoever, chiunque [*kee-oon'-koo-eh*]

whole *n. & adj.*, tutto, intero [*toot'-toh, een-teh'-roh*]

wholehearted, cordiale, sincero, leale [*kohr-dee-ah'-leh, seen-cheh'-roh, leh-ah'-leh*]

wholesale, vendita all'ingrosso [*vehn'-dee-tah ahl-leen-grohs'-soh*]

whom, chi, che, cui [*kee, keh, koo'-ee*]

  whom? chi?, che? [*kee, keh*]

whose, di chi? di cui? [*dee kee, dee koo'-ee*]

why, perchè [*pehr-keh'*]

  why not? perchè no? [*pehr-keh' noh*]

wicked, malvagio [*mahl-vah'-jee-oh*]

wide, largo, ampio [*lahr'-goh, ahm'-pee-oh*]

wide-awake, tutto sveglio [*toot'-toh sveh'-lyoh*]

wide-open, spalancato [*spah-lahn-kah'-toh*]

widespread, diffuso [*deef-foo'-zoh*]

widow, vedova [*veh'-doh-vah*]

widower, vedovo [*veh'-doh-voh*]

width, larghezza [*lahr-gehts'-tsah*]

wife, moglie (f) [*moh'-lyeh*]

wig, parrucca [*pahr-rook'-kah*]

wild, selvaggio [*sehl-vahj'-jee-oh*]

will *n.*, volontà (f, indecl), desiderio [*voh-lohn-tah', deh-zee-deh'-ree-oh*]

will *v.*, volere (irreg), desiderare [*voh-leh'-reh, deh-zee-deh-rah'-reh*]

  I will go, (io) andrò [(*ee'-oh*) *ahn-droh'*]

  Will you have a cigarette? Desidera una sigaretta? [*deh-zee'-deh-rah oo'-nah see-gah-reht'-tah*]

willing, disposto [*dees-pohs'-toh*]

I am willing to . . . Sono disposto a . . . [*soh'-noh dees-pohs'-toh ah*]

willingly, volentieri [*voh-lehn-tee-eh'-ree*]

willpower, forza di volontà [*fohr'-tsah dee voh-lohn-tah'*]

win *v.,* vincere [*veen'-cheh-reh*]

wind *n.,* vento [*vehn'-toh*]

windmill, mulino a vento [*moo-lee'-noh ah vehn'-toh*]

window [car, train], finestrino [*fee-nehs-tree'-noh*]

window [house], finestra [*fee-nehs'-trah*]

windowpane, vetro della finestra [*veh'-troh dehl'-lah fee-nehs'-trah*]

windshield, parabrezza [*pah-rah-brehts'-tsah*]

wine, vino [*vee'-noh*]
   red wine, vino rosso [*vee'-noh rohs'-soh*]
   white wine, vino bianco [*vee'-noh bee-ahn'-koh*]

wing, ala, le ali (pl), [*ah'-lah, leh ah'-lee*]

winner, vincitore (m), vincitrice (f) [*veen-chee-toh'-reh, veen-chee-tree'-cheh*]

winter, inverno [*een-vehr'-noh*]

wipe *v.,* asciugare, pulire [*ah-shee-oo-gah'-reh, poo-lee'-reh*]
   wipe off, cancellare [*kahn-chehl-lah'-reh*]

wire [filament] *n.,* filo [*fee'-loh*]

wire [telegraph] *v.,* telegrafare [*teh-leh-grah-fah'-reh*]

wireless, radio (f), senza filo [*rah'-dee-oh, sehn'-tsah fee'-loh*]

wisdom, saggezza, prudenza [*sahj-jehts'-tsah, proo-dehn'-tsah*]

wise, saggio [*sahj'-jee-oh*]

wish *n.,* desiderio [*deh-zee-deh'-ree-oh*]

wish *v.,* desiderare [*deh-zee-deh-rah'-reh*]
   What do you wish? Cosa desidera? [*koh'-zah deh-zee'-deh-rah*]

wit, ingegno, spirito [*een-jeh'-nyoh, spee'-ree-toh*]

with, con [*kohn*]

withdraw *v.,* ritirare [*ree-tee-rah'-reh*]

withhold *v.,* trattenere (irreg) [*traht-teh-neh'-reh*]

within, dentro, fra [*dehn'-troh, frah*]

without, senza [*sehn'-tsah*]

withstand *v.,* resistere [*reh-zees'-teh-reh*]

witness *n.,* testimone (m, f) [*tehs-tee-moh'-neh*]

witness *v.,* testimoniare [*tehs-tee-moh-nee-ah'-reh*]

witty, intelligente [*een-tehl-lee-jehn'-teh*]

woman, donna [*dohn'-nah*]

wonder v., meravigliarsi [*meh-rah-vee-lyahr'-see*]

wonderful, meraviglioso [*meh-rah-vee-lyoh'-zoh*]

wood, legno [*leh'-nyoh*]

wooden, di legno [*dee leh'-nyoh*]

woods, bosco [*bohs'-koh*]

wool, lana [*lah'-nah*]

word, parola [*pah-roh'-lah*]

work n., lavoro [*lah-voh'-roh*]

   work of art, opera d'arte [*oh'-peh-rah dahr'-teh*]

work v., lavorare [*lah-voh-rah'-reh*]

   Where do you work? Dove lavora? [*doh'-veh lah-voh'-rah*]

workday, giorno feriale [*jee-ohr'-noh feh-ree-ah'-leh*]

worker, lavoratore (m), lavoratrice (f) [*lah-voh-rah-toh'-reh, lah-voh-rah-tree'-cheh*]

working, lavoro, lavorando [*lah-voh'-roh, lah-voh-rahn'-doh*]

   This isn't working, Questo non funziona [*koo-ehs'-toh nohn foon-tsee-oh'-nah*]

workshop, officina, corso di specializzazione [*ohf-fee-chee'-nah, kohr'-soh dee speh-chee-ah-leedz-dzah-tsee-oh'-neh*]

world, mondo [*mohn'-doh*]

worldwide, diffuso [*deef-foo'-zoh*]

world war, guerra mondiale [*goo-ehr'-rah mohn-dee-ah'-leh*]

worn-out [objects], consumato [*kohn-soo-mah'-toh*]

worn-out [persons], esausto [*eh-zah'-oos-toh*]

worried, preoccupato [*preh-ohk-koo-pah'-toh*]

worry n., preoccupazione (f) [*preh-ohk-koo-pah-tsee-oh'-neh*]

worry v., preoccuparsi [*preh-ohk-koo-pahr'-see*]

   Don't worry! Non si preoccupi! [*nohn see preh-ohk'-koo-pee*]

worse, peggio, peggiore [*pehj'-jee-oh, pehj-jee-oh'-reh*]

   worse than, peggiore di [*pehj-jee-oh'-reh dee*]

worship n., adorazione (f) [*ah-doh-rah-tsee-oh'-neh*]

worship v., adorare [*ah-doh-rah'-reh*]

worst adj., il peggiore, la peggiore [*eel pehj-jee-oh'-reh, lah pehj-jee-oh'-reh*]

   the worst of all, il peggiore di tutti [*eel pehj-jee-oh'-reh dee toot'-tee*]

worth, valore (m) [*vah-loh'-reh*]
  be worth *v.,* valere [*vah-leh'-reh*]
  How much is this worth? Quanto vale questo? [*koo-ahn'-toh vah'-leh koo-ehs'-toh*]
worthwhile, (che) ne vale la pena [(*keh*) *neh vah'-leh lah peh'-nah*]
  It is not worthwhile, Non ne vale la pena [*nohn neh vah'-leh lah peh'-nah*]
wounded, ferito [*feh-ree'-toh*]
wrinkle *n.,* ruga [*roo'-gah*]
wrist, polso [*pohl'-soh*]
wristwatch, orologio da polso [*oh-roh-loh'-jee-oh dah pohl'-soh*]
write *v.,* scrivere [*skree'-veh-reh*]
writer, scrittore (m), scrittrice (f) [*skreet-toh'-reh, skreet-tree'-cheh*]
writing, scrittura, scritto [*skreet-too'-rah, skreet'-toh*]
writing paper, carta da scrivere [*kahr'-tah dah skree'-veh-reh*]
written, scritto [*skreet'-toh*]
wrong *adj.,* sbagliato [*zbah-lyah'-toh*]
  be wrong *v.,* avere torto [*ah-veh'-reh tohr'-toh*]

X, Y, Z

x-ray, raggi x (pl) [*rahj'-jee ehks*]

yacht, panfilo [*pahn-fee'-loh*]
yard [courtyard], cortile (m) [*kohr-tee'-leh*]
yard [measure], iarda [*ee-ahr'-dah*]
yawn *v.,* sbadigliare [*zbah-dee-lyah'-reh*]
year, anno [*ahn'-noh*]
  last year, l'anno scorso [*lahn'-noh skohr'-soh*]
  next year, l'anno prossimo [*lahn'-noh prohs'-see-moh*]
yearly, annualmente [*ahn-noo-ahl-mehn'-teh*]
yell *v.,* gridare [*gree-dah'-reh*]
yes, sì [*see'*]

Yes indeed! Per davvero! [*pehr dahv-veh'-roh*]
yesterday, ieri [*ee-eh'-ree*]
   the day before yesterday, l'altro ieri [*lahl'-troh ee-eh'-ree*]
   yesterday evening, ieri sera [*ee-eh'-ree seh'-rah*]
yet *conj.*, tuttavia [*toot-tah-vee'-ah*]
   not yet, non ancora [*nohn ahn-koh'-rah*]
yield *v.*, produrre (irreg), cedere [*proh-door'-reh, cheh'-deh-reh*]
you [polite form], lei (3rd pers. sing); loro (3rd pers. pl) [*leh'-ee, loh'-roh*]
you [informal address], tu (2nd person sing); voi (2nd person pl) [*too, voh'-ee*]
young, giovane [*jee-oh'-vah-neh*]
   (the) young man, il giovane [*eel jee-oh'-vah-neh*]
   (the) young woman, la giovane [*lah jee-oh'-vah-neh*]
your [formal & polite form], suo, sua (m & f sing); suoi, sue (m & f pl) [*soo'-oh, soo'-ah, soo-oh'-ee, soo'-eh*]
your [plural; polite form], il loro, la loro (m & f sing); i loro, le loro (m & f pl) [*eel loh'-roh, lah loh'-roh, ee loh'-roh, leh loh'-roh*]
your [informal form], tuo, tua (m & f sing); tuoi, tue (m & f pl) [*too'-oh, too'-ah, too-oh'-ee, too'-eh*]
your [plural; familiar], vostro, vostra (m & f sing); vostri, vostre (m & f pl) [*vohs'-troh, vohs'-trah, vohs'-tree, vohs'-treh*]
yourself, tu stesso (sing, informal form); lei stesso (sing, polite form) [*too stehs'-soh, leh'-ee stehs'-soh*]
yourselves, voi stessi (pl, informal form); loro stessi (pl, polite form) [*voh'-ee stehs'-see, loh'-roh stehs'-see*]
youth, gioventù (f, indecl) [*jee-oh-vehn-too'*]
youthful, giovanile [*jee-oh-vah-nee'-leh*]

zeal, zelo [*dzeh'-loh*]
zero, zero [*dzeh'-roh*]
zipper, chiusura lampo [*kee-oo-zoo'-rah lahm'-poh*]
zone, zona [*dzoh'-nah*]
zoo, giardino zoologico [*jee-ahr-dee'-noh dzoh-oh-loh'-jee-koh*]

Italian/English

A

a [*ah*] at, to, in
abbaiare *v.* [*ahb-bah-ee-ah'-reh*] bark
abbacchio [*ahb-bahk'-kee-oh*] lamb [food]
abbandonare *v.* [*ahb-bahn-doh-nah'-reh*] abandon
abbasso [*ahb-bahs'-soh*] below
abbastanza [*ahb-bahs-tahn'-tsah*] enough
   più che abbastanza [*pee-oo' keh ahb-bahs-tahn'-tsah*]
     more than enough
abbigliamento [*ahb-bee-lyah-mehn'-toh*] attire
abbonamento [*ahb-boh-nah-mehn'-toh*] subscription
abbondante [*ahb-bohn-dahn'-teh*] abundant
abbondanza [*ahb-bohn-dahn'-tsah*] abundance
   in abbondanza [*een ahb-bohn-dahn'-tsah*] plenty
abbottonare *v.* [*ahb-boht-toh-nah'-reh*] button
abbracciare *v.* [*ahb-brahch-chee-ah'-reh*] hug
abbraccio [*ahb-brach'-chee-oh*] hug
abbreviare *v.* [*ahb-breh-vee-ah'-reh*] shorten
abbronzato [*ahb-brohn-tsah'-toh*] sunburned
abbronzatura [*ahb-brohn-tsah-too'-rah*] tan
abbrustolire *v.* [*ahb-broos-toh-lee'-reh*] toast
abile [*ah'-bee-leh*] skillful, able
abilità *f. indecl.* [*ah-bee-lee-tah'*] ability
abitante [*ah-bee-tahn'-teh*] inhabitant
abitare *v.* [*ah-bee-tah'-reh*] live, inhabit
abitazione *f.* [*ah-bee-tah-tsee-oh'-neh*] home, residence
abito [*ah'-bee-toh*] suit, dress
   abito da sera [*ah'-bee-toh dah seh'-rah*] evening dress
abituale [*ah-bee-too-ah'-leh*] usual, customary
abitualmente [*ah-bee-too-ahl-mehn'-teh*] usually
abituato [*ah-bee-too-ah'-toh*] accustomed
abituarsi *v.* [*ah-bee-too-ahr'-see*] get accustomed
   essere abituato [*ehs'-seh-reh ah-bee-too-ah'-toh*] be
     accustomed
abitudine [*ah-bee-too'-dee-neh*] habit, costume, routine

abolire v. [*ah-boh-lee'-reh*] abolish

aborto [*ah-bohr'-toh*] abortion

abusare v. [*ah-boo-zah'-reh*] abuse

abuso [*ah-boo'-zoh*] abuse

accademia [*ahk-kah-deh'-mee-ah*] academy

accadere v. [*ahk-kah-deh'-reh*] happen, occur

accanto [*ahk-kahn'-toh*] near, beside

accendere v. irreg. [*ahch-chehn'-deh-reh*] light, turn on [light]

accendi-sigaro [*ahch-chehn-dee-see-gah'-roh*] (cigarette) lighter

accenno [*ahch-chen'-noh*] hint

accento [*ahch-chehn'-toh*] accent

accessibile [*ahch-chehss-see'-bee-leh*] accessible

accesso [*ahch-chehss'-soh*] access

accettare v. [*ahch-cheht-tah'-reh*] accept

accettazione f. [*ahch-cheht-tah-tsee-oh'-neh*] acceptance

acciaio [*ahch-chee-ah'-ee-oh*] steel

accidentale [*ahch-chee-dehn-tah'-leh*] accidental

acciuga [*ahch-chee-oo'-gah*] anchovy

acclamazione f. [*ahk-klah-mah-tsee-oh'-neh*] cheer

accludere v. irreg. [*ahk-kloo'-deh-reh*] inclose

accoglienza [*ahk-koh-lyehn'-tsah*] reception

accogliere v. irreg. [*ahk-koh-lyeh-reh*] receive, welcome

accomodamento [*ahk-koh-moh-dah-mehn'-toh*] accommodation

accomodare v. [*ahk-koh-moh-dah'-reh*] accommodate

accomodarsi v. [*ahk-koh-moh-dahr'-see*] make oneself comfortable

  Si accomodi! [*see ahk-koh'-moh-dee*] Sit down! Make yourself at home!

accompagnare v. [*ahk-kohm-pah-nyah'-reh*] accompany

acconsentire v. [*ahk-kohn-sehn-tee'-reh*] consent

accoppiare v., [*ahk-kohp-pee-ah'-reh*] match

accordare v. [*ahk-kohr-dah'-reh*] grant, tune

accordo [*ahk-kohr'-doh*] agreement

  essere v. **d'accordo** [*ehs'-seh-reh dahk-kohr'-doh*] agree

  non essere v. **d'accordo** [*nohn ehs'-seh-reh dahk-kohr'-doh*] disagree

accorgersi v. [*ahk-kohr'-jehr-see*] notice, perceive

accuratezza [*ahk-koo-rah-tehts'-tsah*] accuracy
accurato [*ahk-koo-rah'-toh*] elaborate
accusa [*ahk-koo'-zah*] accusation
accusare *v.* [*ahk-koo-zah'-reh*] accuse
accusato [*ahk-koo-zah'-toh*] accused
accusatore *m.* [*ahk-koo-zah-toh'-reh*] accuser
aceto [*ah-cheh'-toh*] vinegar
acido [*ah'-chee-doh*] sour, acid
acqua [*ahk'-koo-ah*] water
  acqua corrente [*ahk'-koo-ah kohr-rehn'-teh*] running water
  acqua fresca [*ahk'-koo-ah frehs'-kah*] fresh water
  acqua minerale [*ahk'-koo-ah mee-neh-rah'-leh*] mineral
    water
  acqua ossigenata [*ahk'-koo-ah ohs-see-jeh-nah'-tah*]
    peroxide
  acqua seltz [*ahk'-koo-ah sehlts*] soda water
acquarello [*ahk-koo-ah-rehl'-loh*] water colors
acquistare *v.* [*ahk-koo-ees-tah'-reh*] purchase, acquire
acquisto [*ahk-koo-ees'-toh*] acquisition, purchase
adattamento [*ah-daht-tah-mehn'-toh*] adjustment
adattare *v.* [*ah-daht-tah'-reh*] adapt, fit
adatto [*ah-daht'-toh*] suitable
addebitare *v.* [*ahd-deh-bee-tah'-reh*] charge [a customer]
addestramento [*ahd-dehs-trah-mehn'-toh*] training
addestrare *v.* [*ahd-dehs-trah'-reh*] train
addizionare *v.* [*ahd-dee-tsee-oh-nah'-reh*] add up
addizione *f.* [*ahd-dee-tsee-oh'-neh*] addition
addormentarsi *v.* [*ahd-dohr-mehn-tahr'-see*] fall asleep
addormentato [*ahd-dohr-mehn-tah'-toh*] asleep
adeguato [*ah-deh-goo-ah'-toh*] adequate
adesso [*ah-dehs'-soh*] now
adorabile [*ah-doh-rah'-bee-leh*] adorable
adorare *v.* [*ah-doh-rah'-reh*] worship, adore
adorazione *f.* [*ah-doh-rah-tsee-oh'-neh*] worship
adornare *v.* [*ah-dohr-nah'-reh*] adorn
adottare *v.* [*ah-doht-tah'-reh*] adopt
adozione *f.* [*ah-doh-tsee-oh'-neh*] adoption
adulare *v.* [*ah-doo-lah'-reh*] flatter
adulatore *m.*, **adulatrice** *f.* [*ah-doo-lah-toh'-reh, ah-doo-lah-tree'-cheh*] flatterer

adulazione [*ah-doo-lah-tsee-oh'-neh*] flattery

adulto [*ah-dool'-toh*] adult

aereo, aeroplano [*ah-eh'-reh-oh, ah-eh-roh-plah'-noh*] airplane

aeroporto [*ah-eh-roh-pohr'-toh*] airport

affamare v. [*ahf-fah-mah'-reh*] starve

affamato [*ahf-fah-mah'-toh*] hungry

affare m. [*ahf-fah'-reh*] business, affair

  uomo d'affari [*oo-oh'-moh dahf-fah'-ree*] businessman

affascinante [*ahf-fah-shee-nahn'-teh*] charming

affascinare v. [*ahf-fah-shee-nah'-reh*] fascinate, charm

affatto [*ahf-faht'-toh*] at all

  niente affatto [*nee-ehn'-teh ahf-faht'-toh*] not at all

affermare v. [*ahf-fehr-mah'-reh*] affirm

affermativo [*ahf-fehr-mah-tee'-voh*] affirmative

afferrare v. [*ahf-fehr-rah'-reh*] grasp, apprehend

affetto [*ahf-feht'-toh*] affection

affettuosamente [*ahf-feht-too-oh-zah-mehn'-teh*] affectionately

affettuoso [*ahf-feht-too-oh'-zoh*] affectionate

affezione f. [*ahf-feh-tsee-oh'-neh*] affection

affinchè [*ahf-feen-keh'*] in order that

affittare v. [*ahf-feet-tah'-reh*] let, rent, lease

  contratto d'affitto [*kohn-traht'-toh dahf-feet'-toh*] lease

  da affittare [*dah ahf-feet-tah'-reh*] for rent

  stanza d'affittare [*stahn'-tsah dahf-feet-tah'-reh*] room to let

affitto [*ahf-feet'-toh*] rent

affliggere v. irreg. [*ahf-fleej'-jeh-reh*] afflict, grieve

afflusso [*ahf-floos'-soh*] rush

affollato [*ahf-fohl-lah'-toh*] crowded

affondare v. [*ahf-fohn-dah'-reh*] sink

affrancatura [*ahf-frahn-kah-too'-rah*] postage

Africa [*ah'-free-kah*] Africa

africano [*ah-free-kah'-noh*] African

affrontare v. [*ahf-frohn-tah'-reh*] face

agente m. [*ah-jehn'-teh*] agent

  agente di cambio [*ah-jehn'-teh dee kahm'-bee-oh*] stockbroker, money changer

  agente investigativo [*ah-jehn'-teh een-vehs-tee-gah-tee'-voh*] detective

agenzia [*ah-jehn-tsee'-ah*] agency
  agenzia di collocamento [*ah-jehn-tsee'-ah dee kohl-loh-kah-mehn'-toh*] employment agency
  agenzia di viaggi [*ah-jehn-tsee'-ah dee vee-ahj'-jee*] travel agency
aggettivo [*ahj-jeht-tee'-voh*] adjective
aggiornato [*ahj-jee-ohr-nah'-toh*] up-to-date
aggiungere v. [*ahj-jee-oon'-jeh-reh*] add
aggiustare v. [*ahj-jee-oos-tah'-reh*] adjust
aggressione f. [*ahg-grehs-see-oh'-neh*] aggression
aggressivo [*ahg-grehs-see'-voh*] aggressive
agiato [*ah-jee-ah'-toh*] well-off
agile [*ah'-jee-leh*] agile, nimble
agio [*ah'-jee-oh*] leisure
agire v. [*ah-jee'-reh*] act
agitare v. [*ah-jee-tah'-reh*] agitate, shake
agitarsi v. [*ah-jee-tahr'-see*] get excited
  Non si agiti! [*nohn see ah'-jee-tee*] Don't get excited!
agitato [*ah-jee-tah'-toh*] agitated, excited
agli: a gli m. pl. [*ah'-lyee*] to the, at the
aglio [*ah'-lyoh*] garlic
agnello [*ah-nyehl'-loh*] lamb [animal]
ago [*ah'-goh*] needle
agonia [*ah-goh-nee'-ah*] agony
agosto [*ah-gohs'-toh*] August
agricoltura [*ah-gree-kohl-too'-rah*] agriculture
ai m. pl. [*ah'-ee*] to the, at the
aiutare v. [*ah-ee-oo-tah'-reh*] aid, help
aiuto [*ah-ee-oo'-toh*] help, assistance
  Aiuto! [*ah-ee-oo'-toh*] Help!
al: a il [*ahl*] to the, at the
ala, le ali pl. [*ah'-lah, leh ah'-lee*] wing
alba [*ahl'-bah*] dawn
albanese [*ahl-bah-neh'-zeh*] Albanian
Albania [*ahl-bah-nee'-ah*] Albania
albergo [*ahl-behr'-goh*] hotel
  all'albergo [*ahl-lahl-behr'-goh*] at the hotel
albero [*ahl'-beh-roh*] tree
alcool [*ahl'-koh-ohl*] alcohol
alcuni pl. [*ahl-koo'-nee*] some

alcuni uomini [*ahl-koo'-nee oo-oh'-mee-nee*] some men
alcune volte [*ahl-koo'-neh vohl'-teh*] sometimes
alcuno [*ahl-koo'-noh*] any, anyone
alfabeto [*ahl-fah-beh'-toh*] alphabet
alimentare v. [*ah-lee-mehn-tah'-reh*] feed, nourish
aliquota [*ah-lee'-koo-oh-tah*] quota
alito [*ah'-lee-toh*] breath
alla: a la [*ahl*] to the, at the
alla, all' [*ahl-lah, ahl*] in the manner of
all'americana [*ahl-lah-meh-ree-kah'-nah*] in the American
way
allarmare v. [*ahl-lahr-mah'-reh*] alarm
allarmarsi v. [*ahl-lahr-mahr'-see*] get alarmed
allarme m. [*ahl-lahr'-meh*] alarm
alle: a le f. pl. [*ahl'-leh*] to the, at the
alleanza [*ahl-leh-ahn'-tsah*] alliance
alleato [*ahl-leh-ah'-toh*] allied
allegria [*ahl-leh-gree'-ah*] joy
allegro [*ahl-leh'-groh*] cheerful, gay, merry
allergico [*ahl-lehr'-jee-koh*] allergic
allevare v. [*ahl-leh-vah'-reh*] rear
alleviare v. [*ahl-leh-vee-ah'-reh*] relieve
allievo [*ahl-lee-eh'-voh*] pupil
alloggiare v. [*ahl-lohj-jee-ah'-reh*] lodge
alloggio [*ahl-lohj'-jee-oh*] lodging
allontanarsi v. [*ahl-lohn-tah-nahr'-see*] go away
allora [*ahl-loh'-rah*] then
fin da allora [*feen dah ahl-loh'-rah*] since then
da allora in poi [*dah ahl-loh'-rah een poh'-ee*] from that
time
alludere v. [*ahl-loo'-deh-reh*] hint
allusione f. [*ahl-loo-zee-oh'-neh*] allusion, hint
Alpi f. pl. [*ahl'-pee*] Alps
alquanto [*ahl-koo-ahn'-toh*] somewhat, rather
Alt! [*ahlt*] Stop!
altare m. [*ahl-tah'-reh*] altar
altezza [*ahl-tehts'-tsah*] height
altitudine f. [*ahl-tee-too'-dee-neh*] altitude
alto [*ahl'-toh*] high, tall
ad alta voce [*ahd ahl'-tah voh'-cheh*] aloud

più alto [*pee-oo' ahl'-toh*] higher, taller
altoparlante [*ahl-toh-pahr-lahn'-teh*] loudspeaker
altretanto [*ahl-treh-tahn'-toh*] likewise
altrimenti [*ahl-tree-mehn'-tee*] otherwise
altro [*ahl'-troh*] other, else
  in un altro posto [*een oon ahl'-troh pohs'-toh*] somewhere
    else
  l'un l'altro [*loon lahl'-troh*] each other
  nessun altro [*nehs-soon' ahl'-troh*] nobody else
  Nient' altro? [*nee-ehnt-ahl'-troh*] Nothing else?
  Qualche altra cosa? [*koo-ahl'-keh ahl'-trah koh'-zah*]
    Anything else?
  qualcun altro [*koo-ahl-koon' ahl'-troh*] somebody else
  un altro [*oon ahl'-troh*] another
  un' altra persona [*oon ahl'-trah pehr-soh'-nah*] someone
    else
altrove [*ahl-troh'-veh*] somewhere else
alunno [*ah-loon'-noh*] pupil
alveare *m.* [*ahl-veh-ah'-reh*] beehive
alzare *v.* [*ahl-tsah'-reh*] raise, lift up
alzarsi *v.* [*ahl-tsahr'-see*] get up
  Mi sono alzato alle sei [*mi soh'-noh ahl-tsa'-toh ahl'-leh*
    seh'-ee] I got up at six
amante *m., f.* [*ah-mahn'-teh*] lover
amante *adj.* [*ah-mahn'-teh*] fond
amare *v.* [*ah-mah'-reh*] love, like, please
  Ti amo! [*tee ah'-moh*] I love you!
  non amare [*nohn ah-mah'-reh*] dislike
amaro [*ah-mah'-roh*] bitter
ambasciata [*ahm-bah-shee-ah'-tah*] embassy
ambasciatore *m.,* **ambasciatrice** *f.* [*ahm-bah-shee-ah-toh'-*
  reh, ahm-bah-shee-ah-tree'-cheh] ambassador
ambedue [*ahm-beh-doo'-eh*] both
ambiente *m.* [*ahm-bee-ehn'-teh*] environment
ambiguità *f. indecl.* [*ahm-bee-goo-ee-tah'*] ambiguity
ambizione *f.* [*ahm-bee-tsee-oh'-neh*] ambition
ambizioso [*ahm-bee-tsee-oh'-zoh*] ambitious
ambulanza [*ahm-boo-lahn'-tsa*] ambulance
America [*ah-meh'-ree-kah*] America
  America del Nord [*ah-meh'-ree-kah dehl nohrd*] North

America
America del Sud [*ah-meh'-ree-kah dehl sood*] South
America
americano [*ah-meh-ree-kah'-noh*] American
amichevole [*ah-mee-keh'-voh-leh*] friendly
amico [*ah-mee'-koh*] friend
amicizia [*ah-mee-chee'-tsee-ah*] friendship
amido [*ah'-mee-doh*] starch
ammalarsi *v.* [*ahm-mah-lahr'-see*] fall ill
ammalato [*ahm-mah-lah'-toh*] ill
ammazzare *v.* [*ahm-mahts-tsah'-reh*] kill
ammettere *v.* [*ahm-meht'-teh-reh*] admit
ammesso che [*ahm-mehs'-soh keh*] granted that
amministrare *v.* [*ahm-mee-nees-trah'-reh*] manage, administer
amministrazione *f.* [*ahm-mee-nees-trah-tsee-oh'-neh*]
administration
ammirabile [*ahm-mee-rah'-bee-leh*] admirable
ammiraglio [*ahm-mee-rah'-lyoh*] admiral
ammirare *v.* [*ahm-mee-rah'-reh*] admire
ammiratore *m.* [*ahm-mee-rah-toh'-reh*] admirer, fan
ammirazione *f.* [*ahm-mee-rah-tsee-oh'-neh*] admiration
ammissione *f.* [*ahm-mees-see-oh'-neh*] admission, fee
ammobiliare *v.* [*ahm-moh-bee-lee-ah'-reh*] furnish [a house]
ammoniaca [*ahm-moh-nee'-ah-kah*] ammonia
ammonire *v.* [*ahm-moh-nee'-reh*] admonish
ammontare *v.* [*ahm-mohn-tah'-reh*] amount
amnistia [*ahm-nees-tee'-ah*] amnesty
amore *m.* [*ah-moh'-reh*] love, affection
amor proprio [*ah-mohr' proh'-pree-oh*] self-respect
amoreggiare *v.* [*ah-moh-rehj-jee-ah'-reh*] flirt
ampio [*ahm'-pee-oh*] ample
analfabeta [*ah-nahl-fah-beh'-tah*] illiterate
analisi *f. indecl.* [*ah-nah'-lee-zee*] analysis
analisi di sangue [*ah-nah'-lee-zee dee sahn'-goo-eh*]
blood test
analizzare *v.* [*ah-nah-leedz-dzah'-reh*] analyze
ananasso [*ah-nah-nahs'-soh*] pineapple
anarchia [*ah-nahr-kee'-ah*] anarchy
anche [*ahn'-keh*] and, also, even
anche allora [*ahn'-keh ahl-loh'-rah*] even then

anche lui [*ahn'-keh loo'-ee*] also him, even him

anche se [*ahn'-keh seh*] even if

ancora [*ahn'-koh-rah*] anchor

ancora [*ahn-koh'-rɔh*] still, again

ancora una volta [*ahn-koh'-rah oo'-nah vohl'-tah*] once more

non ancora [*nohn ahn-koh'-rah*] not yet

andare *v. irreg.* [*ahn-dah'-reh*] go

andare a piedi [*ahn-dah'-reh ah pee-eh'-dee*] walk

andare in automobile [*ahn-dah'-reh een ah-oo-toh-moh'-bee-leh*] drive

andare via [*ahn-dah'-reh vee'-ah*] go away

Vada via! [*vah'-dah vee'-ah*] Go away!

anello [*ah-nehl'-loh*] ring [jewelry]

angelo [*ahn'-jeh-loh*] angel

angolo [*ahn'-goh-loh*] angle, corner

anguria [*ahn-goo'-ree-ah*] watermelon

anima [*ah'-nee-mah*] soul

animale *m.* [*ah-nee-mah'-leh*] animal

animare *v.* [*ah-nee-mah'-reh*] animate

anitra [*ah'-nee-trah*] duck

annegarsi *v.* [*ahn-neh-gahr'-see*] drown

anniversario [*ahn-nee-vehr-sah'-ree-oh*] anniversary

anno [*ahn'-noh*] year

Buon anno! [*boo-ohn' ahn'-noh*] Happy New Year!

il primo dell'anno [*eel pree'-moh dehl-lahn'-noh*] New Year's day

l'anno scorso [*lahn'-noh skohr'-soh*] last year

l'anno prossimo [*lahn'-noh prohs'-see-moh*] next year

Quanti anni ha? [*koo-ahn'-tee ahn'-nee ah*] How old are you?

annoiare *v.* [*ahn-noh-ee-ah'-reh*] bore, annoy, bother

annoiarsi [*ahn-noh-ee-ahr'-see*] become bored

annoiato [*ahn-noh-ee-ah'-toh*] bored, disturbed

annotare *v.* [*ahn-noh-tah'-reh*] note, take down

annuale [*ahn-noo-ah'-leh*] annual

annualmente [*ahn-noo-ahl-mehn'-teh*] yearly

annullamento [*ahn-nool-lah-mehn'-toh*] annulment

annunciare *v.* [*ahn-noon-chee-ah'-reh*] announce

annunciatore *m.*, **annunciatrice** *f.* [*ahn-noon-chee-ah-toh'-reh,*

ahn-noon-chee-ah-tree'-cheh] announcer
annuncio [*ahn-noon'-chee-oh*] announcement
anonimo [*ah-noh'-nee-moh*] anonymous
ansioso [*ahn-see-oh'-zoh*] anxious
antenato [*ahn-teh-nah'-toh*] ancestor
antichità *f. indecl.* [*ahn-tee-kee-tah'*] antiquity, antique
anticipare *v.* [*ahn-tee-chee-pah'-reh*] anticipate
  in anticipo, anticipato [*een ahn-tee'-chee-poh, ahn-tee-chee-pah'-toh*] in advance
antico [*ahn-tee'-koh*] ancient
antipatia [*ahn-tee-pah-tee'-ah*] dislike
antipasto [*ahn-tee-pahs'-toh*] appetizer
antipatico [*ahn-tee-pah'-tee-koh*] unpleasant person
anzi [*ahn'-tsee*] on the contrary
anziano [*ahn-tsee-ah'-noh*] senior, elderly
  più anziano [*pee-oo' ahn-tsee-ah'-noh*] senior
anziché [*ahn-tsee-keh'*] instead
anzitutto *adv.* [*ahn-tsee-toot'-toh*] first of all
apatia [*ah-pah-tee'-ah*] apathy
ape *f.* [*ah'-peh*] bee
aperitivo [*ah-peh-ree-tee'-voh*] appetizer [liquor]
aperto [*ah-pehr'-toh*] open
  all'aperto [*ahl-lah-pehr'-toh*] outdoors
apertura [*ah-pehr-too'-rah*] opening
apostolo [*ah-pohs'-toh-loh*] apostle
apparato, apparecchio [*ahp-pah-rah'-toh, ahp-pah-rehk'-kee-oh*] apparatus
apparente [*ahp-pah-rehn'-teh*] apparent
apparire *v.* [*ahp-pah-ree'-reh*] appear
apparizione *f.* [*ahp-pah-ree-tsee-oh'-neh*] appearance
appartamento [*ahp-pahr-tah-mehn'-toh*] apartment
appartenere *v. irreg.* [*ahp-pahr-teh-neh'-reh*] belong
  Mi appartiene [*mee ahp-pahr-tee-eh'-neh*] It belongs to me
appassionato [*ahp-pahs-see-oh-nah'-toh*] passionate, fond
appello [*ahp-pehl'-loh*] appeal
  fare *v.* **appello** [*fah'-reh ahp-pehl'-loh*] appeal
appena [*ahp-peh'-nah*] as soon as, barely
  Sono appena arrivato [*soh'-noh ahp-peh'-nah ahr-ree-vah'-toh*] I just arrived
appendere *v. irreg.* [*ahp-pehn'-deh-reh*] hang [an object]

appendicite *f.* [*ahp-pehn-dee-chee'-teh*] appendicitis
Appennini *m. pl.* [*ahp-peh-nee'-nee*] Appennines
appetito [*ahp-peh-tee'-toh*] appetite
appetitoso [*ahp-peh-tee-toh'-zoh*] appetizing
applaudire *v.* [*ahp-plah-oo-dee'-reh*] applaud
applauso [*ahp-plah'-oo-zoh*] applause
applicare *v.* [*ahp-plee-kah'-reh*] apply
appoggiare [*ahp-pohj-jee-ah'-reh*] lean, support
appoggio [*ahp-pohj'-jee-oh*] support
apposta [*ahp-pohs'-tah*] on purpose
apprendere *v. irreg.* [*ahp-prehn'-deh-reh*] learn
apprendista [*ahp-prehn-dees'-tah*] apprentice
apprezzare *v.* [*ahp-preh-tsah'-reh*] appreciate, value
approdo [*ahp-proh'-doh*] landing [of ship]
approfittare di *v.* [*ahp-proh-feet-tah'-reh dee*] take advantage
  of
appropriato [*ahp-proh-pree-ah'-toh*] appropriate
approssimativamente [*ahp-prohs-see-mah-tee-vah-mehn'-teh*]
  approximately
approvare *v.* [*ahp-proh-vah'-reh*] approve
approvazione *f.* [*ahp-proh-vah-tsee-oh'-neh*] approval
appuntamento [*ahp-poon-tah-mehn'-toh*] appointment, date
appuntare *v.* [*ahp-poon-tah'-reh*] pin
appunto [*ahp-poon'-toh*] note, remark
aprile *m.* [*ah-pree'-leh*] April
aprire *v. irreg.* [*ah-pree'-reh*] open, unlock
apriscatola [*ah-pree-skah'-toh-lah*] can opener
aquila [*ah'-koo-ee-lah*] eagle
Arabia [*ah-rah'-bee-ah*] Arabia
arabo [*ah'-rah-boh*] Arab, Arabic
aragosta [*ah-rah-gohs'-tah*] lobster
arancia [*ah-rahn'-chee-ah*] orange
  succo d'arancia [*sook'-koh dah-rahn'-chee-ah*] orange juice
aranciata [*ah-rahn-chee-ah'-tah*] orangeade
arare *v.* [*ah-rah'-reh*] plow
arbitrario [*ahr-bee-trah'-ree-oh*] arbitrary
arbitro [*ahr'-bee-troh*] referee
architetto [*ahr-kee-teht'-toh*] architect
architettura [*ahr-kee-teht-too'-rah*] architecture
archivio [*ahr-kee'-vee-oh*] archives, file

arcipelago [*ahr-chee-peh'-lah-goh*] archipelago

arcivescovo [*ahr-chee-vehs'-koh-voh*] archbishop

arco [*ahr'-koh*] arch, arc, bow

arcobaleno [*ahr-koh-bah-leh'-noh*] rainbow

ardere *v. irreg.* [*ahr'-deh-reh*] burn

area [*ah'-reh-ah*] area, ground

Argentina [*ahr-jehn-tee'-nah*] Argentina

argentino [*ahr-jehn-tee'-noh*] Argentine

argento [*ahr-jehn'-toh*] silver

argine *m.* [*ahr'-jee-neh*] embankment, limit

argomento [*ahr-goh-mehn'-toh*] subject, matter

aria [*ah'-ree-ah*] air, tune

    aria condizionata [*ah'-ree-ah kohn-dee-tsee-oh-nah'-tah*] air conditioning

    darsi *v.* **delle arie** [*dahr'-see dehl'-leh ah'-ree-eh*] show off

    mal d'aria [*mahl dah'-ree-ah*] airsickness

arido [*ah'-ree-doh*] arid

aristocratico [*ah-rees-toh-krah'-tee-koh*] aristocratic

aristocrazia [*ah-rees-toh-krah-tsee'-ah*] aristocracy

aritmetica [*ah-reet-meh'-tee-kah*] arithmetic

arma, le armi *pl.* [*ahr'-mah, leh ahr'-mee*] weapon, arms

armadio [*ahr-mah'-dee-oh*] wardrobe, closet

armata [*ahr-mah'-tah*] army

armato [*ahr-mah'-toh*] armed

armonia [*ahr-moh-nee'-ah*] harmony

aroma [*ah-roh'-mah*] flavor

arrabbiarsi *v.* [*ahr-rahb-bee-ahr'-see*] get angry

arrabbiato [*ahr-rahb-bee-ah'-toh*] angry

arrendersi *v.* [*ahr-rehn'-dehr-see*] surrender

arrestare *v.* [*ahr-rehs-tah'-reh*] arrest

arresto [*ahr-rehs'-toh*] arrest

arretrato [*ahr-reh-trah'-toh*] backward

arricchire *v.* [*ahr-reek-kee'-reh*] enrich

arrivare *v.* [*ahr-ree-vah'-reh*] arrive

    Arrivederci! [*ahr-ree-veh-dehr'-chee*] Goodbye! [familiar form]

    Arrivederla! [*ahr-ree-veh-dehr'-lah*] Goodbye! [polite form]

arrivo [*ahr-ree'-voh*] arrival

arroganza [*ahr-roh-gahn'-tsah*] arrogance

arrossire v. [ahr-rohs-see'-reh] blush
arrostire v. [ahr-rohs-tee'-reh] roast, broil
arrostito [ahr-rohs-tee'-toh] roasted, broiled
arrosto [ahr-rohs'-toh] roast
arrugginito [ahr-rooj-jee-nee'-toh] rusted
arruolare v. [ahr-roo-oh-lah'-reh] enroll
arte f. [ahr'-teh] art
  le belle arti [leh behl'-leh ahr'-tee] the fine arts
arteria [ahr-teh'-ree-ah] artery
articolo [ahr-tee'-koh-loh] item [of things], article
artificiale [ahr-tee-fee-chee-ah'-leh] artificial
artificialmente [ahr-tee-fee-chee-ahl-mehn'-teh] artificially
artigiano [ahr-tee-jee-ah'-noh] craftsman
artista m., f. [ahr-tees'-tah] artist
artistico [ahr-tees'-tee-koh] artistic
arto [ahr'-toh] limb
ascensore m. [ah-shehn-soh'-reh] elevator
ascesso [ah-shehs'-soh] abscess
asciugamano [ah-shee-oo-gah-mah'-noh] towel
asciugare v. [ah-shee-oo-gah'-reh] dry
asciutto [ah-shee-oot'-toh] dry
ascoltare v. [ahs-kohl-tah'-reh] listen
Asia [ah'-zee-ah] Asia
asiatico [ah-zee-ah'-tee-koh] Asiatic
asilo [ah-zee'-loh] asylum
asino [ah'-zee-noh] donkey
asparagi m. pl. [ahs-pah'-rah-jee] asparagus
aspettare v. [ahs-peht-tah'-reh] expect, wait
  Aspetti un momento [ahs-peht'-tee oon moh-mehn'-toh]
    Wait a moment
  Mi aspetti [mee ahs-peht'-tee] Wait for me
aspetto [ahs-peht'-toh] aspect, looks
  bell'aspetto [behl-lahs-peht'-toh] good looks
aspirapolvere m. [ahs-pee-rah-pohl'-veh-reh] vacuum cleaner
aspirare v. [ahs-pee-rah'-reh] aspire
aspirazione f. [ahs-pee-rah-tsee-oh'-neh] aspiration
aspirina [ahs-pee-ree'-nah] aspirin
aspro [ahs'-proh] harsh
assaggiare v. [ahs-sahj-jee-ah'-reh] taste
assai [ahs-sah'-ee] quite, very much

assalire v. [*ahs-sah-lee'-reh*] assault
assalto [*ahs-sahl'-toh*] assault
assassinare v. [*ahs-sahs-see-nah'-reh*] murder
assassinio [*ahs-sahs-see'-nee-oh*] murder
assassino [*ahs-sahs-see'-noh*] murderer
assedio [*ahs-seh'-dee-oh*] siege
assegnare v. [*ahs-seh-nyah'-reh*] assign
assegno [*ahs-seh'-nyoh*] check [bank]
  assegno fisso [*ahs-seh'-nyoh fees'-soh*] allowance
  assegno turistico [*ahs-seh'-nyoh too-rees'-tee-koh*] traveler's
    check
assemblea [*ahs-sehm-bleh'-ah*] assembly
assente [*ahs-sehn'-teh*] absent
assenza [*ahs-sehn'-tsah*] absence
assetato [*ahs-seh-tah'-toh*] thirsty
assicurare v. [*ahs-see-koo-rah'-reh*] assure, insure, secure
assicurazione f. [*ahs-see-koo-rah-tsee-oh'-neh*] assurance,
    insurance
assistente [*ahs-sees-tehn'-teh*] assistant
assistere v. [*ahs-sees'-teh-reh*] assist
  assistere a [*ahs-sees'-teh-reh ah*] attend to
asso [*ahs'-soh*] ace, champion
associare v. [*ahs-soh-chee-ah'-reh*] associate
associazione f. [*ahs-soh-chee-ah-tsee-oh'-neh*] association
assolutamente [*ahs-soh-loo-tah-mehn'-teh*] absolutely
assoluto [*ahs-soh-loo'-toh*] absolute
assolvere v. [*ahs-sohl'-veh-reh*] acquit
assorbente [*ahs-sohr-behn'-teh*] absorbent
assorbire v. [*ahs-sohr-bee'-reh*] absorb
assortimento [*ahs-sohr-tee-mehn'-toh*] assortment, set
assumere v. [*ahs-soo'-meh-reh*] assume, appoint
assunzione [*ahs-soon-tsee-oh'-neh*] assumption
assurdo [*ahs-soor'-doh*] absurd
asta [*ahs'-tah*] auction; lance, pole
astratto [*ahs-traht'-toh*] abstract
astrazione f. [*ahs-trah-tsee-oh'-neh*] abstraction
astronomia [*ahs-troh-noh-mee'-ah*] astronomy
astuto [*ahs-too'-toh*] cunning
Atlantico [*aht-lahn'-tee-koh*] Atlantic
atletica [*aht-leh'-tee-kah*] athletics

atmosfera [*aht-mohs-feh'-rah*] atmosphere
atomico [*ah-toh'-mee-koh*] atomic
atroce [*ah-troh'-cheh*] terrible, outrageous
attaccapanni *m. pl.* [*aht-tahk-kah-pahn'-nee*] hanger [clothes]
attaccare *v.* [*aht-tahk-kah'-reh*] attack, attach
attacco [*aht-tahk'-koh*] attack
atteggiamento [*aht-tehj-jee-ah-mehn'-toh*] attitude
attendere *v.* [*aht-tehn'-deh-reh*] attend, await
attentamente [*aht-tehn-tah-mehn'-teh*] carefully
attento [*aht-tehn'-toh*] attentive, careful
  Attento! [*aht-tehn'-toh*] Watch out!
attenzione *f.* [*aht-tehn-tsee-oh'-neh*] attention
  Attenzione! [*aht-tehn-tsee-oh'-neh*] Caution!
  fare *v.* **attenzione** [*fah'-reh aht-tehn-tsee-oh'-neh*] beware
  Faccia attenzione! [*fahch'-chee-ah aht-tehn-tsee-oh'-neh*]
    Be careful!
atterraggio [*aht-tehr-rahj'-jee-oh*] landing [of airplane]
atterrare *v.* [*aht-tehr-rah'-reh*] land [an airplane]
attesa [*aht-teh'-zah*] wait, waiting
attiguo [*aht-tee'-goo-oh*] adjoining
attimo [*aht'-tee-moh*] instant, moment
attività *f. indecl.* [*aht-tee-vee-tah'*] activity
attivo [*aht-tee'-voh*] active
atto [*aht'-toh*] act, action; document
  atto di nascita [*aht'-toh dee nah'-shee-tah*] birth certificate
attore *m.*, **attrice** *f.* [*aht-toh'-reh, aht-tree'-cheh*] actor, actress
attraente [*aht-trah-ehn'-teh*] attractive
attrarre *v. irreg.* [*aht-trahr'-reh*] attract
attraversare *v.* [*aht-trah-vehr-sah'-reh*] cross
attraverso [*aht-trah-vehr'-soh*] across, through
attuale [*aht-too-ah'-leh*] actual
attualmente [*aht-too-ahl-mehn'-teh*] actually
augurare *v.* [*ah-oo-goo-rah'-reh*] wish
  Auguri! [*ah-oo-goo'-ree*] Best wishes!
aula [*ah'-oo-lah*] classroom, hall
aumentare *v.* [*ah-oo-mehn-tah'-reh*] increase
aumento [*ah-oo-mehn'-toh*] increase
aurora [*ah-oo-roh'-rah*] dawn
Australia [*ah-oos-trah'-lee-ah*] Australia
australiano [*ah-oos-trah-lee-ah'-noh*] Australian

Austria [*ah'-oos-tree-ah*] Austria

austriaco [*ah-oos-tree'-ah-koh*] Austrian

autentico [*ah-oo-tehn'-tee-koh*] authentic

autista *m.* [*ah-oo-tees'-tah*] driver

autobus *m.* [*ah-oo'-toh-boos*] bus

automatico [*ah-oo-toh-mah'-tee-koh*] automatic

automobile *f.* [*ah-oo-toh-moh'-bee-leh*] automobile, car

autonomia [*ah-oo-toh-noh-mee'-ah*] autonomy

autore *m.*, **autrice** *f.* [*ah-oo-toh'-reh, ah-oo-tree'-cheh*]
    author

autorimessa [*ah-oo-toh-ree-mehs'-sah*] garage

autorità *f. indecl.* [*ah-oo-toh-ree-tah'*] authority

autorizzare *v.* [*ah-oo-toh-reedz-dzah'-reh*] authorize

autostop [*ah'-oo-toh-stohp*] hitchhiking

autostrada [*ah-oo-toh-strah'-dah*] roadway, highway

autunno [*ah-oo-toon'-noh*] autumn

avanti [*ah-vahn'-tee*] ahead, before

   Avanti! [*ah-vahn'-tee*] Come in!

   da ora in avanti [*dah oh'-rah een ah-vahn'-tee*] from this
      time on

   Vada avanti! [*vah'-dah ah-vahn'-tee*] Go ahead [in front]!

   avanti e dietro [*ah-vahn'-tee eh dee-eh'-troh*] to and fro

avanzamento [*ah-vahn-tsah-mehn'-toh*] advancement

avanzare *v.* [*ah-vahn-tsah'-reh*] advance

avarizia [*ah-vah-ree'-tsee-ah*] greediness

avaro [*ah-vah'-roh*] miser, stingy

avere *v. irreg.* [*ah-veh'-reh*] have

   Che cosa ha? [*keh koh'-zah ah*] What's up?

avido [*ah'-vee-doh*] eager, greedy

avorio [*ah-voh'-ree-oh*] ivory

avvenimento [*ahv-veh-nee-mehn'-toh*] event, occurrence

avvenire *v.* [*ahv-veh-nee'-reh*] happen

avvenire *m.* [*ahv-veh-nee'-reh*] future

   in avvenire [*een ahv-veh-nee'-reh*] in the future

avventura [*ahv-vehn-too'-rah*] adventure

avventuriero [*ahv-vehn-too-ree-eh'-roh*] adventurer

avverbio [*ahv-vehr'-bee-oh*] adverb

avversario [*ahv-vehr-sah'-ree-oh*] adversary

avvertimento [*ahv-vehr-tee-mehn'-toh*] warning

avvertire *v.* [*ahv-vehr-tee'-reh*] warn

avvicinare *v.* [*ahv-vee-chee-nah'-reh*] approach
avvisare *v.* [*ahv-vee-zah'-reh*] inform
avviso [*ahv-vee'-zoh*] notice
  a mio avviso [*ah mee'-oh ahv-vee'-zoh*] in my opinion
  avviso pubblicitario [*ahv-vee'-zoh poo-blee-chee-tah'-ree-oh*]
    poster, advertisement
avvocato [*ahv-voh-kah'-toh*] lawyer, attorney
avvolgere *v.* [*ahv-vohl'-jeh-reh*] wrap up, roll
azienda [*ah-dzee-ehn'-dah*] business, firm
azione *f.* [*ah-tsee-oh'-neh*] action, deed
azioni *f. pl.* [*ah-tsee-oh'-nee*] stocks, shares
azzardo [*ahdz-dzahr'-doh*] hazard
  gioco d'azzardo [*jee-oh'-koh dahdz-dzahr'-doh*] gambling
azzurro [*ahdz-dzoor'-roh*] azure, light blue

B

baciare *v.* [*bah-chee-ah'-reh*] kiss
bacio [*bah'-chee-oh*] kiss
badare a *v.* [*bah-dah'-reh ah*] mind
baffi *m. pl.* [*bahf'-fee*] moustache
bagaglio [*bah-gah'-lyoh*] luggage
  ufficio-bagagli [*oof-fee'-chee-oh bah-gah'-lyee*] luggage
    counter
bagnarsi *v.* [*bah-nyahr'-see*] get wet, bathe
bagnato [*bah-nyah'-toh*] wet
bagnino [*bah-nyee'-noh*] lifeguard
bagno [*bah'-nyoh*] bath
  costume *m.* **da bagno** [*kohs-too'-meh dah bah'-nyoh*]
    bathing suit
  fare *v.* **il bagno** [*fah'-reh eel bah'-nyoh*] take a bath
  stanza da bagno [*stahn'-tsah dah bah'-nyoh*] bathroom
  vasca da bagno [*vahs'-kah da bah'-nyoh*] bathtub
baia [*bah'-ee-ah*] bay
balcone [*bahl-koh'-neh*] balcony
balena [*bah-leh'-nah*] whale
balia [*bah'-lee-ah*] nurse [for babies]

ballare v. [bahl-lah'-reh] dance
ballerino [bahl-leh-ree'-noh] dancer
balletto [bahl-leht'-toh] ballet
ballo [bahl'-loh] dance
bambinaia [bahm-bee-nah'-ee-ah] nursemaid
bambino [bahm-bee'-noh] child
bambola [bahm'-boh-lah] doll
banana [bah-nah'-nah] banana
banca [bahn'-kah] bank
banchetto [bahn-keht'-toh] banquet
banchiere m. [bahn-kee-eh'-reh] banker
banchina [bahn-kee'-nah] quay, dock
banco [bahn'-koh] bench
banconota [bahn-koh-noh'-tah] bank note
banda [bahn'-dah] band, gang
bandiera [bahn-dee-eh'-rah] flag
bandito [bahn-dee'-toh] bandit
barba [bahr'-bah] beard
  crema da barba [kreh'-mah dah bahr'-bah] shaving cream
  farsi v. **la barba** [fahr'-see lah bahr'-bah] shave
  pennello da barba [pehn-nehl'-loh dah bahr'-bah] shaving
    brush
barbiere m. [bahr-bee-eh'-reh] barber
barca [bahr'-kah] boat
  barca da pesca [bahr'-kah dah pehs'-kah] fishing boat
  barca a vela [bahr'-kah ah veh'-lah] sailboat
barco [bahr'-koh] rowboat
barile m. [bah-ree'-leh] barrel
barone m., **baronessa** [bah-roh'-neh, bah-roh-nehs'-sah]
  baron, baroness
barzelletta [bahr-dzehl-leht'-tah] joke
base f. [bah'-zeh] base
basico [bah'-zee-koh] basic
bassifondi m. pl. [bahs-see-fohn'-dee] gutter
basso [bahs'-soh] low, short
  in basso [een bahs'-soh] down
bastare v. [bahs-tah'-reh] suffice
  Basta! [bahs'-tah] That's enough!
bastone [bahs-toh'-neh] cane, stick
battaglia [baht-tah'-lyah] battle

battello [*baht-tehl'-loh*] boat, skiff
   battello a vapore [*baht-tehl'-loh ah vah-poh'-reh*] steamboat
battere v. [*baht'-teh-reh*] beat, hit; vanquish, overcome
batteria [*baht-teh-ree'-ah*] battery
battesimo [*baht-teh'-zee-moh*] baptism
  nome m. **di battesimo** [*noh'-meh dee baht-teh'-zee-moh*]
    Christian name
battezzare v. [*baht-tehdz-dzah'-reh*] baptize
battito [*baht'-tee-toh*] beat, pulse
battuta [*baht-too'-tah*] beating, beat
battuto [*baht-too'-toh*] beaten
baule m. [*bah-oo'-leh*] trunk
becco [*behk'-koh*] beak
belga [*behl'-gah*] Belgian
Belgio [*behl'-jee-oh*] Belgium
bellezza [*behl-lehts'-tsah*] beauty
bello [*behl'-loh*] good looking, beautiful
belva [*behl'-vah*] wild beast
benchè [*behn-keh'*] although
benda [*behn'-dah*] band, bandage
bene [*beh'-neh*] well, good
  Bene! [*beh'-neh*] Fine!
  abbastanza bene [*ahb-bahs-tahn'-tsah beh'-neh*] fairly well
  stare v. **bene** [*stah'-reh beh'-neh*] be well
  Va bene! [*vah beh'-neh*] All right!
benedire v. [*beh-neh-dee'-reh*] bless
benedizione f. [*beh-neh-dee-tsee-oh'-neh*] blessing
beneficenza [*beh-neh-fee-chehn'-tsah*] charity
beneficio [*beh-neh-fee'-chee-oh*] advantage, benefit
benessere m. [*behn-ehs'-seh-reh*] welfare, comfort
benestante [*beh-neh-stahn'-teh*] well-off
beni m. pl. [*beh'-nee*] property
  beni immobili [*beh'-nee eem-moh'-bee-lee*] real estate
benissimo [*beh-nees'-see-moh*] very well
benvenuto [*behn-veh-noo'-toh*] welcome
  dare v. **il benvenuto** [*dah'-reh eel behn-veh-noo'-toh*]
    welcome
benzina [*behn-dzee'-nah*] gasoline
  pompa di benzina [*pohm'-pah dee behn-dzee'-nah*]
    gasoline station

bere v. irreg. [_beh'-reh_] drink

berretto [_behr-reht'-toh_] cap

bersaglio [_behr-sah'-lyoh_] target

bestemmiare v. [_behs-tehm-mee-ah'-reh_] swear

bestia [_behs'-tee-ah_] beast

bestiame m. [_behs-tee-ah'-meh_] cattle

bevanda [_beh-vahn'-dah_] drink

biancheria [_bee-ahn-keh-ree'-ah_] linen

bianco [_bee-ahn'-koh_] white

  in bianco [_een bee-ahn'-koh_] blank

Bibbia [_beeb'-bee-ah_] Bible

biberon m. [_bee-beh-rohn'_] baby bottle

bibita [_bee'-bee-tah_] drink

biblioteca [_bee-blee-oh-teh'-kah_] library

bicchiere m. [_beek-kee-eh'-reh_] glass [for drinking]

bicicletta [_bee-chee-kleht'-tah_] bicycle

  andare v. **in bicicletta** [_ahn-dah'-reh een bee-chee-kleht'-tah_] ride a bicycle

biglietteria [_bee-lyeht-teh-ree'-ah_] ticket office

biglietto [_bee-lyeht'-toh_] ticket

  biglietto da visita [_bee-lyeht'-toh dah vee'-zee-tah_] calling card

  bigietto di andata e ritorno [_bee-lyeht'-toh dee ahn-dah'-tah eh ree-tohr'-noh_] round trip ticket

bilancia [_bee-lahn'-chee-ah_] balance

bilancio [_bee-lahn'-chee-oh_] budget

bimbo [_beem'-boh_] baby

binario [_bee-nah'-ree-oh_] track [for a train]

biondo [_bee-ohn'-doh_] blond

birra [_beer'-rah_] beer, ale

biscotto [_bees-koht'-toh_] biscuit

bisogno [_bee-zoh'-nyoh_] need

  aver v. **bisogno** [_ah-vehr' bee-zoh'-nyoh_] need

bistecca [_bees-tehk'-kah_] steak

blu [_bloo_] blue

blusa [_bloo'-zah_] blouse

bocca [_bohk'-kah_] mouth

  In bocca al lupo! [_een bohk'-kah ahl loo'-poh_] Good luck!

boccone m. [_bohk-koh'-neh_] mouthful

bolla [_bohl'-lah_] blister

bollettino [*bohl-leht-tee'-noh*] bulletin
bollire *v.* [*bohl-lee'-reh*] boil
bollo [*bohl'-loh*] stamp, seal
bomba [*bohm'-bah*] bomb
bontà *f. indecl.* [*bohn-tah'*] goodness
bordo [*bohr'-doh*] edge, limit
  a bordo [*ah bohr'-doh*] aboard
borghese [*bohr-geh'-zeh*] civilian
borghesia [*bohr-geh-zee'-ah*] bourgeoisie
borsa [*bohr'-sah*] purse, bag
  borsa di studio [*bohr'-sah dee stoo'-dee-oh*] scholarship
  borsa valori [*bohr'-sah vah-loh'-ree*] stock exchange
borsaiuolo [*bohr-sah-ee-oh'-loh*] pickpocket
bosco [*bohs'-koh*] woods
bottiglia [*boht-tee'-lyah*] bottle
bottino [*boht-tee'-noh*] booty
bottone *m.* [*boht-toh'-neh*] button
braccialetto [*brahch-chee-ah-leht'-toh*] bracelet
braccio, le braccia *pl.* [*brahch'-chee-oh, leh brahch'-chee-ah*]
    arm [of body]
branda [*brahn'-dah*] cot
Brasile *m.* [*brah-zee'-leh*] Brazil
brasiliano [*brah-zee-lee-ah'-noh*] Brazilian
bravo [*brah'-voh*] nice, good-natured
  Bravo! [*brah'-voh*] Magnificent!
breve [*breh'-veh*] brief
  in breve [*een breh'-veh*] in short
  tra breve [*trah breh'-veh*] in a short time
brevetto [*breh-veht'-toh*] patent
brezza [*brehts'-tsah*] breeze
briciola [*bree'-chee-oh-lah*] crumb
brigante [*bree-gahn'-teh*] brigand
brillante [*breel-lahn'-teh*] bright, brilliant
brillare *v.* [*breel-lah'-reh*] shine [sun]
brina [*bree'-nah*] frost
brindare *v.* [*breen-dah'-reh*] toast [to one's health]
brindisi *m.* [*breen'-dee-zee*] toast [to one's health]
brio [*bree'-oh*] humor, fine spirits
brivido [*bree'-vee-doh*] shiver
brocca [*brohk'-kah*] jug

brodo di carne [_broh'-doh dee kahr'-neh_] broth

brontolio [_brohn-toh-lee'-oh_] grumble

bronzo [_brohn'-tsoh_] bronze

bruciare _v._ [_broo-chee-ah'-reh_] burn

bruciatura [_broo-chee-ah-too'-rah_] burn

  bruciatura di sole [_broo-chee-ah-too'-rah dee soh'-leh_] sunburn

brunetta [_broo-neht'-tah_] brunette

bruno [_broo'-noh_] brunette, dark

brutale [_broo-tah'-leh_] brutal

brutto [_broot'-toh_] ugly

buca (delle lettere) [_boo'-kah (dehl'-leh leht'-teh-reh)_] (letter) box

bucare _v._ [_boo-kah'-reh_] pierce

bucato [_boo-kah'-reh_] washing [of linen]

buccia [_booch'-chee-ah_] peel, skin

buco [_boo'-koh_] hole

bue _m._ **buoi** _pl._ [_boo'-eh, boo-oh'-ee_] ox

  carne _f._ **di bue** [_kahr'-neh dee boo'-eh_] beef

bufera (di neve) [_boo-feh'-rah (dee neh'-veh)_] (snow)storm

buffo [_boof'-foh_] funny

bugia [_boo-jee'-ah_] lie

bugiardo [_boo-jee-ahr'-doh_] liar

buio [_boo'-ee-oh_] dark [not clear]

  al buio [_ahl boo'-ee-oh_] in the dark

bulbo [_bool'-boh_] eyeball

Bulgaria [_bool-gah-ree'-ah_] Bulgaria

bulgaro [_bool'-gah-roh_] Bulgarian

buongustaio [_boo-ohn-goos-tah'-ee-oh_] connoisseur [of food, drink]

buono [_boo-oh'-noh_] good, nice

  buona fortuna [_boo-oh'-na fohr-too'-nah_] good luck

  buon giorno [_boo-ohn' jee-ohr'-noh_] good day, good morning

  buona notte [_boo-oh'-nah noht'-teh_] good night

  buon pomeriggio [_boo-ohn' poh-meh-reej'-jee-oh_] good afternoon

  buona sera [_boo-oh'-nah seh'-rah_] good evening

buontempone _m._ [_boo-ohn-tehm-poh'-neh_] jolly fellow

burla [_boor'-lah_] jest, trick

burocrazia [*boo-roh-krah-tsee'-ah*] red tape
burrasca [*boor-rahs'-kah*] tornado
burro [*boor'-roh*] butter
bussare *v.* [*boos-sah'-reh*] knock
bussata [*boos-sah'-tah*] knock
bussola [*boos'-soh-lah*] compass
busta [*boos'-tah*] envelope
busto [*boos'-toh*] bust, corset
buttare *v.* [*boot-tah'-reh*] throw
   buttar via [*boot-tahr' vee'-ah*] throw away

C

cabina [*kah-bee'-nah*] cabin, booth
   cabina telefonica [*kah-bee'-nah teh-leh-foh'-nee-kah*]
     telephone booth
cablogramma *m.* [*kah-bloh-grahm'-mah*] cable
cacao [*kah-kah'-oh*] cocoa
caccia [*kahch'-chee-ah*] hunting
cacciare *v.* [*kahch-chee-ah'-reh*] chase, hunt
cacciatore *m.* [*kahch-chee-ah-toh'-reh*] hunter
cacciavite *m.* [*kahch-chee-ah-vee'-teh*] screwdriver
cadavere [*kah-dah'-veh-reh*] corpse
cadere *v. irreg.* [*kah-deh'-reh*] fall
   lasciar cadere [*lah-shee-ahr' kah-deh'-reh*] drop
caduta [*kah-doo'-tah*] fall, collapse
caduto [*kah-doo'-toh*] fallen
caffè *m.* [*kahf-feh'*] cafè, coffeehouse, coffee
calcagno [*kahl-kah'-nyoh*] heel [of foot]
calcio [*kahl'-chee-oh*] football
calcolare *v.* [*kahl-koh-lah'-reh*] calculate
calcolo [*kahl'-koh-loh*] calculation
caldo *n.* [*kahl'-doh*] heat
caldo *adj.* [*kahl'-doh*] warm, hot
   Fa caldo [*fah kahl'-doh*] It is hot [weather]
   avere *v.* **caldo** [*ah-veh'-reh kahl'-doh*] be warm [for
     persons]

calendario [*kah-lehn-dah'-ree-oh*] calendar
calma [*kahl'-mah*] calmness
  Con calma! [*kohn kahl'-mah*] Take it easy!
calmante *m. & adj.* [*kahl-mahn'-teh*] sedative
calmare *v.* [*kahl-mah'-reh*] calm
calmo [*kahl'-moh*] calm, quiet
  Stia calmo! [*stee'-ah kahl'-moh*] Be quiet! [to one person]
calore *m.* [*kah-loh'-reh*] heat, warmth
calorifero [*kah-loh-ree'-feh-roh*] heater
calunnia [*kah-loon'-nee-ah*] slander
calunniare *v.* [*kah-loon-nee-ah'-reh*] slander
calvo [*kahl'-voh*] bald
calza [*kahl'-tsah*] stocking
calzino [*kahl-tsee'-noh*] sock
calzolaio [*kahl-tsoh-lah'-ee-oh*] shoemaker
calzoleria [*kahl-tsoh-leh-ree'-ah*] shoe store
calzoni [*kahl-tsoh'-nee*] pants
cambiale *f.* [*kahm-bee-ah'-leh*] draft [commercial]
cambiamento [*kahm-bee-ah-mehn'-toh*] change
cambiare *v.* [*kahm-bee-ah'-reh*] change, shift
  cambiare idea [*kahm-bee-ah'-reh ee-deh'-ah*] change one's
  mind
cambio [*kahm'-bee-oh*] change, exchange
  corso del cambio [*kohr'-soh dehl kahm'-bee-oh*] rate of
  exchange
  in cambio di [*een kahm'-bee-oh dee*] in exchange for
camera [*kah'-meh-rah*] room
  camera da affittare [*kah'-meh-rah dah ahf-fee-tah'-reh*]
  furnished room
  camera da letto [*kah'-meh-rah dah leht'-toh*] bedroom
  camera d'albergo [*kah'-meh-rah dahl-behr'-goh*] hotel
  room
cameriera, cameriere *m.* [*kah-meh-ree-eh'-rah, kah-meh-ree-eh'-reh*] maid, waitress, waiter
  cameriera d'albergo [*kah-meh-ree-eh'-rah dahl-behr'-goh*]
  chambermaid
  cameriera di bordo [*kah-meh-ree-eh'-rah dee bohr'-doh*]
  stewardess
  cameriere di bordo [*kah-meh-ree-eh'-reh dee bohr'-doh*]
  steward

camicia [*kah-mee'-chee-ah*] shirt
camino [*kah-mee'-noh*] chimney
camion *m.* [*kah-mee-ohn'*] truck
camminare *v.* [*kahm-mee-nah'-reh*] walk
cammino [*kahm-mee'-noh*] way, road, walk
campagna [*kahm-pah'-nyah*] countryside
campana, campanello [*kahm-pah'-nah, kahm-pah-nehl'-loh*] bell
campeggio [*kahm-pehj'-jee-oh*] camping
campione *m.*, **campionessa** [*kahm-pee-oh'-neh, kahm-pee-oh-nehs'-sah*] sample, champion
campo [*kahm'-poh*] camp, field
Canada *m.* [*kah'-nah-dah*] Canada
canadese [*kah-nah-deh'-zeh*] Canadian
canale *m.* [*kah-nah'-leh*] canal, channel
canarino [*kah-nah-ree'-noh*] canary
cancellare *v.* [*kahn-chehl-lah'-reh*] erase, cancel
cancello [*kahn-chehl'-loh*] gate
cancro [*kahn'-kroh*] cancer
candela [*kahn-deh'-lah*] candle
   candela d'accensione [*kahn-deh'-lah dahch-chehn-see-oh'-neh*] spark plug
candelabro [*kahn-deh-lah'-broh*] candlestick
candidato [*kahn-dee-dah'-toh*] candidate
cane *m.* [*kah'-neh*] dog
cannocchiali [*kahn-nohk-kee-ah'-lee*] field glasses
cannone *m.* [*kahn-noh'-neh*] gun, cannon
canottaggio [*kah-noht-tahj'-jee-oh*] boating
cantante *m., f.* [*kahn-tahn'-teh*] singer
cantare *v.* [*kahn-tah'-reh*] sing
cantina [*kahn-tee'-nah*] cellar
canzone *f.* [*kahn-tsoh'-neh*] song
capace [*kah-pah'-cheh*] able, capable
capacità *f. indecl.* [*kah-pah-chee-tah'*] capacity
capella [*kah-pehl'-lah*] chapel
capello, capelli [*kah-pehl'-loh, kah-pehl'-lee*] hair
   taglio di capelli [*tah'-lyoh dee kah-pehl'-lee*] haircut
capezzolo [*kah-pehts'-tsoh-loh*] nipple
capire *v.* [*kah-pee'-reh*] understand
   Capite? [*kah-pee'-teh*] Do you understand?

Non capisco [*nohn kah-pees'-koh*] I don't understand

capire male [*kah-pee'-reh mah'-leh*] be mistaken, misunderstand

capitale *m.* [*kah-pee-tah'-leh*] capital [money]

capitale *f.* [*kah-pee-tah'-leh*] capital [city]

capitano [*kah-pee-tah'-noh*] captain

capitolo [*kah-pee'-toh-loh*] chapter

capo [*kah'-poh*] head, chief, leader

da capo [*dah kah'-poh*] again

capodanno [*kah-poh-dahn'-noh*] New Year's Day

Buon capodanno [*boo-ohn' kah-poh-dahn'-noh*] Happy New Year

capolavoro [*kah-poh-lah-voh'-roh*] masterpiece

capolinea [*kah-poh-lee'-neh-ah*] terminal [bus, train]

capovolgere *v.* [*kah-poh-vohl'-jeh-reh*] overturn

capovolto [*kah-poh-vohl'-toh*] upside down

cappello [*kahp-pehl'-loh*] hat

cappotto [*kahp-poht'-toh*] overcoat

cappuccino [*kahp-pooch-chee'-noh*] capuchin [friar]

capriccio [*kah-preech'-chee-oh*] caprice, fancy

caramella [*kah-rah-mehl'-lah*] candy

caramente [*kah-rah-mehn'-teh*] dearly

carattere *m.* [*kah-raht'-teh-reh*] character

caratteristica [*kah-raht-teh-rees'-tee-kah*] trait

caratteristico [*kah-raht-teh-rees'-tee-koh*] characteristic

carbone *m.* [*kahr-boh'-neh*] charcoal

carburante *m.* [*kahr-boo-rahn'-teh*] gas, fuel

carcere *m.* [*kahr'-cheh-reh*] jail

cardinale *m.* [*kahr-dee-nah'-leh*] cardinal

carezza [*kah-rehts'-tsah*] caress

carezzare *v.* [*kah-rets-tsah'-reh*] caress

carica [*kah'-ree-kah*] charge, office

caricare *v.* [*kah-ree-kah'-reh*] load, wind [a watch]

caricatura [*kah-ree-kah-too'-rah*] cartoon

carico [*kah'-ree-koh*] load, burden, freight

carino [*kah-ree'-noh*] nice, dear, pretty

carità *f. indef.* [*kah-ree-tah'*] charity

Per carità! [*pehr kah-ree-tah'*] For pity's sake!

carnagione *f.* [*kahr-nah-jee-oh'-neh*] complexion

carne *f.* [*kahr'-neh*] meat, flesh

carnevale *m.* [*kahr-neh-vah'-leh*] carnival

caro [*kah'-roh*] dear, darling, expensive

carota [*kah-roh'-tah*] carrot

carpentiere *m.* [*kahr-pehn-tee-eh'-reh*] carpenter

carriera [*kahr-ree-eh'-rah*] career

carro [*kahr'-roh*] truck, cart

carrozza [*kahr-rohts'-tsah*] carriage

carta [*kahr'-tah*] paper

  carta carbone [*kahr'-tah kahr-boh'-neh*] carbon paper

  carta geografica [*kahr'-tah jeh-oh-grah'-fee-kah*] map

  carta igienica [*kahr'-tah ee-jee-eh'-nee-kah*] toilet paper

  carte da giuoco [*kahr'-teh dah jee-oh'-koh*] playing cards

  mazzo di carte [*mahts'-tsoh dee kahr'-teh*] pack of cards

  carta da scrivere [*kahr'-tah dah skree'-veh-reh*] writing paper

  carta velina [*kahr'-tah veh-lee'-nah*] tissue paper

cartellone *m.* [*kahr-tehl-loh'-neh*] sign [street]

cartoleria [*kahr-toh-leh-ree'-ah*] stationery

cartolina [*kahr-toh-lee'-nah*] card

  cartolina di natale [*kahr-toh-lee'-nah dee nah-tah'-leh*] Christmas card

  cartolina postale [*kahr-toh-lee'-nah pohs-tah'-leh*] postcard

  cartolina vaglia [*kahr-toh-lee'-nah vah'-lyah*] money order

cartone *m.* [*kahr-toh'-neh*] cardboard

casa [*kah'-zah*] home, house

  casa di campagna [*kah'-zah dee kahm-pah'-nyah*] cottage

cascata [*kahs-kah'-tah*] waterfall

casella postale [*kah-zehl'-lah pohs-tah'-leh*] post-office box

caso [*kah'-zoh*] case, chance

  in tal caso [*een tahl kah'-zoh*] in that case

  nel caso che [*nehl kah'-zoh keh*] in the event of

  per caso [*pehr kah'-zoh*] by chance

  per puro caso [*pehr poo'-roh kah'-zoh*] by mere chance

cassa [*kahs'-sah*] case

cassetto [*kahs-seht'-toh*] drawer

cassettone *m.* [*kahs-seht-toh'-neh*] chest of drawers

cassiere *m.* [*kahs-see-eh'-reh*] cashier

castagna [*kahs-tah'-nyah*] chestnut

castello [*kahs-tehl'-loh*] castle

casualmente [*kah-zoo-ahl-mehn'-teh*] casually

catalogo [*kah-tah'-loh-goh*] catalog
categoria [*kah-teh-goh-ree'-ah*] category
catena [*kah-teh'-nah*] chain
cattedrale [*kaht-teh-drah'-leh*] cathedral
cattiveria [*kaht-tee-veh'-ree-ah*] mischief
cattivo [*kaht-tee'-voh*] bad, evil
    più cattivo, il più cattivo [*pee-oo' kaht-tee'-voh, eel pee-oo' kaht-tee'-voh*] worse, worst
cattolico [*kaht-toh'-lee-koh*] catholic
causa [*kah'-oo-zah*] cause
    a causa di . . . [*ah kah'-oo-zah dee*] due to . . .
causare v. [*kah-oo-zah'-reh*] cause
cavalcare v. [*kah-vahl-kah'-reh*] ride a horse
cavaliere m. [*kah-vah-lee-eh'-reh*] knight
cavalleria [*kah-vahl-leh-ree'-ah*] cavalry
cavallo [*kah-vahl'-loh*] horse
    andare v. **a cavallo** [*ahn-dah'-reh ah kah-vahl'-loh*] go horseback riding
cavatappi m. sing. [*kah-vah-tahp'-pee*] corkscrew
caverna [*kah-vehr'-nah*] cave
caviglia [*kah-vee'-lyah*] ankle
cavità f. indecl. [*kah-vee-tah'*] cavity
cavo [*kah'-voh*] cable
cavolfiore m. [*kah-vohl-fee-oh'-reh*] cauliflower
cavolo [*kah'-voh-loh*] cabbage
c'e, ci sono [*cheh, chee soh'-noh*] there is, there are
Cecoslovacchia [*cheh-kohs-loh-vahk'-kee-ah*] Czechoslovakia
cecoslovacco [*cheh-koh-sloh-vahk'-koh*] Czechoslovak
cedere v. [*cheh'-deh-reh*] give up
celebrare v. [*cheh-leh-brah'-reh*] celebrate
celebrità f. indecl. [*cheh-leh-bree-tah'*] celebrity
celibe [*cheh'-lee-beh*] single, bachelor
cella [*chehl'-lah*] cell
cementare v. [*cheh-mehn-tah'-reh*] cement
cemento [*cheh-mehn'-toh*] cement
cena [*cheh'-nah*] dinner, supper
cenare v. [*cheh-nah'-reh*] have supper, dinner
cenere f. [*cheh'-neh-reh*] ash
cenno [*chehn'-noh*] sign, wave, nod
    fare v. **cenno** [*fah'-reh chehn'-noh*] wave [one's hand]

censura [*chehn-soo'-rah*] censorship

centesimo [*chehn-teh'-zee-moh*] cent

centimetro [*chehn-tee'-meh-troh*] centimeter

cento [*chehn'-toh*] hundred, one hundred

  due cento [*doo'-eh chehn'-toh*] two hundred

centrale [*chehn-trah'-leh*] central

centro [*chehn'-troh*] center

cera [*cheh'-rah*] wax

cercare v. [*chehr-kah'-reh*] search for, seek

cerchio [*chehr'-kee-oh*] circle, ring, hoop

cereale m. [*cheh-reh-ah'-leh*] cereal

cerimonia [*cheh-ree-moh'-nee-ah*] ceremony

cerino [*cheh-ree'-noh*] match [made of wax]

certamente [*chehr-tah-mehn'-teh*] certainly

certificare v. [*chehr-tee-fee-kah'-reh*] certify

certificato [*chehr-tee-fee-kah'-toh*] certificate

  certificato medico [*chehr-tee-fee-kah'-toh meh'-dee-koh*]
    health certificate

certo [*chehr'-toh*] certain

  fino ad un certo punto [*fee'-noh ahd oon chehr'-toh
    poon'-toh*] to a certain extent

cervello [*chehr-vehl'-loh*] brain

cespuglio [*chehs-poo'-lyoh*] bush

cessare v. [*chehs-sah'-reh*] cease

cestino [*chehs-tee'-noh*] wastebasket

cesto [*chehs'-toh*] basket

cetriolo [*cheh-tree-oh'-loh*] cucumber

che pron. [*keh*] what, who, whom, which

  Che altro? [*keh ahl'-troh*] What else?

  Che peccato! [*keh pehk-kah'-toh*] What a pity!

  Che succede? [*keh sooch-cheh'-deh*] What is the matter?

che conj. [*keh*] than, that

chi [*kee*] who, the one who, which, whom

  Chi parla? [*kee pahr'-lah*] Who is talking?

  Di chi è questo? [*dee kee eh' koo-ehs'-toh*] Whose is this?

chiacchierare v. [*chee-ahk-kee-eh-rah'-reh*] chat

chiamare v. [*kee-ah-mah'-reh*] call

  Ci chiamano [*chee kee-ah'-mah-noh*] They call us

chiamarsi v. [*kee-ah-mahr'-see*] be called, be named

  Come si chiama? [*koh'-meh see kee-ah'-mah*] What is your name?

chiamata [*kee-ah-mah'-tah*] call
  chiamata telefonica [*kee-ah-mah'-tah teh-leh-foh'-nee-kah*]
  telephone call
chiaramente [*kee-ah-rah-mehn'-teh*] clearly
chiarire v. [*kee-ah-ree'-reh*] make clear
chiaro [*kee-ah'-roh*] clear
chiave f., [*kee-ah'-veh*] key
chiedere v. [*kee-eh'-deh-reh*] ask [for something]
  chiedere il permesso [*kee-eh'-deh-reh eel pehr-mehs'-soh*]
  ask permission to
  chiedere scusa [*kee-eh'-deh-reh skoo'-zah*] beg pardon
chiesa [*kee-eh'-zah*] church
chilo [*kee'-loh*] kilogram
chilometro [*kee-loh'-meh-troh*] kilometer [0.621 mile]
chimico [*kee'-mee-koh*] chemical
chinino [*kee-nee'-noh*] quinine
chiodo [*kee-oh'-doh*] nail [carpentry]
chirurgia [*kee-roor-jee'-ah*] surgery
chirurgo [*kee-roor'-goh*] surgeon
chitarra [*kee-tahr'-rah*] guitar
chiudere v. [*kee-oo'-deh-reh*] shut, close
  chiudere a chiave [*kee-oo'-deh-reh ah kee-ah'-veh*] lock up
chiunque [*kee-oon'-koo-eh*] whoever, anybody
chiuso [*kee-oo'-zoh*] shut, closed
chiusura [*kee-oo-zoo'-rah*] closing
  chiusura lampo [*kee-oo-zoo'-rah lahm'-poh*] zipper
ci [*chee*] here, there, of it, to it
  ci sono [*chee soh'-noh*] there are
ci [*chee*] us, to us, ourselves
Ciao! [*chee-ah'-oh*] So long!
ciascuno [*chee-ahs-koo'-noh*] each one, everyone
cibo [*chee'-boh*] food
cicatrice f. [*chee-kah-tree'-cheh*] scar
cieco [*chee-eh'-koh*] blind
cielo [*chee-eh'-loh*] sky, heaven
cifra [*chee'-frah*] figure, amount
ciglia f. pl. [*chee'-lyah*] eyelashes
Cile [*chee'-leh*] Chile
cileno [*chee-leh'-noh*] Chilean

ciliegia [*chee-lee-eh'-jee-ah*] cherry
cilindro [*chee-leen'-droh*] cylinder
cima [*chee'-mah*] peak, summit
cimitero [*chee-mee-teh'-roh*] cemetery
Cina [*chee'-nah*] China
cinema, cinematografo [*chee'-neh-mah, chee-neh-mah-toh'-grah-foh*] movies
cinese [*chee-neh'-zeh*] Chinese
cinquanta [*cheen-koo-ahn'-tah*] fifty
cinque [*cheen'-koo-eh*] five
cinquecento [*cheen-koo-eh-chehn'-toh*] five hundred
cintura [*cheen-too'-rah*] belt
ciò [*chee-oh'*] that, that which
cioccolata [*chee-oh-koh-lah'-tah*] chocolate
cioè [*chee-oh-eh'*] namely
ciononostante [*chee-oh-noh-nohs-tahn'-teh*] nonetheless
cipolla [*chee-pohl'-lah*] onion
cipria [*chee'-pree-ah*] powder [cosmetic]
circa [*cheer'-kah*] about
circo [*cheer'-koh*] circus
circolazione *f.* [*cheer-koh-lah-tsee-oh'-neh*] circulation
circolo [*cheer'-koh-loh*] circle, club
circondare *v.* [*cheer-kohn-dah'-reh*] surround
circostanza [*cheer-kohs-tahn'-tsah*] circumstance
citare *v.* [*chee-tah'-reh*] quote
citazione *f.* [*chee-tah-tsee-oh'-neh*] quotation, summons
città *f. indecl.* [*cheet-tah'*] city
cittadina [*cheet-tah-dee'-nah*] town
cittadinanza [*cheet-tah-dee-nahn'-tsah*] citizenship
cittadino [*cheet-tah-dee'-noh*] citizen
civile [*chee-vee'-leh*] civilized, civil
civilizzazione *f.*, **civiltà** *f.*, *indecl.* [*chee-vee-leedz-dza-tsee-oh'-neh, chee-veel-tah'*] civilization
classe *f.* [*klahs'-seh*] class
classico [*klahs'-see-koh*] classic
clero [*kleh'-roh*] clergy
cliente *m.* [*klee-ehn'-teh*] customer
clima *m.* [*klee'-mah*] climate
clinica [*klee'-nee-kah*] clinic
coda [*koh'-dah*] tail

cogliere v. [koh'-lyeh-reh] pick, gather
cognac m. [koh-nyahk'] brandy
cognata [koh-nyah'-tah] sister-in-law
cognato [koh-nyah'-toh] brother-in-law
cognome m. [koh-nyoh'-meh] last name
coincidenza [koh-een-chee-dehn'-tsah] coincidence
colazione f. [koh-lah-tsee-oh'-neh] breakfast
  fare v. **colazione** [fah'-reh koh-lah-tsee-oh'-neh]
    have breakfast
  seconda colazione [seh-kohn'-dah koh-lah-tsee-oh'-neh]
    lunch
colla [kohl'-lah] glue
collana [kohl-lah'-nah] necklace
colle m., **collina** [cohl'-leh, kohl-lee'-nah] hill
collega m., f. [kohl-leh'-gah] colleague
collegamento [kohl-leh-gah-mehn'-toh] connection
collegio [kohl-leh'-jee-oh] boarding school
colletto [kohl-leht'-toh] collar
collo [kohl'-loh] neck
collocare v. [kohl-loh-kah'-reh] place
colmo n. [kohl'-moh] height, summit
colombo [koh-lohm'-boh] pigeon
colonia [koh-loh'-nee-ah] colony
colonna [koh-lohn'-nah] column
colonnello [koh-loh-nehl'-loh] colonel
colorare v. [koh-loh-rah'-reh] color
colore m. [koh-loh'-reh] color, paint
Colosseo [koh-lohs-seh'-oh] Colosseum
colpa [kohl'-pah] guilt, blame, fault
  attribuire n. **la colpa** [aht-tree-boo-ee'-reh lah kohl'-pah]
    blame
  É colpa mia [eh' kohl'-pah mee'-ah] It's my fault
colpevole [kohl-peh'-voh-leh] guilty
colpire [kohl-pee'-reh] strike, hit
colpo [kohl'-poh] stroke, blow, shot
coltello [kohl-tehl'-loh] knife
coltivare [kohl-tee-vah'-reh] cultivate
colto [kohl'-toh] cultivated, learned
comandare v. [koh-mahn-dah'-reh] order [someone]
combattere v. [kohm-baht'-teh-reh] fight

combinazione *f.* [*kohm-bee-nah-tsee-oh'-neh*] combination
combustibile [*kohm-boos-tee'-bee-leh*] fuel
come [*koh'-meh*] as, like, how
  Com'è? [*koh-meh'*] What is he (she, it) like?
  come lui [*koh'-meh loo'-ee*] like him
  Come mai? [*koh'-meh mah'-ee*] How come?, Why?
  come questo [*koh'-meh koo-ehs'-toh*] like this
  proprio come [*proh'-pree-oh koh'-meh*] just as
  Come sta? [*koh'-meh stah*] How do you do?
comico [*koh'-mee-koh*] comedian, funny
cominciare *v.* [*koh-meen-chee-ah'-reh*] begin
comitato [*koh-mee-tah'-toh*] committee
commedia [*kohm-meh'-dee-ah*] comedy
commentare *v.* [*kohm-mehn-tah'-reh*] comment
commentario [*kohm-mehn-tah'-ree-oh*] commentary
commento [*kohm-mehn'-toh*] comment
commerciale [*kohm-mehr-chee-ah'-leh*] commercial
commerciante *m.* [*kohm-mehr-chee-ahn'-teh*] businessman
commercio [*kohm-mehr'-chee-oh*] trade
commesso [*kohm-mehs'-soh*] salesclerk
commestibile [*kohm-mehs-tee'-bee-leh*] edible
commettere *v.* [*kohm-meht'-teh-reh*] commit
commissione *f.* [*kohm-mees-see-oh'-neh*] commission, errand
commovente [*kohm-moh-vehn'-teh*] touching
commozione *f.* [*kohm-moh-tsee-oh'-neh*] commotion
commuoversi *v.*, [*kohm-moo-oh'-vehr-see*] be moved
  [emotionally]
comodità *f. indecl.* [*koh-moh-dee-tah'*] comfort
comodo [*koh'-moh-doh*] comfortable
  Si faccia comodo! [*see fahch'-chee-ah koh'-moh-doh*]
  Make yourself at home!
compagnia [*kohm-pah-nyee'-ah*] company
  compagnia di navigazione [*kohm-pah-nyee'-ah dee nah-vee-gah-tsee-oh'-neh*] steamship line
compagno [*kohm-pah'-nyoh*] companion, pal, mate
  compagno di scuola [*kohm-pah'-nyoh dee skoo-oh'-lah*]
  schoolmate
  compagno di giochi [*kohm-pah'-nyoh dee jee-oh'-kee*]
  playmate
compassione *f.* [*kohm-pahs-see-oh'-neh*] compassion

compatibile [*kohm-pah-tee'-bee-leh*] consistent
compatriota [*kohm-pah-tree-oh'-tah*] countryman
compensazione *f.* [*kohm-pehn-sah-tsee-oh'-neh*]
    compensation
competente [*kohm-peh-tehn'-teh*] competent
competenza [*kohm-peh-tehn'-tsah*] competence
compiere *v.* [*kohm'-pee-eh-reh*] accomplish, achieve
compilare *v.* [*kohm-pee-lah'-reh*] compile
compimento [*kohm-pee-mehn'-toh*] accomplishment
compito [*kohm'-pee-toh*] task
compleanno [*kohm-pleh-ahn'-noh*] birthday
  Felice compleanno [*feh-lee'-cheh kohm-pleh-ahn'-noh*]
    Happy birthday
complesso [*kohm-plehs'-soh*] complex
completamente [*kohm-pleh-tah-mehn'-teh*] completely
completare *v.* [*kohm-pleh-tah'-reh*] complete
complicare *v.* [*kohm-plee-kah'-reh*] complicate
complimento [*kohm-plee-mehn'-toh*] compliment
  fare *v.* **un complimento** [*fah'-reh oon kohm-plee-mehn'-toh*] pay a compliment
complotto [*kohm-ploht'-toh*] plot
comporre *v.* [*kohm-pohr'-reh*] compose
comportamento [*kohm-pohr-tah-mehn'-toh*] behavior
comportarsi *v.* [*kohm-pohr-tahr'-see*] behave
  Comportati bene! [*kohm-pohr'-tah-tee beh'-neh*] Behave
    yourself!
composizione *f.* [*kohm-poh-zee-tsee-oh'-neh*] composition
compostezza [*kohm-pohs-tehts'-tsah*] composure
compositore *m.* [*kohm-poh-zee-toh'-reh*] composer
comprare *v.* [*kohm-prah'-reh*] buy
compratore *m.* [*kohm-prah-toh'-reh*] buyer
comprendere *v.* [*kohm-prehn'-deh-reh*] understand
  Comprende lei? [*kohm-prehn'-deh leh'-ee*] Do you
    understand?
compromesso [*kohm-proh-mehs'-soh*] compromise
comune *m.* [*koh-moo'-neh*] town
comune [*koh-moo'-neh*] common
comunicare *v.* [*koh-moo-nee-kah'-reh*] communicate
comunicazione *f.* [*koh-moo-nee-kah-tsee-oh'-neh*]
    communication

comunista *m.*, *f.* [*koh-moo-nees'-tah*] communist
comunità *f. indecl.* [*koh-moo-nee-tah'*] community
comunque [*koh-moon'-koo-eh*] however
con [*kohn*] with, by, to
concedere *v.* [*kohn-cheh'-deh-reh*] grant, concede
concentrare *v.* [*kohn-chehn-trah'-reh*] concentrate
concepire *v.* [*kohn-cheh-pee'-reh*] conceive
concerto [*kohn-chehr'-toh*] concert
concetto [*kohn-cheht'-toh*] concept
conchiglia [*kohn-kee'-lyah*] shell [sea]
conciliazione *f.* [*koh-chee-lee-ah-tsee-oh'-neh*] conciliation
conciso [*kohn-chee'-zoh*] concise
concludere *v.* [*kohn-kloo'-deh-reh*] conclude
conclusione *f.* [*kohn-kloo-zee-oh'-neh*] conclusion
concorrenza [*kohn-kohr-rehn'-tsah*] competition
concorso [*kohn-kohr'-soh*] contest
condanna [*kohn-dahn'-nah*] condemnation
condannare *v.* [*kohn-dahn-nah'-reh*] condemn
condannato [*kohn-dah-nah'-toh*] convict(ed)
condensare *v.* [*kohn-dehn-sah'-reh*] condense
condizione *f.* [*kohn-dee-tsee-oh'-neh*] condition
condizioni *pl.* [*kohn-dee-tsee-oh'-nee*] terms
condotta [*kohn-doht'-tah*] conduct, behavior
condurre *v.* [*kohn-door'-reh*] conduct, lead
conduttore *m.* [*kohn-doot-toh'-reh*] conductor [of train]
conferenza [*kohn-feh-rehn'-tsah*] conference
   tenere *v.* **una conferenza** [*teh-neh'-reh oo'-nah kohn-feh-rehn'-tsah*] lecture
confermare *v.* [*kohn-fehr-mah'-reh*] confirm
conferire *v.* [*kohn-feh-ree'-reh*] confer
confessare *v.* [*kohn-fehs-sah'-reh*] confess
confessione *f.* [*kohn-fehs-see-oh'-neh*] confession
confidenziale [*kohn-fee-dehn-tsee-ah'-leh*] confidential
confine [*kohn-fee'-neh*] border
conflitto [*kohn-fleet'-toh*] conflict
confondere *v.* [*kohn-fohn'-deh-reh*] confuse
confortare *v.* [*kohn-fohr-tah'-reh*] comfort
conforto [*kohn-fohr'-toh*] comfort
confusione *f.* [*kohn-foo-zee-oh'-neh*] confusion
confuso [*kohn-foo'-zoh*] confused

congelare v. [*kohn-jeh-lah'-reh*] freeze
congratularsi v. [*kohn-grah-too-lahr'-see*] congratulate
  Congratulazioni! [*kohn-grah-too-lah-tsee-oh'-nee*]
    Congratulations!
congresso [*kohn-grehs'-soh*] congress
coniglio [*koh-nee'-lyoh*] rabbit
connessione f. [*kohn-nehs-see-oh'-neh*] connection
conoscente [*koh-noh-shehn'-teh*] acquaintance
conoscenza [*koh-noh-shehn'-tsah*] knowledge, acquaintance
conoscere v. [*koh-noh'-sheh-reh*] know [somebody or
    something]
conosciuto [*koh-noh-shee-oo'-toh*] well-known
conquistare v. [*kohn-koo-ees-tah'-reh*] conquer
consacrare v. [*kohn-sah-krah'-reh*] dedicate
consapevole [*kohn-sah-peh'-voh-leh*] self-conscious
conscio [*kohn'-shee-oh*] conscious
consecutivo [*kohn-seh-koo-tee'-voh*] consecutive
consegnare v. [*kohn-seh-nyah'-reh*] deliver
conseguenza [*kohn-seh-goo-ehn'-tsah*] consequence
  di conseguenza [*dee kohn-seh-goo-ehn'-tsah*] accordingly
consenso [*kohn-sehn'-soh*] consent
conservare v. [*kohn-sehr-vah'-reh*] preserve
conservativo [*kohn-sehr-vah-tee'-voh*] conservative
considerabile [*koh-see-deh-rah'-bee-leh*] considerable
considerare v. [*kohn-see-deh-rah'-reh*] consider
considerazione f. [*kohn-see-deh-rah-tsee-oh'-neh*]
    consideration
consigliare v. [*kohn-see-lyah'-reh*] advise
consiglio [*kohn-see'-lyoh*] advice, counsel
consistere v. [*kohn-sees'-teh-reh*] consist
consolare v. [*kohn-soh-lah'-reh*] comfort
consolato [*kohn-soh-lah'-toh*] consulate
console m. [*kohn'-soh-leh*] consul
consultare v. [*kohn-sool-tah'-reh*] consult
consumare v. [*kohn-soo-mah'-reh*] consume
consumato [*kohn-soo-mah'-toh*] worn out
consumatore m. [*kohn-soo-mah-toh'-reh*] consumer
contabile m. [*kohn-tah'-bee-leh*] bookkeeper
contadino [*kohn-tah-dee'-noh*] farmer, peasant
contagioso [*kohn-tah-jee-oh'-zoh*] contagious

contare v. [kohn-tah'-reh] count
  contare su [kohn-tah'-reh soo] count on
  denaro contante [deh-nah'-roh kohn-tahn'-teh] cash
  pagare v. **in contanti** [pah-gah'-reh een kohn-tahn'-tee]
    pay cash
contatore m. [kohn-tah-toh'-reh] meter
conte m., **contessa** f. [kohn'-teh, kohn-tehs'-sah] count,
  countess
contegno [kohn-teh'-nyoh] restraint
contemporaneo [kohn-tehm-poh-rah'-neh-oh] contemporary
contenere v. [kohn-teh-neh'-reh] contain
contento [kohn-tehn'-toh] glad, content
contenuto [kohn-teh-noo'-toh] contents
contiguo [kon-tee'-goo-oh] adjacent
continente m. [kohn-tee-nehn'-teh] continent
continuare v. [kohn-tee-noo-ah'-reh] continue
continuazione f. [kohn-tee-noo-ah-tsee-oh'-neh] continuation
conto [kohn'-toh] check, bill, account
  conto corrente [kohn'-toh kohr-rehn'-teh] checking account
  conto in banca [kohn'-toh een bahn'-kah] bank account
  pagare v. **il conto** [pah-gah'-reh eel kohn'-toh] pay the bill
  regolare v. **un conto** [reh-goh-lah'-reh oon kohn'-toh]
    settle an account
  rendere v. **conto di** [rehn'-deh-reh kohn'-toh dee] account
    for
contrabbandiere m. [kohn-trahb-bahn-dee-eh'-reh] smuggler
contraccambiare v. [kohn-trahk-kahm-bee-ah'-reh]
  reciprocate
contradizione f. [kohn-trah-dee-tsee-oh'-neh] contradiction
contrariamente [kohn-trah-ree-ah-mehn'-teh] on the contrary
contrario [kohn-trah'-ree-oh] contrary
  al contrario [ahl kohn-trah'-ree-oh] on the contrary
contrasto [kohn-trahs'-toh] contrast
contratto [kohn-traht'-toh] contract
contravvenzione [kohn-trah-vehn-tsee-oh'-neh] fine, violation
contribuire v. [kohn-tree-boo-ee'-reh] contribute
contribuzione f. [kohn-tree-boo-tsee-oh'-neh] contribution
contro [kohn'-troh] against
controllare v. [kohn-trohl-lah'-reh] control, check
controllo [kohn-trohl'-loh] control

controversia [*kohn-troh-vehr'-see-ah*] controversy
contusione *f.* [*kohn-too-zee-oh'-neh*] bruise
conveniente [*kohn-veh-nee-ehn'-teh*] convenient
convento [*kohn-vehn'-toh*] convent
conversazione *f.* [*kohn-vehr-sah-tsee-oh'-neh*] conversation, talk
convertire *v.* [*kohn-vehr-tee'-reh*] convert
convertito [*kohn-vehr-tee'-toh*] convert
convincere *v.* [*kohn-veen'-cheh-reh*] convince
convinto [*kohn-veen'-toh*] convinced
convitto [*kohn-veet'-toh*] boarding school
convocare *v.* [*kohn-voh-kah'-reh*] summon
cooperazione [*koh-oh-peh-rah-tsee-oh'-neh*] cooperation
coperchio [*koh-pehr'-kee-oh*] lid, cover
coperta [*koh-pehr'-tah*] blanket
coperto [*koh-pehr'-toh*] covered
copertura [*koh-pehr-too'-rah*] cover
copia [*koh'-pee-ah*] copy
copiare *v.* [*koh-pee-ah'-reh*] copy
coppia [*kohp'-pee-ah*] couple
coprire *v. irreg.* [*koh-pree'-reh*] cover
coraggio [*koh-rahj'-jee-oh*] courage
  Che coraggio! [*keh koh-rahj'-jee-oh*] What a nerve!
coraggioso [*koh-rahj-jee-oh'-zoh*] courageous
corallo [*koh-rahl'-loh*] coral
corda [*kohr'-dah*] rope
cordiale [*kohr-dee-ah'-leh*] cordial
coricarsi *v.* [*koh-ree-kahr'-see*] lie down, go to bed
cornice *f.* [*kohr-nee'-cheh*] frame
corno, le corna *pl.* [*kohr'-noh, leh kohr'-nah*] horn [of animal]
coro [*koh'-roh*] chorus
corona [*koh-roh'-nah*] crown
corpo [*kohr'-poh*] body
corporazione *f.* [*kohr-poh-rah-tsee-oh'-neh*] corporation
correggere *v. irreg.* [*kohr-rehj'-jeh-reh*] correct
corrente *f.* [*kohr-rehn'-teh*] current, stream
  al corrente [*ahl koh-rehn'-teh*] well informed
  corrente d'aria [*kohr-rehn'-teh dah'-ree-ah*] draft (of air)
  moneta corrente [*moh-neh'-tah kohr-rehn'-teh*] currency
correre *v. irreg.* [*kohr'-reh-reh*] run

correttezza [*kohr-reht-tehts'-tsah*] decency
corretto [*kohr-reht'-toh*] correct
correzione *f.* [*kohr-reh-tsee-oh'-neh*] correction
corridoio [*kohr-ree-doh'-ee-oh*] corridor
corrispondenza [*kohr-rees-pohn-dehn'-tsah*] correspondence
corrompere *v.* [*kohr-rohm'-peh-reh*] corrupt, bribe
corrotto [*kohr-roht'-toh*] corrupt
corruzione *f.* [*kohr-roo-tsee-oh'-neh*] corruption
corsa [*kohr'-sah*] run, race, trip
   corsa di cavalli [*kohr'-sah dee kah-vahl'-lee*] horse race
corso [*kohr'-soh*] course
corte *f.* [*kohr'-teh*] court
corteggiare *v.* [*kohr-tehj-jee-ah'-reh*] court
corteggiatore *m., f.* [*kohr-tehj-jee-ah-toh'-reh*] suitor
cortese [*kohr-teh'-zeh*] courteous
cortesia [*kohr-teh-zee'-ah*] politeness, kindness
cortile *m.* [*kohr-tee'-leh*] courtyard
corto [*kohr'-toh*] short, brief
cosa [*koh'-zah*] thing, what
   che, che cosa [*keh, keh koh'-zah*] what
   Che cosa c'e? [*keh koh'-zah cheh'*] What's the matter?
   Cosa desidera? [*koh'-zah deh-zee'-deh-rah*] What do you
     wish?
   Che cosa vi prende? [*keh koh'-zah vee prehn'-deh*] What
     is the matter with you?
   Che cosa significa? [*keh koh'-zah see-nyee'-fee-kah*]
     What does it mean?
   Cos' ha? [*kohz-ah'*] What is the matter with him (her, you)?
   Cos'è? [*kohz-eh'*] What is it?
coscienza [*koh-shee-ehn'-tsah*] conscience
coscienzioso [*kohn-shee-ehn-tsee-oh'-zoh*] conscientious
così [*koh-zee'*] so, thus, like this
   così così [*koh-zee' koh-zee'*] so so
   e così via [*eh koh-zee' vee'-ah*] and so forth
cosmetici [*kohz-meh'-tee-chee*] cosmetics
costa [*kohs'-tah*] coast
costare *v.* [*kohs-tah'-reh*] cost
   Quanto costa questo? [*koo-ahn'-toh kohs'-tah koo-ehs'-toh*] How much does this cost?
costante [*kohs-tahn'-teh*] constant

costituire v. [kohs-tee-too-ee'-reh] constitute
costituzione f. [kohs-tee-too-tsee-oh'-neh] constitution
costo [kohs'-toh] cost
  costo della vita [kohs'-toh dehl'-lah vee'-tah] cost of living
costola [kohs'-toh-lah] rib
  costoletta d'agnello [kohs-toh-leht'-tah dah-nyehl'-loh]
    lamb chop
  costoletta di maiale [kohs-toh-leht'-tah dee mah-ee-ah'-leh]
    pork chop
costoso [kohs-toh'-zoh] expensive
costringere v. [kohs-treen'-jeh-reh] compel
costrizione f. [kohs-tree-tsee-oh'-neh] compulsion
costruire v. [kohs-troo-ee'-reh] build, construct
costruzione f. [kohs-troo-tsee-oh'-neh] building, construction
costume m. [kohs-too'-meh] custom
costume da bagno m. [kohs-too'-meh dah bah'-nyoh]
    bathing suit
cotoletta [koh-toh-leht'-tah] cutlet
cotone m. [koh-toh'-neh] cotton
cotto [koht'-toh] done, cooked
  ben cotto [behn koht'-toh] well-done [cooking]
  poco cotto [poh'-koh koht'-toh] rare [cooking]
cranio [krah'-nee-oh] skull
cravatta [krah-vaht'-tah] necktie
creare v. [kreh-ah'-reh] create
creatura [kreh-ah-too'-rah] creature
creazione f. [kreh-ah-tsee-oh'-neh] creation
credente [kreh-dehn'-teh] believer
credere v. [kreh'-deh-reh] believe
credito [kreh'-dee-toh] credit
creditore m. [kreh-dee-toh'-reh] creditor
crema [kreh'-mah] cream
crepuscolo [kreh-poos'-koh-loh] twilight
crescere v. irreg. [kreh'-sheh-reh] grow [up, bigger, taller],
    increase
criminale [kree-mee-nah'-leh] criminal
crimine m. [kree'-mee-neh] crime
crisi f. [kree'-zee] crisis
  crisi economica f. [kree'-zee eh-koh-noh'-mee-kah]
    recession

cristallo [*krees-tahl'-loh*] crystal
cristianesimo [*krees-tee-ah-neh'-zee-moh*] Christianity
cristiano [*krees-tee-ah'-noh*] Christian
Cristo [*krees'-toh*] Christ
criterio [*kree-teh'-ree-oh*] criterion
criticare *v.* [*kree-tee-kah'-reh*] criticize
critico [*kree'-tee-koh*] critical
croce *f.* [*kroh'-cheh*] cross
   Croce Rossa [*kroh'-cheh rohs'-sah*] Red Cross
crociera [*kroh-chee-eh'-rah*] cruise
crollo [*krohl'-loh*] collapse
cronista *m.* [*kroh-nees'-tah*] reporter
cronometro [*kroh-noh'-meh-troh*] stopwatch
crudele [*kroo-deh'-leh*] cruel
crudeltà *f. indecl.* [*kroo-dehl-tah'*] cruelty
crudo [*kroo'-doh*] raw, crude
cubo [*koo'-boh*] cube
cucchiaio [*kook-kee-ah'-ee-oh*] spoon, spoonful
cucchiaino [*kook-kee-ah-ee'-noh*] teaspoon
cucina [*koo-chee'-nah*] kitchen
cucinare *v.* [*koo-chee-nah'-reh*] cook
cucire *v.* [*koo-chee'-reh*] sew, seam
cucitura [*koo-chee-too'-rah*] seam
cugino *m.*, **cugina** *f.* [*koo-jee'-noh, koo-jee'-nah*] cousin
cui [*koo'-ee*] whom, whose, which
culla [*kool'-lah*] cradle
cultura [*kool-too'-rah*] culture
cuocere *v. irreg.* [*koo-oh'-cheh-reh*] bake, cook
cuoco [*koo-oh'-koh*] cook
cuoio [*koo-oh'-ee-oh*] leather
cuore *m.* [*koo-oh'-reh*] heart
cupola [*koo'-poh-lah*] dome
cura [*koo'-rah*] care, cure
   avere *v.* **cura** [*ah-veh'-reh koo'-rah*] take care of
curare *v.* [*koo-rah'-reh*] cure, care
curiosità *f. indecl.* [*koo-ree-oh-zee-tah'*] curiosity
curioso [*koo-ree-oh'-zoh*] curious
curva [*koor'-vah*] curve
cuscino [*koo-shee'-noh*] pillow
custodia [*koos-toh'-dee-ah*] custody

D

da [*dah*] from, by, since, to, for

  da ora in poi [*dah oh'-rah een poh'-ee*] from now on

  Da dove viene? [*dah doh'-veh vee-eh'-neh*] Where do you come from?

  da lontano [*dah lohn-tah'-noh*] from far

dabbene [*dahb-beh'-neh*] good, honest, well educated

dadi [*dah'-dee*] dice

dal, dalla, dallo, dall' [*dahl, dahl'-lah, dahl'-loh, dahl*] from the

damigella d'onore [*dah-mee-jehl'-lah doh-noh'-reh*] bridesmaid

danese [*dah-neh'-zeh*] Danish

danneggiare *v.* [*dahn-nehj-jee-ah'-reh*] damage

danno [*dahn'-noh*] damage

dannoso [*dahn-noh'-zoh*] harmful

danza [*dahn'-tsah*] dance

dappertutto [*dahp-pehr-toot'-toh*] everywhere

dare *v. irreg.* [*dah'-reh*] give

  Me lo da [*meh loh dah*] He, she gives it to me

  Mi dia . . . [*mee dee'-ah*] Give me . . .

  Ci dia . . . [*chee dee'-ah*] Give us . . .

  Dia loro . . . [*dee'-ah loh'-roh*] Give them . . .

  Gli dia . . . , Le dia . . . [*lyee dee'-ah, leh dee'-ah*] Give him . . . , Give her . . .

data [*dah'-tah*] date [day of month]

dato [*dah'-toh*] given

dattilografo [*daht-tee-loh'-grah-foh*] typist

davanti [*dah-vahn'-tee*] before, in front of

  davanti all'albergo [*dah-vahn'-tee ahl-lahl-behr'-goh*] in front of the hotel

Davvero [*dahv-veh'-roh*] Yes, indeed

dazio [*dah'-tsee-oh*] duty [customs]

debito [*deh'-bee-toh*] debt

debole [*deh'-boh-leh*] weak

debolezza [*deh-boh-lehts'-tsah*] weakness

decadenza [*deh-kah-dehn'-tsah*] decay, decline
decadere v. [*deh-kah-deh'-reh*] decay, decline
decennio [*deh-chehn'-nee-oh*] decade
decente [*deh-chehn'-teh*] decent
decidere v. irreg. [*deh-chee'-deh-reh*] decide
decimo [*deh'-chee-moh*] tenth
decisione f. [*deh-chee-zee-oh'-neh*] decision
declarazione f. [*deh-klah-rah-tsee-oh'-neh*] declaration
declinare v. [*deh-klee-nah'-reh*] decline
decollare v. [*deh-kohl-lah'-reh*] take off [plane]
decorare v. [*deh-koh-rah'-reh*] decorate
decorazione f. [*deh-koh-rah-tsee-oh'-neh*] decoration
decreto [*deh-kreh'-toh*] decree
dedicare v. [*deh-dee-kah'-reh*] dedicate
deficiente [*deh-fee-chee-ehn'-teh*] deficient
definire v. [*deh-fee-nee'-reh*] define
definitivamente [*deh-fee-nee-tee-vah-mehn'-teh*] definitely
definito [*deh-fee-nee'-toh*] definite
definizione f. [*deh-fee-nee-tsee-oh'-neh*] definition
defunto [*deh-foon'-toh*] deceased
degno [*deh'-nyoh*] worthy
deliberare v. [*deh-lee-beh-rah'-reh*] deliberate
delicato [*deh-lee-kah'-toh*] delicate
delinquente [*deh-leen-koo-ehn'-teh*] delinquent
delitto [*deh-leet'-toh*] crime
delizioso [*deh-lee-tsee-oh'-zoh*] delicious
deludere v. [*deh-loo'-deh-reh*] disappoint
deluso [*deh-loo'-zoh*] disappointed
democratico [*deh-moh-krah'-tee-koh*] democratic, democrat
democrazia [*deh-moh-krah-tsee'-ah*] democracy
demolire v., [*deh-moh-lee'-reh*] take down, demolish
demoralizzante [*deh-moh-rah-leedz-dzahn'-teh*] discouraging
demoralizzato [*deh-moh-rah-leedz-dzah'-toh*] discouraged
denaro [*deh-nah'-roh*] money
densità f. indecl. [*dehn-see-tah'*] density
denso [*dehn'-soh*] dense, thick
dente m. [*dehn'-teh*] tooth
  mal m. **di denti** [*mahl dee dehn'-tee*] toothache
dentifricio [*dehn-tee-free'-chee-oh*] toothpaste

dentista *m.* [*dehn-tees'-tah*] dentist
dentro [*dehn'-troh*] inside, within
depositare *v.* [*deh-poh-zee-tah'-reh*] deposit
deposito [*deh-poh'-zee-toh*] deposit, stock
depresso [*deh-prehs'-soh*] depressed
deputato [*deh-poo-tah'-toh*] deputy
derubare *v.* [*deh-roo-bah'-reh*] rob
descrivere *v.* [*dehs-kree'-veh-reh*] describe
descrizione *f.* [*dehs-kree-tsee-oh'-neh*] description
deserto [*deh-zehr'-toh*] desert
desiderabile [*deh-zee-deh-rah'-bee-leh*] desirable
desiderare *v.,* [*deh-zee-deh-rah'-reh*] desire
desiderio [*deh-zee-deh'-ree-oh*] wish, desire
destinatario [*dehs-tee-nah-tah'-ree-oh*] addressee
destinazione *f.* [*dehs-tee-nah-tsee-oh'-neh*] destination
destino [*dehs-tee'-noh*] destiny, fate
destra [*dehs'-trah*] right [direction]
determinare *v.* [*deh-tehr-mee-nah'-reh*] determine
dettaglio [*deht-tah'-lyoh*] detail
dettare *v.* [*deht-tah'-reh*] dictate
dettato [*deht-tah'-toh*] dictation
deviazione *f.* [*deh-vee-ah-tsee-oh'-neh*] detour
devoto [*deh-voh'-toh*] devoted
devozione *f.* [*deh-voh-tsee-oh'-neh*] devotion
di *prep.* [*dee*] of
    di cotone [*dee koh-toh'-neh*] made of cotton
    di lana [*dee lah'-nah*] woolen
    di legno [*dee leh'-nyoh*] wooden
    la sorella di Maria [*lah soh-rehl'-lah dee mah-ree'-ah*]
      Mary's sister
    di quando in quando [*dee koo-ahn'-doh een koo-ahn'-doh*]
      now and then
diagnosi *f.* [*dee-ahg-noh'-zee*] diagnosis
diagramma *m.* [*dee-ah-grahm'-mah*] diagram
dialetto [*dee-ah-leht'-toh*] dialect
dialogo [*dee-ah'-loh-goh*] dialogue
diamante *m.* [*dee-ah-mahn'-teh*] diamond
diametro [*dee-ah'-meh-troh*] diameter
diario [*dee-ah'-ree-oh*] diary
diavolo [*dee-ah'-voh-loh*] devil

dicembre *m.* [*dee-chehm'-breh*] December
dichiarare *v.* [*dee-kee-ah-rah'-reh*] declare, state
dichiarazione *f.* [*dee-kee-ah-rah-tsee-oh'-neh*] statement
  dichiarazione di dogana [*dee-kee-ah-rah-tsee-oh'-neh dee doh-gah'-nah*] customs declaration
dicianove [*dee-chee-ah-noh'-veh*] nineteen
diciassette [*dee-chee-ah-seht'-teh*] seventeen
diciotto [*dee-chee-oht'-toh*] eighteen
dieci [*dee-eh'-chee*] ten
dieta [*dee-eh'-tah*] diet
dietro [*dee-eh'-troh*] behind
difendere *v. irreg.* [*dee-fehn'-deh-reh*] defend
difesa [*dee-feh'-zah*] defense
difetto [*dee-feht'-toh*] defect
difettoso [*dee-feht-toh'-zoh*] defective
differente [*deef-feh-rehn'-teh*] different
differenza [*deef-feh-rehn'-tsah*] difference
  a differenza di [*ah deef-feh-rehn'-tsah dee*] unlike
difficile [*deef-fee'-chee-leh*] difficult
difficoltà *f. indecl.* [*deef-fee-kohl-tah'*] difficulty
diffidare *v.* [*deef-fee-dah'-reh*] distrust
diffuso [*deef-foo'-zoh*] widespread
diga [*dee'-gah*] dam
digerire *v.* [*dee-jeh-ree'-reh*] digest
digestione *f.* [*dee-jehs-tee-oh'-neh*] digestion
dignità *f. indecl.* [*dee-nyee-tah'*] dignity
digiunare *v.* [*dee-jee-oo-nah'-reh*] fast
digiuno [*dee-jee-oo'-noh*] fast
dilettare *v.* [*dee-leht-tah'-reh*] delight
diletto [*dee-leht'-toh*] delight
dimagrire *v.* [*dee-mah-gree'-reh*] grow thin, reduce
dimensione *f.* [*dee-mehn-see-oh'-neh*] dimension
dimenticare *v.* [*dee-mehn-tee-kah'-reh*] forget
dimenticato [*dee-mehn-tee-kah'-toh*] forgotten
dimettersi *v.* [*dee-meht'-tehr-see*] resign
diminuire *v.* [*dee-mee-noo-ee'-reh*] diminish
dimissione [*dee-mees-see-oh'-neh*] resignation
dimostrare *v.* [*dee-mohs-trah'-reh*] demonstrate
dimostrazione *f.* [*dee-mohs-trah-tsee-oh'-neh*] demonstration

dinamite *f.* [*dee-nah-mee'-teh*] dynamite
dintorni [*deen-tohr'-nee*] surroundings
Dio [*dee'-oh*] God
dipartimento [*dee-pahr-tee-mehn'-toh*] department
dipendente [*dee-pehn-dehn'-teh*] dependent
dipendere da *v.* [*dee-pehn'-deh-reh dah*] depend on
   dipende [*dee-pehn'-deh*] that depends
dipingere *v. irreg.* [*dee-peen'-jeh-reh*] paint
diploma *m.* [*dee-ploh'-mah*] diploma
diplomatico [*dee-ploh-mah'-tee-koh*] diplomat, diplomatic
diplomato [*dee-ploh-mah'-toh*] graduate
diplomazia [*dee-ploh-mah-tsee'-ah*] diplomacy
dire *v. irreg.* [*dee'-reh*] tell, say
   Mi dica, per favore [*mee dee'-kah, pehr fah-voh'-reh*]
      Tell me, please
   Non mi dica [*nohn mee dee'-kah*] Don't tell me
direttamente [*dee-reht-tah-mehn'-teh*] directly
direttissimo [*dee-reht-tees'-see-moh*] express (train)
diretto [*dee-reht'-toh*] direct
direttore *m.*, **direttrice** *f.* [*dee-reht-toh'-reh, dee-reht-tree'-cheh*] director
direzione *f.* [*dee-reh-tsee-oh'-neh*] direction
dirigere *v. irreg.* [*dee-ree'-jeh-reh*] direct
diritto [*dee-reet'-toh*] right, law
diritto *adj.* [*dee-reet'-toh*] straight, right
   andare *v.* **diritto** [*ahn-dah'-reh dee-reet'-toh*] go straight on
disaccordo [*deez-ahk-kohr'-doh*] disagreement
disagio [*dee-zah'-jee-oh*] discomfort
disapprovare *v.* [*deez-ahp-proh-vah'-reh*] disapprove
disastro [*dee-zahs'-troh*] disaster
discendere *v.* [*dee-shehn'-deh-reh*] descend, come down
disciplina [*dee-shee-plee'-nah*] discipline
disco [*dees'-koh*] record [phono]
discorso [*dees-kohr'-soh*] speech
discussione *f.* [*dees-koos-see-oh'-neh*] discussion
discutere *v. irreg.* [*dees-koo'-teh-reh*] discuss
discutibile [*dees-koo-tee'-bee-leh*] questionable
disegnare *v.* [*dee-zeh-nyah'-reh*] draw [a picture], outline
disegno [*dee-zeh'-nyoh*] design
disertare *v.* [*dee-zehr-tah'-reh*] desert

disfare v. [*dees-fah'-reh*] unpack, undo

disgrazia [*deez-grah'-tsee-ah*] disgrace, bad luck

disgraziatamente [*deez-grah-tsee-ah-tah-mehn'-teh*]
unfortunately

disgraziato [*deez-grah-tsee-ah'-toh*] unfortunate

disgustato [*deez-goos-tah'-toh*] disgusted

disinteressato [*deez-een-teh-rehs-sah'-toh*] unselfish

disobbedire v. [*deez-ohb-beh-dee'-reh*] disobey

disoccupato [*deez-ohk-koo-pah'-toh*] unemployed

disonesto [*deez-oh-nehs'-toh*] dishonest

disonorare v. [*deez-oh-noh-rah'-reh*] disgrace

disonore m. [*deez-oh-noh'-reh*] disgrace

disordine m. [*deez-ohr'-dee-neh*] disorder

disorganizzato [*deez-ohr-gah-needz-dzah'-toh*] unorganized

dispari [*dees'-pah-ree*] odd [number]

disperare v. [*dees-peh-rah'-reh*] despair

disperato [*dees-peh-rah'-toh*] desperate

disperazione f. [*dees-peh-rah-tsee-oh'-neh*] despair

dispetto [*dees-peht'-toh*] spite, vexation

dispiacere m. [*dees-pee-ah-cheh'-reh*] sorrow, regret

dispiacersi v. [*dees-pee-ah-chehr'-see*] be sorry

   Le dispiace se mi siedo qui? [*leh dees-pee-ah'-cheh seh mee
see-eh'-doh koo-ee'*] Do you mind if I sit here?

   Mi dispiace molto [*mee dees-pee-ah'-cheh mohl'-toh*] I am
very sorry

disponibile [*dees-poh-nee'-bee-leh*] available

disporre v. irreg. [*dees-pohr'-reh*] dispose

disposizione f. [*dees-poh-zee-tsee-oh'-neh*] disposition,
arrangement

disposto [*dees-pohs'-toh*] willing

   Sono disposto a . . . [*soh'-noh dees-pohs'-toh ah*] I am
willing to . . .

disprezzare v. [*dees-prehts-tsah'-reh*] despise, scorn

disprezzo [*dees-prehts'-tsoh*] contempt, scorn

disputa, [*dees'-poo-tah*] dispute

disputare v. [*dees-poo-tah'-reh*] argue

dissenteria [*dees-sehn-teh-ree'-ah*] dysentery

dissimile [*dees-see'-mee-leh*] unlike

dissolvere v. [*dees-sohl'-veh-reh*] dissolve

distante [*dees-tahn'-teh*] distant

distanza [*dees-tahn'-tsah*] distance
distensione *f.* [*dees-tehn-see-oh'-neh*] relaxation
distinguere *v.* [*dees-teen'-goo-eh-reh*] distinguish
distintivo [*dees-teen-tee'-voh*] badge, distinctive
distinto [*dees-teen'-toh*] distinct, distinguished
distratto [*dees-traht'-toh*] absent-minded
distrazione *f.* [*dees-trah-tsee-oh'-neh*] distraction
distretto [*dees-treht'-toh*] district
distribuire *v.* [*dees-tree-boo-ee'-reh*] distribute
distribuzione *f.* [*dees-tree-boo-tsee-oh'-neh*] distribution
distruggere *v.* [*dees-trooj'-jeh-reh*] destroy
distruzione *f.* [*dees-troo-tsee-oh'-neh*] destruction
disturbare *v.* [*dees-toor-bah'-reh*] disturb, annoy
   Non si disturbi [*nohn see dees-toor'-bee*] Don't trouble
     yourself
disturbato [*dees-toor-bah'-toh*] annoyed, disturbed
disturbo [*dees-toor'-boh*] trouble, disturbance
disubbidire *v.* [*deez-oo-bee-dee'-reh*] disobey
disuguale [*deez-oo-goo-ah'-leh*] unequal
dito, le dita *pl.* [*dee'-toh, leh dee'-tah*] finger, toe
ditta [*deet'-tah*] firm, company
diurno [*dee-oor'-noh*] daily
divano [*dee-vah'-noh*] couch, sofa
diventare, divenire *v. irreg.* [*dee-vehn-tah'-reh, dee-veh-nee'-*
   reh] become, get, grow
diversi [*dee-vehr'-see*] various
divertente [*dee-vehr-tehn'-teh*] entertaining, amusing
divertimento [*dee-vehr-tee-mehn'-toh*] amusement, fun
   Buon divertimento! [*boo-ohn' dee-vehr-tee-mehn'-toh*]
     Have a good time!
divertire *v.* [*dee-vehr-tee'-reh*] amuse
divertirsi *v.* [*dee-vehr-teer'-see*] amuse oneself
   Si diverta! [*see dee-vehr'-tah*] Enjoy yourself!
dividere *v. irreg.* [*dee-vee'-deh-reh*] split, divide
divino [*dee-vee'-noh*] divine
divisione *f.* [*dee-vee-zee-oh'-neh*] division
diviso [*dee-vee'-zoh*] divided
divorziare *v.* [*dee-vohr-tsee-ah'-reh*] divorce
divorziato [*dee-vohr-tsee-ah'-toh*] divorced
divorzio [*dee-vohr'-tsee-oh*] divorce

dizionario [*dee-tsee-oh-nah'-ree-oh*] dictionary

doccia [*dohch'-chee-ah*] shower

documento [*doh-koo-mehn'-toh*] document

dodicesimo [*doh-dee-cheh'-zee-moh*] twelfth

dodici [*doh'-dee-chee*] twelve

dogana [*doh-gah'-nah*] customs

    agente *m.* **di dogana** [*ah-jehn'-teh dee doh-gah'-nah*] customs officer

    dazio di dogana [*dah'-tsee-oh dee doh-gah'-nah*] customs duty

dolce [*dohl'-cheh*] sweet, cake, dessert

dolore *m.* [*doh-loh'-reh*] ache, pain, grief

doloroso [*doh-loh-roh'-zoh*] painful

dollaro [*dohl'-lah-roh*] dollar

domanda [*doh-mahn'-dah*] question, demand

domandare *v.* [*doh-mahn-dah'-reh*] ask

domandarsi *v.* [*doh-mahn-dahr'-see*] ask [oneself]

domani [*doh-mah'-nee*] tomorrow

    domani mattina [*doh-mah'-nee maht-tee'-nah*] tomorrow morning

    dopodomani [*doh-poh-doh-mah'-nee*] day after tomorrow

domenica [*doh-meh'-nee-kah*] Sunday

domestico [*doh-mehs'-tee-koh*] valet, domestic

domicilio [*doh-mee-chee'-lee-oh*] residence

dominare *v.* [*doh-mee-nah'-reh*] dominate

donare *v.* [*doh-nah'-reh*] donate

donna [*dohn'-nah*] woman, lady

dopo [*doh'-poh*] after, later

doppio [*dohp'-pee-oh*] double

dormire *v.* [*dohr-mee'-reh*] sleep

dormitorio [*dohr-mee-toh'-ree-oh*] dormitory

dose *f.* [*doh'-zeh*] dose

dotato [*doh-tah'-toh*] gifted

dote *f.* [*doh'-teh*] dowry, quality

dottore *m.*, **dottoressa** *f.* [*doht-toh'-reh, doht-toh-rehs'-sah*] doctor, physician

dove [*doh'-veh*] where

    Dov'è? [*doh-veh'*] Where is it (he, she)?

dovere *m.* [*doh-veh'-reh*] duty

dovere *v. irreg., aux.* [*doh-veh'-reh*] have to, ought to, must

Devo andare a casa [*deh'-voh ahn-dah'-reh ah kah'-zah*]
I must go home
Dovrei andare [*doh-vreh'-ee ahn-dah'-reh*] I ought to go
Lei dovrebbe riposare [*leh'-ee doh-vrehb'-beh ree-poh-zah'-reh*] You ought to rest
dovunque [*doh-voon'-koo-eh*] anywhere, wherever
dovuto [*doh-voo'-toh*] due
dozzina [*dohdz-dzee'-nah*] dozen
dramma *m.* [*drahm'-mah*] drama, play
drammatico [*drahm-mah'-tee-koh*] dramatic
droga [*droh'-gah*] drug
drogheria [*droh-geh-ree'-ah*] grocery
dubbio [*doob'-bee-oh*] doubt
  senza dubbio [*sehn'-tsah doob'-bee-oh*] without a doubt
dubbioso [*doob-bee-oh'-zoh*] doubtful
dubitare *v.* [*doo-bee-tah'-reh*] doubt
duca *m.*, **duchessa** [*doo'-kah, doo-kehs'-sah*] duke, duchess
duce *m.* [*doo'-cheh*] leader
due [*doo'-eh*] two
  le due e mezzo [*leh doo'-eh eh mehdz'-dzoh*] half past two
  due volte [*doo'-eh vohl'-teh*] twice
duello [*doo-ehl'-loh*] duel
dunque [*doon'-koo-eh*] then
duomo [*doo-oh'-moh*] cathedral
durante [*doo-rahn'-teh*] during
durare *v.* [*doo-rah'-reh*] last
durata [*doo-rah'-tah*] duration
durevole [*doo-reh'-voh-leh*] durable
duro [*doo'-roh*] hard, tough

E

e, ed [*eh, ehd*] and
è [*eh'*] is
ebbene [*ehb-beh'-neh*] well!, well then
ebreo [*eh-breh'-oh*] Jew, Jewish
eccedere *v.* [*ehch-cheh'-deh-reh*] exceed

eccellente [*ehch-chehl-lehn'-teh*] excellent
eccentrico [*ehch-chehn'-tree-koh*] eccentric
eccessivo [*ehch-chehs-see'-voh*] excessive
eccesso [*ehch-chehs'-soh*] excess
eccetera [*ehch-cheht'-teh-rah*] et cetera
eccetto [*ehch-cheht'-toh*] except
eccezionale [*ehch-cheh-tsee-oh-nah'-leh*] exceptional
eccezione f. [*ehch-cheh-tsee-oh'-neh*] exception
eccitato [*ehch-chee-tah'-toh*] excited
ecco [*ehk'-koh*] here is, there is
  Ecco fatto! [*ehk'-koh faht'-toh*] It is done, Here it is!
  Eccoci! [*ehk'-koh-chee*] Here we are!
  Eccomi! [*ehk'-koh-mee*] Here I am!
  Eccola! [*ehk'-koh-lah*] There she (it) is!
  Eccolo! [*ehk'-koh-loh*] There he (it) is!
eco [*eh'-koh*] echo
economico [*eh-koh-noh'-mee-koh*] economical
edicola [*eh-dee'-koh-lah*] newsstand
edificio [*eh-dee-fee'-chee-oh*] building
edizione f. [*eh-dee-tsee-oh'-neh*] edition
educato [*eh-doo-kah'-toh*] polite, well mannered
educazione f. [*eh-doo-kah-tsee-oh'-neh*] upbringing
effetti personali [*ehf-feht'-tee pehr-soh-nah'-lee*] belongings
effettivo [*ehf-feht-tee'-voh*] effective
effetto [*ehf-feht'-toh*] effect
efficace [*ehf-fee-kah'-cheh*] effective
efficiente [*ehf-fee-chee-ehn'-teh*] efficient
Egitto [*eh-jeet'-toh*] Egypt
egiziano [*eh-jee-tsee-ah'-noh*] Egyptian
egli [*eh'-lyee*] he
egoista [*eh-goh-ees'-tah*] selfish
egregio [*eh-greh'-jee-oh*] distinguished
  Egregio Signore: [*eh-greh'-jee-oh see-nyoh'-reh*] Dear Sir:
eguaglianza [*eh-goo-ah-lyahn'-tsah*] equality
eguale [*eh-goo-ah'-leh*] same, equal
elastico [*eh-lahs'-tee-koh*] elastic
elaborare v. [*eh-lah-boh-rah'-reh*] elaborate
elefante m. [*eh-leh-fahn'-teh*] elephant
elegante [*eh-leh-gahn'-teh*] elegant
eleganza [*eh-leh-gahn'-tsah*] elegance

eleggere v. [eh-lehj'-jeh-reh] elect
elementare [eh-leh-mehn-tah'-reh] elementary
elemento [eh-leh-mehn'-toh] element
elenco [eh-lehn'-koh] list
   elenco telefonico [eh-lehn'-koh teh-leh-foh'-nee-koh]
     telephone directory
elettricità f. indecl. [eh-leht-tree-chee-tah'] electricity
elettrico [eh-leht'-tree-koh] electric
elevato [eh-leh-vah'-toh] elevated, high
elezione f. [eh-leh-tsee-oh'-neh] election
elica [eh'-lee-kah] propeller
eliminare v. [eh-lee-mee-nah'-reh] eliminate
ella [ehl'-lah] she
embargo [ehm-bahr'-koh] embargo
emergenza [eh-mehr-jehn'-tsah] emergency
   in caso di emergenza [een kah'-zoh dee eh-mehr-jehn'-tsah]
     in case of emergency
emigrante m. [eh-mee-grahn'-teh] emigrant
emigrazione f. [eh-mee-grah-tsee-oh'-neh] emigration
emotivo [eh-moh-tee'-voh] emotional
emozionato [eh-moh-tsee-oh-nah'-toh] thrilled
emozione f. [eh-moh-tsee-oh'-neh] emotion
energia [eh-nehr-jee'-ah] energy
energico [eh-nehr'-jee-koh] energetic
enigma [eh-neeg'-mah] puzzle
enorme [eh-nohr'-meh] huge
ente m.[ehn'-teh] institution, corporation
entrare v. [ehn-trah'-reh] enter
   No entri [noh ehn'-tree] Do not enter
entrata [ehn-trah'-tah] entrance
entro [ehn'-troh] in, within
entusiasmo [ehn-too-zee-ahz'-moh] enthusiasm
episodio [eh-pee-soh'-dee-oh] episode
epoca [eh'-poh-kah] epoch
eppure [ehp-poo'-reh] even so, yet, and still
equilibrare v. [eh-koo-ee-lee-brah'-reh] balance
equilibrio [eh-koo-ee-lee'-bree-oh] balance
equipaggiamento [eh-koo-ee-pahj-jee-ah-mehn'-toh] equipment
equipaggio [eh-koo-ee-pahj'-jee-oh] crew
equivalente [eh-koo-ee-vah-lehn'-teh] equivalent

equivoco [*eh-koo-ee'-voh-koh*] misunderstanding
equo [*eh'-koo-oh*] just, fair
era [*eh'-rah*] age, era
erba [*ehr'-bah*] grass
erede [*eh-reh'-deh*] heir, heiress
eredità *f. indecl.* [*eh-reh-dee-tah'*] inheritance
ereditare *v.* [*eh-reh-dee-tah'-reh*] inherit
eroe *m.* [*eh-roh'-eh*] hero
eroico [*eh-roh'-ee-koh*] heroic
errore *m.* [*ehr-roh'-reh*] error, mistake
  errore di stampa [*ehr-roh'-reh dee stahm'-pah*] misprint
esagerare *v.* [*eh-zah-jeh-rah'-reh*] exaggerate
esagerazione *f.* [*eh-zah-jeh-rah-tsee-oh'-neh*] exaggeration
esame *m.* [*eh-zah'-meh*] examination
esaminare *v.* [*eh-zah-mee-nah'-reh*] examine
esattamente [*eh-zaht-tah-mehn'-teh*] exactly
esatto [*eh-zaht'-toh*] accurate, exact
esaurito [*eh-zah-oo-ree'-toh*] exhausted
  tutto esaurito [*toot'-toh eh-zah-oo-ree'-toh*] sold out
escludere *v.* [*ehs-kloo'-deh-reh*] exclude
esclusivo [*ehs-kloo-zee'-voh*] exclusive
escursione *f.* [*ehs-koor-see-oh'-neh*] excursion
esempio [*eh-zehm'-pee-oh*] example
  per esempio [*pehr eh-zehm'-pee-oh*] for example
esente [*eh-zehn'-teh*] exempt, free
esercitare *v.* [*eh-zehr-chee-tah'-reh*] exercise, practice
esercito [*eh-zehr'-chee-toh*] army
esercizio [*eh-zehr-chee'-tsee-oh*] exercise
esibire *v.* [*eh-zee-bee'-reh*] exhibit
esibizione *f.* [*eh-zee-bee-tsee-oh'-neh*] exhibition
esigenza [*eh-zee-jehn'-tsah*] requirement
esigere *v.* [*eh-zee'-jeh-reh*] require
esilio [*eh-zee'-lee-oh*] exile
esistente [*eh-zees-tehn'-teh*] existent, living
esistenza [*eh-zees-tehn'-tsah*] existence
esistere *v.* [*eh-zees'-teh-reh*] exist
esitare *v.* [*eh-zee-tah'-reh*] hesitate
esperienza [*ehs-peh-ree-ehn'-tsah*] experience
esperimento [*ehs-peh-ree-mehn'-toh*] experiment
esperto [*ehs-pehr'-toh*] expert

esplodere v. [ehs-ploh'-deh-reh] burst
esplorare v. [ehs-ploh-rah'-reh] explore
esplosione f. [ehs-ploh-zee-oh'-neh] explosion
esporre v. irreg. [ehs-pohr'-reh] display
esportare v. [ehs-pohr-tah'-reh] export
esportazione f. [ehs-pohr-tah-tsee-oh'-neh] export
esposizione f. [ehs-poh-zee-tsee-oh'-neh] show, exhibition
espressione f. [ehs-prehs-see-oh'-neh] expression
espresso [ehs-prehs'-soh] express
esprimere v. irreg. [ehs-pree'-meh-reh] express
essa [ehs'-sah] she, it
esse f. [ehs'-seh] they
essenza [ehs-sehn'-tsah] essence
essenziale [ehs-sehn-tsee-ah'-leh] essential
essere v. irreg. [ehs'-seh-reh] be
essere umano [ehs'-seh-reh oo-mah'-noh] human being
essi m. [ehs'-see] they
esso [ehs'-soh] he, it
est m. [ehst] East
estate f. [ehs-tah'-teh] summer
estendere v. [ehs-tehn'-deh-reh] extend
estensione f. [ehs-tehn-see-oh'-neh] extent, extension
esteriore [ehs-teh-ree-oh'-reh] exterior
esterno [ehs-tehr'-noh] external
estero [ehs'-teh-roh] foreign
  all'estero [ahl-lehs'-teh-roh] abroad
estinguere v. [ehs-teen'-goo-eh-reh] extinguish
estivo adj. [ehs-tee'-voh] summer, summery
estraneo [ehs-trah'-neh-oh] stranger
estrarre v. irreg. [ehs-trahr'-reh] extract
estremamente [ehs-treh-mah-mehn'-teh] extremely
estremo [ehs-treh'-moh] extreme
età f. indecl. [eh-tah'] age
eterno [eh-tehr'-noh] eternal
etichetta [eh-tee-keht'-tah] label
Europa [eh-oo-roh'-pah] Europe
Europeo [eh-oo-roh-peh'-oh] European
evacuare v. [eh-vah-koo-ah'-reh] evacuate
evento [eh-vehn'-toh] event
eventualmente [eh-vehn-too-ahl-mehn'-teh] eventually

evidente [*eh-vee-dehn'-teh*] evident
evidentemente [*eh-vee-dehn-teh-mehn'-teh*] evidently
evidenza [*eh-vee-dehn'-tsah*] evidence
evitare *v.* [*eh-vee-tah'-reh*] avoid
evo [*eh'-voh*] age, era
  medio evo [*meh'-dee-oh eh'-voh*] middle ages

F

fa [*fah*] he (she, it) makes, does
  Cosa fa? [*koh'-zah fah*] What are you doing?
  Fa caldo [*fah kahl'-doh*] It is warm
  Fa freddo [*fah frehd'-doh*] It is cold
  Non fa niente [*nohn fah nee-ehn'-teh*] It doesn't matter
fa [*fah*] ago
  due settimane fa [*doo'-eh seht-tee-mah'-ne fah*] two weeks
    ago
  molto tempo fa [*mohl'-toh tehm'-poh fah*] long ago
fabbrica [*fahb'-bree-kah*] factory
fabbricante [*fahb-bree-kahn'-teh*] manufacturer
fabbricare *v.* [*fahb-bree-kah'-reh*] manufacture
faccenda [*fahch-chehn'-dah*] business, matter
facchino [*fahk-kee'-noh*] porter
faccia [*fahch'-chee-ah*] face
facile [*fah'-chee-leh*] easy
facilità *f. indecl.* [*fah-chee-lee-tah'*] ease, facility
facilmente [*fah-cheel-mehn'-teh*] easily
facoltà *f. indecl.* [*fah-kohl-tah'*] faculty
faggioli *m. pl.* [*fahj-jee-oh'-lee*] beans
fagotto [*fah-goht'-toh*] bundle
fallimento [*fahl-lee-mehn'-toh*] failure
fallire *v.* [*fahl-lee'-reh*] fail
falsità *f. indecl.* [*fahl-see-tah'*] falsehood
falso [*fahl'-soh*] false
fama [*fah'-mah*] fame
fame *f.* [*fah'-meh*] hunger
  avere *v.* **fame** [*ah-veh'-reh fah'-meh*] be hungry

famiglia [*fah-mee'-lyah*] family
familiare [*fah-mee-lee-ah'-reh*] familiar
famoso [*fah-moh'-zoh*] famous
fanciullezza [*fahn-chee-oo-lehts'-tsah*] childhood
fanciullo, fanciulla [*fahn-chee-ool'-loh, fahn-chee-ool'-lah*]
    young boy, young girl
fango [*fahn'-goh*] mud
fantasia [*fahn-tah-zee'-ah*] fantasy, fancy
fantasma [*fahn-tahz'-mah*] ghost
fantastico [*fahn-tahs'-tee-koh*] fantastic
fare v. irreg. [*fah'-reh*] make, do
   Faccia attenzione! [*fahch'-chee-ah aht-tehn-tsee-oh'-neh*]
    Pay attention!, Look out!
   Faccia presto! [*fahch'-chee-ah prehs'-toh*] Hurry up!
farfalla [*fahr-fahl'-lah*] butterfly
farina [*fah-ree'-nah*] flour
farmacia [*fahr-mah-chee'-ah*] pharmacy
faro [*fah'-roh*] lighthouse
fascino [*fah'-shee-noh*] charm
fase f. [*fah'-zeh*] phase
fastidio [*fahs-tee'-dee-oh*] annoyance
fatale [*fah-tah'-leh*] fatal
fatica [*fah-tee'-kah*] fatigue
faticoso [*fah-tee-koh'-zoh*] tiresome
fatto [*faht'-toh*] fact, deed, made, done
   fatto a mano [*faht'-toh ah mah'-noh*] handmade
fattoria [*faht-toh-ree'-ah*] farm
fattura [*faht-too'-rah*] invoice
favore m. [*fah-voh'-reh*] favor
   per favore [*pehr fah-voh'-reh*] please
favorire v. [*fah-voh-ree'-reh*] favor, please
   Favorisca! [*fah-voh-rees'-kah*] Please!
favorito [*fah-voh-ree'-toh*] favorite
fazzoletto [*fahts-tsoh-leht'-toh*] handkerchief
febbraio [*fehb-brah'-ee-oh*] February
febbre f. [*fehb'-breh*] fever
febbrile [*fehb-bree'-leh*] feverish
fede f. [*feh'-deh*] faith, wedding ring
fedele [*feh-deh'-leh*] faithful
federale [*feh-deh-rah'-leh*] federal

fegato [*feh'-gah-toh*] liver

felice [*feh-lee'-cheh*] happy

felicità *f. indecl.* [*feh-lee-chee-tah'*] happiness

felicitazioni [*feh-lee-chee-tah-tsee-oh'-nee*] congratulations

femmina [*fehm'-mee-nah*] female

femminile [*fehm-mee-nee'-leh*] feminine

ferire *v.* [*feh-ree'-reh*] wound, injure

ferita [*feh-ree'-tah*] wound, injury

ferito [*feh-ree'-toh*] wounded

fermare *v.* [*fehr-mah'-reh*] stop

fermarsi *v.* [*fehr-mahr'-see*] stop [oneself]
  Si fermi qui! [*see fehr'-mee koo-ee'*] Stop here!

fermata [*fehr-mah'-tah*] stop

fermo [*fehr'-meh*] firm, closed

feroce [*feh-roh'-cheh*] ferocious, fierce

ferro [*fehr'-roh*] iron [metal]
  ferro da stiro [*fehr'-roh dah stee'-roh*] flat iron

ferrovia [*fehr-roh-vee'-ah*] railroad, railway

festa [*fehs'-tah*] feast, party

festival *m.* [*fehs'-tee-vahl*] festival

fetta [*feht'-tah*] slice

fettuccine *f. pl.* [*feht-tooch-chee'-neh*] fettucine

fiamma [*fee-ahm'-mah*] flame

fiammifero [*fee-ahm-mee'-feh-roh*] (safety) match

fianco [*fee-ahn'-koh*] side, hip

fiaschetta [*fees-ahs-keht'-tah*] flask

fiato [*fee-ah'-toh*] breath, breathing

fico [*fee'-koh*] fig

fidanzamento [*fee-dahn-tsah-mehn'-toh*] engagement

fidanzato [*fee-dahn-tsah'-toh*] fiancé

fidarsi *v.* [*fee-dahr'-see*] rely, trust

fiducia [*fee-doo'-chee-ah*] trust
  degno di fiducia [*deh'-nyoh dee fee-doo'-chee-ah*] reliable

fiducioso [*fee-doo-chee-oh'-zoh*] confident

fiero [*fee-eh'-roh*] proud

figlia [*fee'-lyah*] daughter

figliastra [*fee-lyahs'-trah*] stepdaughter

figliastro [*fee-lyahs'-troh*] stepson

figli [*fee'-lyee*] children

figlio [*fee'-lyoh*] son

figura [*fee-goo'-rah*] figure
figurarsi *v.* [*fee-goo-rahr'-see*] imagine
  Si figuri!, Figurati! [*see fee-goo'-ree, fee-goo'-rah-tee*]
    Just imagine!
fila [*fee'-lah*] file, line, row
filo [*fee'-loh*] wire [metal], thread
filobus [*fee'-loh-boos*] trolley bus
filosofia [*fee-loh-zoh-fee'-ah*] philosophy
filosofo [*fee-loh'-zoh-foh*] philosopher
filtro [*feel'-troh*] filter
finale [*fee-nah'-leh*] final
finalmente [*fee-nahl-mehn'-teh*] finally
finanziario [*fee-nahn-tsee-ah'-ree-oh*] financial
finchè [*feen-keh'*] until, till
fine *adj.*, [*fee'-neh*] fine, thin, subtle
fine *m.* [*fee'-neh*] purpose, sake, aim
fine *f.* [*fee'-neh*] end, ending
  alla fine [*ahl'-lah fee'-neh*] at last
finestra [*fee-nehs'-trah*] window [of house]
finestrino [*fee-nehs-tree'-noh*] window [of car or train]
fingere *v. irreg.* [*feen'-jeh-reh*] pretend
finire *v.* [*fee-nee'-reh*] end, finish
finito [*fee-nee'-toh*] finished
fino a [*fee'-noh ah*] until, up to
finora [*fee-noh'-rah*] as yet
fintanto che [*feen-tahn'-toh keh*] as long as
fioraio [*fee-oh-rah'-ee-oh*] flower shop
fiore *m.* [*fee-oh'-reh*] flower
  dei fiori [*deh'-ee fee-oh'-ree*] some flowers
Firenze [*fee-rehn'-tseh*] Florence
fiorire *v.* [*fee-oh-ree'-reh*] blossom
fioritura [*fee-oh-ree-too'-rah*] blossom
firma [*feer'-mah*] signature
firmare *v.* [*feer-mah'-reh*] sign
fischiare *v.* [*fees-kee-ah'-reh*] whistle
fischio [*fees'-kee-oh*] whistle
fisica [*fee'-zee-kah*] physics
fisico [*fee'-zee-koh*] physical
fissare *v.* [*fees-sah'-reh*] fix, set, fasten
fiume *m.* [*fee-oo'-meh*] river

fisso [*fees'-soh*] fixed, regular
  prezzo fisso [*prehts'-tsoh fees'-soh*] fixed price
flanella [*flah-nehl'-lah*] flannel
flauto [*flah'-oo-toh*] flute
flessibile [*flehs-see'-bee-leh*] flexible
flotta [*floht'-tah*] fleet
fluente [*floo-ehn'-teh*] fluent
fluentemente [*floo-ehn-teh-mehn'-teh*] fluently
fluido [*floo'-ee-doh*] fluid
focolare *m.* [*foh-koh-lah'-reh*] fireplace
fodera [*foh'-deh-rah*] lining
foglia [*foh'-lyah*] leaf
foglio [*foh'-lyoh*] sheet [paper]
folla [*fohl'-lah*] crowd
fondamentale [*fohn-dah-mehn-tah'-leh*] fundamental
fondare *v.* [*fohn-dah'-reh*] found, establish
fondazione *f.* [*fohn-dah-tsee-oh'-neh*] foundation
fondi [*fohn'-dee*] funds
fondo [*fohn'-doh*] bottom
fonografo [*foh-noh'-grah-foh*] phonograph
fontana [*fohn-tah'-nah*] fountain
fonte *f.* [*fohn'-teh*] spring [of water]
forbici [*fohr'-bee-chee*] scissors
forchetta [*fohr-keht'-tah*] fork
foresta [*foh-rehs'-tah*] forest
forare *v.* [*foh-rah'-reh*] bore [a hole]
forma [*fohr'-mah*] form, shape
formaggio [*fohr-mahj'-jee-oh*] cheese
formale [*fohr-mah'-leh*] formal
formalità *f. indecl.* [*fohr-mah-lee-tah'*] formality
formare *v.* [*fohr-mah'-reh*] form, shape
formica [*fohr'-mee-kah*] ant
formidabile [*fohr-mee-dah'-bee-leh*] formidable
formula [*fohr'-moo-lah*] formula
fornire *v.* [*fohr-nee'-reh*] furnish
forno [*fohr'-noh*] oven
foro [*foh'-roh*] forum
forse [*fohr'-seh*] maybe
forte [*fohr'-teh*] strong
fortezza [*fohr-tehts'-tsah*] fortress

fortuna [*fohr-too'-nah*] fortune, luck
  Buona fortuna! [*boo-oh'-nah fohr-too'-nah*] Good luck!
  per fortuna [*pehr fohr-too'-nah*] luckily
fortunatamente [*fohr-too-nah-tah-mehn'-teh*] fortunately
fortunato [*fohr-too-nah'-toh*] fortunate, lucky
forza [*fohr'-tsah*] strength, force, power
forzare v. [*fohr-tsah'-reh*] force
fossa [*fohs'-sah*] ditch, pit
fotografare v. [*foh-toh-grah-fah'-reh*] photograph
fotografia [*foh-toh-grah-fee'-ah*] photograph, picture
fotografo [*foh-toh'-grah-foh*] photographer
fra [*frah*] between, among
  fra poco [*frah poh'-koh*] in a short while
  fra noi [*frah noh'-ee*] between us
fracassare v. [*frah-kahs-sah'-reh*] smash
fragile [*frah'-jee-leh*] fragile, frail
fragola [*frah'-goh-lah*] strawberry
fragranza [*frah-grahn'-tsah*] fragrance
francese [*frahn-cheh'-zeh*] French, Frenchman
Francia [*frahn'-chee-ah*] France
Franco [*frahn'-koh*] frank
francobollo [*frahn-koh-bohl'-loh*] stamp
frase [*frah'-zeh*] sentence, phrase
fratello [*frah-tehl'-loh*] brother
frattanto [*fraht-tahn'-toh*] meanwhile
freccia [*frehch'-chee-ah*] arrow
freddo [*frehd'-doh*] cold
  avere v. **freddo** [*ah-veh'-reh frehd'-doh*] be cold
  prendere v. **freddo** [*prehn'-deh-reh frehd'-doh*] catch cold
fremere v. [*freh'-meh-reh*] shudder
frenare v. [*freh-nah'-reh*] brake
frenetico [*freh-neh'-tee-koh*] frantic
freno [*freh'-noh*] brake
frequente [*freh-koo-ehn'-teh*] frequent
frequentemente [*freh-koo-ehn-teh-mehn'-teh*] frequently
fresco [*frehs'-koh*] cool, fresh
fretta [*freht'-tah*] haste, hurry
  avere v. **fretta** [*ah-veh'-reh freht'-tah*] be in a hurry
friggere v. [*freej'-jeh-reh*] fry
frigorifero [*free-goh-ree'-feh-roh*] refrigerator

frittata [*freet-tah'-tah*] omelet
frittella [*free-tehl'-lah*] pancake
fritto [*freet'-toh*] fried
fronte *m.* [*frohn'-teh*] front
fronte *f.* [*frohn'-teh*] forehead
frode *f.* [*froh'-deh*] fraud
frugale [*froo-gah'-leh*] thrifty
frusta [*froos'-tah*] whip
frutta [*froot'-tah*] fruit
fruttivendolo [*froot-tee-vehn'-doh-loh*] fruit store
fucile *m.* [*foo-chee'-leh*] gun, rifle
fuga [*foo'-gah*] escape, flight
fuggire *v.* [*fooj-jee'-reh*] flee
fuggitivo [*fooj-jee-tee'-voh*] runaway
fulmine *f.* [*fool'-mee-neh*] lightning
fumare *v.* [*foo-mah'-reh*] smoke
fumo [*foo'-moh*] smoke
fune *f.* [*foo'-neh*] rope
fungo [*foon'-goh*] mushroom
funerale *m.* [*foo-neh-rah'-leh*] funeral
funzione *f.* [*foon-tsee-oh'-neh*] function
fuoco [*foo-oh'-koh*] fire
fuori [*foo-oh'-ree*] out, outside
furbo [*foor'-boh*] smart, crafty
furfante [*foor-fahn'-teh*] villain
furioso [*foo-ree-oh'-zoh*] furious
furore *m.* [*foo-roh'-reh*] rage, fury
furia [*foo'-ree-ah*] fury, anger
furto [*foor'-toh*] theft
futuro [*foo-too'-roh*] future

G

gabbia [*gahb'-bee-ah*] cage
gabinetto [*kah-bee-neht'-toh*] cabinet
galleggiare *v.* [*gahl-lehj-jee-ah'-reh*] float
galleria [*gahl-leh-ree'-ah*] gallery

galleria sotterranea [*gahl-leh-ree'-ah soht-tehr-rah'-neh-ah*] tunnel

gallina [*gahl-lee'-nah*] hen

gallo [*gahl'-loh*] rooster

gallone *m.* [*gahl-loh'-neh*] gallon

gamba [*gahm'-bah*] leg

gambero [*gahm'-beh-roh*] shrimp

gancio [*gahn'-chee-oh*] hook

gara [*gah'-rah*] race, competition

garante *m.* [*gah-rahn'-teh*] voucher

garantire *v.* [*gah-rahn-tee'-reh*] guarantee

garanzia [*gah-rahn-tsee'-ah*] guarantee

gattino [*gaht-tee'-noh*] kitten

gatto [*gaht'-toh*] cat

gelatina [*jeh-lah-tee'-nah*] jelly

gelato [*jeh-lah'-toh*] ice cream

gelato [*jeh-lah'-toh*] frozen

gelo [*jeh'-loh*] frost

geloso [*jeh-loh'-zoh*] jealous

gemello [*jeh-mehl'-loh*] twin

gemito [*jeh'-mee-toh*] groan

gemma [*jehm'-mah*] gem

generale [*jeh-neh-rah'-leh*] general
   in generale [*een jeh-neh-rah'-leh*] in general

generalmente [*jeh-neh-rahl-mehn'-teh*] generally

generatore *m.* [*jeh-neh-rah-toh'-reh*] generator

generazione *f.* [*jeh-neh-rah-tsee-oh'-neh*] generation

genere *m.* [*jeh'-neh-reh*] kind, gender, sort

genero [*jeh'-neh-roh*] son-in-law

generoso [*jeh-neh-roh'-zoh*] generous

gengiva [*jehn-jee'-vah*] gum [anat.]

genio [*jeh'-nee-oh*] genius

genitori [*jeh-nee-toh'-ree*] parents

gennaio [*jehn-nah'-ee-oh*] January

Genova [*jeh'-noh-vah*] Genoa

gente *f.* [*jehn'-teh*] people

gentile [*jehn-tee'-leh*] kind, gentle, polite

gentilezza [*jehn-tee-lehts'-tsah*] kindness

genuino [*jeh-noo-ee'-noh*] genuine

geografia [*jeh-oh-grah-fee'-ah*] geography

geometria [*jeh-oh-meh-tree'-ah*] geometry
gergo [*jehr'-goh*] slang
Germania [*jehr-mah'-nee-ah*] Germany
germe *m.* [*jehr'-meh*] germ
gettare *v.* [*jeht-tah'-reh*] throw
ghiaccio [*gee-ahch'-chee-oh*] ice
già [*jee-ah'*] already
giacca, giacche *pl.* [*jee-ahk'-kah, jee-ahk'-keh*] jacket
giallo [*jee-ahl'-loh*] yellow
Giappone *m.* [*jee-ahp-poh'-neh*] Japan
giapponese [*jee-ahp-poh-neh'-zeh*] Japanese
giardiniere *m.* [*jee-ahr-dee-nee-eh'-reh*] gardener
giardino [*jee-ahr-dee'-noh*] garden
  giardino d'infanzia [*jee-ahr-dee'-noh deen-fahn'-tsee-ah*]
    kindergarten
  giardino zoologico [*jee-ahr-dee'-noh dzoh-oh-loh'-jee-koh*]
    zoo
ginocchio [*jee-nohk'-kee-oh*] knee
giocare *v.* [*jee-oh-kah'-reh*] play [a game]
  giocare d'azzardo [*jee-oh-kah'-reh dahdz-dzahr'-doh*]
    gamble
giocattolo [*jee-oh-kaht'-toh-loh*] toy
gioco [*jee-oh'-koh*] game, play
  gioco del calcio [*jee-oh'-koh dehl kahl'-chee-oh*] football
gioia [*jee-oh'-ee-ah*] joy
gioielliere *m.* [*jee-oh-ee-ehl-lee-eh'-reh*] jeweller
gioielleria [*jee-oh-ee-ehl-leh-ree'-ah*] jeweller's shop
gioiello [*jee-oh-ee-ehl'-loh*] jewel
gioioso [*jee-oh-ee-oh'-zoh*] joyful
giornale *m.* [*jee-ohr-nah'-leh*] newspaper
giornalismo [*jee-ohr-nah-leez'-moh*] journalism
giornalista *m.* [*jee-ohr-nah-lees'-tah*] journalist
giornalmente [*jee-ohr-nahl-mehn'-teh*] daily
giornata [*jee-ohr-nah'-tah*] daylong
giorno [*jee-ohr'-noh*] day
  buon giorno [*boo-ohn' jee-ohr'-noh*] good morning
  giorno feriale [*jee-ohr'-noh feh-ree-ah'-leh*] workday
  ogni giorno [*oh'-nyee jee-ohr'-noh*] every day
  tutto il giorno [*toot'-toh eel jee-ohr'-noh*] all day
giovane [*jee-oh'-vah-neh*] young

(il) giovane [(*eel*) *jee-oh'-vah-neh*] (the) young man
(la) giovane [(*lah*) *jee-oh'-vah-neh*] (the) young woman
più giovane [*pee-oo' jee-oh'-vah-neh*] junior
giovanile [*jee-oh-vah-nee'-leh*] youthful
giovanotto [*jee-oh-vah-noht'-toh*] young man
giovedì *m. indecl.* [*jee-oh-veh-dee'*] Thursday
gioventù *f. indecl.* [*jee-oh-vehn-too'*] youth
gioviale [*jee-oh-vee-ah'-leh*] jovial
girare *v.* [*jee-rah'-reh*] turn; tour; endorse [a check]
giro [*jee'-roh*] tour, turn
gita [*jee'-tah*] short trip, picnic
giù [*jee-oo'*] down, below
giubilante [*jee-oo-bee-lahn'-teh*] jubilant
giubileo [*jee-oo-bee-leh'-oh*] jubilee
giudeo [*jee-oo-deh'-oh*] Jewish
giudicare *v.* [*jee-oo-dee-kah'-reh*] judge
giudice [*jee-oo'-dee-cheh*] judge
giudizio [*jee-oo-dee'-tsee-oh*] judgment
giugno [*jee-oo'-nyoh*] June
giungere *v.* [*jee-oon'-jeh-reh*] arrive, reach
giuramento [*jee-oo-rah-mehn'-toh*] oath
giurare *v.* [*jee-oo-rah'-reh*] swear
giuria [*jee-oo-ree'-ah*] jury
giurisdizione *f.* [*jee-oo-reez-dee-tsee-oh'-neh*] jurisdiction
giustamente [*jee-oos-tah-mehn'-teh*] justly
giustezza [*jee-oos-tehts'-tsah*] fairness
giustizia [*jee-oos-tee'-tsee-ah*] justice
giusto [*jee-oos'-toh*] just, fair
  Sono giusto arrivato [*soh'-noh jee-oos'-toh ahr-ree-vah'-toh*] I just arrived
glandola [*glahn'-doh-lah*] gland
gli *art., m. pl.* [*lyee*] the
gli: a lui *obj. pron., m. sing.* [*lyee, ah loo'-ee*] to him
globo [*gloh'-boh*] globe
gloria [*gloh'-ree-ah*] glory
goccia [*gohch'-chee-ah*] drop
godere *v.* [*goh-deh'-reh*] enjoy
  godere la vita [*goh-deh'-reh lah vee'-tah*] enjoy life
gola [*goh'-lah*] throat
  mal *m.* **di gola** [*mahl dee goh'-lah*] sore throat

gomito [*goh'-mee-toh*] elbow
gomma [*gohm'-mah*] tire [of car]
gomma [*gohm'-mah*] rubber
   gomma da cancellare [*gohm'-mah dah kahn-chehl-lah'-reh*]
     eraser
gonfiare v. [*gohn-fee-ah'-reh*] swell
governante f. **di casa** [*goh-vehr-nahn'-teh dee kah'-zah*]
   housekeeper
governare v. [*goh-vehr-nah'-reh*] govern
governatore m. [*goh-vehr-nah-toh'-reh*] governor
governo [*goh-vehr'-noh*] government
gradito [*grah-dee'-toh*] appreciated
grado [*grah'-doh*] grade, degree
gradualmente [*grah-doo-ahl-mehn'-teh*] gradually
graffio [*grahf'-fee-oh*] scratch
grammatica [*grahm-mah'-tee-kah*] grammar
Gran Bretagna [*grahn breh-tah'-nyah*] Great Britain
granchio [*grahn'-kee-oo*] crab
grande [*grahn'-deh*] big, great
   più grande, il (la) più grande [*pee-oo' grahn'-deh, eel (lah)*
     pee-oo' grahn'-deh] bigger, (the) biggest
   grandissimo [*grahn-dees'-see-moh*] very big
grandezza [*grahn-dehts'-tsah*] greatness
grandine f. [*grahn'-dee-neh*] hail
grano [*grah'-noh*] wheat, grain
grappa [*grahp'-pah*] brandy
grasso n. & adj. [*grahs'-soh*] fat, grease
gratitudine f. [*grah-tee-too'-dee-neh*] gratitude
grato [*grah'-toh*] thankful
grattacielo [*graht-tah-chee-eh'-loh*] skyscraper
gratuito [*grah-too-ee'-toh*] free, granted
grave adj. [*grah'-veh*] grave
gravidanza [*grah-vee-dahn'-tsah*] pregnancy
gravità f. indecl. [*grah-vee-tah'*] gravity
grazia [*grah'-tsee-ah*] grace
Grazie [*grah'-tsee-eh*] Thank you
   Grazie tanto [*grah'-tsee-eh tahn'-toh*] Thanks a lot
grazioso [*grah-tsee-oh'-zoh*] lovely
Grecia [*greh'-chee-ah*] Greece
greco [*greh'-koh*] Greek

grembiule *m.* [*grehm-bee-oo'-leh*] apron
grezzo [*grehdz'-dzoh*] raw
   materiale grezzo [*mah-teh-ree-ah'-leh grehdz'-dzoh*]
    raw material
gridare *v.* [*gree-dah'-reh*] yell
grido [*gree'-doh*] shout
grigio [*gree'-jee-oh*] grey
grosso [*grohs'-soh*] big, bulky
gruppo [*groop'-poh*] group
guadagnare *v.* [*goo-ah-dah-nyah'-reh*] earn, gain
guadagno [*goo-ah-dah'-nyoh*] gain
Guai! [*goo-ah'-ee*] Beware!, Woe!
guancia [*goo-ahn'-chee-ah*] cheek
guanto [*goo-ahn'-toh*] glove
guardare *v.* [*goo-ahr-dah'-reh*] watch, look
   Guardi! [*goo-ahr'-dee*] Look!
guardarobiere *m.* [*goo-ahr-dah-roh-bee-eh'-reh*] dresser
guardia [*goo-ahr'-dee-ah*] guard
guardiano [*goo-ahr-dee-ah'-noh*] guardian
guarire *v.* [*goo-ah-ree'-reh*] heal, get well
guastare *v.* [*goo-ahs-tah'-reh*] spoil
guerra [*goo-ehr'-rah*] war
   guerra mondiale [*goo-ehr'-rah mohn-dee-ah'-leh*] world war
guida [*goo-ee'-dah*] guide
guidare *v.* [*goo-ee-dah'-reh*] drive, lead
guscio [*goo-'shee-oh*] nutshell
gusto [*goos'-toh*] taste
gustoso [*goos-toh'-zoh*] tasty, agreeable

H

ha [*ah*] he (she, it) has, (you) have
hai [*ah'-ee*] you have
hanno [*ahn'-noh*] they have
ho [*oh*] I have

I

i *m. pl.* [*ee*] the
iarda [*ee-ahr'-dah*] yard
Iddio [*ee-dee'-oh*] God
idea [*ee-deh'-ah*] idea
ideale [*ee-deh-ah'-leh*] ideal
identico [*ee-dehn'-tee-koh*] identical
identificare *v.* [*ee-dehn-tee-fee-kah'-reh*] identify
identità *f. indecl.* [*ee-dehn-tee-tah'*] identity
   carta d'identità [*kahr'-tah dee-dehn-tee-tah'*] identification
      card
idiota [*ee-dee-oh'-tah*] idiot
idolo [*ee'-doh-loh*] idol
ieri [*ee-eh'-ree*] yesterday
   l'altro ieri [*lahl'-troh ee-eh'-ree*] the day before yesterday
   ieri sera [*ee-eh'-ree seh'-rah*] yesterday evening
igienico [*ee-jee-eh'-nee-koh*] sanitary
ignorante [*ee-nyoh-rahn'-teh*] ignorant
ignoto [*ee-nyoh'-toh*] unknown
il, lo, l' *m. sing.* [*eel, loh, l*] the
illecito [*eel-leh'-chee-toh*] illicit
illegale [*eel-leh-gah'-leh*] unlawful, illegal
illegibile [*eel-leh-jee'-bee-leh*] illegible
illeso [*eel-leh'-zoh*] unharmed
illogico [*eel-loh'-jee-koh*] irrational
illusione *f.* [*eel-loo-zee-oh'-neh*] illusion
illustrazione *f.* [*eel-loos-trah-tsee-oh'-neh*] illustration
illustre [*eel-loos'-treh*] distinguished
imballaggio [*eem-bahl-lahj'-jee-oh*] packing
imbarazzare *v.* [*eem-bah-rahts-tsah'-reh*] embarrass
imbarazzato [*eem-bah-rahts-tsah'-toh*] embarrassed
imbarcare *v.* [*eem-bahr-kah'-reh*] ship
imbarcarsi *v.* [*eem-bahr-kahr'-see*] embark
imbarco [*eem-bahr'-koh*] shipment
imbroglione *m.* [*eem-broh-lyoh'-neh*] crook

imbucare v. [em-boo-kah'-reh] mail
imitare v. [ee-mee-tah'-reh] imitate
imitazione f. [ee-mee-tah-tsee-oh'-neh] imitation
immacolato [eem-mah-koh-lah'-toh] spotless
immaginare v. [eem-mah-jee-nah'-reh] imagine
immaginazione f. [eem-mah-jee-nah-tsee-oh'-neh] imagination
immagine f. [eem-mah'-jee-neh] image
immateriale [eem-mah-teh-ree-ah'-leh] immaterial
immaturo [eem-mah-too'-roh] immature
immediatamente [eem-meh-dee-ah-tah-mehn'-teh] immediately
immediato [eem-meh-dee-ah'-toh] immediate
immenso [eem-mehn'-soh] immense
immigrazione f. [eem-mee-grah-tsee-oh'-neh] immigration
imminente [eem-mee-nehn'-teh] impending, imminent
immondizia [eem-mohn-dee'-tsee-ah] garbage
immorale [eem-moh-rah'-leh] immoral
immunità f. indecl. [eem-moo-nee-tah'] immunity
impaccare v. [eem-pahk-kah'-reh] pack
imparare v. [eem-pah-rah'-reh] learn
imparentato [eem-pah-rehn-tah'-toh] related
imparziale [eem-pahr-tsee-ah'-leh] impartial
impaurito [eem-pah-oo-ree'-toh] afraid
impaziente [eem-pah-tsee-ehn'-teh] impatient
impedire [eem-peh-dee'-reh] prevent
impegnarsi v., [eem-peh-nyahr'-see] engage [oneself]
impegno [eem-peh'-nyoh] engagement
imperdonabile [eem-pehr-doh-nah'-bee-leh] unforgivable
imperfetto [eem-pehr-feht'-toh] imperfect
imperialismo [eem-pehr-ee-ah-leez'-moh] imperialism
impermeabile [eem-pehr-meh-ah'-bee-leh] waterproof
impero [eem-peh'-roh] empire
impiegare v. [eem-pee-eh-gah'-reh] employ
impiegato [eem-pee-eh-gah'-toh] employee, clerk
impiego [eem-pee-eh'-goh] job, employment, use
imporre v. [eem-pohr'-reh] impose
importante [eem-pohr-tahn'-teh] important
   Che importa? [keh eem-pohr'-tah] What difference does
    it make?
   Non importa [nohn eem-pohr'-tah] It doesn't matter
importanza [eem-pohr-tahn'-tsah] importance

importare v. [*eem-pohr-tah'-reh*] import
importato [*eem-pohr-tah'-toh*] imported
impossibile [*eem-pohs-see'-bee-leh*] impossible
impreparato [*eem-preh-pah-rah'-toh*] unprepared
impresa [*eem-preh'-zah*] enterprise
impressione f. [*eem-prehs-see-oh'-neh*] impression
impressionante [*eem-prehs-see-oh-nahn'-teh*] impressive
imprevisto [*eem-preh-vees'-toh*] unforseen
imprigionare v. [*eem-pree-jee-oh-nah'-reh*] imprison
imprimere v. [*eem-pree'-meh-reh*] print
improbabile [*eem-proh-bah'-bee-leh*] unlikely
improvvisamente [*eem-prohv-vee-zah-mehn'-teh*] suddenly
improvviso [*eem-prohv-vee'-zoh*] sudden
impronta [*eem-prohn'-tah*] print, mark, footprint
  impronta digitale [*eem-prohn'-tah dee-jee-tah'-leh*]
    fingerprint
imprudente [*eem-proo-dehn'-teh*] careless
in [*een*] in, into, at
inatteso [*ee-naht-teh'-zoh*] unexpected
incapace [*een-kah-pah'-cheh*] unable
incapacità f. indecl. [*een-kah-pah-chee-tah'*] inability
incarico [*een-kah'-ree-koh*] appointment, task
incassare v. [*een-kahs-sah'-reh*] cash
incerto [*een-chehr'-toh*] uncertain
inchiesta [*een-kee-ehs'-tah*] inquiry
inchinarsi v. [*een-kee-nahr'-see*] bow
inchino [*een-kee'-noh*] bow, curtsey
inchiodare v. [*een-kee-oh-dah'-reh*] nail
inchiostro [*een-kee-ohs'-troh*] ink
inciampare v. [*een-chee-ahm-pah'-reh*] trip, stumble
incidentalmente [*een-chee-dehn-tahl-mehn'-teh*] incidentally
incidente m. [*een-chee-dehn'-teh*] accident, incident
incinta [*een-cheen'-tah*] pregnant
inclinazione f. [*een-klee-nah-tsee-oh'-neh*] inclination
includere v. [*een-kloo'-deh-reh*] include
incluso [*een-kloo'-zoh*] included
incombustibile [*een-kohm-boos-tee'-bee-leh*] fireproof
incomparabile [*een-kohm-pah-rah'-bee-leh*] incomparable
incompleto [*een-kohm-pleh'-toh*] incomplete
inconsapevole [*een-kohn-sah-peh'-voh-leh*] unconscious,

unaware

incontestabile [*een-kohn-tehs-tah'-bee-leh*] unquestionable

incontrare v. [*een-kohn-trah'-reh*] encounter

  incontrare per caso [*een-kohn-trah'-reh pehr kah'-zoh*] run across

  L'incontro ogni domenica [*leen-kohn'-troh oh'-nyee doh-meh'-nee-kah*] I meet him every Sunday

incontro [*een-kohn'-troh*] match [sport], meeting

incoraggiamento [*een-koh-rahj-jee-ah-mehn'-toh*] encouragement

incoraggiare v. [*een-koh-rahj-jee-ah'-reh*] encourage

incredibile [*een-kreh-dee'-bee-leh*] incredible

incrocio [*een-kroh'-chee-oh*] intersection

incubo [*een'-koo-boh*] nightmare

incursione f. [*een-koor-see-oh'-neh*] raid

indecente [*een-deh-chehn'-teh*] indecent

indeciso [*een-deh-chee'-zoh*] undecided

indefinito [*een-deh-fee-nee'-toh*] indefinite

indelicato [*een-deh-lee-kah'-toh*] tactless

India [*een'-dee-ah*] India

indiano [*een-dee-ah'-noh*] Indian

indicare v. [*een-dee-kah'-reh*] indicate

indicatore m. [*een-dee-kah-toh'-reh*] gauge

indice m. [*een'-dee-cheh*] index

indietro [*een-dee-eh'-troh*] back, backwards

indifferente [*een-deef-feh-rehn'-teh*] indifferent

indigestione f. [*een-dee-jehs-tee-oh'-neh*] indigestion

indignato [*een-dee-nyah'-toh*] indignant

indimenticabile [*een-dee-mehn-tee-kah'-bee-leh*] unforgettable

indipendente [*een-dee-pehn-dehn'-teh*] independent

indipendenza [*een-dee-pehn-dehn'-tsah*] independence

indiretto [*een-dee-reht'-toh*] indirect

indirizzare (una lettera) v. [*een-dee-reets-tsah'-reh (oo'-nah leht'-teh-rah)*] address (a letter)

indirizzo [*een-dee-reets'-tsoh*] address, direction

indiscreto [*een-dees-kreh'-toh*] indiscreet

individuale [*een-dee-vee-doo-ah'-leh*] individual

indossare v. [*een-dohs-sah'-reh*] wear [clothes]

indovinare v. [*een-doh-vee-nah'-reh*] guess

indubbiamente [*een-doob-bee-ah-mehn'-teh*] doubtlessly

indumento [*een-doo-mehn'-toh*] garment
industria [*een-doos'-tree-ah*] industry
industriale [*een-doos-tree-ah'-leh*] industrial
inesatto [*een-ehz-aht'-toh*] inaccurate
inefficiente [*een-ehf-fee-chee-ehn'-teh*] inefficient
inesprimibile [*een-ehs-pree-mee'-bee-leh*] unspeakable
inestimabile [*een-ehs-tee-mah'-bee-leh*] invaluable
inetto [*een-eht'-toh*] unfit
infatti [*een-faht'-tee*] in fact
infedele [*een-feh-deh'-leh*] unfaithful
infelice [*een-feh-lee'-cheh*] unhappy
inferiore [*een-feh-ree-oh'-reh*] inferior
infermiera [*een-fehr-mee-eh'-rah*] nurse [medical]
inferno [*een-fehr'-noh*] hell
infezione *f.* [*een-feh-tsee-oh'-neh*] infection
infine [*een-fee'-neh*] after all, at last
infinito [*een-fee-nee'-toh*] infinite, infinitive
inflessibile [*een-flehs-see'-bee-leh*] unyielding
influenza [*een-floo-ehn'-tsah*] influence
influenzare *v.* [*een-floo-ehn-tsah'-reh*] influence
informare *v.* [*een-fohr-mah'-reh*] inform, acquaint
informarsi *v.* [*een-fohr-mahr'-see*] inquire
informazione *f.* [*een-fohr-mah-tsee-oh'-neh*] information
infrequente [*een-freh-koo-ehn'-teh*] infrequent
ingannare *v.* [*een-gahn-nah'-reh*] deceive
inganno [*een-gahn'-noh*] deceit
ingegnere *m.* [*een-jeh-nyeh'-reh*] engineer
ingegno [*een-jeh'-nyoh*] wit
ingenuo [*een-jeh'-noo-oh*] naive
Inghilterra [*een-geel-tehr'-rah*] England
inghiottire *v.* [*een-gee-oht-tee'-reh*] swallow
inginocchiarsi *v.* [*een-jee-nohk-kee-ahr'-see*] kneel
ingiusto [*een-jee-oos'-toh*] unjust
ingiustizia [*een-jee-oos-tee'-tsee-ah*] injustice
inglese [*een-gleh'-zeh*] British, English
ingranaggio [*een-grah-nahj'-jee-oh*] gear [of a car]
ingrato [*een-grah'-toh*] ungrateful
ingresso [*een-grehs'-soh*] entrance
  Vietato l'ingresso [*vee-eh-tah'-toh leen-grehs'-soh*]
    No admittance

iniezione *f.* [*ee-nee-eh-tsee-oh'-neh*] injection

inimmaginabile [*een-eem-mah-jee-nah'-bee-leh*] unimagined

iniziale *f.* [*ee-nee-tsee-ah'-leh*] initial

iniziare *v.* [*ee-nee-tsee-ah'-reh*] start

inizio [*ee-nee'-tsee-oh*] beginning

innamorarsi *v.* [*een-nah-moh-rahr'-see*] fall in love

innanzi [*een-nahn'-tsee*] before

innocente [*een-noh-chehn'-teh*] innocent

inoltre [*ee-nohl'-treh*] furthermore, besides

inondazione *f.* [*ee-nohn-dah-tsee-oh'-neh*] flood

inquieto [*een-koo-ee-eh'-toh*] uneasy

inquilino [*een-koo-ee-lee'-noh*] tenant

insalata [*een-sah-lah'-tah*] salad

insegnamento [*een-seh-nyah-mehn'-toh*] teaching

insegnante *m.* [*een-seh-nyahn'-teh*] teacher

insegnare *v.* [*een-seh-nyah'-reh*] teach

inseguire *v.* [*een-seh-goo-ee'-reh*] run after

insetto [*een-seht'-toh*] insect

insieme [*een-see-eh'-meh*] together

  nell' insieme [*nehl-een-see-eh'-meh*] altogether

insignificante [*een-see-nyee-fee-kahn'-teh*] unimportant

insistere *v.* [*een-sees'-teh-reh*] insist

insolito [*een-soh'-lee-toh*] unusual

insomma [*een-sohm'-mah*] in conclusion, after all

insopportabile [*een-sohp-pohr-tah'-bee-leh*] unbearable

installare *v.* [*een-stahl-lah'-reh*] install

insufficiente [*een-soo-fee-chee-ehn'-teh*] insufficient

insultare *v.* [*een-sool-tah'-reh*] insult

insulto [*een-sool'-toh*] insult

intanto [*een-tahn'-toh*] meanwhile

inttato [*een-taht'-toh*] intact

integrale [*een-teh-grah'-leh*] unabridged

intellettuale [*een-tehl-leht-too-ah'-leh*] intellectual

intelligente [*een-tehl-lee-jehn'-teh*] intelligent

intendere *v.* [*een-tehn'-deh-reh*] intend, mean

intenso [*een-tehn'-soh*] intense

intenzione *f.* [*een-tehn-tsee-oh'-neh*] intention

internazionale [*een-tehr-nah-tsee-oh-nah'-leh*] international

interno [*een-tehr'-noh*] internal

  all'interno [*ahl-leen-tehr'-noh*] inside

interamente [*een-teh-rah-mehn'-teh*] entirely
interdire v. [*een-tehr-dee'-reh*] ban
interessante [*een-teh-rehs-sahn'-teh*] interesting
  non interessante [*nohn een-teh-rehs-sahn'-teh*] uninteresting
interessarsi v. [*een-teh-rehs-sahr'-see*] care for
  interessato in [*een-teh-rehs-sah'-toh een*] interested in
interesse m. [*een-teh-rehs'-seh*] interest
interferire v. [*een-tehr-feh-ree'-reh*] interfere
interiore [*een-teh-ree-oh'-reh*] interior
intero [*een-teh'-roh*] entire
interprete m. [*een-tehr'-preh-teh*] interpreter
interrompere v. [*een-tehr-rohm'-peh-reh*] discontinue
interruttore m. [*een-tehr-root-toh'-reh*] switch [electric]
intervallo [*een-tehr-vahl'-loh*] intermission
intervista [*een-tehr-vees'-tah*] interview
intervistare v. [*een-tehr-vees-tah'-reh*] interview
intesa [*een-teh'-zah*] understanding
  E inteso [*eh' een-teh'-zoh*] It is understood
intestini m. pl. [*een-tehs-tee'-nee*] bowels
intimità f. indecl. [*een-tee-mee-tah'*] privacy
intimo [*een'-tee-moh*] intimate
intorno [*een-tohr'-noh*] around
intraprendere v. [*een-trah-prehn'-deh-reh*] undertake
intrattenere v. [*een-traht-teh-neh'-reh*] entertain
intrudere v. [*een-troo'-deh-reh*] intrude
intuito [*een-too'-ee-toh*] intuition
inumano [*een-oo-mah'-noh*] inhuman
inutile [*ee-noo'-tee-leh*] useless
invalido [*een-vah'-lee-doh*] invalid
invano [*een-vah'-noh*] in vain
invasione f. [*een-vah-zee-oh'-neh*] invasion
invecchiare v. [*een-vehk-kee-ah'-reh*] age
invece (di) [*een-veh'-cheh (dee)*] instead (of)
inventore m. [*een-vehn-toh'-reh*] inventor
invenzione f. [*een-vehn-tsee-oh'-neh*] invention
inverno [*een-vehr'-noh*] winter
investigare v. [*een-vehs-tee-gah'-reh*] investigate
investire v. [*een-vehs-tee'-reh*] invest, run over
invidia [*een-vee'-dee-ah*] envy
invidiare v. [*een-vee-dee-ah'-reh*] envy

invisibile [*een-vee-zee'-bee-leh*] invisible
invitare v. [*een-vee-tah'-reh*] invite
invito [*een-vee'-toh*] invitation
invocare v. [*een-voh-kah'-reh*] plead
involontario [*een-voh-lohn-tah'-ree-oh*] involuntary
io [*ee'-oh*] I
iodio [*ee-oh'-dee-oh*] iodine
ipnotizzare v. [*eep-noh-teedz-dzah'-reh*] hypnotize
ipocrisia [*ee-poh-kree-zee'-ah*] hypocrisy
ipoteca [*ee-poh'-teh-kah*] mortgage
ira [*ee'-rah*] anger
Irlanda [*eer-lahn'-dah*] Ireland
irlandese [*eer-lahn-deh'-zeh*] Irish
ironico [*ee-roh'-nee-koh*] ironic
irregolare [*eer-reh-goh-lah'-reh*] irregular
irrequieto [*eer-reh-koo-ee-eh'-toh*] restless
irresistibile [*eer-reh-zees-tee'-bee-leh*] irresistible
irrigazione f. [*eer-ree-gah-tsee-oh'-neh*] irrigation
irritare v. [*eer-ree-tah'-reh*] irritate
irritazione f. [*eer-ree-tah-tsee-oh'-neh*] irritation
isola [*ee'-zoh-lah*] island
ispettore m. [*ees-peht-toh'-reh*] inspector
ispezionare v. [*ees-peh-tsee-oh-nah'-reh*] inspect
ispezione f. [*ees-peh-tsee-oh'-neh*] inspection
ispirazione f. [*ees-pee-rah-tsee-oh'-neh*] inspiration
isterico [*ees-teh'-ree-koh*] hysterical
istanza [*ees-tahn'-tsah*] instance
istinto [*ees-teen'-toh*] instinct
istituzione f. [*ees-tee-too-tsee-oh'-neh*] institution
istruire v. [*ees-troo-ee'-reh*] instruct, teach
istruito [*ees-troo-ee'-toh*] learned
istruttore m. [*ees-troot-toh'-reh*] instructor
istruzione f. [*ees-troo-tsee-oh'-neh*] instruction, education
Italia [*ee-tah'-lee-ah*] Italy
italiano [*ee-tah-lee-ah'-noh*] Italian
itinerario [*ee-tee-neh-rah'-ree-oh*] itinerary
Iugoslavia [*ee-oo-gohs-lah'-vee-ah*] Yugoslavia
iugoslavo [*ee-oo-gohs-lah'-voh*] Yugoslav
ivi [*ee'-vee*] there

L

la *art., f. sing.* [*lah*] the
la *obj. pron. f. sing.* [*lah*] her, it, you [polite form]
là, lì [*lah', lee'*] there
  al di là [*ahl dee lah'*] beyond
labbro, le labbra *pl.* [*lahb'-broh, leh lahb'-brah*] lip
laboratorio [*lah-boh-rah-toh'-ree-oh*] laboratory
laccio [*lahch'-chee-oh*] string, shoe lace
lacrima [*lah'-kree-mah*] teardrop
ladro [*lah'-droh*] thief
laggiù [*lahj-jee-oo'*] down there
lagnarsi *v.* [*lah-nyahr'-see*] complain
lago, laghi *pl.* [*lah'-goh, lah'-gee*] lake
laico [*lah'-ee-koh*] secular
lama [*lah'-mah*] blade
lamentare *v.* [*lah-mehn-tah'-reh*] lament, regret
lamentarsi *v.* [*lah-mehn-tahr'-see*] complain, moan
lametta [*lah-meht'-tah*] razor blade
lampada [*lahm'-pah-dah*] lamp
lampadina [*lahm-pah-dee'-nah*] light bulb
lampo [*lahm'-poh*] lightning, flash
lana [*lah'-nah*] wool
lanciare *v.* [*lahn-chee-ah'-reh*] throw, fling
lanterna [*lahn-tehr'-nah*] lantern
lapide *m.* [*lah'-pee-deh*] tombstone
lapis [*lah'-pees*] pencil
lardo [*lahr'-doh*] lard, bacon
larghezza [*lahr-gehts'-tsah*] width
largo [*lahr'-goh*] wide, large
lasagne *f. pl.* [*lah-zah'-nyeh*] lasagna
lasciare *v.* [*lah-shee-ah'-reh*] leave, let
  lasciar stare [*lah-shee-ahr' stah'-reh*] let alone
lassù [*lahs-soo'*] up there
lateralmente [*lah-teh-rahl-mehn'-teh*] sideways
latino [*lah-tee'-noh*] Latin

lato [*lah'-toh*] side

latrina [*lah-tree'-nah*] water closet

latte *m.* [*laht'-teh*] milk

latteria [*laht-teh-ree'-ah*] dairy

laurea [*lah'-oo-reh-ah*] degree

laurearsi *v.* [*lah-oo-reh-ahr'-see*] graduate

laureato [*lah-oo-reh-ah'-toh*] graduate

lavabo [*lah-vah-boh'*] washbasin

lavandaia [*lah-vahn-dah'-ee-ah*] laundress

lavanderia [*lah-vahn-deh-ree'-ah*] laundry

lavare *v.* [*lah-vah'-reh*] wash

  lavarsi [*lah-vahr'-see*] wash [oneself]

lavorare *v.* [*lah-voh-rah'-reh*] work

lavoratore *m.*, **lavoratrice** *f.* [*lah-voh-rah-toh'-reh, lah-voh-rah-tree'-cheh*] worker

lavoro [*lah-voh'-roh*] work, working

  datore *m.* **di lavoro** [*dah-toh'-reh dee lah-voh'-roh*] employer

le *art.*, *f. pl.* [*leh*] the

le *pron.*, *f. pl.* [*leh*] to you, you, her, to her, them

leale [*leh-ah'-leh*] loyal

lega [*leh'-gah*] league

legale [*leh-gah'-leh*] legal

legame *m.*, [*leh-gah'-meh*] bond

legare *v.* [*leh-gah'-reh*] bind, tie

legge *f.* [*lehj'-jeh*] law

leggere *v. irreg.* [*lehj'-jeh-reh*] read

leggermente [*lehj-jehr-mehn'-teh*] slightly

leggero [*lehj-jeh'-roh*] light [not heavy]

leggibile [*lehj-jee'-bee-leh*] legible

legione *f.* [*leh-jee-oh'-neh*] legion

legittimo [*leh-jeet'-tee-moh*] lawful

legno [*leh'-nyoh*] wood

legumi [*leh-goo'-mee*] vegetables

lei *3d pers. sing.*, *f.* [*leh'-ee*] she, her, you [polite form]

  lei scrive [*leh'-ee skree'-veh*] she/you write(s)

  a lei [*ah leh'-ee*] to her, to you

lentamente [*lehn-tah-mehn'-teh*] slowly

lente *m. sing.* [*lehn'-teh*] lens

lento [*lehn'-toh*] slow

lenzuolo, le lenzuola *pl.* [*lehn-tsoo-oh'-loh, leh lehn-tsoo-*

oh'-lah] bedsheet
lettera [*leht'-teh-rah*] letter
  cassetta da lettere [*kahs-seht'-tah dah leht'-teh-reh*]
    letter box
  lettera di presentazione [*leht'-teh-rah dee preh-zehn-tah-tsee-oh'-neh*] letter of introduction
  lettera raccomandata [*leht'-teh-rah rahk-koh-mahn-dah'-tah*] registered letter
letteralmente [*leht-teh-rahl-mehn'-teh*] literally
letteratura [*leht-teh-rah-too'-rah*] literature
letto [*leht'-toh*] bed
lettura [*leht-too'-rah*] reading
leva [*leh'-vah*] draft [military], lever
levante *m.* [*leh-vahn'-teh*] Near East
lezione *f.* [*leh-tsee-oh'-neh*] lesson
li *pron., m. pl.* [*lee*] them
lì [*lee'*] there
  lì per lì [*lee' pehr lee'*] at first
libbra [*leeb'-brah*] pound [weight]
liberale [*lee-beh-rah'-leh*] liberal
liberare *v.* [*lee-beh-rah'-reh*] free
libero [*lee'-beh-roh*] free
libertà *f. indecl.* [*lee-behr-tah'*] freedom
libreria [*lee-breh-ree'-ah*] bookstore
libro [*lee'-broh*] book
licenza [*lee-chehn'-tsah*] permit
licenziare *v.* [*lee-chehn-tsee-ah'-reh*] dismiss
lido [*lee'-doh*] seashore
lieto [*lee-eh'-toh*] glad, happy
  Molto lieto di conoscerla! [*mohl'-toh lee-eh'-toh dee koh-noh'-shehr-lah*] Very happy to meet you!
lima [*lee'-mah*] file [tool]
limitare *v.* [*lee-mee-tah'-reh*] limit
limite [*lee'-mee-teh*] boundary
limonata [*lee-moh-nah'-tah*] lemonade
limone *m.* [*lee-moh'-neh*] lemon
linea [*lee'-neh-ah*] line
  linea aerea [*lee'-neh-ah ah-eh'-reh-ah*] airline
lineamenti *m. pl.* [*lee-neh-ah-mehn'-tee*] features
lingua [*leen'-goo-ah*] tongue, language

liquido [*lee'-koo-ee-doh*] liquid
liquore *m.* [*lee-koo-oh'-reh*] liquor
lira sterlina [*lee'-rah stehr-lee'-nah*] pound [money]
liscio [*lee'-shee-oh*] smooth
lista [*lees'-tah*] list, menu
   lista delle vivande [*lees'-tah dehl'-leh vee-vahn'-deh*]
     bill of fare
lite *f.* [*lee'-teh*] quarrel
litorale [*lee-toh-rah'-leh*] waterfront
litro [*lee'-troh*] liter [approx. 1 quart]
livello [*lee-vehl'-loh*] level
   passaggio a livello [*pahs-sahj'-jee-oh ah lee-vehl'-loh*]
     railroad crossing
lo *art., m. sing.* [*loh*] the
lo *pron., m. sing.* [*loh*] him, it
locale [*loh-kah'-leh*] local
località *f. indecl.* [*loh-kah-lee-tah'*] location
locomotiva [*loh-koh-moh-tee'-vah*] locomotive
locanda [*loh-kahn'-dah*] inn
lodare *v.* [*loh-dah'-reh*] praise
logico [*loh'-jee-koh*] logical
lontano [*lohn-tah'-noh*] far
   Quanto lontano? [*koo-ahn'-toh lohn-tah'-noh*] How far?
   molto lontano [*mohl'-toh lohn-tah'-noh*] far away
loro *subj. pron., m. & f. pl.* [*loh'-roh*] they, you [polite form]
loro *m., f. pl.*, **essi** *m. pl.*, **esse** *f. pl.* [*loh'-roh, ehs'-see,*
   ehs'-seh] them
   il loro *m. sing.*, **la loro** *f. sing.*, **i loro** *m. pl.*, **le loro** *f. pl.*
   [*eel loh'-roh, lah loh'-roh, ee loh'-roh, leh loh'-roh*]
   theirs, yours [polite form]
   a loro [*ah loh'-roh*] to them, to you
   per loro [*pehr loh'-roh*] for them, for you
lotta [*loht'-tah*] struggle
   lotta libera [*loht'-tah lee'-beh-rah*] wrestling
lottare *v.* [*loht-tah'-reh*] fight
lotto [*loht'-toh*] lot [real estate]
lozione *f.* [*loh-tsee-oh'-neh*] lotion
   lozione da barba [*loh-tsee-oh'-neh dah bahr'-bah*] shaving
     lotion
lubrificare *v.* [*loo-bree-fee-kah'-reh*] lubricate

luce *f.* [*loo'-cheh*] light
  accendere *v.* **la luce** [*ahch-chehn'-deh-reh lah loo'-cheh*]
    turn on the light
  spegnere *v.* **la luce** [*speh'-nyeh-reh lah loo'-cheh*] turn out
    the light
lucidare *v.* [*loo-chee-dah'-reh*] polish
lucido [*loo'-chee-doh*] polish
luglio [*loo'-lyoh*] July
lui [*loo'-ee*] he, him
luna [*loo'-nah*] moon
  chiaro di luna [*kee-ah'-roh dee loo'-nah*] moonlight
  luna di miele [*loo'-nah dee mee-eh'-leh*] honeymoon
lunedì [*loo-neh-dee'*] Monday
lunghezza [*loon-gehts'-tsah*] length
lungo [*loon'-goh*] long
  più a lungo [*pee-oo' ah loon'-goh*] longer [time]
  più lungo [*pee-oo' loon'-goh*] longer [measure]
luogo [*loo-oh'-goh*] place
  aver *v.* **luogo** [*ah-vehr' loo-oh'-goh*] take place, happen
  in luogo di [*een loo-oh'-goh dee*] in place of
lupo [*loo'-poh*] wolf
lusingare *v.* [*loo-zeen-gah'-reh*] flatter
lusso [*loos'-soh*] luxury
lussuoso [*loos-soo-oh'-zoh*] luxurious
lustrascarpe *m.* [*loos-trah-skahr'-peh*] shoeshine boy
lutto [*loot'-toh*] mourning

M

ma [*mah*] but, however, yet
macchia [*mahk'-kee-ah*] spot, stain
macchina [*mahk'-kee-nah*] car, machine, engine
  macchina da scrivere [*mahk'-kee-nah dah skree'-veh-reh*]
    typewriter
  macchina da cucire [*mahk'-kee-nah dah koo-chee'-reh*]
    sewing machine
  macchina fotografica [*mahk'-kee-nah foh-toh-grah'-fee-kah*]

camera

macchinario [*mahk-kee-nah'-ree-oh*] machinery

macellaio [*mah-chehl-lah'-ee-oh*] butcher

macelleria [*mah-chehl-leh-ree'-ah*] butcher shop

macinare v. [*mah-chee-nah'-reh*] grind

madre f. [*mah'-dreh*] mother

madrigna [*mah-dree'-nyah*] stepmother

madrina [*mah-dree'-nah*] godmother

maestà f. indecl. [*mah-ehs-tah'*] majesty

maestro m., **maestra** f. [*mah-ehs'-troh, mah-ehs'-trah*]
   schoolteacher

magazzino [*mah-gahdz-dzee'-noh*] warehouse, storage

maggio [*mahj'-jee-oh*] May

maggiore [*mahj-jee-oh'-reh*] bigger, greater, elder
   la maggior parte [*lah mahj'-jee-ohr pahr'-teh*] most,
      the majority

maggioranza [*mahj-jee-oh-rahn'-tsah*] majority

maggiorenne [*mahj-jee-oh-rehn'-neh*] of age

magico [*mah'-jee-koh*] magic

magnifico [*mah-nyee'-fee-koh*] magnificent

magro [*mah'-groh*] skinny, thin

mai [*mah'-ee*] never, ever

maiale m. [*mah-ee-ah'-leh*] pork

malato [*mah-lah'-toh*] sick, ill

malattia [*mah-laht-tee'-ah*] sickness, disease
   malattia del cuore [*mah-laht-tee'-ah del koo-oh'-reh*]
      heart disease

maldisposto [*mahl-dees-pohs'-toh*] unwilling

male m. [*mah'-leh*] evil, ill

male adj. & adv. [*mah'-leh*] bad, badly
   far male v. [*fahr mah'-leh*] ache
   fare male a [*fah'-reh mah'-le ah*] hurt [somebody]
   mal di denti [*mahl dee dehn'-tee*] toothache
   mal di stomaco [*mahl dee stoh'-mah-koh*] stomachache
   mal di testa [*mahl dee tehs'-tah*] headache

maledire v. [*mah-leh-dee'-reh*] curse

maledizione f. [*mah-leh-dee-tsee-oh'-neh*] curse

malgrado [*mahl-grah'-doh*] regardless, despite

maligno [*mah-lee'-nyoh*] evil, bad

malinteso [*mahl-een-teh'-zoh*] misunderstanding

malissimo [*mah-lees'-see-moh*] very bad

malsano [*mahl-sah'-noh*] unhealthy

malvagio [*mahl-vah'-jee-oh*] wicked

mancanza [*mahn-kahn'-tsah*] lack

   sentire v. **la mancanza** [*sehn-tee'-reh lah mahn-kahn'-tsah*] miss [someone]

   Sento molto la sua mancanza [*sehn'-toh mohl'-toh lah soo'-ah mahn-kahn'-tsah*] I miss you very much

mancare v. [*mahn-kah'-reh*] be lacking

mancia [*mahn'-chee-ah*] tip, gratuity

mandare v. [*mahn-dah'-reh*] send

   mandare a chiamare [*mahn-dah'-reh ah kee-ah-mah'-reh*] send for

mandato [*mahn-dah'-toh*] warrant

maneggiare v. [*mah-nehj-jee-ah'-reh*] handle

mangiare v. [*mahn-jee-ah'-reh*] eat

mania [*mah-nee'-ah*] fad

manica [*mah'-nee-kah*] sleeve

manicure f. [*mah-nee-koo'-reh*] manicure

maniera [*mah-nee-eh'-rah*] manner, way

manifesto [*mah-nee-fehs'-toh*] poster, bill

maniglia [*mah-nee'-lyah*] handle

mano, le mani pl. [*mah'-noh, leh mah'-nee*] hand

   darsi v. **la mano** [*dahr'-see lah mah'-noh*] shake hands

manoscritto [*mah-nohs-kreet'-toh*] manuscript

mansueto [*mahn-soo-eh'-toh*] tame

mantenere v. irreg. [*mahn-teh-neh'-reh*] maintain, keep, support

manuale [*mah-noo-ah'-leh*] manual

manzo [*mahn'-tsoh*] beef

marca [*mahr'-kah*] brand

   marca di fabbrica [*mahr'-kah dee fahb'-bree-kah*] trademark

marchese m., **marchesa** f. [*mahr-keh'-zeh, mahr-keh'-zah*] marquis, marchioness

marcia [*mahr'-chee-ah*] march

marciapiede m. [*mahr-chee-ah-pee-eh'-deh*] sidewalk

marcio [*mahr'-chee-oh*] rotten

mare m. [*mah'-reh*] sea

marea [*mah-reh'-ah*] tide

margherita [*mahr-geh-ree'-tah*] daisy
marina [*mah-ree'-nah*] navy
marinaio [*mah-ree-nah'-ee-oh*] sailor
marionetta [*mah-ree-oh-neht'-tah*] puppet
marito [*mah-ree'-toh*] husband
marmellata [*mahr-mehl-lah'-tah*] jam
marmo [*mahr'-moh*] marble
marrone [*mahr-roh'-neh*] brown
martedì [*mahr-teh-dee'*] Tuesday
martello [*mahr-tehl'-loh*] hammer
marzo [*mahr'-tsoh*] March
mascella [*mah-shehl'-lah*] jaw
maschera [*mahs'-keh-rah*] mask
maschio [*mahs'-kee-oh*] male
massa [*mahs'-sah*] mass [quantity]
massaggio [*mahs-sahj'-jee-oh*] massage
massaia [*mahs-sah'-ee-ah*] housewife
massimo [*mahs'-see-moh*] greatest
masticare v. [*mahs-tee-kah'-reh*] chew
matematica [*mah-teh-mah'-tee-kah*] mathematics
materasso [*mah-teh-rahs'-soh*] mattress
materia [*mah-teh'-ree-ah*] matter
materiale m. [*mah-teh-ree-ah'-leh*] material
maternità f. indecl. [*mah-tehr-nee-tah'*] motherhood
materno [*mah-tehr'-noh*] maternal
matita [*mah-tee'-tah*] pencil
mattina [*maht-tee'-nah*] morning
mattone m. [*maht-toh'-neh*] brick
matrimonio [*mah-tree-moh'-nee-oh*] marriage
matto [*maht'-toh*] crazy
maturità f. indecl. [*mah-too-ree-tah'*] maturity
maturo [*mah-too'-roh*] mature, ripe
me [*meh*] me
meccanico [*mehk-kah'-nee-koh*] mechanic, mechanical
meccanismo [*mehk-kah-neez'-moh*] device
medaglia [*meh-dah'-lyah*] medal
medesimo [*meh-deh'-zee-moh*] same
media [*meh'-dee-ah*] average
medicina [*meh-dee-chee'-nah*] medicine
medico adj. [*meh'-dee-koh*] medical

medico *n.* [*meh'-dee-koh*] physician
  professione medica [*proh-fehs-see-oh'-neh meh'-dee-kah*]
    medical profession
medio [*meh'-dee-oh*] medium
mediterraneo [*meh-dee-tehr-rah'-neh-oh*] Mediterranean
meglio [*meh'-lyoh*] better, best
  meglio così [*meh'-lyoh koh-zee'*] better like that
  tanto meglio [*tahn'-toh meh'-lyoh*] so much the better
mela [*meh'-lah*] apple
  torta di mele [*tohr'-tah dee meh'-leh*] apple pie
melodia [*meh-loh-dee'-ah*] melody
melone *m.* [*meh-loh'-neh*] melon
membro [*mehm'-broh*] member
memoria [*meh-moh'-ree-ah*] memory
  a memoria [*ah meh-moh'-ree-ah*] by heart
mendicante *m.* [*mehn-dee-kahn'-teh*] beggar
meno [*meh'-noh*] less, minus
  a meno che [*ah meh'-noh keh*] unless
  al meno [*ahl meh'-noh*] at least
  di meno [*dee meh'-noh*] fewer
  il meno possibile [*eel meh'-noh pohs-see'-bee-leh*] the least
    possible
mensile [*mehn-see'-leh*] monthly
mentale [*mehn-tah'-leh*] mental
mente *f.* [*mehn'-teh*] mind
mentire *v.* [*mehn-tee'-reh*] lie, tell a lie
mento [*mehn'-toh*] chin
mentre *conj.* [*mehn'-treh*] while, as
  Mentre mangiavo [*mehn'-treh mahn-jee-ah'-voh*] While
    I was eating
menzionare *v.* [*mehn-tsee-oh-nah'-reh*] mention
meraviglia [*meh-rah-vee'-lyah*] amazement, wonder
  Che meraviglia! [*keh meh-rah-vee'-lyah*] How wonderful!
meravigliare *v.* [*meh-rah-vee-lyah'-reh*] amaze, astonish
meravigliarsi *v.* [*meh-rah-vee-lyahr'-see*] wonder
meraviglioso [*meh-rah-vee-lyoh'-zoh*] wonderful
mercante *m.* [*mehr-kahn'-teh*] merchant
mercato [*mehr-kah'-toh*] market
  a buon mercato [*ah boo-ohn' mehr-kah'-toh*] cheap
merce *f.* [*mehr'-cheh*] merchandise, goods

mercoledì [*mehr-koh-leh-dee'*] Wednesday
meridionale [*meh-ree-dyoh-nah'-leh*] southern
meritare *v.* [*meh-ree-tah'-reh*] deserve, merit
merito [*meh'-ree-toh*] merit
meschino [*mehs-kee'-noh*] mean, wretched
mescolare *v.* [*mehs-koh-lah'-reh*] mix
mescuglio [*mehs-koo'-lyoh*] mixture
mese *m.* [*meh'-zeh*] month
messa [*mehs'-sah*] mass [eccl.]
messaggero [*mehs-sahj-jeh'-roh*] messenger
messaggio [*mehs-sahj'-jee-oh*] message
messicano [*mehs-see-kah'-noh*] Mexican
Messico [*mehs'-see-koh*] Mexico
meta [*meh'-tah*] goal
metà *f. indecl.* [*meh-tah'*] half
  a metà strada [*ah meh-tah' strah'-dah*] halfway
  la metà [*lah meh-tah'*] one half
metallo [*meh-tahl'-loh*] metal
metodo [*meh'-toh-doh*] method
metro [*meh'-troh*] meter
  sistema *m.* **metrico** [*sees-teh'-mah meh'-ıree-koh*] metric
  system
mettere *v. irreg.* [*meht'-teh-reh*] set, put, lay
  mettere da parte [*meht'-teh-reh dah pahr'-teh*] set aside
  mettere in azione [*meht'-teh-reh een ah-tsee-oh'-neh*] set off
mezzo [*mehdz'-dzoh*] half, middle
  mezz'ora [*mehdz-dzoh'-rah*] half an hour
  in mezzo a [*een mehdz'-dzoh ah*] among, between
mezzogiorno [*mehdz-dzoh-jee-ohr'-noh*] noon
mezzanotte *f.* [*mehdz-dzah-noht'-teh*] midnight
mi [*mee*] me, to me
  Mi dia [*mee dee'-ah*] Give me
  Mi dica [*mee dee'-kah*] Tell me
  Mi scusi [*mee skoo'-zee*] Excuse me
miele *m.* [*mee-eh'-leh*] honey [food]
mietere *v.* [*mee-eh'-teh-reh*] harvest
miglio, miglia *pl.* [*mee'-lyoh, mee'-lyah*] mile
miglioramento [*mee-lyoh-rah-mehn'-toh*] improvement
migliorare *v.* [*mee-lyoh-rah'-reh*] improve
migliore *adj.,* [*mee-lyoh'-reh*] better

il (la) migliore [*eel (lah) mee-lyoh'-reh*] (the) best

Milano [*mee-lah'-noh*] Milan

milionario [*mee-lee-oh-nah'-ree-oh*] millionaire

milione *m.* [*mee-lee-oh'-neh*] million

   un milione, due milioni [*oon mee-lee-oh'-neh, doo'-eh mee-lee-oh-nee*] one million, two millions

militare [*mee-lee-tah'-reh*] military

mille, mila *pl.* [*meel'-leh, mee'-lah*] thousand, one thousand

   due mila [*doo'-eh mee'-lah*] two thousand

minaccia [*mee-nahch'-chee-ah*] threat

minacciare *v.* [*mee-nahch-chee-ah'-reh*] threaten

minatore *m.* [*mee-nah-toh'-reh*] miner

minerale *m.* [*mee-neh-rah'-leh*] mineral

minestra [*mee-nehs'-trah*] soup

miniera [*mee-nee-eh'-rah*] mine

minimo [*mee'-nee-moh*] least, minimum

ministero [*mee-nees-teh'-roh*] ministry, office

   ministero degli affari esteri [*mee-nees-teh'-roh deh'-lyee ahf-fah'-ree ehs'-teh-ree*] foreign office

ministro [*mee-nees'-troh*] minister

minoranza [*mee-noh-rahn'-tsah*] minority

minore [*mee-noh'-reh*] minor [of age]

minorenne [*mee-noh-rehn'-neh*] underage, minor

minuto *m. & adj.* [*mee-noo'-toh*] minute

   Aspetti un minuto! [*ahs-peht'-tee oon mee-noo'-toh*] Wait a minute!

mio *m.*, **mia** *f.*; **miei, mie** *pl.* [*mee'-oh, mee'-ah, mee-eh'-ee, mee'-eh*] my, mine

miope [*mee'-oh-peh*] shortsighted

miracolo [*mee-rah'-koh-loh*] miracle

mirare *v.* [*mee-rah'-reh*] aim

miscela [*mee-sheh'-lah*] blend

miserabile [*mee-zeh-rah'-bee-leh*] miserable

miseria [*mee-zeh'-ree-ah*] misery

misericordia [*mez-zeh-ree-kohr'-dee-ah*] mercy

misero [*mee'-zeh-roh*] woeful, wretched

missionario [*mees-see-oh-nah'-ree-oh*] missionary

missione *f.* [*mees-see-oh'-neh*] mission

misterioso [*mees-teh-ree-oh'-zoh*] mysterious

mistero [*mees-teh'-roh*] mystery

mistico [*mees'-tee-koh*] mystic
misura [*mee-zoo'-rah*] measure, size
misurare *v.* [*mee-zoo-rah'-reh*] measure
mite [*mee'-teh*] mild
mittente *m.* [*mee-tehn'-teh*] sender
mito [*mee'-toh*] myth
mobili *pl. m.* [*moh'-bee-lee*] furniture
moda [*moh'-dah*] fashion
  di moda [*dee moh'-dah*] fashionable
modello [*moh-dehl'-loh*] model, pattern
moderno [*moh-dehr'-noh*] modern
modestia [*moh-dehs'-tee-ah*] modesty
modesto [*moh-dehs'-toh*] modest
modificare *v.* [*moh-dee-fee-kah'-reh*] modify, alter
modo [*moh'-doh*] way, manner
  ad ogni modo [*ahd oh'-nyee moh'-doh*] in any case
  di modo che [*dee moh'-doh keh*] so that
  in nessun modo [*een nehs-soon' moh'-doh*] in no way
moglie [*moh'-lyeh*] wife
molo [*moh'-loh*] dock, pier, wharf
molti [*mohl'-tee*] many
moltissimo [*mohl-tees'-see-moh*] very much, a great many
molto [*mohl'-toh*] much, a lot, very
  Molto male! [*mohl'-toh mah'-leh*] Too bad!
  molto tempo [*mohl'-toh tehm'-poh*] a long time
  molto tempo fa [*mohl'-toh tehm'-poh fah*] long ago
momento [*moh-mehn'-toh*] moment
  al momento [*ahl moh-mehn'-toh*] at present
monaca [*moh'-nah-kah*] nun
monarchia [*moh-nahr-kee'-ah*] monarchy
monastero [*moh-nahs-teh'-roh*] monastery
mondo [*mohn'-doh*] world
moneta [*moh-neh'-tah*] coin, currency
monotono [*moh-noh'-toh-noh*] monotonous
montagna [*mohn-tah'-nyah*] mountain
  catena di montagne [*kah-teh'-nah dee mohn-tah'-nyeh*]
    mountain range
montare *v.* [*mohn-tah'-reh*] mount, set up
monte *m.* [*mohn'-teh*] mountain
monumento [*moh-noo-mehn'-toh*] monument

morale [*moh-rah'-leh*] moral, morale
moralità *f. indecl.* [*moh-rah-lee-tah'*] morality
morbido [*mohr'-bee-doh*] soft
morbillo [*mohr-beel'-loh*] measles
mordere *v. irreg.* [*mohr'-deh-reh*] bite
morire *v. irreg.* [*moh-ree'-reh*] die
mormorio [*mohr-moh-ree'-oh*] whisper, murmur
morso [*mohr'-soh*] bite, bitten
mortale [*mohr-tah'-leh*] deadly
morte *f.* [*mohr'-teh*] death
morto [*mohr'-toh*] dead
mosca [*mohs'-kah*] fly
mostarda [*mohs-tahr'-dah*] mustard
mostra [*mohs'-trah*] exhibition
mostrare *v.* [*mohs-trah'-reh*] show
mostruoso [*mohs-troo-oh'-zoh*] monstrous
motivo [*moh-tee'-voh*] motive
motocicletta [*moh-toh-chee-kleht'-tah*] motorcycle
motore *m.* [*moh-toh'-reh*] motor, engine
movimento [*moh-vee-mehn'-toh*] motion
mucchio [*mook'-kee-oh*] pile
mulino a vento [*moo-lee'-noh ah vehn'-toh*] windmill
multa [*mool'-tah*] fine, penalty
municipio [*moo-nee-chee'-pee-oh*] city hall
munizione *f.* [*moo-nee-tsee-oh'-neh*] ammunition
muovere *v. irreg.* [*moo-oh'-veh-reh*] move
muro [*moo'-roh*] wall
muscolo [*moos'-koh-loh*] muscle
museo [*moo-zeh'-oh*] museum
musica [*moo'-zee-kah*] music
musicale [*moo-zee-kah'-leh*] musical
musicista *m., f.* [*moo-zee-chees'-tah*] musician
muto [*moo'-toh*] dumb, mute

N

Napoli [*nah'-poh-lee*] Naples
narcotico [*nahr-koh'-tee-koh*] drug

narrativa [*nahr-rah-tee'-vah*] fiction
narrare *v.* [*nahr-rah'-reh*] narrate
nascere *v. irreg.* [*nah'-sheh-reh*] be born
  Dove è nato? [*doh'-veh eh' nah'-toh*] Where were you
    born?
nascita [*nah'-shee-tah*] birth
nascondere *v. irreg.* [*nahs-kohn'-deh-reh*] hide
naso [*nah'-zoh*] nose
nastro [*nahs'-troh*] ribbon, tape
Natale *m.* [*nah-tah'-leh*] Christmas
  Buon Natale! [*boo-ohn' nah-tah'-leh*] Merry Christmas!
nativo [*nah-tee'-voh*] native
nato [*nah'-toh*] born
  Dove è nato Lei? [*doh'-veh eh nah'-toh leh'-ee*] Where
    were you born?
natura [*nah-too'-rah*] nature
naturale [*nah-too-rah'-leh*] natural
naturalmente [*nah-too-rahl-mehn'-teh*] naturally
navale [*nah-vah'-leh*] naval
nave *f.* [*nah'-veh*] ship
  nave da carico [*nah'-veh dah kah'-ree-koh*] cargo ship
  nave da guerra [*nah'-veh dah goo-ehr'-rah*] warship
  nave traghetto [*nah'-veh trah-geht'-toh*] ferryboat
navigare *v.* [*nah-vee-gah'-reh*] sail
nazionale [*nah-tsee-oh-nah'-leh*] national
nazionalità *f. indecl.* [*nah-tsee-oh-nah-lee-tah'*] nationality
nazione *m.* [*nah-tsee-oh'-neh*] nation, country
nè, neppure [*neh, nehp-poo'-reh*] nor
nè . . . nè [*neh' . . . neh'*] neither . . . nor
  nè l'uno nè l'altro [*neh loo'-noh neh lahl'-troh*] neither
ne [*neh*] from there, from it
  ne vengono [*neh vehn'-goh-noh*] they come (from there)
ne [*neh*] of (about, from) him (her, it, you, them); some,
    any
  Di Pietro, ne abbiamo parlato [*dee pee-eh'-troh neh ahb-
    bee-ah'-moh pahr-lah'-toh*] Of Peter [of him] we spoke
neanche [*neh-ahn'-keh*] neither, not even
nebbia [*nehb'-bee-ah*] fog
nebbioso [*nehb-bee-oh'-zoh*] foggy
necessario [*neh-chehs-sah'-ree-oh*] necessary

necessità *f. indecl.* [*neh-chehs-see-tah'*] need, necessity
negare *v.* [*neh-gah'-reh*] deny
negativo [*neh-gah-tee'-voh*] negative
negligenza [*neh-glee-jehn'-tsah*] neglect
negli : in gli *m. pl.* [*neh'-lyee*] in the
negoziante *m.* [*neh-goh-tsee-ahn'-teh*] dealer
negoziare *v.* [*neh-goh-tsee-ah'-reh*] trade
negozio [*neh-goh'-tsee-oh*] store, shop
negro [*neh'-groh*] Negro
nemico [*neh-mee'-koh*] enemy
nemmeno [*nehm-meh'-noh*] not even
neppure [*nehp-poo'-reh*] not even
nero [*neh'-roh*] black
nervi [*nehr'-vee*] nerves
nervoso [*nehr-voh'-zoh*] nervous
nessuno [*nehs-soo'-noh*] nobody, none
   Non c'è nessuno [*nohn cheh' nehs-soo'-noh*] There is none
   per nessun motivo [*pehr nehs-soon' moh-tee'-voh*] by no
    means
netto *adj.*, [*neht'-toh*] net
neutrale [*neh-oo-trah'-leh*] neutral
neve *f.* [*neh'-veh*] snow
nevicare *v.* [*neh-vee-kah'-reh*] snow
nido [*nee'-doh*] nest
niente [*nee-ehn'-teh*] nothing
   niente affatto [*nee-ehn'-teh ahf-faht'-toh*] not in the least
   Non fa niente! [*nohn fah nee-ehn'-teh*] Never mind!
nipote *m.* [*nee-poh'-teh*] nephew
nipote *f.* [*nee-poh'-teh*] niece
nipotino *m.*, **nipotina** *f.* [*nee-poh-tee'-noh, nee-poh-tee'-nah*]
   grandchild
no [*noh*] no
nobile [*noh'-bee-leh*] noble
nocivo [*noh-chee'-voh*] harmful
nodo [*noh'-doh*] knot
noi [*noh'-ee*] we, us
   a noi [*ah noh'-ee*] to us
noia [*noh'-ee-ah*] boredom
noioso [*noh-ee-oh'-zoh*] boring
noleggiare *v.* [*noh-lehj-jee-ah'-reh*] charter

nome *m.* [*noh'-meh*] name, noun
  Quale è il suo nome? [*koo-ah'-leh eh' eel soo'-oh noh'-meh*] What is your name?
  Mi chiamo . . . [*mee kee-ah'-moh*] My name is . . .
  primo nome [*pree'-moh noh'-meh*] first name
nomignolo [*noh-mee'-nyoh-loh*] nickname
nominare *v.* [*noh-mee-nah'-reh*] name, elect
non [*nohn*] not
  Non . . . [*nohn*] Don't . . .
  No, non ci vado [*noh, nohn chee vah'-doh*] No, I don't go
  Non è buono [*nohn eh' boo-oh'-noh*] It is no good
  non più [*nohn pee-oo'*] no longer, no more
  non una volta [*nohn oo'-nah vohl'-tah*] not once
nondimeno [*nohn-dee-meh'-noh*] nevertheless
nonna [*nohn'-nah*] grandmother
nonno [*nohn'-noh*] grandfather
nono [*noh'-noh*] ninth
nonostante [*noh-nohs-tahn'-teh*] in spite of
  ciò nonostante [*chee-oh' noh-nohs-tahn'-teh*] even so
nord *m.* [*nohrd*] north
nord-est [*nohrd-ehst'*] northeast
nord-ovest [*nohrd-oh'-vehst*] northwest
normale [*nohr-mah'-leh*] normal
norvegese [*nohr-veh-jeh'-zeh*] Norwegian
Norvegia [*nohr-veh'-jee-ah*] Norway
nostalgico [*nohs-tahl'-jee-koh*] homesick
nostro *m.*, **nostra** *f.* [*nohs'-troh, nohs'-trah*] our
  il nostro, la nostra [*eel nohs'-troh, lah nohs'-trah*] ours
nostri *m. pl.*, **nostre** *f. pl.* [*nohs'-tree, nohs'-treh*] our
  i nostri, le nostre [*ee nohs'-tree, leh nohs'-treh*] ours
nota [*noh'-tah*] note
notare *v.* [*noh-tah'-reh*] notice
  far notare *v.* [*fahr noh-tah'-reh*] point out
notevole [*noh-teh'-voh-leh*] remarkable
notifica [*noh-tee'-fee-kah*] notice
notificare *v.* [*noh-tee-fee-kah'-reh*] notify
notizia [*noh-tee'-tsee-ah*] news
notte *f.* [*noht'-teh*] night
  Buona notte! [*boo-oh'-nah noht'-teh*] Good night!
  la notte scorsa [*lah noht'-teh skohr'-sah*] last night

locale notturno [*loh-kah'-leh noht-toor'-noh*] nightclub
novanta [*noh-vahn'-tah*] ninety
nove [*noh'-veh*] nine
novecento [*noh-veh-chehn'-toh*] nine hundred
novembre *m.* [*noh-vehm'-breh*] November
novità *f. indecl.* [*noh-vee-tah'*] novelty, news
   Che novità? [*keh noh-vee-tah'*] What's new?
nozione *f.* [*noh-tsee-oh'-neh*] notion
nozze *f. pl.* [*nohts'-tseh*] wedding
nubile [*noo'-bee-leh*] single, unmarried woman
nudo [*noo'-doh*] naked
nulla [*nool'-lah*] nothing
   Non c'è nulla [*nohn cheh' nool'-lah*] There is nothing
   Non serve a nulla [*nohn sehr'-veh ah nool'-lah*]
     It's good for nothing
   nulla di particolare [*nool'-lah dee pahr-tee-koh-lah'-reh*]
     nothing special
nullaosta [*nool-lah-ohs'-tah*] official permission
numero [*noo'-meh-roh*] number
numeroso [*noo-meh-roh'-zoh*] numerous
numberare *v.* [*noo-meh-rah'-reh*] number
nuocere *v.* [*noo-oh'-cheh-reh*] harm
nuora [*noo-oh'-rah*] daughter-in-law
nuotare *v.* [*nooh-oh-tah'-reh*] swim
nuotatore *m.* [*noo-oh-tah-toh'-reh*] swimmer
nuovo [*noo-oh'-voh*] new
   di nuovo [*dee noo-oh'-voh*] again
   niente di nuovo [*nee-ehn'-teh dee noo-oh'-voh*] nothing new
nutrimento [*noo-tree-mehn'-toh*] nourishment
nutrire *v.* [*noo-tree'-reh*] feed
nuvola [*noo'-voh-lah*] cloud
nuvoloso [*noo-voh-loh'-zoh*] cloudy
nylon *m.* [*nah'-ee-lohn*] nylon

O

o, od [*oh, ohd*] or, either
obbedire *v.* [*ohb-beh-dee'-reh*] obey

obbligare v. [*ohb-blee-gah'-reh*] oblige
obbligato [*ohb-blee-gah'-toh*] obliged
  molto obbligato [*mohl'-toh ohb-blee-gah'-toh*] much
    obliged
obbligo [*ohb'-blee-goh*] obligation
obiezione f. [*oh-bee-eh-tsee-oh'-neh*] objection
occasione f. [*ohk-kah-zee-oh'-neh*] occasion
occhiali m. pl. [*ohk-kee-ah'-lee*] eyeglasses
occhiata [*ohk-kee-ah'-tah*] glance
  dare v. **un'occhiata** [*dah'-reh oon ohk-kee-ah'-tah*] glance
occhio, occhi pl. [*ohk'-kee-oh, ohk'-kee*] eye
occorrere v. irreg. [*ohk-kohr'-reh-reh*] occur, need
occidentale [*ohch-chee-dehn-tah'-leh*] western
occidente [*ohch-chee-dehn'-teh*] west
occupare v. [*ohk-koo-pah'-reh*] occupy
occupato [*ohk-koo-pah'-toh*] busy, engaged, occupied
occupazione f. [*ohk-koo-pah-tsee-oh'-neh*] occupation
oceano [*oh-cheh'-ah-noh*] ocean
oculista m. [*oh-koo-lees'-tah*] eye doctor
odiare v. [*oh-dee-ah'-reh*] hate
odio [*oh'-dee-oh*] hate
odorare v. [*oh-doh-rah'-reh*] smell
odore m. [*oh-doh'-reh*] smell, odor
offendere v. irreg. [*ohf-fehn'-deh-reh*] offend
offendersi v. [*ohf-fehn'-dehr-see*] feel offended
offensivo [*ohf-fehn-see'-voh*] offensive
offerta [*ohf-fehr'-tah*] offer
offesa [*ohf-feh'-zah*] offence
officina [*ohf-fee-chee'-nah*] workshop
offrire v. irreg. [*ohf-free'-reh*] offer
oggetto [*ohj-jeht'-toh*] object
oggi [*ohj'-jee*] today
oggigiorno [*ohj-jee-jee-ohr'-noh*] nowadays
ogni [*oh'-nyee*] every, each, any
  ogni altro giorno [*oh'-nyee ahl'-troh jee-ohr'-noh*] every
    other day
  ogni cosa [*oh'-nyee koh'-zah*] everything
  ogni giorno [*oh'-nyee jee-ohr'-noh*] every day
  ogni volta [*oh'-nyee vohl'-tah*] every time
ognuno [*oh-nyoo'-noh*] everybody

Olanda [*oh-lahn'-dah*] Holland
olandese [*oh-lahn-deh'-zeh*] Dutch
olio [*oh'-lee-oh*] oil
   olio di oliva [*oh'-lee-oh dee oh-lee'-vah*] olive oil
oliva [*oh-lee'-vah*] olive
oltremare [*ohl-treh-mah'-reh*] overseas
ombra [*ohm'-brah*] shade, shadow
ombrello [*ohm-brehl'-loh*] umbrella
omettere *v.* [*oh-meht'-teh-reh*] omit
omissione *f.* [*oh-mees-see-oh'-neh*] omission
onda, ondata [*ohn'-dah, ohn-dah'-tah*] wave
ondeggiare *v.* [*ohn-dehj-jee-ah'-reh*] wave
onesto [*oh-nehs'-toh*] honest
onorare *v.* [*oh-noh-rah'-reh*] honor
onorario [*oh-noh-rah'-ree-oh*] fee
onore *m.* [*oh-noh'-reh*] honor
opera [*oh'-peh-rah*] opera, work
   mano d'opera [*mah'-noh doh'-peh-rah*] labor
   opera d'arte [*oh'-peh-rah dahr'-teh*] work of art
operaio [*oh-peh-rah'-ee-oh*] laborer
operare *v.* [*oh-peh-rah'-reh*] operate [surgery]
operazione *f.* [*oh-peh-rah-tsee-oh'-neh*] operation
opinione *f.* [*oh-pee-nee-oh'-neh*] opinion
opporre *v. irreg.* [*ohp-pohr'-reh*] oppose
opportunità *f. indecl.* [*ohp-pohr-too-nee-tah'*] opportunity
opposto [*ohp-pohs'-toh*] opposite
oppure [*ohp-poo'-reh*] or (else)
ora [*oh'-rah*] hour, now, time
   or sono [*ohr soh'-noh*] ago
   Che ore sono? [*keh oh'-reh soh'-noh*] What time is it?
orale [*oh-rah'-leh*] oral
orario [*oh-rah'-ree-oh*] schedule
oratore *m.* [*oh-rah-toh'-reh*] speaker
orchestra [*ohr'-kehs-trah*] orchestra
ordinare *v.* [*ohr-dee-nah'-reh*] order, arrange, command
ordinariamente [*ohr-dee-nah-ree-ah-mehn'-teh*] ordinarily
ordinario [*ohr-dee-nah'-ree-oh*] ordinary
ordinato [*ohr-dee-nah'-toh*] orderly
ordine *m.* [*ohr'-dee-neh*] order
   ai suoi ordini [*ah'-ee soo-oh'-ee ohr'-dee-nee*] at your

service

orecchino [*oh-rehk-kee'-noh*] earring

orecchio, le orecchie *pl.* [*oh-rehk'-kee-oh, leh oh-rehk'-kee-eh*] ear

organico [*ohr-gah'-nee-koh*] organic

organizzare *v.* [*ohr-gah-needz-dzah'-reh*] organize

organizzazione *f.* [*ohr-gah-needz-dzah-tsee-oh'-neh*] organization

organo [*ohr'-gah-noh*] organ

orgoglio [*ohr-goh'-lyoh*] pride

orgoglioso [*ohr-goh-lyoh'-zoh*] proud

orfano [*ohr'-fah-noh*] orphan

orientale [*oh-ree-ehn-tah'-leh*] eastern

Oriente *m.* [*oh-ree-ehn'-teh*] Far East

   Medio Oriente [*meh'-dee-oh oh-ree-ehn'-teh*] Middle East

originale [*oh-ree-jee-nah'-leh*] original

originalmente [*oh-ree-jee-nahl-mehn'-teh*] originally

orizzonte *m.* [*oh-reedz-dzohn'-teh*] horizon

orlo [*ohr'-loh*] edge

ormai [*ohr-mah'-ee*] by now, already

ornamento [*ohr-nah-mehn'-toh*] ornament

oro [*oh'-roh*] gold

   d'oro [*doh'-roh*] golden

orologiaio [*oh-roh-loh-jee-ah'-ee-oh*] watchmaker

orologio [*oh-roh-loh'-jee-oh*] watch, clock

   orologio da polso [*oh-roh-loh'-jee-oh dah pohl'-soh*] wristwatch

orribile [*ohr-ree'-bee-leh*] horrible

orso [*ohr'-soh*] bear

ortografia [*ohr-toh-grah-fee'-ah*] spelling

osare *v.* [*oh-zah'-reh*] dare

osceno [*oh-sheh'-noh*] obscene

oscurità *f. indecl.* [*ohs-koo-ree-tah'*] darkness

oscuro [*ohs-koo'-roh*] obscure, dim

ospedale *m.* [*ohs-peh-dah'-leh*] hospital

ospitalità *f. indecl.* [*ohs-pee-tah-lee-tah'*] hospitality

ospite *m.* [*ohs'-pee-teh*] host, guest

osservare *v.* [*ohs-sehr-vah'-reh*] observe

osservatore *m.*, **osservatrice** *f.* [*ohs-sehr-vah-toh'-reh, ohs-sehr-vah-tree'-cheh*] observer

osservazione *f.* [*ohs-sehr-vah-tsee-oh′-neh*] observation
ossigeno [*ohs-see′-jeh-noh*] oxygen
osso, le ossa *pl.* [*ohs′-soh, leh ohs′-sah*] bone
ostacolo [*ohs-tah′-koh-loh*] obstacle
oste [*ohs′-teh*] innkeeper
ostile [*ohs-tee′-leh*] hostile
ostinato [*ohs-tee-nah′-toh*] stubborn
ostrica [*ohs′-tree-kah*] oyster
ottanta [*oht-tahn′-tah*] eighty
ottavo [*oht-tah′-voh*] eighth
ottenere *v. irreg.* [*oht-teh-neh′-reh*] obtain, get
ottimista *m., f.* [*oht-tee-mees′-tah*] optimistic, optimist
ottimo [*oht′-tee-moh*] excellent
otto [*oht′-toh*] eight
ottobre *m.* [*oht-toh′-breh*] October
ottocento [*oht-toh-chehn′-toh*] eight hundred
ottone *m.* [*oht-toh′-neh*] brass
ovale [*oh-vah′-leh*] oval
ovest *m.* [*oh′-vehst*] west
ovunque [*oh-voon′-koo-eh*] everywhere
ovvio [*ohv′-vee-oh*] obvious
ozioso [*oh-tsee-oh′-zoh*] lazy

P

pacchetto [*pahk-keht′-toh*] package
  pacchetto di sigarette [*pahk-keht′-toh dee see-gah-reht′teh*]
    pack of cigarettes
pacco [*pahk′-koh*] pack, package, parcel
pace *f.* [*pah′-cheh*] peace
pacifico [*pah-chee′-fee-koh*] peaceful, easy-going
padella [*pah-dehl′-lah*] frying pan
padre *m.* [*pah′-dreh*] father
padrigno [*pah-dree′-nyoh*] stepfather
padrino [*pah-dree′-noh*] godfather
padrona *f.* [*pah-droh′-nah*] boss, owner [female]
  padrona di casa [*pah-droh′-nah dee kah′-zah*] landlady

padrone *m.* [*pah-droh'-neh*] boss, owner, master
  padrone di casa [*pah-droh'-neh dee kah'-zah*] landlord
paesaggio [*pah-eh-zahj'-jee-oh*] landscape
paese *m.* [*pah-eh'-zeh*] country
paga [*pah'-gah*] pay
pagamento [*pah-gah-mehn'-toh*] payment, pay
  tratta di pagamento [*traht'-tah dee pah-gah-mehn'-toh*]
    draft [bank]
pagare *v.* [*pah-gah'-reh*] pay
  pagare in contanti [*pah-gah'-reh een kohn-tahn'-tee*]
    pay cash
  pagare mensilmente [*pah-gah'-reh mehn-seel-mehn'-teh*]
    pay by instalments
  pagare una multa [*pah-gah'-reh oo'-nah mool'-tah*]
    pay a fine
pagina [*pah'-jee-nah*] page
paglia [*pah'-lyah*] straw
paio, paia *pl.* [*pah'-ee-oh, pah'-ee-ah*] pair
palazzo [*pah-lahts'-tsoh*] palace, mansion
palcoscenico [*pahl-koh-sheh'-nee-koh*] stage [theater]
palestra [*pah-lehs'-trah*] gymnasium [sports]
palla [*pahl'-lah*] ball [for playing]
pallido [*pahl'-lee-doh*] pale
pallone *m.* [*pahl-loh'-neh*] balloon
palma [*pahl'-mah*] palm
palo [*pah'-loh*] pole, post
palpebra [*pahl'-peh-brah*] eyelid
pane *m.* [*pah'-neh*] bread
  del pane [*dehl pah'-neh*] some bread
pane abbrustolito [*pah'-neh ahb-broos-toh-lee'-toh*] toast
panetteria [*pah-neht-teh-ree'-ah*] bakery
panfilo [*pahn-fee'-loh*] yacht
panico [*pah'-nee-koh*] panic
panino [*pah-nee'-noh*] sandwich, bun
panna [*pahn'-nah*] cream
  panna montata [*pahn'-nah mohn-tah'-tah*] whipped cream
panno [*pahn'-noh*] cloth
pantaloni lunghi *m. pl.* [*pahn-tah-loh'-nee loon'-gee*]
    trousers
pantofole *f. pl.* [*pahn-toh'-foh-leh*] slippers

papa *m.* [*pah'-pah*] pope
papà [*pah-pah'*] dad, daddy
parabrezza [*pah-rah-brehts'-tsah*] windshield
paracadute *m.* [*pah-rah-kah-doo'-teh*] parachute
paradiso [*pah-rah-dee'-zoh*] paradise
paragonare *v.* [*pah-rah-goh-nah'-reh*] compare
paragone *m.* [*pah-rah-goh'-neh*] comparison
paragrafo [*pah-rah'-grah-foh*] paragraph
paralizzare *v.* [*pah-rah-leedz-dzah'-reh*] paralyze
parallelo [*pah-rahl-leh'-loh*] parallel
parata [*pah-rah'-tah*] parade
parcheggiare *v.* [*pahr-kehj-jee-ah'-reh*] park
parcheggio [*pahr-kehj'-jee-oh*] parking
parco [*pahr'-koh*] park
parecchi [*pah-rehk'-kee*] several
parente *m.* [*pah-rehn'-teh*] relative
parere *v. irreg.* [*pah-reh'-reh*] seem
  Che le pare? [*keh leh pah'-reh*] How does it seem to you?
  Mi pare che . . . [*mee pah'-reh keh*] It seems to me
    that . . .
parete *f.* [*pah-reh'-teh*] wall
pari [*pah'-ree*] even, equal, same
  numero pari [*noo'-meh-roh pah'-ree*] even number
parlare *v.* [*pahr-lah'-reh*] speak, talk
  Parla italiano? [*pahr'-lah ee-tah-lee-ah'-noh*] Do you
    speak Italian?
parlamento [*pahr-lah-mehn'-toh*] parliament
parola [*pah-roh'-lah*] word
  parola d'ordine [*pah-roh'-lah dohr'-dee-neh*] watchword
parrocchia [*pahr-rohk'-kee-ah*] parish
parrucca [*pahr-rook'-kah*] wig
parrucchiere *m.* [*pahr-rook-kee-eh'-reh*] hairdresser
parte *f.* [*pahr'-teh*] part, share
  a parte [*ah pahr'-teh*] beside
  da parte [*dah pahr'-teh*] aside
  d'altra parte [*dahl'-trah pahr'-teh*] on the other hand
  da parte mia [*dah pahr'-teh mee'-ah*] on my part
  in parte [*een pahr'-teh*] partly
partecipare *v.* [*pahr-teh-chee-pah'-reh*] participate
partenza [*pahr-tehn'-tsah*] departure

particolare [*pahr-tee-koh-lah'-reh*] particular
particolarmente [*pahr-tee-koh-lahr-mehn'-teh*] particularly
partire *v.* [*pahr-tee'-reh*] leave, depart
partita [*pahr-tee'-tah*] game, shipment [commerce]
partito [*pahr-tee'-toh*] party [political]
parto [*pahr'-toh*] childbirth, delivery
partorire *v.* [*pahr-toh-ree'-reh*] give birth
patria [*pah'-tree-ah*] native land
parzialmente [*pahr-tsee-ahl-mehn'-teh*] partially
Pasqua [*pahs'-koo-ah*] Easter
passaggio [*pahs-sahj'-jee-oh*] passage
   passaggio a livello [*pahs-sahj'-jee-oh ah lee-vehl'-loh*]
     railroad crossing
passante *m.* [*pahs-sahn'-teh*] passerby
passaporto [*pahs-sah-pohr'-toh*] passport
passare *v.* [*pahs-sah'-reh*] pass, come by
   passare il tempo [*pahs-sah'-reh eel tehm'-poh*] spend time
passato [*pahs-sah'-toh*] past
   la settimana passata [*lah seht-tee-mah'-nah pahs-sah'-tah*]
     last week
passeggero [*pahs-sehj-jeh'-roh*] passenger
   treno passeggeri [*treh'-noh pahs-sehj-jeh'-ree*] passenger
     train
passeggiare *v.* [*pahs-sehj-jee-ah'-reh*] stroll
passeggiata [*pahs-sehj-jee-ah'-tah*] ride, walk
   fare *v.* **una passeggiata** [*fah'-reh oo'-nah pahs-sehj-jee-*
    ah'-tah] take a walk
passione *f.* [*pahs-see-oh'-neh*] passion
passivo [*pahs-see'-voh*] passive
passo [*pahs'-soh*] pace, step, pass [mountain]
pasta [*pahs'-tah*] paste, pastry
pasticceria [*pahs-teech-cheh-ree'-ah*] pastry shop
pasto [*pahs'-toh*] meal
patata [*pah-tah'-tah*] potato
patente *f.* [*pah-tehn'-teh*] license
patetico [*pah-teh'-tee-koh*] pathetic
patria [*pah'-tree-ah*] fatherland, country
patriotico [*pah-tree-oh'-tee-koh*] patriotic
pattinare *v.* [*paht-tee-nah'-reh*] skate
pattini *m. pl.* [*paht'-tee-nee*] skates

paura [*pah-oo'-rah*] fear
  avere *v.* **paura** [*ah-veh'-reh pah-oo'-rah*] be afraid
pausa [*pah'-oo-zah*] pause
pavimento [*pah-vee-mehn'-toh*] floor, pavement
paziente *n. & adj.* [*pah-tsee-ehn'-teh*] patient
pazienza [*pah-tsee-ehn'-tsah*] patience
pazzo [*pahts'-tsoh*] crazy, mad
peccato [*pehk-kah'-toh*] sin
  Che peccato! [*keh pehk-kah'-toh*] That's too bad!, What
    a pity!
pecora [*peh'-koh-rah*] sheep
pedaggio [*peh-dahj'-jee-oh*] toll
pedale *m.* [*peh-dah'-leh*] pedal
pedata [*peh-dah'-tah*] kick
pedestre *adj.* [*peh-dehs'-treh*] pedestrian
peggio [*pehj'-jee-oh*] worse
peggiore [*pehj-jee-oh'-reh*] worse
  il, la peggiore [*eel, lah pehj-jee-oh'-reh*] (the) worst
  peggiore di [*pehj-jee-oh'-reh dee*] worse than
pelare *v.* [*peh-lah'-reh*] peel, skin
pelle *f.* [*pehl'-leh*] skin
pellicia [*pehl-lee'-chee-ah*] fur
pellicola [*pehl-lee'-koh-lah*] film
pelo [*peh'-loh*] hair, fur
peloso [*peh-loh'-zoh*] hairy
pena [*peh'-nah*] pain
  a mala pena [*ah mah'-lah peh'-nah*] hardly
  Non vale la pena [*nohn vah'-leh lah peh'-nah*] It isn't
    worthwhile
penalità *f. indecl.* [*peh-nah-lee-tah'*] penalty
pendente [*pehn-dehn'-teh*] leaning
penisola [*peh-nee'-zoh-lah*] peninsula
penna [*pehn'-nah*] pen
pennello [*pehn-nehl'-loh*] paintbrush
pensare *v.* [*pehn-sah'-reh*] think
pensato [*pehn-sah'-toh*] thought
  ben pensato [*behn pehn-sah'-toh*] well-thought
pensiero [*pehn-see-eh'-roh*] thought, thinking
pensione *f.* [*pehn-see-oh'-neh*] boardinghouse, pension
pentola [*pehn'-toh-lah*] pot

pentolino [*pehn-toh-lee'-noh*] kettle

pepe *m.* [*peh'-peh*] pepper

per [*pehr*] for

    per esempio [*pehr eh-zehm'-pee-oh*] for example

    Per favore! [*pehr fah-voh'-reh*] Please!

    per me, per lei [*pehr meh, pehr leh'-ee*] for me, for you

pera [*peh'-rah*] pear

percento [*pehr-chehn'-toh*] percent

percentuale *m.* [*pehr-chehn-too-ah'-leh*] percentage

percepire *v.* [*pehr-cheh-pee'-reh*] perceive

perchè [*pehr-keh'*] why, because

    Perchè? [*pehr-keh'*] What for?, Why?

    Perchè no? [*pehr-keh' noh*] Why not?

    Perchè non voglio [*pehr-keh' nohn voh'-lyoh*] Because I
       don't want to

perciò [*pehr-chee-oh'*] therefore

perdere *v. irreg.* [*pehr'-deh-reh*] lose

    perdere (l'autobus, ecc.) [*pehr'-deh-reh*] miss (the bus, etc.)

    Ho perduto l'autobus [*oh pehr-doo'-toh lah'-oo-toh-boos*]
       I missed the bus

perdita [*pehr'-dee-tah*] loss, leakage

perdonare *v.* [*pehr-doh-nah'-reh*] pardon, forgive

perdonato [*pehr-doh-nah'-toh*] forgiven

perdono [*pehr-doh'-noh*] pardon

perduto [*pehr-doo'-toh*] lost

perfetto [*pehr-feht'-toh*] perfect

perfezione *f.* [*pehr-feh-tsee-oh'-neh*] perfection

pericolo [*peh-ree'-koh-loh*] danger

pericoloso [*peh-ree-koh-loh'-zoh*] dangerous, unsafe

periferia [*peh-ree-feh-ree'-ah*] suburb

periodico [*peh-ree-oh'-dee-koh*] periodical

periodo [*peh-ree'-oh-doh*] period

perla [*pehr'-lah*] pearl

permaloso [*pehr-mah-loh'-zoh*] touchy

permanente [*pehr-mah-nehn'-teh*] permanent

    ondulazione permanente [*ohn-doo-lah-tsee-oh'-neh pehr-
      mah-nehn'-teh*] permanent wave

permesso [*pehr-mehs'-soh*] permission, permit

permettere *v.* [*pehr-meht'-teh-reh*] permit, allow

    Mi permetta di . . . [*mee pehr-meht'-tah dee*] Allow me

to . . .
però [*peh-roh'*] but
persecuzione f. [*pehr-seh-koo-tsee-oh'-neh*] persecution
perseguire v. [*pehr-seh-goo-ee'-reh*] pursue
persiana di finestra [*pehr-see-ah'-nah dee fee-nehs'-trah*]
    shutter
persiano [*pehr-see-ah'-noh*] Persian
persistere v. [*pehr-sees'-teh-reh*] persist
persona [*pehr-soh'-nah*] person
personale [*pehr-soh-nah'-leh*] personal
personale m. [*pehr-soh-nah'-leh*] personnel
personalità f. indecl. [*pehr-soh-nah-lee-tah'*] personality
personalmente [*pehr-soh-nahl-mehn'-teh*] personally
persuadere v. irreg. [*pehr-soo-ah-deh'-reh*] persuade
persuasivo [*pehr-soo-ah-zee'-voh*] persuasive
pertinente [*pehr-tee-nehn'-teh*] relevant
pesante [*peh-zahn'-teh*] heavy
pesare v. [*peh-zah'-reh*] weigh
pesca [*pehs'-kah*] peach
pesca [*pehs'-kah*] fishing
pescare v. [*pehs-kah'-reh*] fish
pescatore m. [*pehs-kah-toh'-reh*] fisherman
pesce m. [*peh'-sheh*] fish
peso [*peh'-zoh*] weight
pessimista [*pehs-see-mees'-tah*] pessimist, pessimistic
peste f. [*pehs'-teh*] pest
petizione f. [*peh-tee-tsee-oh'-neh*] petition
petrolio [*peh-troh'-lee-oh*] oil [fuel]
pettegolo [*peht-teh'-goh-loh*] gossip
pettinare v. [*peht-tee-nah'-reh*] comb
    pettinarsi [*peht-tee-nahr'-see*] comb [oneself]
    Mi pettino i capelli [*mee peht'-tee-noh ee kah-pehl'-lee*]
        I comb my hair
pettine m. [*peht'-tee-neh*] comb
petto [*peht'-toh*] bosom, breast
pezzetto [*pehts-tseht'-toh*] bit, little bit
pezzo [*pehts'-tsoh*] piece, part [of a machine]
    pezzi di ricambio [*pehts'-tsee dee ree-kahm'-bee-oh*]
        spare parts
    pezzo grosso [*pehts'-tsoh grohs'-soh*] big shot

piacere *v. irreg.* [*pee-ah-cheh'-reh*] like, please, be pleasing

piacere *m.* [*pee-ah-cheh'-reh*] pleasure, favor

  con piacere [*kohn pee-ah-cheh'-reh*] with pleasure

  con molto piacere [*kohn mohl'-toh pee-ah-cheh'-reh*]
    with much pleasure

  Il piacere è mio [*eel pee-ah-cheh'-reh eh' mee'-oh*]
    The pleasure is mine

  Le fa piacere? [*leh fah pee-ah-cheh'-reh*] Does it please
    you?

  Le piacerebbe . . . ? [*leh pee-ah-cheh-rehb'-beh*] Would
    you like . . . ?

  Mi piace moltissimo [*mee pee-ah'-cheh mohl-tees'-see-moh*] I like it very much

  Non mi piace [*nohn mee pee-ah'-cheh*] I don't like it

  Per piacere! [*pehr pee-ah-cheh'-reh*] Please!

  Piacere di conoscerla! [*pee-ah-cheh'-reh dee koh-noh'-shehr-lah*] Pleased to meet you!

  vaggio di piacere [*vee-ahj'-jee-oh dee pee-ah-cheh'-reh*]
    pleasure trip

piacevole [*pee-ah-cheh'-voh-leh*] pleasant, likeable

piaga [*pee-ah'-gah*] sore, wound

pianeta *m.* [*pee-ah-neh'-tah*] planet

piangere *v. irreg.* [*pee-ahn'-jeh-reh*] cry, weep

pianista *m., f.* [*pee-ah-nees'-tah*] pianist

piano *adj.* [*pee-ah'-noh*] level, plane

piano *adv.* [*pee-ah'-noh*] slowly, softly

piano (di casa) [*pee-ah'-noh (dee kah'-zah)*] floor, plan

  al piano superiore [*ahl pee-ah'-noh soo-peh-ree-oh'-reh*]
    upstairs

pianoforte *m.* [*pee-ah-noh-fohr'-teh*] piano

pianta [*pee-ahn'-tah*] plant

pianterreno [*pee-ahn-tehr-reh'-noh*] ground floor

piattaforma [*pee-aht-tah-fohr'-mah*] platform

piattino [*pee-aht-tee'-noh*] saucer

piatto [*pee-aht'-toh*] plate, dish

piatto [*pee-aht'-toh*] plain, flat

piazza [*pee-ahts'-tsah*] square [of a city]

piccione *m.* [*peech-chee-oh'-neh*] pigeon

piccolo [*peek'-koh-loh*] small, little

  più piccolo [*pee-oo' peek'-koh-loh*] smaller

piede *m.* [*pee-eh'-deh*] foot
  a piedi [*ah pee-eh'-dee*] on foot
piegare *v.* [*pee-eh-gah'-reh*] bend, fold
pieno [*pee-eh'-noh*] full
pietà *f. indecl.* [*pee-eh-tah'*] mercy, pity
pietra [*pee-eh'-trah*] stone
pigiama *m.* [*pee-jee-ah'-mah*] pajamas
pigione *f.* [*pee-jee-oh'-neh*] rent
pigro [*pee'-groh*] lazy
pillola [*peel'-loh-lah*] pill
pilota *m.* [*pee-loh'-tah*] pilot
pinta [*peen'-tah*] pint
pio [*pee'-oh*] pious
pioggia [*pee-ohj'-jee-ah*] rain
piombo [*pee-ohm'-boh*] lead [metal]
piovere *v.* [*pee-oh'-veh-reh*] rain
  Piove [*pee-oh'-veh*] It is raining
pipa [*pee'-pah*] pipe [smoking]
piroscafo [*pee-rohs'-kah-foh*] steamship
piscina [*pee-shee'-nah*] swimming pool
pista [*pees'-tah*] track, runway
pistola [*pees-toh'-lah*] pistol
pittore *m.*, **pittrice** *f.* [*peet-toh'-reh, peet-tree'-cheh*] painter
pittura [*peet-too'-rah*] painting
più [*pee-oo'*] more, most, plus
  il più [*eel pee-oo'*] the most
  mai più [*mah'-ee pee-oo'*] nevermore
  non più [*nohn pee-oo'*] no more
  più o meno [*pee-oo' oh meh'-noh*] more or less
  tanto più [*tahn'-toh pee-oo'*] all the more
piuma [*pee-oo'-mah*] feather
piuttosto [*pee-oot-tohs'-toh*] rather
  Vorrebbe piuttosto . . . ? [*vohr-rehb'-beh pee-oot-tohs'-toh*]
    Would you rather . . . ?
  Io preferisco piuttosto . . . [*ee'-oh preh-feh-rees'-koh pee-*
    oo-tohs'-toh] I rather prefer . . .
pizzicare *v.* [*peets-tsee-kah'-reh*] pinch
pizzicotto [*peets-tsee-koht'-toh*] pinching
plastico [*plahs'-tee-koh*] plastic
pleurite *f.* [*pleh-oo-ree'-teh*] pleurisy

plurale [*ploo-rah'-leh*] plural
pneumatico (di ricambio) [*pneh-oo-mah'-tee-koh (dee ree-kahm'-bee-oh)*] (spare) tire
pochi *m.*, **poche** *f.* [*poh'-kee, poh'-keh*] few
pochissimo [*poh-kees'-see-moh*] very little
poco [*poh'-koh*] little
   dopo poco [*doh'-poh poh'-koh*] shortly afterwards
   in poco tempo [*een poh'-koh tehm'-poh*] in a short time
   poco a poco [*poh'-koh ah poh'-koh*] little by little
   un poco [*oon poh'-koh*] somewhat
poema *m.* [*poh-eh'-mah*] poem
poesia [*poh-eh-zee'-ah*] poetry
poeta *m.*, **poetessa** *f.* [*poh-eh'-tah, poh-eh-tehs'-sah*] poet
poi [*poh'-ee*] then, afterwards
poichè *conj.* [*poh-ee-keh'*] since
polacco [*poh-lahk'-koh*] Polish
polare [*poh-lah'-reh*] polar
politica [*poh-lee'-tee-kah*] politics, policy
politico [*poh-lee'-tee-koh*] political
polizia [*poh-lee-tsee'-ah*] police
poliziotto [*poh-lee-tsee-oht'-toh*] policeman
polizza di assicurazione [*poh-leets'-tsah dee ahs-see-koo-rah-tsee-oh'-neh*] insurance policy
pollice *m.* [*pohl'-lee-cheh*] thumb, inch
pollo [*pohl'-loh*] chicken
polmone *m.* [*pohl-moh'-neh*] lung
polmonite *f.* [*pohl-moh-nee'-teh*] pneumonia
polo [*poh'-loh*] pole [geog.]
Polonia [*poh-loh'-nee-ah*] Poland
polpetta [*pohl-peht'-tah*] meatball
polso [*pohl'-soh*] pulse, wrist
poltrona [*pohl-troh'-nah*] armchair
polvere *f.* [*pohl'-veh-reh*] dust
polveroso [*pohl-veh-roh'-zoh*] dusty
pomeriggio [*poh-meh-reej'-jee-oh*] afternoon
pomodoro [*poh-moh-doh'-roh*] tomato
   sugo di pomodoro [*soo'-goh dee poh-moh-doh'-roh*] tomato juice
pompa [*pohm'-pah*] pump
pompare *v.* [*pohm-pah'-reh*] pump

pompelmo [*pohm-pehl'-moh*] grapefruit

pompiere *m.* [*pohm-pee-eh'-reh*] fireman

ponte *m.* [*pohn'-teh*] bridge, deck [of ship]

popolare [*poh-poh-lah'-reh*] popular

popolarità *f. indecl.* [*poh-poh-lah-ree-tah'*] popularity

popolazione *f.* [*poh-poh-lah-tsee-oh'-neh*] population

popolo [*poh'-poh-loh*] people

porcellana [*pohr-chehl-lah'-nah*] porcelain, china

porco [*pohr'-koh*] pig

porpora [*pohr'-poh-rah*] purple

porre *v. irreg.* [*pohr'-reh*] put, place

porta [*pohr'-tah*] door, gate

   Apra la porta [*ah'-prah lah pohr'-tah*] Open the door

   Chiuda la porta! [*kee-oo'-dah lah pohr'-tah*] Close the
    door!

portabile [*pohr-tah'-bee-leh*] portable

portacenere *m.* [*pohr-tah-cheh'-neh-reh*] ashtray

portafoglio [*pohr-tah-foh'-lyoh*] wallet

portare *v.* [*pohr-tah'-reh*] carry, bring, wear

   Per favore, mi porti . . . [*pehr fah-voh'-reh, mee pohr'-tee*]
    Please bring me . . .

   Portamelo [*pohr'-tah-meh-loh*] Bring it to me

portata [*pohr-tah'-tah*] reach

portico [*pohr'-tee-koh*] porch

portiere *m.* [*pohr-tee-eh'-reh*] janitor, doorman

porto [*pohr'-toh*] seaport, harbor

Portogallo [*pohr-toh-gahl'-loh*] Portugal

portoghese [*pohr-toh-geh'-zeh*] Portuguese

porzione *f.* [*pohr-tsee-oh'-neh*] portion, part

posa [*poh'-zah*] pose

posare *v.* [*poh-zah'-reh*] pose

positivo [*poh-zee-tee'-voh*] positive

posizione [*poh-zee-tsee-oh'-neh*] position

possedere *v. irreg.* [*pohs-seh-deh'-reh*] own, possess

possesso [*pohs-sehs'-soh*] possession

possible [*pohs-see'-bee-leh*] possible

possibilità *f. indecl.* [*pohs-see-bee-lee-tah'*] possibility

possibilmente [*pohs-see-beel-mehn'-teh*] possibly

posta [*pohs'-tah*] mail, post

   fermo-posta [*fehr-moh-pohs'-tah*] post-office box,

general delivery

postino [*pohs-tee'-noh*] mailman

posto [*pohs'-toh*] place, spot, seat

  in nessun posto [*een nehs-soon' pohs'-toh*] nowhere

potente [*poh-tehn'-teh*] powerful

potere *m.* [*poh-teh'-reh*] power [authority]

potere *v. irreg., aux.* [*poh-teh'-reh*] be able, can, may

  Può essere [*poo-oh' ehs'-seh-reh*] It may be

  Può darsi che . . . [*poo-oh' dahr'-see keh*] It may be that . . .

  Può venire Lei? [*poo-oh' veh-nee'-reh leh'-ee*] Can you come?

  Sì io posso [*see', ee'-oh pohs'-soh*] Yes, I can

  Posso entrare? [*pohs'-soh ehn-trah'-reh*] May I come in?

potere (fare qualcosa) *v.* [*poh-teh'-reh* (*fah'-reh koo-ahl-koh'-zah*)] afford to

  Non posso pagare [*nohn pohs'-soh pah-gah'-reh*] I can't afford to pay

  Non posso bere [*nohn pohs'-soh beh'-reh*] I can't afford to drink

  Io potrei andare domani [*ee'-oh poh-treh'-ee ahn-dah'-reh doh-mah'-nee*] I might go tomorrow

povero [*poh'-veh-roh*] poor

povertà *f. indecl.* [*poh-vehr-tah'*] poverty

pozzo [*pohts'-tsoh*] well [water]

pranzare *v.* [*prahn-tsah'-reh*] lunch

pranzo [*prahn'-tsoh*] lunch

  Il pranzo è pronto! [*eel prahn'-tsoh eh' prohn'-toh*] Lunch is ready!

  sala da pranzo [*sah'-lah dah prahn'-tsoh*] dining room

praticare *v.* [*prah-tee-kah'-reh*] practice

pratico [*prah'-tee-koh*] practical

prato [*prah'-toh*] lawn

precauzione *f.* [*preh-kah·oo-tsee-oh'-neh*] caution

precedente [*preh-cheh-dehn'-teh*] former, previous

precedentemente [*preh-cheh-dehn-teh-mehn'-teh*] formerly

precedere *v.* [*preh-cheh'-deh-reh*] precede

precisamente [*preh-chee-zah-mehn'-teh*] precisely

preciso [*preh-chee'-zoh*] precise

predica [*preh'-dee-kah*] sermon, preaching

prediletto [*preh-dee-leht'-toh*] pet

preferenza [*preh-feh-rehn'-tsah*] preference
preferibile [*preh-feh-ree'-bee-leh*] preferable
preferire v. [*preh-feh-ree'-reh*] prefer
preferito [*preh-feh-ree'-toh*] favorite
pregare v. [*preh-gah'-reh*] pray, beg
  Prego . . . [*preh'-goh*] (You are) welcome . . .
  Prego, entri! [*preh'-goh, ehn'-tree*] Please come in!
preghiera [*preh-gee-eh'-rah*] prayer
pregiudizio [*preh-jee-oo-dee'-tsee-oh*] prejudice
preliminare [*preh-lee-mee-nah'-reh*] preliminary
prematuro [*preh-mah-too'-roh*] premature
premere v. [*preh'-meh-reh*] press, squeeze
premio [*preh'-mee-oh*] award, prize
prendere v. irreg. [*prehn'-deh-reh*] take
  Prenda! [*prehn'-dah*] Take it!
prenotare v. [*preh-noh-tah'-reh*] reserve, book
prenotazione f. [*preh-noh-tah-tsee-oh'-neh*] reservation
preoccuparsi v. [*preh-ohk-koo-pahr'-see*] take care of, worry
  Non si preoccupi! [*nohn see preh-ohk'-koo-pee*] Don't
    worry!
preoccupato [*preh-ohk-koo-pah'-toh*] upset, worried
preoccupazione f. [*preh-ohk-koo-pah-tsee-oh'-neh*] worry
preparare v. [*preh-pah-rah'-reh*] prepare
preparazione f. [*preh-pah-rah-tsee-oh'-neh*] preparation
presa [*preh'-zah*] plug [electric]
presentabile [*preh-zehn-tah'-bee-leh*] presentable
presentare v. [*preh-zehn-tah'-reh*] present, introduce
  presentarsi [*preh-zehn-tahr'-see*] introduce oneself
presentazione f. [*preh-zehn-tah-tsee-oh'-neh*] introduction
presente [*preh-zehn'-teh*] present
presentemente [*preh-zehn-teh-mehn'-teh*] presently
presentimento [*preh-sehn-tee-mehn'-toh*] premonition
presenza [*preh-zehn'-tsah*] presence
preservare v. [*preh-sehr-vah'-reh*] preserve
presidente m. [*preh-zee-dehn'-teh*] president
  vice-presidente [*vee'-cheh preh-zee-dehn'-teh*]
    vice-president
preso [*preh'-zoh*] taken
pressare v. [*prehs-sah'-reh*] press
pressione f. [*prehs-see-oh'-neh*] pressure

prestare *v.* [*prehs-tah'-reh*] lend

prestigio [*prehs-tee'-jee-oh*] prestige

prestito [*prehs'-tee-toh*] loan
    chiedere *v.* **in prestito** [*kee-eh'-deh-reh een prehs'-tee-toh*]
      borrow

presto [*prehs'-toh*] soon, early
    il più presto possibile [*eel pee-oo' prehs'-toh pohs-see'-bee-*
      leh] as soon as possible
    Presto, presto! [*prehs'-toh, prehs'-toh*] Hurry up!
    più presto [*pee-oo' prehs'-toh*] sooner
    presto o tardi [*prehs'-toh oh tahr'-dee*] sooner or later

presupporre *v. irreg.* [*preh-zoop-pohr'-reh*] presume

presupposto [*preh-zoop-pohs'-toh*] assumption

prete *m.* [*preh'-teh*] priest

pretendere *v.* [*preh-tehn'-deh-reh*] pretend

pretenzioso [*preh-tehn-tsee-oh'-zoh*] pretentious

pretesa [*preh-teh'-zah*] pretense

prevalente [*preh-vah-lehn'-teh*] prevalent

prevenire *v.* [*preh-veh-nee'-reh*] prevent

prevenzione *f.* [*preh-vehn-tsee-oh'-neh*] prevention

prezioso [*preh-tsee-oh'-zoh*] precious

prezzo [*prehts'-tsoh*] price, rate
    al prezzo di [*ahl prehts'-tsoh dee*] at the rate of
    prezzo fisso [*prehts'-tsoh fees'-soh*] fixed price
    prezzo del viaggio [*prehts'-tsoh dehl vee-ahj'-jee-oh*] fare

prigione *f.* [*pree-jee-oh'-neh*] prison

prigioniero [*pree-jee-oh-nee-eh'-roh*] prisoner

prima (di) [*pree'-mah (dee)*] before
    prima che venga [*pree'-mah keh vehn'-gah*] before he
      (she) comes
    prima classe [*pree'-mah klahs'-seh*] first class
    prima di lei [*pree'-mah dee leh'-ee*] before you

primavera [*pree-mah-veh'-rah*] spring [season]

primitivo [*pree-mee-tee'-voh*] primitive

primo [*pree'-moh*] first
    primo nome [*pree'-moh noh'-meh*] first name

principale *m.* [*preen-chee-pah'-leh*] chief, principal, master

principale *adj.* [*preen-chee-pah'-leh*] main, leading

principalmente [*preen-chee-pahl-mehn'-teh*] mainly

principe *m.*, **principessa** *f.* [*preen'-chee-peh, preen-chee-*

pehs'-sah] prince, princess

principiante m. [preen-chee-pee-ahn'-teh] beginner

principio [preen-chee'-pee-oh] principle, beginning

   al principio [ahl preen-chee'-pee-oh] at the beginning

privare v. [pree-vah'-reh] deprive

privato [pree-vah'-toh] private

privilegio [pree-vee-lehj'-jee-oh] privilege

privo di [pree'-voh dee] lacking in

probabile [proh-bah'-bee-leh] likely

probabilmente [proh-bah-beel-mehn'-teh] probably

problema m. [proh-bleh'-mah] problem

procedere v. [proh-cheh'-deh-reh] proceed

procedimento [proh-cheh-dee-mehn'-toh] procedure

processo [proh-chehs'-soh] process, trial

procurarsi v. [proh-koo-rahr'-see] obtain

prodotto [proh-doht'-toh] product

produrre v. irreg. [proh-door'-reh] produce

produzione f. [proh-doo-tsee-oh'-neh] production

   produzione in serie [proh-doo-tsee-oh'-neh een seh'-ree-eh]
   mass production

professione f. [proh-fehs-see-oh'-neh] profession

professore m., **professoressa** f. [proh-fehs-soh'-reh, proh-
   fehs-soh-rehs'-sah] professor

profezia [proh-feh-tsee'-ah] prophecy

profilo [proh-fee'-loh] profile

profittare v. [proh-feet-tah'-reh] profit

profitto [proh-feet'-toh] profit

profondità f. indecl. [proh-fohn-dee-tah'] depth

profondo [proh-fohn'-doh] deep

   poco profondo [poh'-koh proh-fohn'-doh] shallow

profugo [proh'-foo-goh] refugee

profumo [proh-foo'-moh] perfume

progetto [proh-jeht'-toh] project, plan

programma m. [proh-grahm'-mah] program

progredire v. [proh-greh-dee'-reh] progress

progressivo [proh-grehs-see'-voh] progressive

progresso [proh-grehs'-soh] progress

proibire v. [proh-ee-bee'-reh] prohibit

proibito [proh-ee-bee'-toh] forbidden

promessa [proh-mehs'-sah] promise

promettente [*proh-meht-tehn'-teh*] promising
promettere v. [*proh-meht'-teh-reh*] promise
prominente [*proh-mee-nehn'-teh*] prominent
promozione f. [*proh-moh-tsee-oh'-neh*] promotion
pronome m. [*proh-noh'-meh*] pronoun
pronto [*prohn'-toh*] ready
   pronto soccorso [*prohn'-toh sohk-kohr'-soh*] first aid
pronuncia [*proh-noon'-chee-ah*] pronunciation
pronunciare v. [*proh-noon-chee-ah'-reh*] pronounce
  Come si pronuncia . . . ? [*koh'-meh see proh-noon'-chee-ah*]
    How do you pronounce . . . ?
propaganda [*proh-pah-gahn'-dah*] propaganda
proporre v. irreg. [*proh-pohr'-reh*] propose
proporzione f. [*proh-pohr-tsee-oh'-neh*] proportion
proposizione f. [*proh-poh-zee-tsee-oh'-neh*] proposition
proposito [*proh-poh'-zee-toh*] purpose, design
  a proposito [*ah proh-poh'-zee-toh*] by the way
  di proposito [*dee proh-poh'-zee-toh*] on purpose
proposta [*proh-pohs'-tah*] proposal
proprietà f. indecl. [*proh-pree-eh-tah'*] property
proprietario [*proh-pree-eh-tah'-ree-oh*] owner
proprio [*proh'-pree-oh*] just, exactly, own
  la mia propria casa [*lah mee'-ah proh'-pree-ah kah'-zah*]
    my own house
  proprio così [*proh'-pree-oh koh-zee'*] just so
  proprio un poco [*proh'-pree-oh oon poh'-koh*] a little bit
prosciutto [*proh-shee-oot'-toh*] ham
prosperità f. indecl. [*prohs-peh-ree-tah'*] prosperity
prospero [*prohs'-peh-roh*] prosperous
prossimo [*prohs'-see-moh*] next
  il prossimo anno [*eel prohs'-see-moh ahn'-noh*] next year
  il prossimo mese [*eel prohs'-see-moh meh'-zeh*] next month
  la prossima settimana [*lah prohs'-see-mah seht-tee-mah'-nah*] next week
  la prossima volta [*lah prohs'-see-mah vohl'-tah*] next time
proteggere v. irreg. [*proh-tehj'-jeh-reh*] protect
protesta [*proh-tehs'-tah*] protest, complain
protestante [*proh-tehs-tahn'-teh*] Protestant
protestare v. [*proh-tehs-tah'-reh*] protest
protezione f. [*proh-teh-tsee-oh'-neh*] protection

prova [*proh'-vah*] trial, test, proof
provare *v.* [*proh-vah'-reh*] prove, test, try
proverbio [*proh-vehr'-bee-oh*] proverb
provincia [*proh-veen-chee-ah*] province
provinciale [*proh-veen-chee-ah'-leh*] provincial
provisorio [*proh-vee-zoh'-ree-oh*] temporary
provista [*proh-vees'-tah*] supply
provvedere *v.* [*prohv-veh-deh'-reh*] provide
prudente [*proo-dehn'-teh*] prudent, careful
prugna [*proo'-nyah*] plum
  prugna secca [*proo'-nyah sehk'-kah*] prune
psichiatra *m., f.* [*psee-kee-ah'-trah*] psychiatrist
psicoanalisi *f.* [*psee-koh-ah-nah'-lee-zee*] psychoanalysis
psicologico [*psee-koh-loh'-jee-koh*] psychological
pubblicare *v.* [*poob-blee-kah'-reh*] publish
pubblicazione *f.* [*poob-blee-kah-tsee-oh'-neh*] publication
pubblicità *f. indecl.* [*poob-blee-chee-tah'*] publicity, advertising
pubblico *n. & adj.* [*poob'-blee-koh*] public
pugilato [*poo-jee-lah'-toh*] boxing
pugno [*poo'-nyoh*] fist, punch
pulire *v.* [*poo-lee'-reh*] clean
  pulire a secco [*poo-lee'-reh ah sehk'-koh*] dry clean
pulito [*poo-lee'-toh*] clean
pulizia [*poo-lee-tsee'-ah*] cleaning
punire *v.* [*poo-nee'-reh*] punish
punizione *f.* [*poo-nee-tsee-oh'-neh*] punishment
punta [*poon'-tah*] point [form], tip
puntare *v.* [*poon-tah'-reh*] point
punto [*poon'-toh*] point, period [punctuation]
  punto di vista [*poon'-toh dee vees'-tah*] standpoint
  punto interrogativo [*poon'-toh een-tehr-roh-gah-tee'-voh*]
    question mark
puntuale [*poon-too-ah'-leh*] punctual
puntura [*poon-too'-rah*] sting, prick
pure [*poo'-reh*] also, as well
  Fate pure! [*fah'-teh poo'-reh*] Go ahead!, Certainly!
puro [*poo'-roh*] pure
purtroppo [*poor-trohp'-poh*] unfortunately

Q

qua [*koo-ah'*] here
quadrato [*koo-ah-drah'-toh*] square
quadro [*koo-ah'-droh*] picture
quaggiù [*koo-ahj-jee-oo'*] down here
qualche [*koo-ahl'-keh*] some, any
  in qualche luogo [*een koo-ahl'-keh loo-oh'-goh*] somewhere
  qualche volta [*koo-ahl'-keh vohl'-tah*] sometimes
qualcosa [*koo-ahl-koh'-zah*] something
qualcuno [*koo-ahl-koo'-noh*] somebody, someone
quale [*koo-ah'-leh*] what, which, who, whom
qualifica [*koo-ah-lee'-fee-kah*] qualification
qualificare *v.* [*koo-ah-lee-fee-kah'-reh*] qualify
qualificato [*koo-ah-lee-fee-kah'-toh*] qualified
qualità *f. indecl.* [*koo-ah-lee-tah'*] quality
qualora [*koo-ah-loh'-rah*] if, when
qualsiasi [*koo-ahl-see'-ah-see*] any, whatever
qualunque [*koo-ah-loon'-koo-eh*] whatever
  qualunque cosa [*koo-ah-loon'-koo-eh koh'-zah*] anything
quando [*koo-ahn'-doh*] when, how soon
  Da quando? [*dah koo-ahn'-doh*] Since when?
quanti *m. pl.*, **quante** *f. pl.* [*koo-ahn'-tee, koo-ahn'-teh*]
  how many
  Quanti anni ha? [*koo-ahn'-tee ahn'-nee ah*] How old are
    you?
quantità *f. indecl.* [*koo-ahn-tee-tah'*] quantity
quanto *m.*, **quanta** *f.* [*koo-ahn'-toh, koo-ahn'-tah*] how much?
  Quanto le devo? [*koo-ahn'-toh leh deh'-voh*] How much
    do I owe you?
  Quanto è lontano? [*koo-ahn'-toh eh' lohn-tah'-noh*]
    How far is it?
  Quanto tempo? [*koo-ahn'-toh tehm'-poh*] How long?
  Quanto vale questo? [*koo-ahn'-toh vah'-leh koo-ehs'-toh*]
    How much is this worth?
  in quanto a . . . [*een koo-ahn'-toh ah*] as for . . .

Per quanto tempo? [*pehr koo-ahn'-toh tehm'-poh*]
  For how long? [time]
quaranta [*koo-ah-rahn'-tah*] forty
quartiere *m.* [*koo-ahr-tee-eh'-reh*] neighborhood
  quartiere generale [*koo-ahr-tee-eh'-reh jeh-neh-rah'-leh*]
    headquarters [army]
quarto [*koo-ahr'-toh*] quarter, fourth
quasi [*koo-ah'-zee*] nearly, almost
  quasi mai [*koo-ah'-zee mah'-ee*] hardly ever
quattordici [*koo-aht-tohr'-dee-chee*] fourteen
quattrini *m. pl.* [*koo-aht-tree'-nee*] money
quattro [*koo-aht'-troh*] four
quattrocento [*koo-aht-troh-chehn'-toh*] four hundred
quelli *m. pl.,* **quelle** *f. pl.* [*koo-ehl'-lee, koo-ehl'-leh*] those
quello *m.* **quella** *f.* [*koo-ehl'-loh, koo-ehl'-lah*] that, that one
  quello che [*koo-ehl'-loh keh*] that which
  quello che desidera [*koo-ehl'-loh keh deh-zee'-deh-rah*]
    whatever you wish
questi *m. pl.,* **queste** *f. pl.* [*koo-ehs'-tee, koo-ehs'-teh*] these
questionario [*koo-ehs-tee-oh-nah'-ree-oh*] questionaire, form
questione *f.* [*koo-ehs-tee-oh'-neh*] question
questo *m.,* **questa** *f.* [*koo-ehs'-toh, koo-ehs'-tah*] this one
  in questa maniera [*een koo-ehs'-tah mah-nee-eh'-rah*]
    in this way
  Che cosa è questo? [*keh koh'-zah eh' koo-ehs'-toh*]
    What is this?
  È questa la via giusta? [*eh' koo-ehs'-tah lah vee'-ah jee-oos'-tah*] Is this the right way?
qui [*koo-ee'*] here
  Eccolo qui [*ehk'-koh-loh koo-ee'*] Here it is
  proprio qui [*proh'-pree-oh koo-ee'*] right here
  Venga qui! [*vehn'-gah koo-ee'*] Come here!
quieto [*koo-ee-eh'-toh*] quiet
quindi [*koo-een'-dee*] therefore
quindici [*koo-een'-dee-chee*] fifteen
quinto [*koo-een'-toh*] fifth
quotazione *f.* [*koo-oh-tah-tsee-oh'-neh*] quotation
quotidiano [*koo-oh-tee-dee-ah'-noh*] daily
quoziente *m.* [*koo-oh-tsee-ehn'-teh*] quotient

R

rabbia [*rahb'-bee-ah*] anger
rabbino [*rahb-bee'-noh*] rabbi
raccogliere *v.* [*rahk-koh'-lyeh-reh*] collect, pick up
raccolta [*rahk-kohl'-tah*] collection, harvest
raccolto [*rahk-kohl'-toh*] crop
raccomandare *v.* [*rahk-koh-mahn-dah'-reh*] recommend
raccomandazione *f.* [*rahk-koh-mahn-dah-tsee-oh'-neh*]
    recommendation
raccontare *v.* [*rahk-kohn-tah'-reh*] tell, relate
racconto [*rahk-kohn'-toh*] tale, story
radere *v. irreg.*, **radersi** [*rah-deh'-reh*, *rah-dehr'-see*] shave
radicale [*rah-dee-kah'-leh*] radical
radice *f.* [*rah-dee'-cheh*] root
radio *f.* [*rah'-dee-oh*] radio
radunarsi *v.* [*rah-doo-nahr'-see*] get together
raffinato [*rahf-fee-nah'-toh*] refined
raffineria [*rahf-fee-neh-ree'-ah*] refinery
raffreddare *v.* [*rahf-frehd-dah'-reh*] cool
  raffreddarsi [*rahf-frehd-dahr'-see*] catch cold
  Mi sono raffreddato [*mee soh'-noh rahf-frehd-dah'-toh*]
    I have caught a cold
raffreddore *m.* [*rahf-frehd-doh'-reh*] cold [illness]
ragazza [*rah-gahts'-tsah*] girl
ragazzo [*rah-gahts'-tsoh*] boy
raggiungere *v.* [*rahj-jee-oon'-jeh-reh*] reach, arrive
raggio [*rahj'-jee-oh*] ray
ragionare *v.* [*rah-jee-oh-nah'-reh*] reason
ragione *f.* [*rah-jee-oh'-neh*] reason
  avere *v.* **ragione** [*ah-veh'-reh rah-jee-oh'-neh*] be right
ragionevole [*rah-jee-oh-neh'-voh-leh*] reasonable
rallentare *v.* [*rahl-lehn-tah'-reh*] slow down
rame *m.* [*rah'-meh*] copper
ramo [*rah'-moh*] branch [of tree]
rana [*rah'-nah*] frog

rancore *m.* [*rahn-koh'-reh*] grudge
rapidamente [*rah-pee-dah-mehn'-teh*] quickly
rapido [*rah'-pee-doh*] rapid, fast
rapire *v.* [*rah-pee'-reh*] kidnap
rapporto [*rahp-pohr'-toh*] report
   in rapporto a [*een rahp'-pohr-toh ah*] in reference to
rappresentante [*rahp-preh-zehn-tahn'-teh*] representative
rappresentare *v.* [*rahp-preh-zehn-tah'-reh*] represent
raramente [*rah-rah-mehn'-teh*] seldom
raro [*rah'-roh*] rare, unusual
rasoio [*rah-zoh'-ee-oh*] razor
   rasoio di sicurezza [*rah-zoh'-ee-oh dee see-koo-rehts'-tsah*] safety razor
   rasoio elettrico [*rah-zoh'-ee-oh eh-leht'-tree-koh*] electric razor
rassicurare *v.* [*rahs-see-koo-rah'-reh*] reassure
rassomiglianza [*rahs-soh-mee-lyahn'-tsah*] resemblance
rassomigliare *v.* [*rahs-soh-mee-lyah'-reh*] resemble
razza [*rahts'-tsah*] (human) race
re *m.* [*reh*] king
reale [*reh-ah'-leh*] royal, real
realizzare *v.* [*reh-ah-leedz-dzah'-reh*] realize
realmente [*reh-ahl-mehn'-teh*] really
reazione *f.* [*reh-ah-tsee-oh'-neh*] reaction
recente [*reh-chehn'-teh*] recent
recentemente [*reh-chehn-teh-mehn'-teh*] recently
recentissimo [*reh-chehn-tees'-see-moh*] latest
recipiente *m.* [*reh-chee-pee-ehn'-teh*] container
reciproco [*reh-chee'-proh-koh*] mutual
recitare *v.* [*reh-chee-tah'-reh*] recite
reclamare *v.* [*reh-klah-mah'-reh*] claim
reclame *f.* [*reh-klah'-meh*] advertising
record *m.* [*reh'-kohrd*] record [sports]
redattore *m.* [*reh-daht-toh'-reh*] editor
reddito [*rehd'-dee-toh*] income
  imposta sul reddito [*eem-pohs'-tah sool rehd'-dee-toh*] income tax
redimere *v.* [*reh-dee'-meh-reh*] redeem
regalo [*reh-gah'-loh*] gift, present
reggimento [*rehj-jee-mehn'-toh*] regiment

reggipetto [*rehj-jee-peht'-toh*] bra, brassiere
regina [*reh-jee'-nah*] queen
regione *f.* [*reh-jee-oh'-neh*] region
registrare *v.* [*reh-jees-trah'-reh*] register
registro [*reh-jees'-troh*] register
regnare *v.* [*reh-nyah'-reh*] reign
regno [*reh'-nyoh*] kingdom
regola [*reh'-goh-lah*] rule
regolamento [*reh-goh-lah-mehn'-toh*] regulation
regolare *v.* [*reh-goh-lah'-reh*] settle, regulate
relativo [*reh-lah-tee'-voh*] relative
   relativo a [*reh-lah-tee'-voh ah*] pertaining to
religione *f.* [*reh-lee-jee-oh'-neh*] religion
religioso [*reh-lee-jee-oh'-zoh*] religious
remare *v.* [*reh-mah'-reh*] row
remo [*reh'-moh*] oar
remoto [*reh-moh'-toh*] remote
reparto [*reh-pahr'-toh*] department [of store]
republica [*reh-poob'-lee-kah*] republic
reputazione *f.* [*reh-poo-tah-tsee-oh'-neh*] reputation
requisito [*reh-koo-ee-zee'-toh*] requirement
residente [*reh-zee-dehn'-teh*] resident
residenza [*reh-zee-dehn'-tsah*] residence
residuo [*reh-zee'-doo-oh*] remainder
resoconto [*reh-zoh-kohn'-toh*] report
respingere *v.* [*rehs-peen'-jeh-reh*] repel
respirare *v.* [*rehs-pee-rah'-reh*] breathe
respirazione *f.* [*rehs-pee-rah-tsee-oh'-neh*] breathing
respiro [*rehs-pee'-roh*] breath
responsabile [*rehs-pohn-sah'-bee-leh*] responsible
responsabilità *f. indecl.* [*rehs-pohn-sah-bee-lee-tah'*]
   responsibility
resistenza [*reh-zees-tehn'-tsah*] resistance
resistere *v.* [*reh-zees'-teh-reh*] resist
restare *v.* [*rehs-tah'-reh*] remain, stay
restaurare *v.* [*rehs-tah-oo-rah'-reh*] restore
resto [*rehs'-toh*] change [money], rest, remainder
rete *f.* [*reh'-teh*] net
retina [*reh-tee'-nah*] (hair) net
rettangolo [*reht-tahn'-goh-loh*] rectangle

reumatismo [*reh-oo-mah-teez'-moh*] rheumatism
riacquistare v. [*ree-ahk-koo-ees-tah'-reh*] regain
ribellarsi v. [*ree-behl-lahr'-see*] rebel
ribelle m., f. [*ree-behl'-leh*] rebel
ricatto [*ree-kaht'-toh*] blackmail
ricchezza [*reek-kehts'-tsah*] wealth
ricciuto [*reech-chee-oo'-toh*] curly
ricco [*reek'-koh*] rich
ricerca [*ree-chehr'-kah*] search
   fare v. **ricerche** [*fah'-reh ree-chehr'-keh*] research
ricetta [*ree-cheht'-tah*] prescription
ricevere v. [*ree-cheh'-veh-reh*] receive
ricevimento [*ree-cheh-vee-mehn'-toh*] reception, party
ricevuta [*ree-cheh-voo'-tah*] receipt
richiamare (alla memoria) v. [*ree-kee-ah-mah'-reh*
   (*ahl'-lah meh-moh'-ree-ah*)] recall
richiedente [*ree-kee-eh-dehn'-teh*] applicant
richiedere v. [*ree-kee-eh'-deh-reh*] request
richiesta [*ree-kee-ehs'-tah*] request
   fare v. **la richiesta** [*fah'-reh lah ree-kee-ehs'-tah*] apply for
ricompensa [*ree-kohm-pehn'-sah*] reward
ricompensare v. [*ree-kohm-pehn-sah'-reh*] reward
riconoscente [*ree-koh-noh-shehn'-teh*] grateful
riconoscere v. [*ree-koh-noh'-sheh-reh*] recognize
ricordare a v. [*ree-kohr-dah'-reh ah*] remind
ricordarsi v. [*ree-kohr-dahr'-see*] remember
   Si ricorda di me? [*see ree-kohr'-dah dee meh*] Do you
     remember me?
ricordo [*ree-kohr'-doh*] souvenir
ricorrere a v. [*ree-kohr'-reh-reh ah*] resort to
ricorso [*ree-kohr'-soh*] appeal
ricreazione f. [*ree-kreh-ah-tsee-oh'-neh*] recreation
ricuperare v. [*ree-koo-peh-rah'-reh*] recover
ricupero [*ree-koo'-peh-roh*] recovery
ridere v. irreg. [*ree'-deh-reh*] laugh
ridicolo [*ree-dee'-koh-loh*] ridicule, ridiculous
ridurre v. irreg. [*ree-door'-reh*] reduce
riduzione f. [*ree-doo-tsee-oh'-neh*] reduction
riempire v. [*ree-ehm-pee'-reh*] fill
riesaminare v. [*ree-eh-zah-mee-nah'-reh*] review

riferire v. [ree-feh-ree'-reh] report
  riferirsi [ree-feh-reer'-see] refer to
riferimento [ree-feh-ree-mehn'-toh] reference
  punto di riferimento [poon'-toh dee ree-feh-ree-mehn'-toh]
    landmark
rifiutare v. [ree-fee-oo-tah'-reh] refuse
rifiuto [ree-fee-oo'-toh] refusal
riflessione f. [ree-flehs-see-oh'-neh] reflection, consideration
riflesso [ree-flehs'-soh] reflex
riflettere v. [ree-fleht'-teh-reh] reflect
riformare v. [ree-fohr-mah'-reh] reform
rifugio [ree-foo'-jee-oh] refuge, shelter
riga [ree'-gah] ruler [measure]
rigido [ree'-jee-doh] stiff
riguardo [ree-goo-ahr'-doh] regard
  riguardo a [ree-goo-ahr'-doh ah] concerning
  in riguardo a [een ree-goo-ahr'-doh ah] in regard to
rilassare v. [ree-lahs-sah'-reh] relax
rilievo [ree-lee-eh'-voh] projection
  mettere v. **in rilievo** [meht'-teh-reh een ree-lee-eh'-voh]
    emphasize
rilluttante [reel-loot-tahn'-teh] reluctant
rima [ree'-mah] rhyme
rimandare v. [ree-mahn-dah'-reh] postpone
rimanere v. irreg. [ree-mah-neh'-reh] remain
rimborsare v. [reem-bohr-sah'-reh] repay
rimborso [reem-bohr'-soh] refund
rimedio [ree-meh'-dee-oh] remedy
rimessa [ree-mehs'-sah] remittance
rimorchiare v. [ree-mohr-kee-ah'-reh] tow
rimorso [ree-mohr'-soh] remorse
rimpiangere v. [reem-pee-ahn'-jeh-reh] regret
rimproverare v. [reem-proh-veh-rah'-reh] scold
rimuovere v. [ree-moo-oh'-veh-reh] remove
rinascimento [ree-nah-shee-mehn'-toh] renaissance
rinchiudere v. [reen-kee-oo'-deh-reh] enclose
rinfrescante [reen-frehs-kahn'-teh] refreshing
rinfrescare v. [reen-frehs-kah'-reh] refresh
rinfresco [reen-frehs'-koh] refreshment
ringraziare v. [reen-grah-tsee-ah'-reh] thank

rinnovare v. [*reen-noh-vah'-reh*] renew
rintracciare v. [*reen-trahch-chee-ah'-reh*] trace
riparare v. [*ree-pah-rah'-reh*] repair
riparazione f. [*ree-pah-rah-tsee-oh'-neh*] repair
ripetere v. [*ree-peh'-teh-reh*] repeat
  Per favore ripeta! [*pehr fah-voh'-reh ree-peh'-tah*]
    Please repeat!
riposare v. [*ree-poh-zah'-reh*] rest
riposo [*ree-poh'-zoh*] rest
riprendere v. [*ree-prehn'-deh-reh*] resume
riproduzione f. [*ree-proh-doo-tsee-oh'-neh*] reproduction
risata [*ree-zah'-tah*] laughter
riscaldamento [*rees-kahl-dah-mehn'-toh*] heating
riscaldare v. [*rees-kahl-dah'-reh*] warm
rischiare v. [*rees-kee-ah'-reh*] take a chance, risk
rischio [*rees'-kee-oh*] risk
risentimento [*ree-sehn-tee-mehn'-toh*] resentment
riservare v. [*ree-zehr-vah'-reh*] reserve
riso [*ree'-zoh*] laugh
riso [*ree'-zoh*] rice
risoluzione f. [*ree-zoh-loo-tsee-oh'-neh*] resolution
risolvere v. [*ree-zohl'-veh-reh*] solve
risparmiare v. [*rees-pahr-mee-ah'-reh*] save, spare
risparmio [*rees-pahr'-mee-oh*] saving
  libretto di risparmio [*lee-breht'-toh dee rees-pahr'-mee-oh*]
    savings account
rispettabile [*rees-peht-tah'-bee-leh*] respectable
rispettare v. [*rees-peht-tah'-reh*] respect
rispettivo [*rees-peht-tee'-voh*] respective
rispetto [*rees-peht'-toh*] respect
rispettoso [*rees-peht-toh'-zoh*] respectful
rispondere v. irreg. [*rees-pohn'-deh-reh*] answer, reply
risposta [*rees-pohs'-toh*] response
rissa [*rees'-sah*] row
ristorante m. [*rees-toh-rahn'-teh*] restaurant
  vagone ristorante m. [*vah-goh'-neh rees-toh-rahn'-teh*]
    dining car
risultato [*ree-zool-tah'-toh*] result
risveglio [*ree-zveh'-lyoh*] awakening
ritardare v. [*ree-tahr-dah'-reh*] delay

essere v. **in ritardo** [*ehs'-seh-reh een ree-tahr'-doh*] be late

ritenere v. *irreg.* [*ree-teh-neh'-reh*] retain

ritirare v. [*ree-tee-rah'-reh*] withdraw

  ritirarsi [*ree-tee-rahr'-see*] retire

ritmo [*reet'-moh*] rhythm

ritornare v. [*ree-tohr-nah'-reh*] return

  Quando ritornerà? [*koo-ahn'-doh ree-tohr-neh-rah'*]
    When will you return?

ritorno [*ree-tohr'-noh*] return

  andata e ritorno [*ahn-dah'-tah eh ree-tohr'-noh*] round
    trip

ritratto [*ree-traht'-toh*] portrait

rituale m. & adj. [*ree-too-ah'-leh*] ritual

riunione f. [*ree-oo-nee-oh'-neh*] meeting

riuscire v. [*ree-oo-shee'-reh*] succeed

riva [*ree'-vah*] shore

rivale m. & adj. [*ree-vah'-leh*] rival

rivelare v. [*ree-veh-lah'-reh*] reveal

rivelazione f. [*ree-veh-lah-tsee-oh'-neh*] revelation

riverenza [*ree-veh-rehn'-tsah*] reverence

rivista [*ree-vees'-tah*] magazine, review

rivolgere v. [*ree-vohl'-jeh-reh*] address

rivolta [*ree-vohl'-tah*] riot

rivoltarsi v. [*ree-vohl-tahr'-see*] turn around, rebel

rivoltato [*ree-vohl-tah'-toh*] inside out

rivoltella [*ree-vohl-tehl'-lah*] revolver

rivoluzione f. [*ree-voh-loo-tsee-oh'-neh*] revolution

roba [*roh'-bah*] goods, things, stuff

roccia [*rohch'-chee-ah*] rock

rognone m. [*roh-nyoh'-neh*] kidney

Romania [*roh-mah-nee'-ah*] Roumania

Roma [*roh'-mah*] Rome

romano [*roh-mah'-noh*] Roman

romantico [*roh-mahn'-tee-koh*] romantic

romanza [*roh-mahn'-tsah*] romance

romanziere m. [*roh-mahn-tsee-eh'-reh*] novelist

romanzo [*roh-mahn'-tsoh*] novel

Romeno [*roh-meh'-noh*] Roumanian

rompere v. *irreg.* [*rohm'-peh-reh*] break

rondine f. [*rohn'-dee-neh*] swallow

rosa [*roh'-zah*] rose
rossetto [*rohs-seht'-toh*] lipstick
rosso [*rohs'-soh*] red
rotondo [*roh-tohn'-doh*] round
rotta [*roht'-tah*] route
rotto [*roht'-toh*] broken
rottura [*roht-too'-rah*] fracture
rovesciare *v.* [*roh-veh-shee-ah'-reh*] reverse, overturn, upset
rovina [*roh-vee'-nah*] ruin
rovinare *v.* [*roh-vee-nah'-reh*] ruin
rovinato [*roh-vee-nah'-toh*] ruined
rubare *v.* [*roo-bah'-reh*] steal
rubato [*roo-bah'-toh*] stolen
rubinetto [*roo-bee-neht'-toh*] faucet
rude [*roo'-deh*] rude
ruga [*roo'-gah*] wrinkle
ruggine *f.* [*rooj'-jee-neh*] rust
rumore *m.* [*roo-moh'-reh*] rumor, noise
rumoroso [*roo-moh-roh'-zoh*] noisy
ruota [*roo-oh'-tah*] wheel
rurale [*roo-rah'-leh*] rural
ruscello [*roo-shehl'-loh*] brook
russare *v.* [*roos-sah'-reh*] snore
Russia [*roos'-see-ah*] Russia
russo [*roos'-soh*] Russian
rustico [*roos'-tee-koh*] rustic
ruvido [*roo'-vee-doh*] rough

S

sabato [*sah'-bah-toh*] Saturday
sabbia [*sahb'-bee-ah*] sand.
sabbioso [*sahb-bee-oh'-zoh*] sandy
sabotaggio [*sah-boh-tahj'-jee-oh*] sabotage
sacco [*sahk'-koh*] sack
sacerdote *m.* [*sah-chehr-doh'-teh*] clergyman
sacrificare *v.* [*sah-kree-fee-kah'-reh*] sacrifice

sacrificio [*sah-kree-fee'-chee-oh*] sacrifice
sacro [*sah'-kroh*] sacred
saggezza [*sahj-jehts'-tsah*] wisdom
saggio [*sahj'-jee-oh*] wise
sala [*sah'-lah*] hall
  sala d'aspetto [*sah'-lah dahs-peht'-toh*] waiting room
salario [*sah-lah'-ree-oh*] salary
salato [*sah-lah'-toh*] salty
sale *m.* [*sah'-leh*] salt
salire *v. irreg.* [*sah-lee'-reh*] climb, go up
  salire su [*sah-lee'-reh soo*] board
salmone *m.* [*sahl-moh'-neh*] salmon
salone [*sah-loh'-neh*] room, hall
  salone di bellezza [*sah-loh'-neh dee behl-lehts'-tsah*]
    beauty parlor
salotto [*sah-loht'-toh*] parlor, living room
salsa [*sahl'-sah*] sauce
salsiccia [*sahl-seech'-chee-ah*] sausage
saltare *v.* [*sahl-tah'-reh*] jump
salto [*sahl'-toh*] jump
salutare *v.* [*sah-loo-tah'-reh*] greet, salute
salutare *adj.* [*sah-loo-tah'-reh*] healthy
salute *f.* [*sah-loo'-teh*] health
  Alla sua salute! [*ahl'-lah soo'-ah sah-loo'-teh*]
    To your health!
  in buona salute [*een boo-oh'-nah sah-loo'-teh*] in good
    health
saluti [*sah-loo'-tee*] greetings
saluto [*sah-loo'-toh*] salute
salvacondotta *m.* [*sahl-vah-kohn-doht'-tah*] safe conduct
salvagente *m.* [*sahl-vah-jehn'-teh*] life jacket
salvaggio [*sahl-vahj'-jee-oh*] rescue
salvare *v.* [*sahl-vah'-reh*] save, rescue
Salve! [*sahl'-veh*] Hello!
salvo *adj.* [*sahl'-voh*] safe
salvo *prep.* [*sahl'-voh*] except, excepting
sanatorio [*sah-nah-toh'-ree-oh*] sanatorium
sangue *m.* [*sahn'-goo-eh*] blood
sano [*sah'-noh*] sound, healthy
  sano di mente [*sah'-noh dee mehn'-teh*] sane

sano e salvo [*sah'-noh eh sahl'-voh*] safe and sound

santo [*sahn'-toh*] saint, holy

sanzione *f.* [*sahn-tsee-oh'-neh*] sanction

sapere *v. irreg.* [*sah-peh'-reh*] know [in general sense]

  Sa lei? [*sah leh'-ee*] Do you know?

  Non so [*nohn soh*] I don't know

  Chi sa? [*kee sah*] Who knows?

sapere *m.* [*sah-peh'-reh*] knowledge

sapienza [*sah-pee-ehn'-tsah*] knowledge

sapone *m.* [*sah-poh'-neh*] soap

sapore *m.* [*sah-poh'-reh*] flavor, taste

saporito [*sah-poh-ree'-toh*] tasty

sarà [*sah-rah'*] (he, she, it, you) will be

saranno [*sah-rahn'-noh*] (they, you [polite form]) will be

sarcastico [*sahr-kahs'-tee-koh*] sarcastic

Sardegna [*sahr-deh'-nyah*] Sardinia

sardina [*sahr-dee'-nah*] sardine

saremo [*sah-reh'-moh*] we will be

sarò [*sah-roh'*] I will be

sarta [*sahr'-tah*] dressmaker

sarto [*sahr'-toh*] tailor

sartoria [*sahr-toh-ree'-ah*] tailor shop

sasso [*sahs'-soh*] stone

satira [*sah'-tee-rah*] satire

satirico [*sah-tee'-ree-koh*] satirical

sbadigliare *v.* [*zbah-dee-lyah'-reh*] yawn

sbadiglio [*zbah-dee'-lyoh*] yawn

sbagliare *v.* [*zbah-lyah'-reh*] err, make an error

  sbagliarsi [*zbah-lyahr'-see*] be mistaken

sbagliato [*zbah-lyah'-toh*] mistaken, wrong

sbaglio [*zbah'-lyoh*] error, mistake

sbarazzarsi di *v.* [*zbah-rahts-tsahr'-see dee*] get rid of

sbarcare *v.* [*zbahr-kah'-reh*] land [ship]

sbarra [*zbahr'-rah*] bar [metal]

sbarrare *v.* [*zbahr-rah'-reh*] bar

sbucciare *v.* [*zbooch-chee-ah'-reh*] peel [food]

scacchi *m. pl.* [*skahk'-kee*] chess

scadenza [*skah-dehn'-tsah*] expiration

scadere *v.* [*skah-deh'-reh*] expire, fall due

scaduto [*skah-doo'-toh*] expired, due

scaffale *m.* [*skahf-fah'-leh*] shelf
scala [*skah'-lah*] ladder, stairs
scalzo [*skahl'-tsoh*] barefoot
scambiare *v.* [*skahm-bee-ah'-reh*] exchange
scandalo [*skahn'-dah-loh*] scandal
scapolo [*skah'-poh-loh*] bachelor
scappare *v.* [*skahp-pah'-reh*] escape
scaricare *v.* [*skah-ree-kah'-reh*] unload
scarico [*skah'-ree-koh*] discharge, unloading
scarlatto [*skahr-laht'-toh*] scarlet
scarpa [*skahr'-pah*] shoe
scarso [*skahr'-soh*] scarce, scanty
scatola [*skah'-toh-lah*] box, can
scattare *v.* [*skaht-tah'-reh*] spring up
scavare *v.* [*skah-vah'-reh*] dig
scegliere *v. irreg.* [*sheh'-lyeh-reh*] choose
scelta [*shehl'-tah*] choice
scelto [*shehl'-toh*] chosen
scena [*sheh'-nah*] scene
scenario [*sheh-nah'-ree-oh*] scenery
scendere *v. irreg.* [*shehn'-deh-reh*] descend, go down, get off
scheletro [*skeh'-leh-troh*] skeleton
schema *m.* [*skeh'-mah*] scheme
scherma [*skehr'-mah*] fencing
schermo [*skehr'-moh*] screen
scherzare *v.* [*skehr-tsah'-reh*] joke, kid
   Senza scherzi [*sehn'-tsah skehr'-tsee*] No kidding
scherzo [*skehr'-tsoh*] joke, trick
scherzoso [*skehr-tsoh'-zoh*] playful
schiacciare *v.* [*skee-ahch-chee-ah'-reh*] crush
schiaffeggiare *v.* [*skee-ahf-fehj-jee-ah'-reh*] slap
schiaffo [*skee-ahf'-foh*] slap
schiavitù *f. indecl.* [*skee-ah-vee-too'*] slavery
schiavo [*skee-ah'-voh*] slave
schiena [*skee-eh'-nah*] back [anat.]
schiuma [*skee-oo'-mah*] foam
sci *m.* [*shee*] ski
scialle *m.* [*shee-ahl'-leh*] shawl
scialuppa [*shee-ah-loo'-pah*] lifeboat
sciampagna [*shee-ahm-pah'-nyah*] champagne

sciacquare v. [*shee-ahk-koo-ah'-reh*] rinse
sciare v. [*shee-ah'-reh*] ski
sciarpa [*shee-ahr'-pah*] scarf
scienza [*shee-ehn'-tsah*] science
scienziato [*shee-ehn-tsee-ah'-toh*] scientist
scimmia [*sheem'-mee-ah*] monkey, ape
sciocchezza [*shee-ohk-kehts'-tsah*] nonsense
sciocco [*shee-ohk'-koh*] foolish
sciogliere v. irreg. [*shee-oh'-lyeh-reh*] melt, untie, dissolve
sciolto [*shee-ohl'-toh*] melted
sciopero [*shee-oh'-peh-roh*] strike
scintilla [*sheen-teel'-lah*] spark
sciupare v. [*shee-oo-pah'-reh*] waste
scivolare v. [*shee-voh-lah'-reh*] slip, slide
scivoloso [*shee-voh-loh'-zoh*] slippery
scodella [*skoh-dehl'-lah*] bowl
scolpire v. [*skohl-pee'-reh*] carve
scommessa [*skohm-mehs'-sah*] bet
scommettere v. [*skoh-meht'-teh-reh*] bet
scomodo [*skohm'-moh-doh*] uncomfortable
scomparire v. irreg. [*skohm-pah-ree'-reh*] disappear
scomparso [*skohm-pahr'-soh*] missing
scompartimento [*skohm-pahr-tee-mehn'-toh*] compartment
sconfiggere v. [*skohn-feej'-jeh-reh*] defeat
sconfitta [*skohn-feet'-tah*] defeat
sconosciuto [*skoh-noh-shee-oo'-toh*] unknown
sconto [*skohn'-toh*] discount
scontrino [*skohn-tree'-noh*] check, ticket, coupon
scontro [*skohn'-troh*] collision
sconvenienza [*skohn-veh-nee-ehn'-tsah*] inconvenience
scopa [*skoh'-pah*] broom
scopare v. [*skoh-pah'-reh*] sweep
scoperta [*skoh-pehr'-tah*] discovery
scopo [*skoh'-poh*] purpose, sake, aim
scoppio [*skohp'-pee-oh*] burst
scoprire v. irreg. [*skohp-pree'-reh*] discover
scoraggiare v. [*skoh-rahj-jee-ah'-reh*] discourage
scorciatoia [*skohr-chee-ah-toh'-ee-ah*] shortcut
scorrere v. [*skohr'-reh-reh*] flow
scorso [*skohr'-soh*] past

la notte scorsa [*lah noht'-teh skohr'-sah*] last night

scortese [*skohr-teh'-zeh*] unkind, impolite

scortesia [*skohr-teh-zee'-ah*] rudeness

scozzese [*skohts-tseh'-zeh*] Scotch

Scozia [*skoh'-tsee-ah*] Scotland

scritto [*skreet'-toh*] writing, written

scrittore *m.*, **scrittrice** *f.* [*skreet-toh'-reh, skreet-tree'-cheh*] writer

scrittura [*skreet-too'-rah*] writing

scrivania [*skree-vah-nee'-ah*] desk

scrivere *v. irreg.* [*skree'-veh-reh*] write

  Come si scrive? [*koh'-meh see skree'-veh*] How do you spell it?

  scrivere a macchina [*skree'-veh-reh ah mahk'-kee-nah*] type

scultura [*skool-too'-rah*] sculpture

scuola [*skoo-oh'-lah*] school

  scuola elementare [*skoo-oh'-lah eh-leh-mehn-tah'-reh*] elementary school

  scuola media [*skoo-oh'-lah meh'-dee-ah*] high school

scuotere *v.* [*skoo-oh'-teh-reh*] rock, shake

scusa [*skoo'-zah*] excuse, apology

scusare *v.* [*skoo-zah'-reh*] excuse

  scusarsi [*skoo-zahr'-see*] apologize

  Mi scusi! [*mee skoo'-zee*] Excuse me!

sdraiarsi *v.* [*zdrah-ee-ahr'-see*] lie down

se [*seh*] whether, if

  se è possibile [*seh eh' pohs-see'-bee-leh*] if it is possible

  se no [*seh noh*] otherwise

sè [*seh'*] one's self, himself, herself, themselves

sebbene [*sehb-beh'-neh*] although

seccare *v.* [*sehk-kah'-reh*] vex, dry

secco [*sehk'-koh*] dry

secchio [*sehk'-kee-oh*] pail

secolo [*seh'-koh-loh*] century

secondario [*seh-kohn-dah'-ree-oh*] secondary

secondo *adj.* [*seh-kohn'-doh*] second

secondo a . . . [*seh-kohn'-doh ah*] according to . . .

secondo [*seh-kohn'-doh*] second [of a minute]

sede *f.* [*seh'-deh*] residence

sede centrale [*seh'-deh chehn-trah'-leh*] headquarters
[business]
sedere *v. irreg.* [*seh-deh'-reh*] sit
　sedersi [*seh-dehr'-see*] sit (down)
　Si sieda, per favore! [*see see-eh'-dah, pehr fah-voh'-reh*]
　　Have a seat, please!
sedia [*seh'-dee-ah*] chair
　sedia a dondolo [*seh'-dee-ah ah dohn'-doh-loh*] rocking
　　chair
sedici [*seh'-dee-chee*] sixteen
sedurre *v. irreg.* [*seh-door'-reh*] seduce
seduto [*seh-doo'-toh*] seated
segnalare *v.* [*seh-nyah-lah'-reh*] signal
segnale [*seh-nyah'-leh*] signal
segnare *v.* [*seh-nyah'-reh*] mark, point out
segno [*seh'-nyoh*] sign
segretario [*seh-greh-tah'-ree-oh*] secretary
segreto *n. & adj.* [*seh-greh'-toh*] secret
seguente [*seh-goo-ehn'-teh*] following
seguire *v.* [*seh-goo-ee'-reh*] follow
　Mi segua! [*mee seh'-goo-ah*] Follow me!
seguito [*seh'-goo-ee-toh*] following
　in seguito [*een seh'-goo-ee-toh*] afterwards
sei [*seh'-ee*] six
seicento [*seh-ee-chehn'-toh*] six hundred
sella [*sehl'-lah*] saddle
selvaggio [*sehl-vahj'-jee-oh*] savage
sembrare *v.* [*sehm-brah'-reh*] seem
　Come le sembra? [*koh'-meh leh sehm'-brah*] How does it
　　seem to you?
　Mi sembra che . . . [*mee sehm'-brah keh*] It seems to me
　　that . . .
seme *m.* [*seh'-meh*] seed
semiaperto [*seh-mee-ah-pehr'-toh*] half-open
seminare *v.* [*seh-mee-nah'-reh*] sow
semplice [*sehm'-plee-cheh*] simple
semplicemente [*sehm-plee-cheh-mehn'-teh*] simply
sempre [*sehm'-preh*] always
　come sempre [*koh'-meh sehm'-preh*] as ever, like always
　per sempre [*pehr sehm'-preh*] forever

senato [*seh-nah'-toh*] senate
senatore *m.* [*seh-nah-toh'-reh*] senator
seno [*seh'-noh*] bosom
sensible [*sehn-see'-bee-leh*] sensible
sensitivo [*sehn-see-tee'-voh*] sensitive
senso [*sehn'-soh*] sense
  buon senso [*boo-ohn' sehn'-soh*] common sense
  senso unico [*sehn'-soh oo'-nee-koh*] one-way street
sentiero [*sehn-tee-eh'-roh*] path
sentimentale [*sehn-tee-mehn-tah'-leh*] sentimental
sentimento [*sehn-tee-mehn'-toh*] feeling
sentire *v.* [*sehn-tee'-reh*] hear, listen
  Senta! [*sehn'-tah*] Listen!
sentirsi *v.* [*sehn-teer'-see*] feel
  Come si sente? [*koh'-meh see sehn'-teh*] How do you feel?
senza [*sehn'-tsah*] without
separare *v.* [*seh-pah-rah'-reh*] separate
separatamente [*seh-pah-rah-tah-mehn'-teh*] separately
separato [*seh-pah-rah'-toh*] separate
separazione *f.* [*seh-pah-rah-tsee-oh'-neh*] separation
sera [*seh'-rah*] evening
  Buona sera! [*boo-oh'-nah seh'-rah*] Good evening
  Domani sera [*doh-mah'-nee seh'-rah*] tomorrow evening
  durante la sera [*doo-rahn'-teh lah seh'-rah*] in the evening
  ieri sera [*ee-eh'-ree seh'-rah*] yesterday evening
serata [*seh-rah'-tah*] evening
serbatoio [*sehr-bah-toh'-ee-oh*] tank
serenata [*seh-reh-nah'-tah*] serenade
sereno [*seh-reh'-noh*] serene
seriamente [*seh-ree-ah-mehn'-teh*] seriously
serie *f. sing. & pl.* [*seh'-ree-eh*] series
serio [*seh'-ree-oh*] serious
serpente *m.* [*sehr-pehn'-teh*] snake
serratura [*sehr-rah-too'-rah*] lock
servire *v.* [*sehr-vee'-reh*] serve, wait on, be good for
  Che cosa serve questo? [*keh koh'-zah sehr'-veh koo-ehs'-toh*] What is this used for?
  In che posso servirla? [*een keh pohs'-soh sehr-veer'-lah*] What can I do for you?
  Non serve a nulla! [*nohn sehr'-veh ah nool'-lah*] It's not

good for anything!

Si serva! [*see sehr'-vah*] Help yourself!

servitore *m.*, **servitrice** *f.* [*sehr-vee-toh'-reh, sehr-vee-tree'-cheh*] servant

servizio [*sehr-vee'-tsee-oh*] service

  di servizio [*dee sehr-vee'-tsee-oh*] on duty

  essere *v.* **di servizio** [*ehs'-seh-reh dee sehr-vee'-tsee-oh*] be on duty

  fuori servizio [*foo-oh'-ree sehr-vee'-tsee-oh*] out of order

  servizio compreso [*sehr-vee'-tsee-oh kohm-preh'-zoh*] no tipping

  servizio militare [*sehr-vee'-tsee-oh mee-lee-tah'-reh*] military service

sessanta [*sehs-sahn'-tah*] sixty

sessione *f.* [*sehs-see-oh'-neh*] session

sesso [*sehs'-soh*] sex

sesto [*sehs'-toh*] sixth

seta [*seh'-tah*] silk

  seta artificiale [*seh'-tah ahr-tee-fee-chee-ah'-leh*] rayon

sete *f.* [*seh'-teh*] thirst

  avere *v.* **sete** [*ah-veh'-reh seh'-teh*] be thirsty

setta [*seht'-tah*] sect

settanta [*seht-tahn'-tah*] seventy

sette [*seht'-teh*] seven

settembre *m.* [*seht-tehm'-breh*] September

settentrionale [*seht-tehn-tree-oh-nah'-leh*] northern

settimana [*seht-tee-mah'-nah*] week

  la settimana scorsa [*lah seht-tee-mah'-nah skohr'-sah*] last week

  la settimana prossima [*lah seht-tee-mah'-nah prohs'-see-mah*] next week

  fine-settimana [*fee'-neh seht-tee-mah'-nah*] weekend

settimanale [*seht-tee-mah-nah'-leh*] weekly

settimo [*seht'-tee-moh*] seventh

severo [*seh-veh'-roh*] severe

sezione *f.* [*seh-tsee-oh'-neh*] section

sfavorevole [*sfah-voh-reh'-voh-leh*] unfavorable

sfida [*sfee'-dah*] challenge

sfidare *v.* [*sfee-dah'-reh*] challenge

sfiducia [*sfee-doo'-chee-ah*] distrust

sfigurare v. [sfee-goo-rah'-reh] mar
sfondo [sfohn'-doh] background
sfortuna [sfohr-too'-nah] hard luck
sfortunato [sfohr-too-nah'-toh] unlucky
sforzo [sfohr'-tsoh] effort
sgradevole [zgrah-deh'-voh-leh] unpleasant
sgradito [zgrah-dee'-toh] unwelcome
sgomberare v. [zgohm-beh-rah'-reh] vacate
sguardo [zgoo-ahr'-doh] look
si refl. & impers. pron. [see] oneself, himself, herself, etc;
    one, they, we; one another, each other
sì [see'] yes
sia . . . sia [see'-ah . . . see'-ah] both . . . and
siccome [seek-koh'-meh] as, inasmuch as
Sicilia [see-chee'-lee-ah] Sicily
siciliano [see-chee-lee-ah'-noh] Sicilian
sicuramente [see-koo-rah-mehn'-teh] surely
sicurezza [see-koo-rehts'-tsah] security
sicuro [see-koo'-roh] sure, secure

  È sicuro? [eh' see-koo'-roh] Are you sure?

siesta [see-ehs'-tah] afternoon nap
sigaretta [see-gah-reht'-tah] cigarette
sigaro [see'-gah-roh] cigar
sigillare v. [see-jeel-lah'-reh] seal
sigillo [see-jeel'-loh] seal [for document]
significato [see-nyee-fee-kah'-toh] meaning
significare v. [see-nyee-fee-kah'-reh] mean
signora [see-nyoh'-rah] madam, lady

  Sigra. Mrs.

  per signore [pehr see-nyoh'-reh] ladies' room

signore m. [see-nyoh'-reh] gentleman, sir, mister

  Sig. Mr.

  Gentile Signore: [jehn-tee'-leh see-nyoh'-reh] Dear Sir:
  Il signor tal dei tali [eel see-nyohr' tahl deh'-ee tah'-lee]
    Mr. So and So

signorina [see-nyoh-ree'-nah] miss, young girl
silenzio [see-lehn'-tsee-oh] silence

  Silenzio! [see-lehn'-tsee-oh] Quiet!, Shut up!

silenziosamente [see-lehn-tsee-oh-zah-mehn'-teh] silently
silenzioso [see-lehn-tsee-oh'-zoh] silent

sillaba [*seel'-lah-bah*] syllable
simile [*see'-mee-leh*] similar, alike, like
similmente [*see-meel-mehn'-teh*] likewise
simpatia [*seem-pah-tee'-ah*] sympathy
simpatico [*seem-pah'-tee-koh*] nice, pleasant, likable
simultaneo [*see-mool-tah'-neh-oh*] simultaneous
sinceramente [*seen-cheh-rah-mehn'-teh*] sincerely
sincero [*seen-cheh'-roh*] sincere
sindaco [*seen'-dah-koh*] mayor
sinfonia [*seen-foh-nee'-ah*] symphony
sinistro [*see-nees'-troh*] left
  a sinistra [*ah see-nees'-trah*] to the left
sinora [*seen-oh'-rah*] so far
sintetico [*seen-teh'-tee-koh*] synthetic
sintomo [*seen'-toh-moh*] symptom
sistema *m.* [*sees-teh'-mah*] system
sistemare *v.* [*sees-teh-mah'-reh*] arrange
sistematico [*sees-teh-mah'-tee-koh*] systematic
situato [*see-too-ah'-toh*] situated
situazione *f.* [*see-too-ah-tsee-oh'-neh*] situation
sleale [*sleh-ah'-leh*] disloyal
slittare *v.* [*zleet-tah'-reh*] slide
smacchiare *v.* [*zmahk-kee-ah'-reh*] clean [clothes]
smarrire *v.* [*zmahr-ree'-reh*] lose
  smarrirsi [*zmahr-reer'-see*] get lost
smentire *v.* [*zmehn-tee'-reh*] deny
smettere *v.* [*zmeht'-teh-reh*] stop [doing something]
  La smetta! [*lah zmeht'-tah*] Stop it!
smorfia [*zmohr'-fee-ah*] grin
snello [*znehl'-loh*] slender
soave [*soh-ah'-veh*] gentle, soft, mild
sobrio [*soh'-bree-oh*] sober
sobborgo [*sohb-bohr'-goh*] suburb
soccorso [*sohk-kohr'-soh*] help, aid
  pronto soccorso [*prohn'-toh sohk-kohr'-soh*] first aid
sociale [*soh-chee-ah'-leh*] social
socialista *m.*, *f.* [*soh-chee-ah-lees'-tah*] socialist
società *f. indecl.* [*soh-chee-eh-tah'*] society
socio [*soh'-chee-oh*] associate, member
soda [*soh'-dah*] soda

soddisfacente [*sohd-dees-fah-chehn'-teh*] satisfactory

soddisfare v. [*sohd-dees-fah'-reh*] satisfy

soddisfatto [*sohd-dees-faht'-toh*] satisfied

soddisfazione f. [*sohd-dees-fah-tsee-oh'-neh*] satisfaction

soffiare v. [*sohf-fee-ah'-reh*] blow

soffitta [*sohf-feet'-tah*] attic

soffitto [*sohf-feet'-toh*] ceiling

soffocare v. [*sohf-foh-kah'-reh*] suffocate, choke

soffrire v. irreg. [*sohf-free'-reh*] suffer

soggetto [*sohj-jeht'-toh*] topic, subject

soggiorno [*sohj-jee-ohr'-noh*] stay, living room

sognare v. [*soh-nyah'-reh*] dream

sogno [*soh'-nyoh*] dream

solamente [*soh-lah-mehn'-teh*] only

soldato [*sohl-dah'-toh*] soldier

soldi m. pl. [*sohl'-dee*] money

soldo [*sohl'-doh*] penny

sole m. [*soh'-leh*] sun

    calar m. **del sole** [*kah-lahr' dehl soh'-leh*] sunset

    luce f. **del sole** [*loo'-cheh dehl soh'-leh*] sunshine

    levar m. **del sole** [*leh-vahr' dehl soh'-leh*] sunrise

    occhiali m. pl. **da sole** [*ohk-kee-ah'-lee dah soh'-leh*] sunglasses

solido [*soh'-lee-doh*] solid

solitario [*soh-lee-tah'-ree-oh*] lonely

solito [*soh'-lee-toh*] usual, customary

    di solito [*dee soh'-lee-toh*] usually

sollevamento [*sohl-leh-vah-mehn'-toh*] upheaval

sollevare v. [*sohl-leh-vah'-reh*] lift

sollievo [*sohl-lee-eh'-voh*] relief [from discomfort]

solo [*soh'-loh*] alone, single, only

    da solo [*dah soh'-loh*] all alone

soltanto [*sohl-tahn'-toh*] only

soluzione f. [*soh-loo-tsee-oh'-neh*] solution

somma [*sohm'-mah*] sum

sommare v. [*sohm-mah'-reh*] sum up

sommario [*sohm-mah'-ree-oh*] summary

sommità f. indecl. [*sohm-mee-tah'*] top, summit, peak

somministrare v. [*sohm-mee-nees-trah'-reh*] minister

sommo [*sohm'-moh*] very great

sonnecchiare v. [*sohn-nehk-kee-ah'-reh*] doze
sonnellino [*sohn-nehl-lee'-noh*] nap
sonno [*sohn'-noh*] sleep
   avere v. **sonno** [*ah-veh'-reh sohn'-noh*] be sleepy
sopportare v. [*sohp-pohr-tah'-reh*] support, bear
sopportabile [*sohp-pohr-tah-bee-leh*] bearable
sopra [*soh'-prah*] above, on, over
sopracciglio, le sopracciglia pl. [*soh-prahch-chee'-lyoh, leh
   sohp-prahch-chee'-lyah*] eyebrow
soprano [*soh-prah'-noh*] soprano
soprattutto [*soh-praht-toot'-toh*] above all
sopravvivere v. [*soh-prahv-vee'-veh-reh*] survive
sopprimere v. [*sohp-pree'-meh-reh*] suppress, put down
sordo [*sohr'-doh*] deaf
sorella [*soh-rehl'-lah*] sister
sorgente f. [*sohr-jehn'-teh*] source, spring
sorgere v. [*sohr'-jeh-reh*] rise, arise
sorpassare [*sohr-pahs-sah'-reh*] overtake
sorprendente [*sohr-prehn-dehn'-teh*] surprising
sorprendere v. [*sohr-prehn'-deh-reh*] surprise
   sorprendersi di [*sohr-prehn'-dehr-see dee*] be surprised at
sorpresa [*sohr-preh'-zah*] surprise
sorridere v. irreg. [*sohr-ree'-deh-reh*] smile
sorriso [*sohr-ree'-zoh*] smile
sorvegliare v. [*sohr-veh-lyah'-reh*] guard
sospendere [*sohs-pehn'-deh-reh*] call off, suspend
sospettare v. [*sohs-peht-tah'-reh*] suspect
sospetto [*sohs-peht'-toh*] suspicion
sospettoso [*sohs-peht-too-oh'-zoh*] suspicious
sospirare v. [*sohs-pee-rah'-reh*] sigh
sospiro [*sohs-pee'-roh*] sigh
sosta [*sohs'-tah*] halt, rest, stop
   Sosta vietata [*sohs'-tah vee-eh-tah'-tah*] No parking
sostanziale [*sohs-tahn-tsee-ah'-leh*] substantial
sostare v. [*sohs-tah'-reh*] pause
sostegno [*sohs-teh'-nyoh*] support
sostenere v. [*sohs-teh-neh'-reh*] support
sostituire v. [*sohs-tee-too-ee'-reh*] replace
sostituto [*sohs-tee-too'-toh*] substitute
sostituzione f. [*sohs-tee-too-tsee-oh'-neh*] substitution

sottana [*soht-tah'-nah*] skirt
sotterranea [*soht-tehr-rah'-neh-ah*] subway
sotterraneo [*soht-tehr-rah'-neh-oh*] basement
sottile [*soht-tee'-leh*] thin, subtle
sotto [*soht'-toh*] below, under
sottomarino [*soht-toh-mah-ree'-noh*] submarine
sottomettere v. [*soht-toh-meht'-teh-reh*] submit
sottoporre v. [*soht-toh-pohr'-reh*] subject
sottoscritto [*soht-toh-skreet'-toh*] undersigned
sottosopra [*soht-toh-soh'-prah*] upside down
sottosuolo [*soht-toh-soo-oh'-loh*] underground
sottoveste f. [*soht-toh-vehs'-teh*] slip, underskirt
sottovoce [*soht-toh-voh'-cheh*] in a low voice
sottrazione f. [*soht-trah-tsee-oh'-neh*] subtraction
sovente [*soh-vehn'-teh*] often
spada [*spah'-dah*] sword
spaghetti m. pl. [*spah-geht'-tee*] spaghetti
  spaghetti alle vongole [*spah-geht'-tee ahl'-leh vohn'-goh-leh*] spaghetti in clam sauce
Spagna [*spah'-nyah*] Spain
spagnolo [*spah-nyoh'-loh*] Spanish, Spaniard
spago [*spah'-goh*] string
spalancato [*spah-lahn-kah'-toh*] wide-open
spalla [*spahl'-lah*] shoulder
spalliera [*spahl-lee-eh'-rah*] back of a seat
spalmare v. [*spahl-mah'-reh*] spread on
sparare v. [*spah-rah'-reh*] shoot
spargere v. irreg. [*spahr'-j-reh*] spread, scatter
sparire v. [*spah-ree'-reh*] disappear
sparo [*spah'-roh*] shot
spartire v. [*spahr-tee'-reh*] part, divide
spaventare v. [*spah-vehn-tah'-reh*] frighten
spavento [*spah-vehn'-toh*] fear, fright
spaventoso [*spah-vehn-toh'-zoh*] dreadful
spazio [*spah'-tsee-oh*] room, space
  Non c'è spazio [*nohn cheh' spah'-tsee-oh*] There is no room
spazioso [*spah-tsee-oh'-zoh*] spacious
spazzola [*spahts'-tsoh-lah*] brush
  spazzolino da denti [*spahts-tsoh-lee'-noh dah dehn'-tee*]

toothbrush

spazzolare v. [*spahts-tsoh-lah'-reh*] brush

specchio [*spehk'-kee-oh*] mirror

speciale [*speh-chee-ah'-leh*] special

specialmente [*speh-chee-ahl-mehn'-teh*] especially

specialista [*speh-chee-ah-lees'-tah*] specialist

specialità f. indecl. [*speh-chee-ah-lee-tah'*] specialty

specie [*speh'-chee-eh*] sort, kind

specificazione f. [*speh-chee-fee-kah-tsee-oh'-neh*] specification

spedire v. [*speh-dee'-reh*] send, forward, ship

spedizione f. [*speh-dee-tsee-oh'-neh*] expedition

spegnere v. irreg. [*speh'-nyeh-reh*] turn off, extinguish

spendere v. irreg. [*spehn'-deh-reh*] spend [money]

spensierato [*spehn-see-eh-rah'-toh*] carefree

speranza [*speh-rahn'-tsah*] hope

sperare v. [*speh-rah'-reh*] hope

spesa [*speh'-zah*] expense

  fare v. **le spese** [*fah'-reh leh speh'-zeh*] go shopping

spesso adv. [*spehs'-soh*] often, frequently

spesso adj. [*spehs'-soh*] thick

spettacolo [*speht-tah'-koh-loh*] spectacle

spettatore m., **spettatrice** f. [*speht-tah-toh'-reh, speht-tah-tree'-cheh*] spectator

spia [*spee'-ah*] spy

spiacente [*spee-ah-chehn'-teh*] sorry

  essere v. **spiacente** [*ehs'-seh-reh spee-ah-chehn'-teh*] be sorry

spiaggia [*spee-ahj'-jee-ah*] beach

spiare v. [*spee-ah'-reh*] spy

spiccioli m. pl. [*speech'-chee-oh-lee*] small change

spiegare v. [*spee-eh-gah'-reh*] explain

  Mi spieghi questo, per favore [*mee spee-eh'-gee koo-ehs'-toh, pehr fah-voh'-reh*] Explain this to me, please

spiegazione f. [*spee-eh-gah-tsee-oh'-neh*] explanation

spillo, spilla [*speel'-loh, speel'-lah*] pin

spina [*spee'-nah*] spine, thorn

  spina dorsale [*spee'-nah dohr-sah'-leh*] spine, backbone

  spina elettrica [*spee'-nah eh-leht'-tree-kah*] plug

spinaci m. pl. [*spee-nah'-chee*] spinach

spingere v. irreg. [speen'-jeh-reh] push, drive, shove
spirito [spee'-ree-toh] spirit
spirituale [spee-ree-too-ah'-leh] spiritual
splendido [splehn'-dee-doh] splendid
splendore m. [splehn-doh'-reh] glitter
spogliarsi v. [spoh-lyahr'-see] undress oneself
spontaneo [spohn-tah'-neh-oh] spontaneous
sporcizia [spohr-chee'-tsee-ah] dirt
sporco [spohr'-koh] dirty
sport m. [spohrt] sport
sportello [spohr-tehl'-loh] ticket window
sposa [spoh'-zah] bride
sposo [spoh'-zoh] bridegroom
sposare v. [spoh-zah'-reh] marry
sposarsi v. [spoh-zahr'-see] get married
sposato [spoh-zah'-toh] married
sprecare v. [spreh-kah'-reh] waste
spremere v. [spreh'-meh-reh] press, squeeze
spremuta di limone [spreh-moo'-tah dee lee-moh'-neh]
    lemon juice
spruzzare v. [sproots-tsah'-reh] spray
spugna [spoo'-nyah] sponge
sputare v. [spoo-tah'-reh] spit
squadra [skoo-ah'-drah] team, square
squisito [skoo-ee-zee'-toh] exquisite
stabile [stah'-bee-leh] stable
stabilire v. [stah-bee-lee'-reh] establish
staccare v. [stahk-kah'-reh] disconnect, detach
stadio [stah'-dee-oh] stadium
stagione f. [stah-jee-oh'-neh] season
stamane [stah-mah'-neh] this morning
stampa [stahm'-pah] press, print
stampare v. [stahm-pah'-reh] print
stampato [stahm-pah'-toh] printed matter
stancarsi v. [stahn-kahr'-see] get tired
stanco [stahn'-koh] tired
stanotte [stah-noht'-teh] tonight
stanza [stahn'-tsah] room
    stanza soggiorno [stahn'-tsah sohj-jee-ohr'-noh] living room
stare v. irreg. [stah'-reh] be, feel, stay, remain

Come sta? [*koh'-meh stah*] How are you?

Sto bene, grazie [*stoh beh'-neh, grah'-tsee-eh*]
I am fine, thanks

Sono stanco [*soh'-noh stahn'-koh*] I am tired

stare in piedi [*stah'-reh een pee-eh'-dee*] stand up

starnutire v. [*stahr-noo-tee'-reh*] sneeze

starnuto [*stahr-noo'-toh*] sneeze

stasera [*stah-seh'-rah*] this evening

statista m. [*stah-tees'-tah*] statesman

stato [*stah'-toh*] state, condition

   in buono stato [*een boo-oh'-noh stah'-toh*] in good
   condition

   gli Stati Uniti [*lyee stah'-tee oo-nee'-tee*] United States

statua [*stah'-too-ah*] statue

stazione f. [*stah-tsee-oh'-neh*] station

   stazione climatica [*stah-tsee-oh'-neh klee-mah'-tee-kah*]
   resort

   stazione ferroviaria [*stah-tsee-oh'-neh fehr-roh-vee-ah'-
   ree-ah*] railway station

   stazione di polizia [*stah-tsee-oh'-neh dee poh-lee-tsee'-ah*]
   police station

   stazione radio [*stah-tsee-oh'-neh rah'-dee-oh*] radio station

stella [*stehl'-lah*] star

stendere v. [*stehn'-deh-reh*] stretch

stenografo [*steh-noh'-grah-foh*] stenographer

stesso [*stehs'-soh*] self, same

   allo stesso tempo [*ahl'-loh stehs'-soh tehm'-poh*] at the
   same time

   È la stessa cosa [*eh' lah stehs'-sah koh'-zah*] It does not
   make any difference

   Per me è la stessa cosa [*pehr meh eh' lah stehs'-sah koh'-
   zah*] It's all the same to me

   io stesso [*ee'-oh stehs'-soh*] I myself

   Lei stesso [*leh'-ee stehs'-soh*] you [polite form], yourself

   lei stessa [*leh'-ee stehs'-sah*] she herself

   lui stesso [*loo'-ee stehs'-soh*] he himself

   voi stessi [*voh'-ee stehs'-see*] you yourselves

   loro stessi [*loh'-roh stehs'-see*] they themselves

sterilizzato [*steh-ree-leedz-dzah'-toh*] sterilized

stile m. [*stee'-leh*] style

stimare v. [*stee-mah'-reh*] esteem, value
stimolante [*stee-moh-lahn'-teh*] stimulant
stipendio [*stee-pehn'-dee-oh*] salary
stirare v. [*stee-rah'-reh*] press [clothes]
stivale m. [*stee-vah'-leh*] boot
stoffa [*stohf'-fah*] cloth
stomaco [*stoh'-mah-koh*] stomach
stordire v. [*stohr-dee'-reh*] stun
stordito [*stohr-dee'-toh*] dizzy
storia [*stoh'-ree-ah*] history, story
storta [*stohr'-tah*] sprain
storto [*stohr'-toh*] crooked
straccio [*strahch'-chee-oh*] rag
strada [*strah'-dah*] street, road
straniero [*strah-nee-eh'-roh*] foreign, foreigner
strano [*strah'-noh*] strange, odd
   Che strano! [*keh strah'-noh*] How queer!
straordinario [*strah-ohr-dee-nah'-ree-oh*] extraordinary
strappare v. [*strahp-pah'-reh*] tear, rip
stravagante [*strah-vah-gahn'-teh*] extravagant
strega [*streh'-gah*] witch
stretto [*streht'-toh*] tight, narrow
strillare v. [*streel-lah'-reh*] shout, scream
striscia [*stree'-shee-ah*] stripe
stringere v. irreg. [*streen'-jeh-reh*] tighten, grasp, bind fast
strofinare v. [*stroh-fee-nah'-reh*] rub
strumento [*stroo-mehn'-toh*] instrument
struttura [*stroot-too'-rah*] structure
studente m., **studentessa** f. [*stoo-dehn'-teh, stoo-dehn-tehs'-sah*] student
studiare v. [*stoo-dee-ah'-reh*] study
studio [*stoo'-dee-oh*] study
studioso [*stoo-dee-oh'-zoh*] scholar
stufa [*stoo'-fah*] stove
stupido [*stoo'-pee-doh*] stupid
stuzzicadenti [*stoots-tsee-kah-dehn'-tee*] toothpick
su [*soo*] on, above, over, up
   su e giù [*soo eh jee-oo'*] up and down
subire v. [*soo-bee'-reh*] undergo, suffer
subito [*soo'-bee-toh*] at once, right away

succedere v. [*sooch-cheh'-deh-reh*] happen, occur
  Che succede? [*keh sooch-cheh'-deh*] What is the matter?
successivo [*sooch-chehs-see'-voh*] successive
successo [*sooch-chehs'-soh*] success
successore [*sooch-chehs-soh'-reh*] successor
succo [*sook'-koh*] juice
  succo di frutta [*sook'-koh dee froot'-tah*] fruit juice
succursale f. [*sook-koor-sah'-leh*] branch [business]
sud m. [*sood*] south
sudamericano [*sood-ah-meh-ree-kah'-noh*] South American
sudare v. [*soo-dah'-reh*] perspire
suddetto [*sood-deht'-toh*] abovementioned
sudore m. [*soo-doh'-reh*] sweat
sudicio [*soo-dee'-chee-oh*] filth
sufficiente [*soof-fee-chee-ehn'-teh*] sufficient
suggerimento [*sooj-jeh-ree-mehn'-toh*] suggestion, advice
sugo [*soo'-goh*] gravy, sauce
suicidio [*soo-ee-chee'-dee-oh*] suicide
suo, sua, suoi m. pl. **sue** f. pl. [*soo'-oh, soo'-ah, soo-oh'-ee,*
  soo'-eh] yours [polite form], his, hers
suocera [*soo-oh'-cheh-rah*] mother-in-law
suocero [*soo-oh'-cheh-roh*] father-in-law
suolo [*soo-oh'-loh*] soil, ground
suonare v. [*soo-oh-nah'-reh*] sound, ring, play
  suonare il companello [*soo-oh-nah'-reh eel kahm-pah-*
    nehl'-loh] ring the bell
  suonare il pianoforte [*soo-oh-nah'-reh eel pee-ah-noh-*
    fohr'-teh] play the piano
  Non suona bene [*nohn soo-oh'-nah beh'-neh*] It doesn't
    sound good
suonata [*soo-oh-nah'-tah*] ringing
suono [*soo-oh'-noh*] sound
suora [*soo-oh'-rah*] nun
superbo [*soo-pehr'-boh*] superb
superficiale [*soo-pehr-fee-chee-ah'-leh*] superficial
superficie f. [*soo-pehr-fee'-chee-eh*] surface
superfluo [*soo-pehr'-floo-oh*] superfluous
superiore [*soo-peh-ree-oh'-reh*] superior, upper
superiorità f. indecl. [*soo-peh-ree-oh-ree-tah'*] superiority
superstizioso [*soo-pehr-stee-tsee-oh'-zoh*] superstitious

supplementare [*soop-pleh-mehn-tah'-reh*] extra
supporre *v. irreg.* [*soop-pohr'-reh*] suppose
supposizione *f.* [*soop-poh-zee-tsee-oh'-neh*] supposition, guess
supremo [*soo-preh'-moh*] supreme
sussurrare *v.* [*soos-soor-rah'-reh*] whisper
svanire *v.* [*zvah-nee'-reh*] vanish
svantaggio [*zvahn-tahj'-jee-oh*] disadvantage
svedese [*zveh-deh'-zeh*] Swedish
sveglia [*zveh'-lyah*] alarm clock
svegliare *v.* [*zveh-lyah'-reh*] awake
   svegliarsi [*zveh-lyahr'-see*] wake up
sveglio [*zveh'-lyoh*] alert
sveltezza [*zvehl-tehts'-tsah*] quickness
svelto [*zvehl'-toh*] quick
svenimento [*zveh-nee-mehn'-toh*] faint
svenire *v. irreg.* [*zveh-nee'-reh*] faint
svestire *v.* [*zvehs-tee'-reh*] undress
   svestirsi [*zvehs-teer'-see*] undress oneself
Svezia [*zveh'-tsee-ah*] Sweden
sviare *v.* [*zvee-ah'-reh*] mislead
sviluppare *v.* [*zvee-loop-pah'-reh*] develop
sviluppo [*zvee-loop'-poh*] development
Svizzera [*zveets'-tseh-rah*] Switzerland
svizzero [*zveets'-tseh-roh*] Swiss
svolgere *v.* [*zvohl'-jeh-reh*] develop, unroll
svolta [*zvohl'-tah*] turn, turning point

T

tabacco [*tah-bahk'-koh*] tobacco
   sale *m.* **e tabacchi** [*sah'-leh eh tah-bahk'-kee*] tobacco shop
tacco [*tahk'-koh*] heel [of shoe]
tacchino [*tahk-kee'-noh*] turkey
taccuino [*tahk-koo-ee'-noh*] notebook
tacere *v. irreg.* [*tah-cheh'-reh*] be silent
taglia [*tah'-lyah*] size [of clothes]
tagliare *v.* [*tah-lyah'-reh*] cut

tagliatelle [*tah-lyah-tehl'-leh*] noodles
taglio [*tah'-lyoh*] cut [of dress]
   taglio di capelli [*tah'-lyoh dee kah-pehl'-lee*] haircut
tale [*tah'-leh*] such
talento [*tah-lehn'-toh*] talent
talvolta [*tahl-vohl'-tah*] sometimes
tamburo [*tahm-boo'-roh*] drum
tanto [*tahn'-toh*] so, so much, so long
   tanto quanto [*tahn'-toh koo-ahn'-toh*] as much as
   di tanto in tanto [*dee tahn'-toh een tahn'-toh*] occasionally
   tanto . . . quanto [*tahn'-toh . . . koo-ahn'-toh*] as . . . as
tappeto [*tahp-peh'-toh*] carpet
tappezzeria [*tahp-pehts-tseh-ree'-ah*] tapestry
tappo [*tahp'-poh*] cork
tardi [*tahr'-dee*] late
   più tardi [*pee-oo' tahr'-dee*] later
   Noi siamo tardi [*noh'-ee see-ah'-moh tahr'-dee*] We are late
tariffa [*tah-reef'-fah*] rate, tariff
tartaruga [*tahr-tah-roo'-gah*] turtle
tasca, tasche *pl.* [*tahs'-kah, tahs'-keh*] pocket
tassa [*tahs'-sah*] tax
   esente da tassa [*eh-zehn'-teh dah tahs'-sah*] duty-free
tassare *v.* [*tahs-sah'-reh*] tax
tassì *m.* [*tahs-see'*] taxi
tastiera [*tahs-tee-eh'-rah*] keyboard
tasto [*tahs'-toh*] key [of piano]
tatto [*taht'-toh*] tact
taverna [*tah-vehr'-nah*] tavern, inn
tavola [*tah'-voh-lah*] table
   preparare *v.* **la tavola** [*preh-pah-rah'-reh lah tah'-voh-lah*] set the table
tazza [*tahts'-tsah*] cup
   tazza di tè [*tahts'-tsah dee teh'*] teacup
tè *m.* [*teh'*] tea
teatro [*teh-ah'-troh*] theater
tecnico [*tehk'-nee-koh*] technical
tedesco [*teh-dehs'-koh*] German
teiera [*teh-ee-eh'-rah*] teapot
telefonare *v.* [*teh-leh-foh-nah'-reh*] telephone
   chiamata telefonica [*kee-ah-mah'-tah teh-leh-foh'-nee-kah*]

telephone call

elenco telefonico [*eh-lehn'-koh teh-leh-foh'-nee-koh*] telephone book

telefonista [*teh-leh-foh-nees'-tah*] telephone operator

telefono [*teh-leh'-foh-noh*] telephone

   per telefono [*pehr teh-leh'-foh-noh*] by phone

telegrafare v. [*teh-leh-grah-fah'-reh*] cable

telegramma m. [*teh-leh-grahm'-mah*] telegram

telescopo [*teh-lehs'-koh-poh*] telescope

televisione f. [*teh-leh-vee-zee-oh'-neh*] television

televisore m. [*teh-leh-vee-zoh'-reh*] television set

tema m. [*teh'-mah*] theme, subject

temere v. [*teh-meh'-reh*] fear

temperatura [*tehm-peh-rah-too'-rah*] temperature

temperino [*tehm-peh-ree'-noh*] penknife

tempesta [*tehm-pehs'-tah*] storm

tempio [*tehm'-pee-oh*] temple

tempo [*tehm'-poh*] time [extent], weather

   a tempo [*ah tehm'-poh*] on time

   allo stesso tempo [*ahl'-loh stehs'-soh tehm'-poh*] at the same time

   Come e il tempo? [*koh'-meh eh' eel tehm'-poh*] How is the weather?

   poco tempo fa [*poh'-koh tehm'-poh fah*] a while ago

temporale m. [*tehm-poh-rah'-leh*] thunderstorm

temporaneo [*tehm-poh-rah'-neh-oh*] temporary

tenda [*tehn'-dah*] curtain

tendenza [*tehn-dehn'-tsah*] tendency

tenere v. irreg. [*teh-neh'-reh*] keep

tenero [*teh'-neh-roh*] tender, soft

tenore m. [*teh-noh'-reh*] tenor

tensione f. [*tehn-see-oh'-neh*] stress, tension

tentare v. [*tehn-tah'-reh*] try

tentativo [*tehn-tah-tee'-voh*] attempt, try

tentazione f. [*tehn-tah-tsee-oh'-neh*] temptation

teoria [*teh-oh-ree'-ah*] theory

terminare v. [*tehr-mee-nah'-reh*] finish, end

termine m. [*tehr'-mee-neh*] term, limit, end

termometro [*tehr-moh'-meh-troh*] thermometer

termosifone m. [*tehr-moh-see-foh'-neh*] radiator [heating]

terra [*tehr'-rah*] ground, land
  a terra [*ah tehr'-rah*] ashore
terrazza [*tehr-rahts'-tsah*] terrace
terreno di gioco [*tehr-reh'-noh dee jee-oh'-koh*] playground
terremoto [*tehr-reh-moh'-toh*] earthquake
terribile [*tehr-ree'-bee-leh*] terrible
terribilmente [*tehr-ree-beel-mehn'-teh*] terribly
territorio [*tehr-ree-toh'-ree-oh*] territory
terrore [*tehr-roh'-reh*] terror
terzo [*tehr'-tsoh*] third
tesoreria [*teh-zoh-reh-ree'-ah*] treasury
tesoriere m. [*teh-zoh-ree-eh'-reh*] treasurer
tesoro [*teh-zoh'-roh*] treasure
  buono del tesoro [*boo-oh'-noh dehl teh-zoh'-roh*] bond
tessere v. [*tehs'-seh-reh*] weave
tessile [*tehs'-see-leh*] textile
tessitore m., **tessitrice** f. [*tehs-see-toh'-reh, tehs-see-tree'-cheh*] weaver
tessuto [*tehs-soo'-toh*] fabric, cloth, tissue
testa [*tehs'-tah*] head
  a testa [*ah tehs'-tah*] apiece
teste, testimone m., f. [*tehs'-teh, tehs-tee-moh'-neh*] witness
  testimone oculare m. [*tehs-tee-moh'-neh oh-koo-lah'-reh*] eye witness
testimoniare v. [*tehs-tee-moh-nee-ah'-reh*] testify
testo [*tehs'-toh*] text
tetto [*teht'-toh*] roof
Tevere m. [*teh'-veh-reh*] Tiber
ti [*tee*] you, to you, yourself
tifoso [*tee-foh'-zoh*] fan [sports]
tigre f. [*tee'-greh*] tiger
timido [*tee'-mee-doh*] timid
timbrare v. [*teem-brah'-reh*] stamp
tingere v. [*teen'-jeh-reh*] dye
tintura [*teen-too'-rah*] dye
tipico [*tee'-pee-koh*] typical
tipo [*tee'-poh*] type
tipografo [*tee-poh'-grah-foh*] printer
tirannia [*tee-rahn-nee'-ah*] tyranny
tiranno [*tee-rahn'-noh*] tyrant

tirare *v.* [*tee-rah'-reh*] pull
  tirar calci [*tee-rahr' kahl'-chee*] kick
titolo [*tee'-toh-loh*] title
toccare *v.* [*tohk-kah'-reh*] touch
tocco [*tohk'-koh*] touch
togliere *v. irreg.* [*toh'-lyeh-reh*] take away, remove
toletta [*toh-leht'-tah*] toilet, dressing table
tollerare *v.* [*tohl-leh-rah'-reh*] tolerate
tomba [*tohm'-bah*] tomb, grave
tonnellata [*tohn-nehl-lah'-tah*] ton
tonno [*tohn'-noh*] tuna
tono [*toh'-noh*] tone
tonsille *f. pl.* [*tohn-seel'-leh*] tonsils
topo [*toh'-poh*] rat
torace [*toh-rah'-cheh*] chest
torbido [*tohr'-bee-doh*] turbid, muddy
torcere *v.* [*tohr'-cheh-reh*] twist
Torino [*toh-ree'-noh*] Turin
tormento [*tohr-mehn'-toh*] anguish
tornare *v.* [*tohr-nah'-reh*] return, come back
toro [*toh'-roh*] bull
torpedone *m.* [*tohr-peh-doh'-neh*] bus, motor coach
torre *f.* [*tohr'-reh*] tower
torta [*tohr'-tah*] pie, cake
torto [*tohr'-toh*] wrong
  avere *v.* **torto** [*ah-veh'-reh tohr'-toh*] be wrong
tortura [*tohr-too'-rah*] torture
torturare *v.* [*tohr-too-rah'-reh*] torture
tosse *f.* [*tohs'-seh*] cough
tossire *v.* [*tohs-see'-reh*] cough
tostapane *m.* [*tohs-tah-pah'-neh*] toaster
totale [*toh-tah'-leh*] total
tovaglia [*toh-vah'-lyah*] tablecloth
tovagliolo [*toh-vah-lyoh'-loh*] napkin
tra [*trah*] among, between
traccia [*trahch'-chee-ah*] trace
tradimento [*trah-dee-mehn'-toh*] betrayal
tradire *v.* [*trah-dee'-reh*] betray
traditore *m.*, **traditrice** *f.* [*trah-dee-toh'-reh, trah-dee-tree'-cheh*] traitor

tradizionale [*trah-dee-tsee-oh-nah'-leh*] traditional
tradizione *f.* [*trah-dee-tsee-oh'-neh*] tradition
tradurre *v. irreg.* [*trah-door'-reh*] translate
traduttore *m.*, **traduttrice** *f.* [*trah-doot-toh'-reh, trah-doot-tree'-cheh*] translator
traduzione *f.* [*trah-doo-tsee-oh'-neh*] translation
traffico [*trahf'-fee-koh*] traffic
tragedia [*trah-jeh'-dee-ah*] tragedy
tragico [*trah'-jee-koh*] tragic
tram *m.* [*trahm*] streetcar
tramite [*trah'-mee-teh*] through
tramonto [*trah-mohn'-toh*] sunset
tranne [*trahn'-neh*] except, save
tranquillo [*trahn-koo-eel'-loh*] quiet
transito [*trahn'-zee-toh*] transit
transitorio [*trahn-zee-toh'-ree-oh*] transient
trappola [*trahp'-poh-lah*] trap
trarre *v. irreg.* [*trahr'-reh*] draw, get
trascinare *v.* [*trah-shee-nah'-reh*] drag
trascurare *v.* [*trahs-koo-rah'-reh*] neglect
trasferimento [*trahs-feh-ree-mehn'-toh*] transfer
trasferire *v.* [*trahs-feh-ree'-reh*] transfer
trasformare *v.* [*trahs-fohr-mah'-reh*] transform
trasgredire *v.* [*trahz-greh-dee'-reh*] trespass
trasmettere *v.* [*trahz-meht'-teh-reh*] broadcast, transmit
trasmissione *f.* [*trahz-mees-see-oh'-neh*] broadcast, transmission
trasparente [*trahs-pah-rehn'-teh*] transparent
trasportare *v.* [*trahs-pohr-tah'-reh*] transport
trasporto [*trahs-pohr'-toh*] transportation
trattamento [*traht-tah-mehn'-toh*] treatment
trattare [*traht-tah'-reh*] treat, deal
trattative [*traht-tah-tee'-veh*] negotiations
trattato [*traht-tah'-toh*] treaty
trattenimento [*traht-teh-nee-mehn'-toh*] entertainment, party
trattenere *v. irreg.* [*traht-teh-neh'-reh*] withhold
trattoria [*traht-toh-ree'-ah*] restaurant
traversata [*trah-vehr-sah'-tah*] crossing
travestimento [*trah-vehs-tee-mehn'-toh*] disguise
tre [*treh*] three

trecento [*treh-chehn'-toh*] three hundred

tredici [*treh'-dee-chee*] thirteen

tregua [*treh'-goo-ah*] truce

tremare v. [*treh-mah'-reh*] tremble, shake

tremendo [*treh-mehn'-doh*] tremendous

tremulo [*treh'-moo-loh*] quivering

treno [*treh'-noh*] train

trenta [*trehn'-tah*] thirty

triangolo [*tree-ahn'-goh-loh*] triangle

tribunale m. [*tree-boo-nah'-leh*] tribunal, court

tributo [*tree-boo'-toh*] tribute

trimestre m. [*tree-mehs'-treh*] quarter [three months]

trionfante [*tree-ohn-fahn'-teh*] triumphant

trionfo [*tree-ohn'-foh*] triumph

trippa [*treep'-pah*] tripe

triste [*trees'-teh*] sad

tristezza [*trees-tehts'-tsah*] sadness

triviale [*tree-vee-ah'-leh*] trivial

tromba [*trohm'-bah*] horn [musical instrument]

troncare v. [*trohn-kah'-reh*] cut off, break off

trono [*troh'-noh*] throne

tropicale [*troh-pee-kah'-leh*] tropical

troppi [*trohp'-pee*] too many

troppo [*trohp'-poh*] too much, too many

trovare v. [*troh-vah'-reh*] find

trovato [*troh-vah'-toh*] found

truccarsi v. [*trook-kahr'-see*] make up [oneself]

trucco [*trook'-koh*] trick

truffare v. [*troof-fah'-reh*] cheat

truppa [*troop'-pah*] troop

tu pron., 2d pers. sing., **voi** pl. [*too, voh'-ee*] you [informal address]

tubercolosi [*too-behr-koh-loh'-zee*] tuberculosis

tubo [*too'-boh*] tube

tuffarsi v. [*toof-fahr'-see*] dive

tumulto [*too-mool'-toh*] uproar

tuo m., **tua** f.; **tuoi** m. pl., **tue** f. pl. [*too'-oh, too'-ah, too-oh'-ee, too'-eh*] your

tuonare v. [*too-oh-nah'-reh*] thunder, roar

tuono [*too-oh'-noh*] thunder

turbare *v.* [*toor-bah'-reh*] upset
Turchia [*toor-kee'-ah*] Turkey
turco [*toor'-koh*] Turkish, Turk
turismo [*too-reez'-moh*] tourism
turista [*too-rees'-tah*] tourist
turno [*toor'-noh*] turn [order]
tuttavia [*toot-tah-vee'-ah*] nevertheless, yet, still
tutto [*toot'-toh*] all, whole
   Ecco tutto [*ehk'-koh toot'-toh*] That's all
   dopo tutto [*doh'-poh toot'-toh*] after all

U

ubbidiente [*oob-bee-dee-ehn'-teh*] obedient
ubbidire *v.* [*oob-bee-dee'-reh*] obey
ubriaco [*oo-bree-ah'-koh*] drunk
uccello [*ooch-chehl'-loh*] bird
uccidere *v. irreg.* [*ooch-chee'-deh-reh*] kill, slay
ucciso [*ooch-chee'-zoh*] killed
udienza [*oo-dee-ehn'-tsah*] audience
udire *v. irreg.* [*oo-dee'-reh*] hear
udito [*oo-dee'-toh*] hearing
ufficiale *m. & adj.* [*oof-fee-chee-ah'-leh*] officer, official
ufficio [*oof-fee'-chee-oh*] office
   ufficio postale [*oof-fee'-chee-oh pohs-tah'-leh*] post office
uguale [*oo-goo-ah'-leh*] equal
ulteriore [*ool-teh-ree-oh'-reh*] further
ultimo [*ool'-tee-moh*] last
umanità *f. indecl.* [*oo-mah-nee-tah'*] humanity
umano [*oo-mah'-noh*] human
umidità *f. indecl.* [*oo-mee-dee-tah'*] humidity, moisture
umido [*oo'-mee-doh*] humid
umile [*oo'-mee-leh*] humble
umiltà *f. indecl.* [*oo-meel-tah'*] humility
umore *m.* [*oo-moh'-reh*] mood, humor
   essere *v.* **di buonumore** [*ehs'-seh-reh dee boo-ohn-oo-moh'-reh*] be in a good mood

essere *v.* **di malumore** [*ehs'-seh-reh dee mahl-oo-moh'-reh*] be in a bad mood

umoristico [*oo-moh-rees'-tee-koh*] humorous

un, uno, una, un' [*oon, oo'-noh, oo'-nah, oon*] a, an, one

unanime [*oo-nah'-nee-meh*] unanimous

undici [*oon'-dee-chee*] eleven

ungherese [*oon-geh-reh'-zeh*] Hungarian

Ungheria [*oon-geh-ree'-ah*] Hungary

unghia [*oon'-gee-ah*] (finger)nail

unico [*oo'-nee-koh*] only, unique

uniforme *f. & adj.* [*oo-nee-fohr'-meh*] uniform

unione *f.* [*oo-nee-oh'-neh*] union

unire *v.* [*oo-nee'-reh*] join, unite

unirsi *v.* [*oo-neer'-see*] unite together

unità *f. indecl.* [*oo-nee-tah'*] unity

unitamente [*oo-nee-tah-mehn'-teh*] jointly

unito [*oo-nee'-toh*] united

universale [*oo-nee-vehr-sah'-leh*] universal

università *f. indecl.* [*oo-nee-vehr-see-tah'*] university, college

universo [*oo-nee-vehr'-soh*] universe

uomo, uomini *pl.* [*oo-oh'-moh, oo-oh'-mee-nee*] man

uovo, le uova *pl.* [*oo-oh'-voh, leh oo-oh'-vah*] egg

uova a la coque [*oo-oh'-vah ah lah kohk*] soft-boiled eggs

uova fritte [*oo-oh'-vah freet'-teh*] fried eggs

uova sode [*oo-oh'-vah soh'-deh*] hard-boiled eggs

uova strapazzate [*oo-oh'-vah strah-pahts-tsah'-teh*] scrambled eggs

(L')Urbe [*(l)oor'-beh*] Rome, the Eternal City

uragano [*oo-rah-gah'-noh*] hurricane

urbano [*oor-bah'-noh*] urban

urgente [*oor-jehn'-teh*] urgent

urgenza [*oor-jehn'-tsah*] urgency

urtare *v.* [*oor-tah'-reh*] collide

urto [*oor'-toh*] shock

usanza [*oo-zahn'-tsah*] custom

usare *v.* [*oo-zah'-reh*] use

usato [*oo-zah'-toh*] used

usciere *m.* [*oo-shee-eh'-reh*] usher

uscire *v. irreg.* [*oo-shee'-reh*] go out, come out

uscita [*oo-shee'-tah*] exit

uso [*oo'-zoh*] use
   fuori uso [*foo-oh'-ree oo'-zoh*] out of order
usuale [*oo-zoo-ah'-leh*] usual
utensile *m.* [*oo-tehn-see'-leh*] tool
utile [*oo'-tee-leh*] useful
utilizzare *v.* [*oo-tee-leedz-dzah'-reh*] utilize
uva [*oo'-vah*] grape
   uva secca [*oo'-vah sehk'-kah*] raisin

V

vacante [*vah-kahn'-teh*] vacant
   posto vacante [*pohs'-toh vah-kahn'-teh*] vacancy
vacca [*vahk'-kah*] cow
vacanza [*vah-kahn'-tsah*] vacation
vaccinazione *f.* [*vahch-chee-nah-tsee-oh'-neh*] vaccination
vagabondo [*vah-gah-bohn'-doh*] vagabond
vagamente [*vah-gah-mehn'-teh*] vaguely
vago [*vah'-goh*] vague
vagone *m.* [*vah-goh'-neh*] wagon
   vagone ferroviario [*vah-goh'-neh fehr-roh-vee-ah'-ree-oh*]
     railroad car
   vagone letto [*vah-goh'-neh leht'-toh*] sleeping car
valere *v. irreg.* [*vah-leh'-reh*] be worth
   Non ne vale la pena [*nohn neh vah'-leh lah peh'-nah*]
     It is not worthwhile
   vale a dire [*vah'-leh ah dee'-reh*] that is to say
valido [*vah'-lee-doh*] valid
valigia [*vah-lee'-jee-ah*] suitcase
valle *f.* [*vahl'-leh*] valley
valore *m.* [*vah-loh'-reh*] value
valorosamente [*vah-loh-roh-zah-mehn'-teh*] bravely
valuta [*vah-loo'-tah*] value, currency
   valuta estera [*vah-loo'-tah ehs'-teh-rah*] foreign currency
valutare *v.* [*vah-loo-tah'-reh*] value, estimate
valutazione *f.* [*vah-loo-tah-tsee-oh'-neh*] estimate
valvola [*vahl'-voh-lah*] valve

vaniglia [*vah-nee'-lyah*] vanilla
vanità *f. indecl.* [*vah-nee-tah'*] vanity
vanitoso [*vah-nee-toh'-zoh*] vain
vano [*vah'-noh*] vain
  in vano [*een vah'-noh*] vainly, in vain
vantaggio [*vahn-tahj'-jee-oh*] advantage
vantarsi *v.* [*vahn-tahr'-see*] boast, brag
vapore *m.* [*vah-poh'-reh*] steam
vari [*vah'-ree*] various
variabile [*vah-ree-ah'-bee-leh*] variable, changeable
variare *v.* [*vah-ree-ah'-reh*] vary
varicella [*vah-ree-chel'-lah*] smallpox
varietà *f. indecl.* [*vah-ree-eh-tah'*] variety
vasca [*vahs'-kah*] tub
  vasca da bagno [*vahs'-kah dah bah'-nyoh*] bathtub
vasellame *m.* [*vah-zehl-lah'-meh*] pottery
vaso [*vah'-zoh*] vase
vassoio [*vahs-soh'-ee-oh*] tray
vasto [*vahs'-toh*] vast
Vaticano [*vah-tee-kah'-noh*] Vatican
vecchiaia [*vehk-kee-ah'-ee-ah*] old age
vecchio [*vehk'-kee-oh*] old
vedere *v. irreg.* [*veh-deh'-reh*] see
  Mi faccia vedere [*mee fahch'-chee-ah veh-deh'-reh*]
    Let me see
  Vede la luna? [*veh'-deh lah loo'-nah*] Do you see the moon?
  Sì, la vedo [*see, lah veh'-doh*] Yes, I see it
  Vede il libro? [*veh'-deh eel lee'-broh*] Do you see the book?
  Sì, lo vedo [*see, loh veh'-doh*] Yes, I see it
  Vediamo un po [*veh-dee-ah'-moh oon poh*] Let's see
vedova, vedovo [*veh'-doh-vah, veh'-doh-voh*] widow, widower
veduta [*veh-doo'-tah*] view
veicolo [*veh-ee'-koh-loh*] vehicle
vela [*veh'-lah*] sail
veleno [*veh-leh'-noh*] poison
velenoso [*veh-leh-noh'-zoh*] poisonous
velluto [*vehl-loo'-toh*] velvet
velo [*veh'-loh*] veil
veloce [*veh-loh'-cheh*] fast
velocità *f. indecl.* [*veh-loh-chee-tah'*] speed

a tutta velocità [*ah toot'-tah veh-loh-chee-tah'*] at full speed
velocità massima [*veh-loh-chee-tah' mahs'-see-mah*] speed
   limit
vena [*veh'-nah*] vein
vendere v. [*vehn'-deh-reh*] sell
vendetta [*vehn-deht'-tah*] vengeance
vendicare v. [*vehn-dee-kah'-reh*] avenge
vendita [*vehn'-dee-tah*] sale
  in vendita [*een vehn'-dee-tah*] for sale
  vendita all'ingrosso [*vehn'-dee-tah ahl-leen-grohs'-soh*]
   wholesale
  vendita al minuto [*vehn'-dee-tah ahl mee-noo'-toh*] retail
  vendita all'asta [*vehn'-dee-tah ahl-lahs'-tah*] auction sale
venditore m. [*vehn-dee-toh'-reh*] seller
  venditore ambulante [*vehn-dee-toh'-reh ahm-boo-lahn'-teh*]
   peddler
venduto [*vehn-doo'-toh*] sold
venerdì m. [*veh-nehr-dee'*] Friday
Venezia [*veh-neh'-tsee-ah*] Venice
venire v. irreg. [*veh-nee'-reh*] come
ventaglio [*vehn-tah'-lyoh*] fan
venti [*vehn'-tee*] twenty
ventilatore m. [*vehn-tee-lah-toh'-reh*] ventilator
vento [*vehn'-toh*] wind
verbo [*vehr'-boh*] verb
verde [*vehr'-deh*] green
verdetto [*vehr-deht'-toh*] verdict
verdura [*vehr-doo'-rah*] vegetables
vergine f. & adj. [*vehr'-jee-neh*] virgin
vergogna [*vehr-goh'-nyah*] shame
vergognoso [*vehr-goh-nyoh'-zoh*] shameful
verificare v. [*veh-ree-fee-kah'-reh*] verify
verità f. indecl. [*veh-ree-tah'*] truth
  in verità [*een veh-ree-tah'*] indeed
verme m. [*vehr'-meh*] worm
vernice f. [*vehr-nee'-cheh*] paint [house]
vero [*veh'-roh*] true
  È vero [*eh' veh'-roh*] It is true
  Non è vero [*nohn eh' veh'-roh*] It isn't true
versare v. [*vehr-sah'-reh*] pour, spill

versatile [*vehr-sah'-tee-leh*] versatile
versione *f.* [*vehr-see-oh'-neh*] version
verso *n.* [*vehr'-soh*] verse
verso *prep.* [*vehr'-soh*] toward, about
verticale [*vehr-tee-kah'-leh*] veritcal
vertigine *f.* [*vehr-tee'-jee-nee*] dizziness
  avere *v.* **le vertigini** [*ah-veh'-reh leh vehr-tee'-jee-nee*]
    feel dizzy
vescovo [*vehs'-koh-voh*] bishop
vestibolo [*vehs-tee'-boh-loh*] lobby
vestire *v.* [*vehs-tee'-reh*] dress
  vestirsi [*vehs-teer'-see*] get dressed
Vesuvio [*veh-zoo'-vee-oh*] Vesuvius
veterano [*veh-teh-rah'-noh*] veteran
veterinario [*veh-teh-ree-nah'-ree-oh*] veterinary
vetrina [*veh-tree'-nah*] shopwindow
vetro [*veh'-troh*] glass [material]
vi *adv.* [*vee*] there
vi *pron.* [*vee*] you, to you
via *n.* [*vee'-ah*] street, road, way
via *adv.* [*vee'-ah*] away, off
  Via! [*vee'-ah*] Come on!
via aerea [*vee'-ah ah-eh'-reh-ah*] air mail
viaggiare *v.* [*vee-ahj-jee-ah'-reh*] travel
viaggiatore *m.*, **viaggiatrice** *f.* [*vee-ahj-jee-ah-toh'-reh, vee-ahj-jee-ah-tree'-cheh*] traveller
viaggio [*vee-ahj'-jee-oh*] travel, trip
  agenzia di viaggi [*ah-jehn-tsee'-ah dee vee-ahj'-jee*]
    travel agency
viale *m.* [*vee-ah'-leh*] avenue
vibrare *v.* [*vee-brah'-reh*] vibrate
viceversa [*vee-cheh-vehr'-sah*] vice versa
vicinanza [*vee-chee-nahn'-tsah*] vicinity
vicino [*vee-chee'-noh*] near, neighbor
  vicino a [*vee-chee'-noh ah*] next to
vicolo [*vee'-koh-loh*] alley
vietare *v.* [*vee-eh-tah'-reh*] forbid
  vietato fumare [*vee-eh-tah'-toh foo-mah'-reh*] no smoking
  vietato l'ingresso [*vee-eh-tah'-toh leen-grehs'-soh*]
    no admittance

vigile *m. & adj.* [*vee'-jee-leh*] city policeman, alert

vigilia [*vee-jee'-lee-ah*] eve

  vigilia di Natale [*vee-jee'-lee-ah dee nah-tah'-leh*]
    Christmas Eve

vigliacco [*vee-lyahk'-koh*] coward

vigneto [*vee-nyeh'-toh*] vineyard

vigoroso [*vee-goh-roh'-zoh*] vigorous

villa [*veel'-lah*] villa

villaggio [*veel-lahj'-jee-oh*] village

villeggiatura [*veel-lehj-jee-ah-too'-rah*] vacation [in the
    country]

vincere *v. irreg.* [*veen'-cheh-reh*] win

vincita [*veen'-chee-tah*] victory, winning

vincitore *m.*, **vincitrice** *f.* [*veen-chee-toh'-reh, veen-chee-
    tree'-cheh*] winner

vincolo [*veen'-koh-loh*] tie, bond

vino [*vee'-noh*] wine

  vino bianco [*vee'-noh bee-ahn'-koh*] white wine

  vino rosso [*vee'-noh rohs'-soh*] red wine

vinto [*veen'-toh*] conquered

viola [*vee-oh'-lah*] violet [color]

violare *v.* [*vee-oh-lah'-reh*] violate

violazione *f.* [*vee-oh-lah-tsee-oh'-neh*] violation

violetta [*vee-oh-leht'-tah*] violet [flower]

violenza [*vee-oh-lehn'-tsah*] violence

violino [*vee-oh-lee'-noh*] violin

virgola [*veer'-goh-lah*] comma

virtù *f. indecl.* [*veer-too'*] virtue

virtuoso [*veer-too-oh'-zoh*] virtuous

visibile [*vee-zee'-bee-leh*] visible

visionario [*vee-zee-oh-nah'-ree-oh*] visionary

visione *f.* [*vee-zee-oh'-neh*] vision

visita [*vee'-zee-tah*] visit

  biglietto da visita [*bee-lyeht'-toh dah vee'-zee-tah*]
    visiting card

  fare *v.* **una visita** [*fah'-reh oo'-nah vee'-zee-tah*]
    pay a visit to

visitare *v.* [*vee-zee-tah'-reh*] visit

visitatore *m.*, **visitatrice** *f.* [*vee-zee-tah-toh'-reh, vee-zee-tah-
    tree'-cheh*] visitor

viso [*vee'-zoh*] face

visone *m.* [*vee-zoh'-neh*] mink

vista [*vees'-tah*] eyesight, view

   punto di vista [*poon'-toh dee vees'-tah*] point of view

visto [*vees'-toh*] visa

vita [*vee'-tah*] life, waist

   assicurazione *f.* **sulla vita** [*ahs-see-koo-rah-tsee-oh'-neh sool'-lah vee'-tah*] life insurance

vitale [*vee-tah'-leh*] vital

vitamina [*vee-tah-mee'-nah*] vitamin

vite *f.* [*vee'-teh*] screw, vineyard

vitello [*vee-tehl'-loh*] calf

   carne *f.* **di vitello** [*kahr'-neh dee vee-tehl'-loh*] veal

vittima [*veet'-tee-mah*] victim

vitto [*veet'-toh*] food, board

vittoria [*veet-toh'-ree-ah*] victory

vivace [*vee-vah'-cheh*] lively

vivere *v. irreg.* [*vee'-veh-reh*] live

viveri *m. pl.* [*vee'-veh-ree*] food supplies

vivido [*vee'-vee-doh*] vivid

vivo [*vee'-voh*] alive

viziare *v.* [*vee-tsee-ah'-reh*] spoil

vizio [*vee'-tsee-oh*] vice

vizioso [*vee-tsee-oh'-zoh*] vicious

vocabolario [*voh-kah-boh-lah'-ree-oh*] vocabulary

vocale *f.* [*voh-kah'-leh*] vowel, vocal

vocazione *f.* [*voh-kah-tsee-oh'-neh*] vocation

voce *f.* [*voh'-cheh*] voice

   ad alta voce [*ahd ahl'-tah voh'-cheh*] loud

voglia [*voh'-lyah*] desire, wish

voi [*voh'-ee*] you [informal]

volante *m.* [*voh-lahn'-teh*] steering wheel

volare *v.* [*voh-lah'-reh*] fly

volentieri [*voh-lehn-tee-eh'-ree*] willingly

volere *v. irreg.* [*voh-leh'-reh*] want

volgare [*vohl-gah'-reh*] vulgar

volgere *v. irreg.* [*vohl'-jeh-reh*] turn, revolve

volo [*voh'-loh*] flight

volontà *f. indecl.* [*voh-lohn-tah'*] will

   forza di volontà [*fohr'-tsah dee voh-lohn-tah'*] willpower

volontario [*voh-lohn-tah'-ree-oh*] voluntary, volunteer
volta [*vohl'-tah*] time [occasion], vault
  ancora una volta [*ahn-koh'-rah oo'-nah vohl'-tah*]
    once again
  ogni volta [*oh'-nyee vohl'-tah*] each time
  una volta [*oo'-nah vohl'-tah*] once
  a volte [*ah vohl'-teh*] at times
voltare *v.* [*vohl-tah'-reh*] turn
volto [*vohl'-toh*] face
volume *m.* [*voh-loo'-meh*] volume
voluminoso [*voo-loo-mee-noh'-zoh*] bulky
vomitare *v.* [*voh-mee-tah'-reh*] vomit
vostro, vostra [*vohs'-troh, vohs'-trah*] your
il vostro, la vostra [*eel vohs'-troh, lah vohs'-trah*] yours
votare *v.* [*voh-tah'-reh*] vote
voto [*voh'-toh*] vote, vow
vulcano [*vool-kah'-noh*] volcano
vulnerabile [*vool-neh-rah'-bee-leh*] vulnerable
vuoto [*voo-oh'-toh*] empty

Z

zaffiro [*dzahf-fee'-roh*] sapphire
zaino [*dzah'-ee-noh*] knapsack
zampa [*dzahm'-pah*] paw
zanzara [*dzahn-dzah'-rah*] mosquito
zebra [*dzeh'-brah*] zebra
zelante [*dzeh-lahn'-teh*] zealous
zelo [*dzeh'-loh*] zeal
zero [*dzeh'-roh*] zero
zia [*dzee'-ah*] aunt
zinco [*dzeen'-koh*] zinc
zingaro [*dzeen'-gah-roh*] gypsy
zio, zii *pl.* [*dzee'-oh, dzee'-ee*] uncle
Zitto! [*dzeet'-toh*] Be quiet! [to several persons]
zona [*dzoh'-nah*] zone
zoo [*zoh'-oh*] zoo

zoppo [*dzohp'-poh*] lame
zucca [*dzook'-kah*] pumpkin
zucchero [*dzook'-keh-roh*] sugar
zucchino [*dzook-kee'-noh*] squash
zuppa [*dzoop'-pah*] soup

Phrases for Use Abroad

Helpful Expressions

Good morning./Good evening.
Buon giorno./Buona sera.
Boo-ohn' jee-ohr'-noh./Boo-oh'-nah seh'-rah.

How do you do?/How are you?
Come sta?
Koh'-meh stah?

This is Mr./Mrs./Miss. . . .
Le presento il signor/la signora/la signorina. . . .
Leh preh-zehn'-toh eel see-nyohr'/lah see-nyoh'-rah/lah see-nyoh-ree'-nah. . . .

What is your name?
Lei, come si chiama?
Leh'-ee, koh'-meh see kee-ah'-mah?

My name is. . . .
Mi chiamo . . . .
Mee kee-ah'-moh . . . .

I am pleased to meet you.
Piacere di conoscerla.
Pee-ah-cheh'-reh dee koh-noh'-shehr-lah.

I don't understand.
Non capisco.
Nohn kah-pees'-koh.

Could you speak more slowly, please?
Può parlare più lentamente, per favore?
Poo-oh' pahr-lah'-reh pee-oo' lehn-tah-mehn'-teh, pehr fah-voh'-reh?

327

Could you repeat, please?
Può ripetere, per favore?
Poo-oh' ree-peh'-teh-reh, pehr fah-voh'-reh?

Goodbye./See you later.
Arrivederla.
Ahr-ree-veh-dehr'-lah.

Thank you.
Grazie.
Grah'-tsee-eh.

You're welcome.
Prego.
Preh'-goh.

Excuse me.
Mi scusi.
Mee skoo'-zee.

Do you speak English?
Scusi, lei parla inglese?
Skoo'-zee, leh'-ee pahr'-lah een-gleh'-zeh?

How do you say . . . in Italian?
Come si dice . . . in italiano?
Koh'-meh see dee'-cheh . . . een ee-tah-lee-ah'-noh?

What does . . . mean?
Cosa vuol dire . . . ?
Koh'-zah voo-ohl' dee'-reh . . . ?

Customs

May I see your passport/visa, please?
Mi fa vedere il suo passaporto/visto, per favore?
Mee fah veh-deh'-reh eel soo'-oh pahs'-sah-pohr-toh/vees'-toh, pehr fah-voh'-reh?

Do you have anything to declare?
Ha qualcosa da dichiarare?
Ah koo-ahl-koh'-zah dah dee-kee-ah-rah'-reh?

It is for my personal use.
È per mio uso personale.
Eh pehr mee'-oh oo'-zoh pehr-soh-nah'-leh.

How long are you staying?
Quanto tempo si ferma?
Koo-ahn'-toh tehm'-poh see fehr'-mah?

I will be here for ... days/weeks/months.
Ci starò per ... giorni/settimane/mesi.
Chee stah-roh' pehr ... jee-ohr'-nee/seht-tee-mah'-neh/meh'-zee.

Money

Where can I cash this traveler's check?
Dove posso cambiare questo assegno turistico?
Doh'-veh pohs'-soh kahm-bee-ah'-reh koo-ehs'-toh ahs-seh'-nyoh too-rees'-tee-koh?

Please give me some small change.
Per favore, mi dia della moneta spicciola.
Pehr fah-voh'-reh, mee dee'-ah dehl'-lah moh-neh'-tah speech'-chee-oh-lah.

What is the rate of exchange for dollars?
Quant'è il cambio del dollaro?
Koo-ahn-teh' eel kahm'-bee-oh dehl dohl'-lah-roh?

At the Hotel

I want a room with/without bath.
Vorrei una camera con/senza bagno.
Vohr-reh'-ee oo'-nah kah'-meh-rah kohn/sehn'-tsah bah'-nyoh.

How much is the room?
Quant'è la camera?
Koo-ahn-teh' lah kah'-meh-rah?

Are meals included?
Sono inclusi i pasti?
Soh'-noh een-kloo'-zee ee pahs'-tee?

I would like something cheaper.
Vorrei qualcosa meno caro.
Vohr-reh'-ee koo-ahl-koh'-zah meh'-noh kah'-roh.

Where is the manager?
Dove è il direttore?
Doh'-veh eh eel dee-reht-toh'-reh?

Laundry/Dry Cleaning

Where is a laundry/dry cleaner?
Dove c'è una lavanderia/tintoria?
Doh'-veh cheh oo'-nah lah-vahn-deh-ree'-ah/teen-toh-ree'-ah?

When will my clothes be ready?
Quando saranno pronti i miei vestiti?
Koo-ahn'-doh sah-rahn'-noh prohn'-tee ee mee-eh'-ee vehs-tee'-tee?

Please wash these clothes.
Vorrei far lavare questa biancheria.
Vohr-reh'-ee fahr lah-vah'-reh koo-ehs'-tah bee-ahn-keh-ree'-ah

I want these clothes dry cleaned.
Vorrei questi vestiti lavati a secco.
Vohr-reh'-ee koo-ehs'-tee vehs-tee'-tee lah-vah'-tee ah sehk'-koh.

Please press these trousers.
Per favore, vorrei far stirare questi pantaloni.
Pehr fah-voh'-reh, vohr-reh'-ee fahr stee-rah'-reh koo-ehs'-tee pahn-tah-loh'-nee.

Barber/Hairdresser

I would like a haircut/trim.
Vorrei farmi tagliare/aggiustare i capelli.
Vohr-reh'-ee fahr'-mee tah-lyah'-reh/aj-jee-oos-tah'-reh ee kah-pehl'-lee.

Make it shorter, please.
Li tagli un pò più corti, per favore.
Lee tah'-lyee oon poh pee-oo' kohr'-tee, pehr fah-voh'-reh.

I would like a shampoo and set.
Vorrei uno shampoo e la messa in piega.
Vohr-reh'-ee oo'-noh shahm'-poo eh lah mehs'-sah een pee-eh'-gah.

Getting Around

When is the next flight to . . . ?
Quand è il prossimo volo per . . . ?
Koo-ahn-deh' eel prohs'-see-moh voh'-loh pehr . . . ?

I want a ticket to . . . .
Vorrei un biglietto per . . . .
Vohr-reh'-ee oon bee-lyeht'-toh pehr . . . .

Is lunch/dinner served on this flight?
Servono il pranzo/la cena sull'aereo?
Sehr'-voh-noh eel prahn'-tsoh/lah cheh'-nah sool-lah-eh'-reh-oh?

I want to confirm my flight.
Vorrei riconfermare il mio volo.
Vohr-reh'-ee ree-kohn-fehr-mah'-reh eel mee'-oh voh'-loh.

Take my bags to my cabin, please.
Porti le valigie nella mia cabina, per favore.
Pohr'-tee leh vah-lee'-jee-eh nehl'-lah mee'-ah kah-bee'-nah, pehr fah-voh'-reh.

At what time does the boat dock?
A che ora arriva la nave al molo?
Ah keh oh'-rah ahr-ree'-vah lah nah'-veh ahl moh'-loh?

Where is the ticket window?
Dove è la biglietteria?
Doh'-veh eh lah bee-lyeht-teh-ree'-ah?

May I have a timetable?
Posso avere un orario?
Pohs'-soh ah-veh'-reh oon oh-rah'-ree-oh?

How much is a one-way/round-trip first-class/second-class ticket to . . . ?
Quanto costa un biglietto di andata/andata e ritorno di prima classe/seconda classe per . . . ?
Koo-ahn'-toh kohs'-tah oon bee-lyeht'-toh dee ahn-dah'-tah/ ahn-dah'-tah eh ree-tohr'-noh dee pree'-mah klahs'-seh/seh-kohn'-dah klahs'-seh pehr . . . ?

From which track does the train for . . . leave?
Su che binario parte il treno per . . . ?
Soo keh bee-nah'-ree-oh pahr'-teh eel treh'-noh pehr . . . ?

At what time does this train leave?
A che ora parte questo treno?
Ah keh oh'-rah pahr'-teh koo-ehs'-toh treh'-noh?

Is this seat taken?
È occupato questo posto?
Eh ohk-koo-pah'-toh koo-ehs'-toh pohs'-toh?

When is the dining car open?
Quando è aperto il vagone ristorante?
Koo-ahn'-doh eh ah-pehr'-toh eel vah-goh'-neh rees-toh-rahn'-teh?

Where is the bus station?
Dove è la stazione degli autobus?
Doh'-veh eh lah stah-tsee-oh'-neh deh'-lyee ah'-oo-toh-boos?

When is the next bus to . . . ?
Quando parte il prossimo autobus per . . . ?
Koo-ahn'-doh pahr'-teh eel prohs'-see-moh ah-oo'-toh-boos pehr . . . ?

Where do I get off to go to . . . ?
Dove devo scendere per andare a . . . ?
Doh'-veh deh'-voh shehn'-deh-reh pehr ahn-dah'-reh ah . . . ?

Take me to . . . .
Mi porti a . . . .
Mee pohr'-tee ah . . .

Where can I rent a car?
Dove posso prendere in affito un'automobile?
Doh'-veh pohs'-soh prehn'-deh-reh een ahf-feet'-toh oon-ah-oo-toh-moh'-bee-leh?

Do you charge by the day or by the mile?
Come si paga, per giorni o per chilometraggio?
Koh'-meh see pah'-gah, pehr jee-ohr'-nee oh pehr kee-loh-meh-trahj'-jee-oh?

Where is the nearest gas station?
Dove è la stazione di servizio più vicina?
Doh'-veh eh lah stah-tsee-oh'-neh dee sehr-vee'-tsee-oh pee-oo' vee-chee'-nah?

Fill it up with regular/premium.
Mi faccia il pieno con benzina normale/super.
Mee fahch'-chee-ah eel pee-eh'-noh kohn behn-dzee'-nah nohr-mah'-leh/soo'-pehr.

Please check the oil/the tires.
Verifichi l'olio/le gomme, per favore.
Veh-ree'-fee-kee loh'-lee-oh/leh gohm'-meh, pehr fah-voh'-reh.

Shopping

Where is there a bookstore?
Dove c'è una libreria?
Doh'-veh cheh oo'-nah lee-breh-ree'-ah?

How much does this cost?
Quanto costa questo?
Koo-ahn'-toh kohs'-tah koo-ehs'-toh?

Have you anything better/cheaper?
Ha qualcosa di meglio/meno costoso?
Ah koo-ahl-koh'-zah dee meh'-lyoh/meh'-noh kohs-toh'-soh?

This is too large/small.
Questo è troppo grande/piccolo.
Koo-ehs'-toh eh trohp'-poh grahn'-deh/peek'-koh-loh.

Do you accept checks/traveler's checks?
Accettate assegni/assegni turistici?
Ahch-cheht-tah'-teh ahs-seh'-nyee/ahs-seh'-nyee too-rees'-tee-chee?

I would like a roll of color/black and white film.
Vorrei un film a colori/in bianco e nero.
Vohr-reh'-ee oon feelm ah koh-loh'-ree/een bee-ahn'-koh eh neh'-roh.

Here are some films to develop.
Vorrei far sviluppare questi film.
Vohr-reh'-ee fahr svee-loop-pah'-reh koo-ehs'-tee feelm.

Sightseeing

Where is the museum/zoo?
Dove è il museo/lo zoo?
Doh'-veh eh eel moo-zeh'-oh/loh dzoh'-oh?

Do we have to pay to go in?
Dobbiamo pagare per entrare?
Dohb-bee-ah'-moh pah-gah'-reh pehr ehn-trah'-reh?

What hours are the museums open?
Quando sono aperti i musei?
Koo-ahn'-doh soh'-noh ah-pehr'-tee ee moo-zeh'-ee?

Entertainment

I would like to see an opera.
Vorrei vedere un'opera.
Vohr-reh'-ee veh-deh'-reh oon-oh'-peh-rah.

We would like a table for two, please.
Un tavolo per due, per favore.
Oon tah'-voh-loh pehr doo'-eh, pehr fah-voh'-reh.

May we have a menu/wine list, please?
Vuol darci il menù/la lista dei vini, per favore?
Voo-ohl' dahr'-chee eel meh-noo'/lah lees'-tah deh'-ee vee'-nee, pehr fah-voh'-reh?

What do you recommend?
Lei, che cosa raccomanda?
Leh'-ee, keh koh'-zah rahk-koh-mahn'-dah?

Please bring the check.
Il conto, per favore.
Eel kohn'-toh, pehr fah-voh'-reh.

Is the tip included?
È incluso il servizio?
Eh een-kloo'-zoh eel sehr-vee'-tsee-oh?

Where do I pay?
Dove pago?
Doh'-veh pah'-goh?

There is a mistake in the bill.
C'è un errore nel conto.
Cheh oon ehr-roh'-reh nehl kohn'-toh.

Health

I don't feel well.
Non mi sento bene.
Nohn mee sehn'-toh beh'-neh.

I need a doctor/dentist.
Ho bisogno di un medico/dentista.
Oh bee-zoh'-nyoh dee oon meh'-dee-koh/dehn-tees'-tah.

I have a headache/stomachache/toothache.
Ho mal di testa/stomaco/denti.
Oh mahl dee tehs'-tah/stoh'-mah-koh/dehn'-tee.

I have a bad cold/fever.
Ho un brutto raffreddore/ho la febbre.
Oh oon broot'-toh rahf-frehd-doh'-reh/oh lah fehb'-breh.

I have burned myself.
Mi sono bruciato.
Mee soh'-noh broo-chee-ah'-toh.

My . . . hurts.
Mi fa male il/la . . . .
Mee fah mah'-leh eel/lah . . . .

My . . . is bleeding.
Mi sanguina il/la . . . .
Mee sahn-goo-ee'-nah eel/lah . . . .

Please fill this prescription.
Vorrei questa medicina.
Vohr-reh'-ee koo-ehs'-tah meh-dee-chee'-nah

Emergencies

Help!
Aiuto!
Ah-ee-oo'-toh.

Police!
Polizia!
Poh-lee-tsee'-ah.

Please call a policeman/an ambulance.
Chiami la polizia/l'ambulanza, per favore.
Kee-ah'-mee lah poh-lee-tsee'-ah/lahm-boo-lahn'-tsah, pehr fah-voh'-reh.

I need a lawyer.
Ho bisogno di un avvocato.
Oh bee-zoh'-nyoh dee oon ahv-voh-kah'-toh.

I have been robbed.
Mi hanno derubato.
Mee ahn'-noh deh-roo-bah'-toh.

Is there anyone here who speaks English?
C'è qualcuno qui che parli inglese?
Cheh koo-ahl-koo'-noh koo-ee' keh pahr'-lee een-gleh'-zeh?

I am lost.
Ho perso la giusta direzione.
Oh pehr'-soh lah jee-oos'-tah dee-reh-tsee-oh'-neh.

Someone is injured.
Qualcuno si è fatto male
Koo-ahl-koo'-noh see eh faht'-toh mah'-leh.

Menu Reader

Beverages

acqua [*ah'-koo-ah*] water
  fresca [*frehs'-kah*] cold water
  minerale [*mee-neh-rah'-leh*] mineral water
acquavite [*ahk-koo-ah-vee'-teh*] liquor, brandy
aperitivo [*ah-peh-ree-tee'-voh*] aperitif (drink before meals)
aranciata [*ah-rahn-chee-ah'-tah*] orangeade
bibite [*bee'-bee-teh*] soft drinks
birra [*beer'-rah*] beer
caffè [*kahf-feh'*] coffee
  espresso [*ehs-prehs'-soh*] strong black coffee (Italian style)
  americano [*ah-meh-ree-kah'-noh*] American-style coffee
  freddo [*frehd'-doh*] iced coffee
  latte [*laht'-teh*] coffee with milk (sugar)
  macchiato [*mahk-kee-ah'-toh*] light coffee
  cappuccino [*kahp-poo-chee'-noh*] coffee with cream
  nero [*neh'-roh*] black coffee
cioccolata [*chee-ohk-koh-lah'-tah*] chocolate
  con latte [*kohn laht'-teh*] hot chocolate
ghiacciata [*gee-ahch-chee-ah'-tah*] fruit drink over ice
grappa [*grahp'-pah*] grape brandy
latte [*laht'-teh*] milk
limonata [*lee-moh-nah'-tah*] lemonade
succo [*sook'-koh*] juice
  d'arancia [*dah-rahn'-chee-ah*] orange
  di pomodoro [*dee poh-moh-doh'-roh*] tomato
  di frutta [*dee froot'-tah*] fruit
tè [*teh*] tea
vino [*vee'-noh*] wine
  bianco [*bee-ahn'-koh*] white wine
  da tavola [*dah tah'-voh-lah*] table wine
  Marsala [*mahr-sah'-lah*] renowned Sicilian red dessert wine

rosato, rosatello [*roh-zah'-toh, roh-zah-tehl'-loh*] rosé wine
rosso [*rohs'-soh*] red wine
spumante [*spoo-mahn'-teh*] sparkling wine

The Menu

acciughe [*ahch-chee-oo'-geh*] anchovies
aceto [*ah-cheh'-toh*] vinegar
aglio [*ah'-lyoh*] garlic
agnello [*ah-nyehl'-loh*] lamb
  abbacchio alla cacciatora [*ahb-bahk'-kee-oh ahl'-lah kahch-chee-ah-toh'-rah*] lamb with garlic and white wine
agnolotti [*ah-nyoh-loht'-tee*] small filled envelopes of dough
alla casalinga [*ahl'-lah kah-zah-leen'-gah*] homemade
alla francese [*ahl'-lah frahn-cheh'-zeh*] cooked in butter
all'inglese [*ahl-leen-gleh'-zeh*] boiled
all'italiana [*ahl-lee-tah-lee-ah'-nah*] with pasta
alla napoletana [*ahl'-lah nah-poh-leh-tah'-nah*] breaded
alla romana [*ahl'-lah roh-mah'-nah*] sautéed
alla spagnola [*ahl'-lah spah-nyoh'-lah*] with tomatoes
al sangue/poco cotto [*ahl sahn-goo-eh/poh'-koh koht'-toh*] rare
antipasto [*ahn-tee-pahs'-toh*] hors d'oeuvres
arancia [*ah-rahn'-chee-ah*] orange
arrosto di vitello [*ahr-rohs'-toh dee vee-tehl'-loh*] roast veal
asparagi [*ahs-pah'-rah-jee*] asparagus
ben cotto [*behn koht'-toh*] well done
biscotti [*bees-koht'-tee*] cookies, crackers
bistecca [*bees-tehk'-kah*] steak
  all'inglese [*ahl-leen-gleh'-zeh*] rare
  ben cotto [*behn koht'-toh*] well done
bollito [*bohl-lee'-toh*] boiled
braciola [*brah-chee-oh'-lah*] rib steak
  di maiale [*dee mah-ee-ah'-lee*] pork chop
  di manzo [*dee mahn'-tsoh*] rolled beef
  spezzatino di manzo [*spehts-tsah-tee'-noh dee mahn'-tsoh*] beef stew
broccoli [*brohk'-koh-lee*] broccoli
brodo di pesce [*broh'-doh dee peh'-sheh*] seafood chowder
burro [*boor'-roh*] butter

cannelloni [*kahn-nehl-loh'-nee*] meat-filled pasta
carciofi [*kahr-chee-oh'-fee*] artichokes
carne [*kahr'-neh*] meat
carote [*kah-roh'-teh*] carrots
cavolfiore [*kah-vohl-fee-oh'-reh*] cauliflower
cavoli [*kah'-voh-lee*] cabbages
cervello [*chehr-vehl'-loh*] brains
cetriolo [*cheh-tree-oh'-loh*] cucumber
ciliege [*chee-lee-eh'-jeh*] cherries
cipolle [*chee-pohl'-leh*] onions
composta di frutta [*kohm-pohs'-tah dee froot'-tah*] stewed fruit
coscia di montone [*koh'-shee-ah dee mohn-toh'-neh*] leg of lamb
costoletta [*kohs-toh-leht'-tah*] chop, cutlet
   alla bolognese [*ahl'-lah boh-loh-nyeh'-zeh*] with melted
   cheese
   alla milanese [*ahl'-lah mee-lah-neh'-zeh*] breaded
cotto [*koht'-toh*] cooked, stewed
crudo [*kroo'-doh*] raw
dolce [*dohl'-cheh*] dessert
dolci [*dohl'-chee*] pastries, cakes
fagioli [*fah-jee-oh'-lee*] beans
fagiolini [*fah-jee-oh-lee'-nee*] stringbeans
fave [*fah'-veh*] broad beans
fegato [*feh'-gah-toh*] liver
fettuccine [*feht-too-chee'-neh*] noodles
fichi [*fee'-kee*] figs
filetto [*fee-leht'-toh*] fillet
   di bue [*dee boo'-eh*] fillet of beef
   di sogliola [*dee soh-lyoh'-lah*] fillet of sole
formaggio [*fohr-mahj'-jee-oh*] cheese
fragole [*frah'-goh-leh*] strawberries
frittata [*freet-tah'-tah*] omelet
fritelle [*free-tehl'-leh*] pancakes
fritto [*freet'-toh*] fried
fritto misto [*freet'-toh mees'-toh*] assorted tiny fried fish
frutta [*froot'-tah*] fruit
gamberi [*gahm'-beh-ree*] shrimp
gelato [*jeh-lah'-toh*] ice cream
gnocchi [*nyohk'-kee*] dumplings

granchio [*grahn'-kee-oh*] crab, crabmeat

insalata [*een-sah-lah'-tah*] salad
  mista [*mees'-tah*] mixed
  russa [*roos'-sah*] potato
  verde [*vehr'-deh*] lettuce

lasagne [*lah-zah'-nyeh*] a kind of large, flat spaghetti

lattuga [*laht-too'-gah*] lettuce

legumi [*leh-goo'-mee*] vegetables

maccheroni [*mahk-keh-roh'-nee*] macaroni

maiale [*mah-ee-ah'-leh*] pork

manicotti [*mah-nee-koht'-tee*] pasta with a filling of chopped ham and ricotta cheese

manzo [*mahn'-tsoh*] beef
  arrosto ripieno [*ahr-rohs'-toh ree-pee-eh'-noh*] stuffed roast
  lesso [*lehs'-soh*] boiled

marinata [*mah-ree-nah'-tah*] marinated, pickled

marmellata [*mahr-mehl-lah'-tah*] jam

mela [*meh'-lah*] apple

melanzana [*meh-lahn-dzah'-nah*] eggplant

melone [*meh-loh'-neh*] melon

minestra [*mee-nehs'-trah*] soup
  in brodo [*een broh'-doh*] bouillon with noodles or rice
  di funghi [*dee foon'-gee*] cream of mushroom soup

minestrone [*mee-nehs-troh'-neh*] thick vegetable soup

mostarda [*mohs-tahr'-dah*] mustard

olio [*oh'-lee-oh*] oil
  d'oliva [*doh-lee'-vah*] olive oil

olive [*oh-lee'-veh*] olives

osso buco [*ohs'-soh boo'-koh*] veal shank stewed in wine and tomatoes

ostriche [*ohs'-tree-keh*] oysters

pan di Genova [*pahn dee jeh'-noh-vah*] almond cake

pan di spagna [*pahn dee spah'-nyah*] sponge cake

pancetta [*pahn-cheht'-tah*] bacon

pagnotta [*pah-nyoht'-tah*] long loaf of bread

pane [*pah'-neh*] bread
  tostato [*tohs-tah'-toh*] toasted bread

panettone [*pah-neht-toh'-neh*] raisin cake (Milan)

panino [*pah-nee'-noh*] roll, bun

imbottito [*eem-boht-tee'-toh*] sandwich

pasta (asciutta) [*pahs'-tah (ah-shee-oot'-tah)*] the traditional Italian first course (macaroni)

  al burro [*ahl boor'-roh*] with butter

  al sugo [*ahl soo'-goh*] with tomato sauce

  al sugo di carne/al ragù [*ahl soo'-goh dee kahr'-neh/ahl rah-goo'*] with meat sauce

pasticceria [*pahs-teech-cheh-ree'-ah*] pastry

patate [*pah-tah'-teh*] potatoes

  al forno [*ahl fohr'-noh*] baked

  fritte [*freet'-teh*] French fried

  lesse [*lehs'-seh*] boiled

  in padella [*een pah-dehl'-lah*] home fried

  purèe di patate [*poo-reh' dee pah-tah'-teh*] mashed

pepe [*peh'-peh*] black pepper

peperoni [*peh-peh-roh'-nee*] green peppers

pera [*peh'-rah*] pear

pesca [*pehs'-kah*] peach

pesce [*peh'-sheh*] fish

piselli [*pee-zehl'-lee*] peas

pollo [*pohl'-loh*] chicken

  alla diavola [*ahl'-lah dee-ah'-voh-lah*] grilled with pepper, pimiento, mustard

  alla cacciattora [*ahl'-lah kahch-chee-ah-toh'-rah*] chicken with tomato and vegetable sauce

polpette [*pohl-peht'-teh*] meat balls

polpettone [*pohl-peht-toh'-neh*] meat loaf

pomodori [*poh-moh-doh'-ree*] tomatoes

pompelmo [*pohm-pehl'-moh*] grapefruit

prosciutto [*proh-shee-oot'-toh*] ham

ravioli [*rah-vee-oh'-lee*] pasta stuffed with meat, cheese, etc.

  alla fiorentina [*ahl'-lah fee-oh-rehn-tee'-nah*] with cheese

  alla vegetariana [*ahl'-lah veh-jeh-tah-ree-ah'-nah*] with tomato sauce

  fatti in casa [*faht'-tee een kah'-zah*] homemade

ripieno con carne [*ree-pee-eh'-noh kohn kahr'-neh*] stuffed with meat

riso [*ree'-zoh*] rice

risotto [*ree-zoht'-toh*] rice with butter, white wine, etc.

alla milanese [*ahl'-lah mee-lah-neh'-zeh*] with white wine, parmesan cheese, and saffron
rosbif [*rohz-beef'*] roast beef
salame [*sah-lah'-meh*] salami
sale [*sah'-leh*] salt
salmone affumicato [*sahl-moh'-neh ahf-foo-mee-kah'-toh*] smoked salmon
salsiccia [*sahl-seech'-chee-ah*] sausage
saltimbocca [*sahl-teem-bohk'-kah*] veal and ham dish
scaloppine al Marsala [*skah-lohp-pee'-neh ahl mahr-sah'-lah*] thin sautéed slices of veal with Marsala wine sauce
sedano [*seh'-dah-noh*] celery
spaghetti [*spah-geht'-tee*] spaghetti
alla bolognese [*ahl'-lah boh-loh-nyeh'-zeh*] with meat sauce
alla bosaiola [*ahl'-lah boh-zah-ee-oh'-lah*] with tuna, mushrooms and cheese
alla carbonara [*ahl'-lah kahr-boh-nah'-rah*] cooked with eggs and bacon
al sugo di carne [*ahl soo'-goh dee kahr'-neh*] with meat sauce
spinaci [*spee-nah'-chee*] spinach
tagliatelle [*tah-lyah-tehl'-leh*] long, narrow noodles
tonno [*tohn'-noh*] tuna
torta [*tohr'-tah*] cake, open pie
uova [*oo-oh'-vah*] eggs
a la coque [*ah lah kohk*] soft-boiled
fritte [*freet'-teh*] fried
sode [*soh'-deh*] hard-boiled
strapazzate [*strah-pahts-tsah'-teh*] scrambled
uva [*oo'-vah*] grapes
verdura [*vehr-doo'-rah*] vegetables
vermicelli [*vehr-mee-chehll'-lee*] thin noodles
vitello al forno [*vee-tehl'-loh ahl fohr'-noh*] roast veal
vongole [*vohn'-goh-leh*] small clams
zabaglione [*dzah-bah-lyoh'-neh*] dessert of beaten egg yolks, sugar and Marsala wine, usually served warm
zucchero [*dzook'-keh-roh*] sugar
zucchini [*dzook-kee'-nee*] squash
zuppa [*dzoop'-pah*] soup
alla pavese [*ahl'-lah pah-veh'-zeh*] consommé

A Concise Italian Grammar

Nouns

1. Italian nouns have grammatical gender. Nouns ending in *-o* are usually masculine, and those ending in *-a* feminine. Singular nouns ending in *-e* may be masculine or feminine, and they are marked *m.* or *f.* in the Dictionary. To form the plural, the *-o* and *-e* endings regularly become *-i*; the *-a* ending becomes *-e*.

2. Some nouns do not change in the plural, such as masculine nouns ending in *-a*, *il cinema, i cinema*, and those nouns ending in an accented vowel, *la città, le città*. The plurals of nouns (and adjectives) ending in *-co* and *-go* are *-ci* and *-gi* in some cases, but in others *-chi* and *-ghi*.

lago	lake	**laghi**	**amico**	friend	**amici**
fuoco	fire	**fuochi**	**fico**	fig	**fichi**

Irregular plurals and other exceptions to these rules are shown in the Dictionary.

Articles

1. An article agrees with the noun it precedes, and is sometimes the best clue to the gender and number of the noun. In the masculine, the form of the article depends on the first letter of the word which follows it, whether noun or adjective.

2. The forms of the *definite article*, the, are:

	Masculine		Feminine	
	Sing.	Pl.	Sing.	Pl.
Before most consonants	**il**	**i**	**la**	**le**
Before impure s, z, gn, ps	**lo**	**gli**	**la**	**le**
Before vowels	**l'**	**gli (gl')**	**l'**	**le (l')**
	lo stato	**gli stati**	**il grande stato**	

343

3. When *a*, *di*, *da*, *in*, and *su* precede a definite article, the two words contract:

	il	lo	i	gli	la	le	l'
a	al	allo	ai	agli	alla	alle	all'
di	del	dello	dei	degli	della	delle	dell'
da	dal	dallo	dai	dagli	dalla	dalle	dall'
in	nel	nello	nei	negli	nella	nelle	nell'
su	sul	sullo	sui	sugli	sulla	sulle	sull'

4. The forms of the *indefinite article*, a, an, are:

	Masculine		Feminine	
	Sing.	*Pl.*	*Sing.*	*Pl.*
Before most consonants	**un**	**dei**	**una**	**delle**
Before impure s, z, gn, ps	**uno**	**degli**	**una**	**delle**
Before vowels	**un**	**degli**	**un'**	**delle**

uno specchio   degli specchii   un grande specchio

5. The *partitive article* (*dei*, *delle*, etc.) is used when speaking of an indefinite quantity. The nearest English equivalent is "some" or "any," but often English does not express the idea at all. The partitive is formed by the contraction of the preposition *di* and the definite article, as shown above.

Qualifying Adjectives

1. There are two classes of adjectives: (*a*) gender adjectives ending in -*o* in the masculine and having four forms: -*o*, -*a* in the singular, -*i*, -*e* in the plural; (*b*) neuter adjectives having two forms: -*e* in the singular, -*i* in the plural, the masculine and feminine being identical. Adjectives agree in number and gender with the nouns they modify. An adjective which modifies two or more nouns is always masculine plural if at least one noun is masculine.

2. The adjective normally follows the noun, but certain adjectives usually precede it — demonstratives, numerals, possessives, and the following (unless they are modified by an adverb or unless special emphasis is desired): *molto*, *tutto*,

giovane, vecchio, buono, cattivo, bello, brutto, lungo, largo, breve, grande, piccolo, nuovo, antico, altro.

3. The comparative of adjectives is formed by using *più*, more, or *meno*, less, before the adjective. The equivalent of "than" in comparisons is *di* before nouns, pronouns, and numbers, and *che* before adjectives, adverbs, prepositions, participles, and infinitives.

Pietro è più intelligente di Marco.

Peter is more intelligent than Mark.

Dino è meno forte che intelligente.

Dino is less strong than intelligent.

The relative superlative is formed by the definite article and *più* or *meno*.

The absolute superlative is formed either by adding *-issimo*, which changes according to gender and number, or by using modifying adverbs *molto, assai*, etc., with the adjective.

Certain adjectives have irregular as well as regular forms of comparison, for example, *grande*, big, great, *maggiore*, bigger, greater; *cattivo*, bad, *peggiore*, worse.

Personal Pronouns

1. Italian has different pronoun forms for subject, object, and indirect object, plus a special category called disjunctives.

	Subj.	Dir. Obj.	Indir. Obj.	Disjunctive
			Singular	
I	io	mi	mi	me
you (familiar)	tu	ti	ti	te
he, she, it	lui	lo	gli	lui
	lei	la	le	lei
you (polite)	lei	la	le	lei, sè
			Plural	
we	noi	ci	ci	noi
you (familiar)	voi	vi	vi	voi
they	loro	li, le	loro (gli)	loro
you (polite)	loro	li, le	loro	loro, sè

2. Subject pronouns are often omitted when the verb ending clearly indicates the subject.

3. The second person singular form *tu* and its corresponding verb forms are used familiarly, with relatives and close friends. The polite or formal form of address is *lei, loro*.

4. All pronouns except disjunctives and the plural indirect object *loro* precede the verb. If both direct and indirect objects occur in the same clause, the indirect object precedes the direct object. When *gli* or *le* precedes a direct object pronoun, it is written *glie* and combined with the direct object.

> **Glielo do.** I give it to him.

5. Personal pronouns contract with words beginning with a vowel. Exceptions are *li, le,* and *loro*; and *ci* does not contract with the letters *u, o, a*.

> **T'aspetto.** I wait for you.
> **Ci amano.** They love us.

6. The word *stesso*, self, is used with a personal pronoun for emphasis, as in English.

> **È venuto lui stesso.** He himself came.

7. The disjunctive form, so called because it is independent of the verb, is used after prepositions, in exclamations and for emphasis, after *come* and *quanto*, after comparisons, and after *essere*.

> **Parlava con me.** He was talking to me.

Other Pronouns and Adjectives

An adjective is used with a noun; a pronoun is used instead of a noun. In Italian, the two are often the same for the possessives, demonstratives, and interrogatives.

1. *Possessive adjectives and pronouns.* Possessives are usually preceded by the definite article. The adjectives usually precede the noun, but may follow it for emphasis.

| | Masculine | | Feminine | |
	Sing.	Pl.	Sing.	Pl.
my	**il mio**	**i miei**	**la mia**	**le mie**
your	**il tuo**	**i tuoi**	**la tua**	**le tue**
his, her, its, your	**il suo**	**i suoi**	**la sua**	**le sue**
our	**il nostro**	**i nostri**	**la nostra**	**le nostre**
your	**il vostro**	**i vostri**	**la vostra**	**le vostre**
their, your	**il loro**	**i loro**	**la loro**	**le loro**

Since possessives agree in gender and number with the object possessed, not the possessor, the phrase *il suo libro* can mean either "his book" or "her book," depending on the context. To avoid ambiguity you may rephrase the sentence. Instead of saying *la sua casa*, you may say *la casa di Carlo* if you mean "Charles's house."

2. *Demonstrative adjectives and pronouns.* The demonstratives have the following forms:

| | THIS, THIS ONE | | THESE | |
| | THE LATTER | | | |
	m. sing.	*f. sing.*	*m. pl.*	*f. pl.*
	questo	**questa**	**questi**	**queste**
	THAT, THAT ONE		THOSE	
	THE FORMER			
Before most consonants	**quel**	**quella**	**quei**	**quelle**
Before impure s, z, gn, ps	**quello**	**quella**	**quegli**	**quelle**

When the singular adjective precedes words beginning with a vowel, the final vowel of the adjective is dropped.

3. *Interrogative adjectives and pronouns.* (*a*) The interrogative *what?* is expressed by *che* as an adjective, *che cosa* (or simply *che* or *cosa*) as a pronoun. The pronoun is always singular, and the adjective has the same form with nouns of any gender and number.

> **Che libri hai letto?** What books have you read?
> **Che cosa/Che/Cosa vuoi?** What do you want?

(*b*) *Who, whom, whose,* is expressed by *chi* for both genders, and as a pronoun it is followed by a singular verb, unless the verb is a form of *essere*, to be. *Chi* is used with the preposition *di* to mean *whose*.

> **Chi va prima?**   Who goes first?
> **Con chi parlavi?**   Whom were you talking to?
> **Chi sono quelle donne?**   Who are those women?
> **Di chi è questo libro?**   Whose book is this?

(*c*) *Quale* and *quali* are the singular and plural forms, respectively, for *which?*, *which one?* They are used with both masculine and feminine.

> **Quale di quelle case e la sua?**
>   Which one of those houses is yours?
> **Di quali ragazzi parli?**
>   Which boys are you talking about?

(*d*) The adjective *quanto* has four regular endings, -*o* and -*a* in the singular, meaning *how much*, and -*i* and -*e* in the plural, meaning *how many*.

4. *Relative pronouns*. (*a*) The most common relative pronoun is *che*, who, whom, that, which. It is used as the subject or direct object of a verb, but not after a preposition.

> **La ragazza che parlava è mia sorella.**
>   The girl who was speaking is my sister.
> **Mi piaciono i libri che mi hai dato.**
>   I like the books (that) you gave me.

Note in the second sentence that the word for "that" may not be omitted in Italian, though it often is in English.

(*b*) *Cui* means *whom* or *which* as the object of a preposition, the one form functioning for persons and things of all genders and numbers. When preceded by a noun and the definite article, *cui* means *whose*.

> **i ragazzi di cui parlo**
>   the boys of whom I am talking
> **la signora la cui madre è morta**
>   the lady whose mother is dead

(*c*) *Quale* (plural *quali*) is used sparingly in place of *che* and *cui* when there is a possibility of ambiguity. It is used with the article agreeing in gender and number with its reference noun.

La figlia del professore, della quale parlavamo, è qui.
The daughter of the professor, of whom (f.) we were speaking, is here.

Quel libro e la penna con la quale scrivo sono miei.
That book and the pen with which I am writing are mine.

(*d*) *Quel che*, *ciò che*, and *quello* are different ways of saying *what*. They are singular and refer to things.

Io so quel che lui vuole.
I know what he wants.

Ciò che egli dice non è vero.
What he says is not true.

(*e*) *Chi*, meaning he who, she who, the one who, those who, is always singular, even though the English translation may be plural. It may be replaced by *colui che* (m.), *colei che* (f.), or *coloro che* (plural, using plural verb).

Chi visita l'Italia è colpito dalla sua bellezza.
He who visits (One who visits/Those who visit) Italy is (are) struck by its beauty.

Chi is at times used as a correlative pronoun, repeated before each verb.

Chi giocava, chi ballava.
Some were playing, some were dancing.

Adverbs

In Italian, adverbs are formed from adjectives in two ways. The usual form is by adding -*mente* to the feminine form, unless the ending is -*le* or -*re*, in which case the -*e* is dropped before -*mente*. Some adverbs can be formed from an adjective preceded by a preposition.

rapido	**rapidamente**	rapidly
felice	**felicemente**	happily
abile	**abilmente**	ably
recente	**recentemente** *or* **di recente**	recently
breve	**brevemente** *or* **in breve**	briefly

Some words function as both adjective and adverb: *basso, caro, certo, lontano, molto, piano, poco, proprio, sicuro, vero, vicino.*

Some adverbs, like adjectives, have irregular comparative and superlative forms:

Positive	*Comparative*	*Relative Superlative*	*Absolute Superlative*
bene, well	**meglio**	**il meglio**	**ottimamente**
male, badly	**peggio**	**il peggio**	**pessimamente**
molto, much	**più**	**il più**	**massimamente**
poco, little	**meno**	**il meno**	**minimamente**

Prepositions

Preposition usage is idiomatic in any language and it must be learned by exposure. The dictionary gives most equivalences. Prepositions contract with the definite article, as shown in the chart on page 344. The following prepositions, when used with a personal pronoun, must be followed by *di*:

contro	against	**dopo**	after	**sopra**	on, upon
dentro	inside	**fra**	between	**sotto**	under
dietro	behind	**senza**	without	**su**	on, over

Verbs

Italian verbs have different forms for the different persons and numbers, as well as for the different tenses. The infinitive form of the verb is given in the dictionary. For a special category of verbs in Italian, the reflexive, the subject and object are the same. The infinitive form of a reflexive verb is formed by the regular infinitive without the final vowel and with an added -*si* (*lavare*, to wash; *lavarsi*, to wash oneself). These verbs are conjugated like any active verb, but they take the reflexive pronoun (*mi, ti, si, ci, vi, si*) that agrees in person and number with the subject. The plural form of the reflexive can express reciprocity: *Si amano.* They love each other.

Infinitives are regularly of three classes, ending in *-are*, *-ere*, or *-ire*. Conjugation tables for these regular verbs, as well as for the auxiliaries *avere* and *essere* and for many irregular verbs, are given at the end of this section.

1. Principle parts. (*a*) The *infinitive* itself is often used as a noun, (*i*) with the article as a subject of a clause, just as English uses the gerund:

>**Il mangiare troppo fa male.**
>Eating too much is harmful.

(*ii*) without the article, just as in English:

>**È importante dire la verità.**
>It is important to tell the truth.

(*iii*) as object of another verb or of a preposition:

>**una casa da affitare**   a house for rent
>**preferire dormire**   prefer to sleep

(*iv*) as an imperative:

>**Non fumare!**   Don't smoke! *or* No smoking!

(*b*) The *present gerund*, formed by dropping the infinitive ending and adding to the verb stem *-ando* for the first conjugation verbs or *-endo* for the second and third, translates the English present participle, whether or not preceded by a preposition.

>**Leggendo si imparano molte cose.**
>By reading one learns many things.
>**Vedendo che non c'era, andai via.**
>Seeing that he wasn't there, I went away.

(*c*) The *past gerund*, formed by the present gerund of the auxiliary verb and the past participle of the desired verb, is used as in English.

>**Essendo arrivato prima del tempo, dovetti aspettare.**
>Having arrived before time, I had to wait.

The gerund is also used with the present or past imperfect of the verb *stare*, stay, be, feel, to form a progressive tense.

>**Sto scrivendo una lettera.**
>I am writing a letter.

Stavo scrivendo una lettera.
I was writing a letter.

(*d*) The *present participle* of a verb is formed by adding the following endings to the verb stem: *-ante* for the first conjugation, *-ente* for the second or third. The present participle is rarely used, and some verbs do not have this form. When used it has the function of an adjective or noun: *cane dormente*, sleeping dog; *acqua corrente*, running water.

(*e*) The *past participle* of regular verbs is formed by adding to the stem *-ato*, *-uto*, or *-ito*, respectively, for the three conjugations. Many verbs, especially *-ere* verbs, have irregular past participles. The past participle is mainly used in the formation of compound tenses. In such compounds it agrees with a preceding direct object, whether noun or pronoun.

la signorina che ho invitata
the young lady I invited

The past participle is often used in an absolute construction, without the auxiliary verb.

Tornato dal lavoro è andato a dormire.
Having returned from work, he went (has gone) to sleep.

2. Verb tenses. (*a*) The *present tense* translates the English present: *parlo*, I speak, I do speak, I am speaking. Unlike English, Italian also uses the present to indicate an action that began in the past and continues in the present.

È all'ospedale da due settimane.
He (she) has been in the hospital for two weeks.

(*b*) The *imperfect* corresponds to the past progressive or to expressions showing habitual action: *piangevo*, I was crying, I used to cry, I would cry (for hours).

(*c*) The *past definite* or remote past or past absolute expresses a state of action definitely completed in the past with no relation to the present.

Prima finì gli studi e poi si sposò.
First he completed his studies and then got married.

(*d*) The *future tense* corresponds to the English future: *canterò*, I will sing. It may also be used to express probability.

Chi fischia così? Sarà Giuseppe.
Who is whistling so? It must be Joe.

(*e*) The *present conditional* is similar in form to the future tense and is used in expressing probability.

Io uscirei volentieri con quella signorina.
I would willingly go out with that young lady.
Egli non farebbe mai una cosa simile.
He would never do such a thing.

(*f*) The *imperative* is used as it is in English: the first person plural *Andiamo!* means Let's go! For the negative, the affirmative form is preceded by *non*: *Non parlate!* Don't speak! (plural you).

(*g*) The *subjunctive* in all its tenses is always used in a subordinate clause. Its use is determined by the verb in the main clause. The subjunctive is used primarily: (*i*) when the verb in the main clause is one of emotion, opinion, desire, command or wishes:

Speriamo che sia venuto.
We hope that he has come.
Crede lei che ella sia qui?
Do you think she is here?

(*ii*) after verbs referring to indefinite subjects and after impersonal expressions which do not express certainty:

Qui non c'è nessuno che capisca l'Italiano.
There is no one here who understands Italian.
È probabile che vengano anch'essi.
It is probable that they too will come.

BUT: **È evidente che ella non capisce questa lingua.**
It is evident that she does not understand this language.

(*iii*) after a relative superlative:

Questo è il libro più vecchio che io abbia.
This is the oldest book I have.

(*iv*) after adverbial expressions of time, purpose, condition;
(*v*) in the imperfect or pluperfect tense in *if*-clauses ex-

pressing a condition contrary to fact, with the verb of the main clause in the conditional:

Se io avessi denaro farei quel viaggio.
If I had money, I would take that trip.

(*h*) All *compound tenses* of verbs are a combination of a form of an auxiliary verb *avere*, have, or *essere*, be, and the past participle of the main verb. Most Italian verbs are conjugated with *avere*; *essere* is used with reflexive verbs, verbs used in the passive voice, impersonal verbs, and verbs of motion, the most common of which are:

andare	go	**ritornare**	return
venire	come	**diventare**	become
entrare	enter	**nascere**	be born
uscire	go out	**morire**	die
cadere	fall	**essere**	be
partire	leave	**salire**	climb
arrivare	arrive	**scendere**	descend
giungere	arrive	**rimanere**	remain
	restare	stay, remain	

The past participle of verbs conjugated with *essere* agrees with the subject in gender and number, unless the verb is reflexive and followed by a direct object. In that case, the participle agrees with the object.

The past participle of verbs conjugated with *avere* agrees with the subject unless the verb is preceded by a direct object, in which case the participle agrees with the object.

3. Conjugating verbs. An Italian verb has two parts: the stem, which is different for each verb, and the ending, which varies according to person, number, and tense. Conjugating a verb is a matter of finding the right stem and adding the proper ending: *parl-o*, *parl-avo*, etc. A regular verb has one stem for all tenses, while an irregular verb's stem may change. The endings remain basically the same.

There are three groups of regular verbs which you will recognize by the ending of the infinitive: verbs in *-are* (*parlare*, to speak); verbs in *-ere* (*credere*, to believe); and verbs in *-ire* (*partire*, to leave; *capire*, to understand). Within the third group are two subgroups, those adding -isc- to the stem in some tenses and those not. In general, -ire verbs having a single consonant before the infinitive ending (cap-ire) do add -isc-, and those having a double consonant (part-ire) do not. The list which follows give three basic forms for each conjugation: infinitive, present participle, and past participle. The stem precedes the hyphen. The endings which follow it must be added to the stem of the verb you are using.

4. Model Conjugation.

1st Group	2nd Group	3rd Group	
INFINITIVE			
parl-are	**cred-ere**	**part-ire**	**cap-ire**
to speak	to believe, think	to leave	to understand
PAST PART.:			
parl-ato	cred-uto	part-ito	cap-ito
PRESENT PART.:			
parl-ante	cred-ente	part-ente	——

INDICATIVE

PRESENT:			
parl-o	cred-o	part-o	cap-isco
parl-i	cred-i	part-i	cap-isci
parl-a	cred-e	part-e	cap-isce
parl-iamo	cred-iamo	part-iamo	cap-iamo
parl-ate	cred-ete	part-ite	cap-ite
parl-ano	cred-ono	part-ono	cap-iscono
IMPERFECT:			
parl-avo	cred-evo	part-ivo	cap-ivo
parl-avi	cred-evi	part-ivi	cap-ivi
parl-ava	cred-eva	part-iva	cap-iva
parl-avamo	cred-evamo	part-ivamo	cap-ivamo
parl-avate	cred-evate	part-ivate	cap-ivate
parl-avano	cred-evano	part-ivano	cap-ivano
PAST DEFINITE:			
parl-ai	cred-ei	part-ii	cap-ii
parl-asti	cred-esti	part-isti	cap-isti
parl-ò	cred-è	part-ì	cap-ì
parl-ammo	cred-emmo	part-immo	cap-immo

| parl-aste | cred-este | part-iste | cap-iste |
| parl-arono | cred-erono | part-irono | cap-irono |

FUTURE:

parl-erò	cred-erò	part-irò	cap-irò
parl-erai	cred-erai	part-irai	cap-irai
parl-erà	cred-erà	part-irà	cap-irà
parl-eremo	cred-eremo	part-iremo	cap-iremo
parl-erete	cred-erete	part-irete	cap-irete
parl-eranno	cred-eranno	part-iranno	cap-ranno

CONDITIONAL:

parl-erei	cred-erei	part-irei	cap-irei
parl-eresti	cred-eresti	part-iresti	cap-iresti
parl-erebbe	cred-erebbe	part-irebbe	cap-irebbe
parl-eremmo	cred-emmo	part-iremmo	cap-iremmo
parl-ereste	cred-este	part-ireste	cap-ireste
parl-erebbero	cred-erebbero	part-irebbero	cap-irebbero

IMPERATIVE:

___	___	___	___
parl-a	cred-i	part-i	cap-isci
parl-i	cred-a	part-a	cap-isca
parl-iamo	cred-iamo	part-iamo	cap-iamo
parl-ate	cred-ete	part-ite	cap-ite
parl-ino	cred-ano	part-ano	cap-iscano

SUBJUNCTIVE

PRESENT:

parl-i	cred-a	part-a	cap-isca
parl-i	cred-a	part-a	cap-isca
parl-i	cred-a	part-a	cap-isca
parl-iamo	cred-iamo	part-iamo	cap-iamo
parl-iate	cred-iate	part-iate	cap-iate
parl-ino	cred-ano	part-ano	cap-iscano

IMPERFECT:

parl-assi	cred-essi	part-issi	cap-issi
parl-assi	cred-essi	part-issi	cap-issi
parl-asse	cred-esse	part-isse	cap-isse
parl-assimo	cred-essimo	part-issimo	cap-issimo

parl-aste	cred-este	part-iste	cap-iste
parl-assero	cred-essero	part-issero	cap-issero

PERFECT:

ho parlato, creduto, capito, etc.; sono partito, -a, etc.

PAST PERFECT:

avevo parlato, creduto, capito, etc.; ero partito, -a, etc.

FUTURE PERFECT:

avrò parlato, creduto, capito, etc.; sarò partito, -a, etc.

CONDITIONAL PERFECT:

avrei parlato, creduto, capito, etc.; sarei partito, -a, etc.

PERFECT SUBJUNCTIVE:

abbia parlato, creduto, capito, etc.; sia partito, -a, etc.

5. Auxiliary Verbs.

INF.:   **avere,** to have

PAST PART.:   avuto

INDICATIVE

PRESENT:

ho	abbiamo
hai	avete
ha	hanno

IMPERFECT:

avevo	avevamo
avevi	avevate
aveva	avevano

PAST DEFINITE:

ebbi	avemmo
avesti	aveste
ebbe	ebbero

FUTURE:

avrò	avremo
avrai	avrete
avrà	avranno

CONDITIONAL:

avrei	avremmo
avresti	avreste
avrebbe	avrebbero

PERFECT:
  ho avuto, etc.
PAST PERFECT:
  avevo avuto, etc.
FUTURE PERFECT:
  avrò avuto, etc.
CONDITIONAL PERFECT:
  avrei avuto, etc.
IMPERATIVE:

——	abbiamo
abbi	abbiate
abbia	abbiano

SUBJUNCTIVE

PRESENT:

abbia	abbiamo
abbia	abbiate
abbia	abbiano

IMPERFECT:

avessi	avessimo
avessi	aveste
avesse	avessere

PERFECT:
  abbia avuto, etc.

INF.:   **essere,** to be
PAST PART.:   stato

INDICATIVE

PRESENT:

sono	siamo
sei	siete
è	sono

IMPERFECT:

ero	eravamo
eri	eravate
era	erano

PAST DEFINITE:

fui	fummo
fosti	foste

fu	furono

FUTURE:

sarò	saremo
sarai	sarete
sarà	saranno

CONDITIONAL:

sarei	saremmo
saresti	sareste
sarebbe	sarebbero

PERFECT:
sono stato, etc.

PAST PERFECT:
ero stato, etc.

FUTURE PERFECT:
sarò stato, etc.

CONDITIONAL PERFECT:
sarei stato, etc.

IMPERATIVE:

———	siamo
sii	siate
sia	siano

SUBJUNCTIVE

PRESENT:

sia	siamo
sia	siate
sia	siano

IMPERFECT:

fossi	fossimo
fossi	foste
fosse	fossero

PERFECT:
sia stato, etc.

6. Irregular verbs. This list shows the conjugations of those tenses containing irregular forms; that is, the tenses shown here cannot be derived from the "Model Conjugations." Tenses not shown are regularly formed.

accendere light PAST PART. acceso

PAST DEFINITE accesi, accendesti, accese, accendemmo, accendeste, accesero

accogliere receive, welcome PAST PART. accolto
PRESENT accolgo, accogli, accoglie, accogliamo, accogliete, accolgono
PAST DEFINITE accolsi, accogliesti, accolse, accogliemmo, accoglieste, accolsero

andare go (*Aux.*: ESSERE)
PRESENT vado, vai, va, andiamo, andate, vanno
FUTURE andrò, andrai, andrà, andremo, andrete, andranno
CONDITIONAL andrei, andresti, andrebbe, andremmo, andreste, andrebbero
IMPERATIVE và, vada, andiamo, andate, vadano
PRESENT SUBJUNCTIVE vada, vada, vada, andiamo, andiate, vadano

appartenere belong *See* TENERE

aprire open PAST PART. aperto
PAST DEFINITE aprii *or* apersi, apristi, apri *or* aperse, aprimmo, apriste, aprirono *or* apersero

assumere assume, take, hire PAST PART. assunto
PAST DEFINITE assunsi, assumesti, assunse, assunemmo, assumeste, assunsero

bere drink (Conjugated from the old infinitive *bevere*)
PAST PART. bevuto
PAST DEFINITE bevvi, bevesti, bevve, bevemmo, beveste, bevvero
FUTURE berrò, berrai, berrà, berremo, berrete, berranno
CONDITIONAL berrei, berresti, berrebbe, berremmo, berreste, berrebbero

cadere fall (*Aux.*: ESSERE)
PAST DEFINITE caddi, cadesti, cadde, cademmo, cadeste, caddero
FUTURE cadrò, cadrai, cadrà, cadremo, cadrete, cadranno
CONDITIONAL cadrei, cadresti, cadrebbe, cadremmo, cadreste, cadrebbero

chiedere ask PAST PART. chiesto
PAST DEFINITE chiesi, chiedesti, chiese, chiedemmo, chiedeste, chiesero

chiudere close PAST PART. chiuso
PAST DEFINITE chiusi, chiudesti, chiuse, chiudemmo, chiudeste, chiusero

concedere grant, concede PAST PART. concesso
PAST DEFINITE concessi, concedesti, concesse, concedemmo, concedeste, concessero

conoscere know PAST PART. conosciuto
PAST DEFINITE conobbi, conoscesti, conobbe, conoscemmo, conosceste, conobbero

coprire cover PAST PART. coperto

correggere correct PAST PART. corretto
PAST DEFINITE corressi, correggesti, corresse, correggemmo, correggeste, corressero

correre run (*Aux.*: ESSERE when it means from one place to another; otherwise AVERE) PAST PART. corso
PAST DEFINITE corsi, corresti, corse, corremmo, correste, corsero

crescere grow (*Aux.*: ESSERE except when it has a direct object) PAST PART. cresciuto
PAST DEFINITE crebbi, crescesti, crebbe, crescemmo, cresceste, crebbero

cuocere cook PAST PART. cotto
PRESENT cuocio, cuoci, cuoce, cuociamo *or* cociamo, cuocete *or* cocete, cuociono
PAST DEFINITE cossi, cocesti, cosse, cuocemmo, cuoceste, cossero
PRESENT SUBJUNCTIVE cuocia, cuocia, cuocia, cuociamo, cuociate, cuociano

dare give PAST PART. dato
PRESENT do, dai, dà, diamo, date, danno
PAST DEFINITE diedi, desti, diede, demmo, deste, diedero

IMPERFECT davo, davi, dava, davamo, davate, davano
FUTURE darò, darai, darà, daremo, darete, daranno
CONDITIONAL darei, daresti, darebbe, daremmo, dareste, darebbero
IMPERATIVE dà, dia, daimo, date, diano
PRESENT SUBJUNCTIVE dia, dia, dia, diamo, diate, diano
IMPERFECT SUBJUNCTIVE dessi, dessi, desse, dessimo, deste, dessero

decidere decide PAST PART. deciso
PAST DEFINITE decisi, decidesti, decise, decidemmo, decideste, decisero

difendere defend PAST PART. difeso
PAST DEFINITE difesi, difendesti, difese, difendemmo, difendeste, difesero

dire say, tell (Conjugated from old infinitive *dicere*) PAST PART. detto
PRESENT GERUND dicendo
PRESENT dico, dici, dice, diciamo, dite, dicono
PAST DEFINITE dissi, dicesti, disse, dicemmo, diceste, dissero
IMPERFECT dicevo, dicevi, diceva, dicevamo, dicevate, dicevano
FUTURE dirò, dirai, dirà, diremo, direte, diranno
CONDITIONAL direi, diresti, direbbe, diremmo, direste, direbbero
IMPERATIVE di' *or* dici, dica, diciamo, dite, dicano
PRESENT SUBJUNCTIVE dica, dica, dica, diciamo, diciate, dicano
IMPERFECT SUBJUNCTIVE dicessi, dicessi, dicesse, dicessimo, diceste, dicessero

discutere discuss PAST PART. discusso
PAST DEFINITE discussi, discutesti, discusse, discutemmo, discuteste, discussero

dividere divide PAST PART. diviso
PAST DEFINITE divisi, dividesti, divise, dividemmo, divideste, divisero

dovere have, must PAST PART. dovuto

PRESENT devo *or* debbo, devi, deve, dobbiamo, dovete, devono *or* debbono
PAST DEFINITE dovei *or* dovetti, dovesti, dovè *or* dovette, dovemmo, doveste, doverono *or* dovettero
FUTURE dovrò, dovrai, dovrà, dovremo, dovrete, dovranno
CONDITIONAL dovrei, dovresti, dovrebbe, dovremmo, dovreste, dovrebbero
PRESENT SUBJUNCTIVE deva, deva, deva (*or* debba, debba, debba), dobbiamo, dobbiate, devano *or* debbano

fare do, make (Conjugated from the old infinitive *facere*)
PAST PART. fatto
PRESENT GERUND facendo
PRESENT faccio, fai, fa, facciamo, fate, fanno
PAST DEFINITE feci, facesti, fece, facemmo, faceste, fecero
IMPERFECT facevo, facevi, faceva, facevamo, facevate, facevano
FUTURE farò, farai, farà, faremo, farete, faranno
CONDITIONAL farei, faresti, farebbe, faremmo, fareste, farebbero
IMPERATIVE fà, faccia, facciamo, fate, facciano
PRESENT SUBJUNCTIVE faccia, faccia, faccia, facciamo, facciate, facciano
IMPERFECT SUBJUNCTIVE facessi, facessi, facesse, facessimo, faceste, facessero

giungere arrive, reach (*Aux.*: ESSERE) PAST PART. giunto
PAST DEFINITE giunsi, giungesti, giunse, giungemmo, giungeste, giunsero

leggere read PAST PART. letto
PAST DEFINITE lessi, leggesti, lesse, leggemmo, leggeste, lessero

mantenere maintain, keep, support *See* TENERE

mettere put PAST PART. messo
PAST DEFINITE misi, mettesti, mise, mettemmo, metteste, misero

mordere bite PAST PART. morso

PAST DEFINITE morsi, mordesti, morse, mordemmo, mordeste, morsero

morire die (*Aux.*: ESSERE) PAST PART. morto
PRESENT muoio, muori, muore, moriamo, morite, muoiono
FUTURE morrò, morrai, morrà, morremo, morrete, morranno
CONDITIONAL morrei, morresti, morrebbe, morremmo, morreste, morrebbero
IMPERATIVE muori, muoia, moriamo, morite, muoiano
PRESENT SUBJUNCTIVE muoia, muoia, muoia, moriamo, moriate, muoiano
NOTE: The regular forms for the future and conditional are also used.

muovere move (*Not* to change residence) PAST PART. mosso
PRESENT muovo, muovi, muove, moviamo, movete, muovono
PAST DEFINITE mossi, movesti, mosse, movemmo, moveste, mossero
IMPERATIVE muovi, muova, muoviamo, movete, muovano
PRESENT SUBJUNCTIVE muova, muova, muova, moviamo, moviate, muovano

nascere be born (*Aux.*: ESSERE) PAST PART. nato
PAST DEFINITE egli nacque, essi nacquero

nascondere hide, conceal PAST PART. nascosto
PAST DEFINITE nascosi, nascondesti, nascose, nascondemmo, nascondeste, nascosero

offendere offend PAST PART. offeso
PAST DEFINITE offesi, offendesti, offese, offendemmo, offendeste, offesero

offrire offer PAST PART. offerto
PAST DEFINITE offrii *or* offersi, offristi, offrì *or* offerse, offrimmo, offriste, offrirono *or* offersero

perdere lose PAST PART. perduto *or* perso
PAST DEFINITE persi *or* perdei *or* perdetti, perdesti, perse *or*

perdè *or* perdette, perdemmo, perdeste, persero *or* per-
derono *or* perdettero

persuadere persuade PAST PART. persuaso
PAST DEFINITE persuasi, persuadesti, persuase, persuadem-
mo, persuadeste, persuasero

piacere like, please (*Aux.*: ESSERE) PAST PART. piaciuto
PRESENT piaccio, piaci, piace, piacciamo, piacete, piacciono
PAST DEFINITE piacqui, piacesti, piacque, piacemmo, pia-
ceste, piacquero
PRESENT SUBJUNCTIVE piaccia, piaccia, piaccia, piacciamo,
piacciate, piacciano
NOTE: This verb is used mostly in the third person singular
and plural.

piangere cry, weep PAST PART. pianto
PAST DEFINITE piansi, piangesti, pianse, piangemmo, pian-
geste, piansero

porre (ponere) put, place PAST PART. posto
PRESENT GERUND ponendo
PRESENT pongo, poni, pone, poniamo, ponete, pongono
PAST DEFINITE posi, ponesti, pose, ponemmo, poneste,
posero
FUTURE porrò, porrai, porrà, porremo, porrete, porranno
CONDITIONAL porrei, porresti, porrebbe, porremmo, por-
reste, porrebbero
IMPERFECT ponevo, ponevi, poneva, ponevamo, ponevate,
ponevano
IMPERATIVE poni, ponga, poniamo, ponete, pongano
PRESENT SUBJUNCTIVE ponga, ponga, ponga, poniamo,
poniate, pongano
IMPERFECT SUBJUNCTIVE ponessi, ponessi, ponesse, pones-
simo, poneste, ponessero

potere be able to, can, may
PRESENT posso, puoi, può, possiamo, potete, possono
FUTURE potrò, potrai, potrà, potremo, potrete, potranno
CONDITIONAL potrei, potresti, potrebbe, potremmo, po-
treste, potrebbero

IMPERATIVE possa, possa, possiamo, possiate, possano
PRESENT SUBJUNCTIVE possa, possa, possa, possiamo, possiate, possano

prendere take PAST PART. preso
PAST DEFINITE presi, prendesti, prese, prendemmo, prendeste, presero

produrre produce *See* CONDURRE

radere shave PAST PART. raso
PAST DEFINITE rasi, radesti, rase, rademmo, radeste, rasero

rendere render, give back PAST PART. reso
PAST DEFINITE resi, rendesti, rese, rendemmo, rendeste, resero

ridere laugh PAST PART. riso
PAST DEFINITE risi, ridesti, rise, ridemmo, rideste, risero

rimanere remain (*Aux.*: ESSERE) PAST PART. rimasto
PRESENT rimango, rimani, rimane, rimaniano, rimanete, rimangono
PAST DEFINITE rimasi, rimanesti, rimase, rimanemmo, rimaneste, rimasero
FUTURE rimarrò, rimarrai, rimarrà, rimarremo, rimarrete, rimarranno
CONDITIONAL rimarrei, rimarresti, rimarrebbe, rimarremmo, rimarreste, rimarrebbero
IMPERATIVE rimani, rimanga, rimaniamo, rimanete, rimangano
PRESENT SUBJUNCTIVE rimanga, rimanga, rimanga, rimaniamo, rimaniate, rimangano

rispondere answer, reply PAST PART. risposto
PAST DEFINITE risposi, rispondesti, rispose, rispondemmo, rispondeste, risposero

ritenere retain *See* TENERE

rompere break PAST PART. rotto
PAST DEFINITE ruppi, rompesti, ruppe, rompemmo, rompeste, ruppero

salire go up, climb, ascend, get on (*Aux.*: ESSERE)
PRESENT salgo, sali, sale, saliamo, salite, salgono
IMPERATIVE sali, salga, saliamo, salite, salgano
PRESENT SUBJUNCTIVE salga, salga, salga, saliamo, saliate, salgano

sapere know, know how
PRESENT so, sai, sa, sappiamo, sapete, sanno
PAST DEFINITE seppi, sapesti, seppe, sapemmo, sapeste, seppero
FUTURE saprò, saprai, saprà, sapremo, saprete, sapranno
CONDITIONAL saprei, sapresti, saprebbe, sapremmo, sapreste, saprebbero
IMPERATIVE sappi, sappia, sappiamo, sappiate, sappiano
PRESENT SUBJUNCTIVE sappia, sappia, sappia, sappiamo, sappiate, sappiano

scendere descend, go down, get off (*Aux.*: ESSERE)
PAST PART. sceso
PAST DEFINITE scesi, scendesti, scese, scendemmo, scendeste, scesero

sciogliere untie, dissolve, melt PAST PART. sciolto
PAST DEFINITE sciolsi, sciogliesti, sciolse, sciogliemmo, scioglieste, sciolsero
IMPERATIVE sciogli, sciolga, sciogliamo, sciogliete, sciolgano
PRESENT SUBJUNCTIVE sciolga, sciolga, sciolga, sciogliamo, sciogliate, sciolgano

scoprire discover PAST PART. scoperto
PAST DEFINITIVE scoprii *or* scopersi, scopristi, scoprì *or* scoperse, scoprimmo, scopriste, scoprirono *or* scopersero

scrivere write PAST PART. scritto
PAST DEFINITIVE scrissi, scrivesti, scrisse, scrivemmo, scriveste, scrissero

sedere sit (*Aux.*: ESSERE, except with a direct object)
PRESENT siedo *or* seggo, siedi, siede, sediamo, sedete, siedono *or* seggano
IMPERATIVE siedi, segga, sediamo, sedete, seggano

PRESENT SUBJUNCTIVE segga, segga, segga (*or* sieda, sieda, sieda), sediamo, sediate, seggano *or* siedano

sorgere arise, rise PAST PART. sorto
PAST DEFINITE sorsi, sorgesti, sorse, sorgemmo, sorgeste, sorsero

spendere spend PAST PART. speso
PAST DEFINITE spesi, spendesti, spese, spendemmo, spendeste, spesero

stare stay, be, stand, feel (*Aux.*: ESSERE) PAST PART. stato
PRESENT sto, stai, sta, stiamo, state, stanno
PAST DEFINITE stetti, stesti, stette, stemmo, steste, stettero
IMPERFECT stavo, stavi, stava, stavamo, stavate, stavano
FUTURE starò, starai, starà, staremo, starete, staranno
CONDITIONAL starei, staresti, starebbe, staremmo, stareste, starebbero
IMPERATIVE stà, stia, stiamo, state, stiano
PRESENT SUBJUNCTIVE stia, stia, stia, stiamo, stiate, stiano
IMPERFECT SUBJUNCTIVE stessi, stessi, stesse, stessimo, steste, stessero

supporre suppose *See* PORRE

tacere be silent, keep quiet PAST PART. taciuto
PRESENT taccio, taci, tace, taciamo, tacete, tacciono
PAST DEFINITE tacqui, tacesti, tacque, tacemmo, tacete, tacquero
IMPERATIVE taci, taccia, taciamo, tacete, tacciano
PRESENT SUBJUNCTIVE taccia, taccia, taccia, tacciamo, tacciate, tacciano (May also be written with one *c*.)

tenere hold, have, keep
PRESENT tengo, tieni, tiene, teniamo, tenete, tengono
PAST DEFINITE tenni, tenesti, tenne, tenemmo, teneste, tennero
FUTURE terrò, terrai, terrà, terremo, terrete, terranno
CONDITIONAL terrei, terresti, terrebbe, terremmo, terreste, terrebbero
IMPERATIVE tieni, tenga, teniamo, tenete, tengano
PRESENT SUBJUNCTIVE tenga, tenga, tenga, teniamo, teniate, tengano

trarre draw out; drag, haul, derive PAST PART. tratto
PRESENT GERUND traendo
PRESENT traggo, trai, trae, traiamo, traete, traggono
PAST DEFINITE trassi, traesti, trasse, traemmo, traeste, trassero
IMPERFECT traevo, traevi, traeva, traevamo, traevate, traevano
FUTURE trarrò, trarrai, trarrà, trarremo, trarrete, trarranno
CONDITIONAL trarrei, trarresti, trarrebbe, trarremmo, trarreste, trarrebbero
IMPERATIVE trai, tragga, traiamo, traete, traggano
PRESENT SUBJUNCTIVE tragga, tragga, tragga, traiamo, traiate, traggano
IMPERFECT SUBJUNCTIVE traessi, traessi, traesse, traessimo, traeste, traessero

uccidere kill PAST PART. ucciso
PAST DEFINITE uccisi, uccidesti, uccise, uccidemmo, uccideste, uccisero

udire hear
PRESENT odo, odi, ode, udiamo, udite, odono
IMPERATIVE odi, oda, udiamo, udite, odano
PRESENT SUBJUNCTIVE oda, oda, oda, udiamo, udiate, odano

uscire go out (*Aux.*: ESSERE)
PRESENT esco, esci, esce, usciamo, uscite, escono
IMPERATIVE esci, esca, usciamo, uscite, escano

valere be worth (*Aux.*: ESSERE) PAST PART. valso
PRESENT valgo, vali, vale, valiamo, valete, valgono
PAST DEFINITE valsi, valesti, valse, valemmo, valeste, valsero
FUTURE varrò, varrai, varrà, varremo, varrete, varranno
CONDITIONAL varrei, varresti, varrebbe, varremmo, varreste, varrebbero
IMPERATIVE vali, valga, valiamo, valete, valgano
PRESENT SUBJUNCTIVE valga, valga, valga, valiamo, valiate, valgano

NOTE: Usually only the third person singular and plural of this verb are used.

vedere see PAST PART. visto *or* veduto
PAST DEFINITE vidi, vedesti, vide, vedemmo, vedeste, videro
FUTURE vedrò, vedrai, vedrà, vedremo, vedrete, vedranno
CONDITIONAL vedrei, vedresti, vedrebbe, vedremmo, vedreste, vedrebbero

venire come (*Aux.*: ESSERE) PAST PART. venuto
PRESENT vengo, vieni, viene, veniamo, venite, vengono
PAST DEFINITE venni, venisti, venne, venimmo, veniste, vennero
FUTURE verrò, verrai, verrà, verremo, verrete, verranno
CONDITIONAL verrei, verresti, verrebbe, verremmo, verreste, verrebbero
IMPERATIVE vieni, venga, veniamo, venite, vengano
PRESENT SUBJUNCTIVE venga, venga, venga, veniamo, veniate, vengano

vincere win PAST PART. vinto
PAST DEFINITE vinsi, vincesti, vinse, vincemmo, vinceste, vinsero

vivere live (*Aux.*: AVERE if followed by a direct object; otherwise ESSERE.) PAST PART. vissuto
PAST DEFINITE vissi, vivesti, visse, vivemmo, viveste, vissero
FUTURE vivrò, vivrai, vivrà, vivremo, vivrete, vivranno
CONDITIONAL vivrei, vivresti, vivrebbe, vivremmo, vivreste, vivrebbero

volere want, be willing, desire, wish
PRESENT voglio, vuoi, vuole, vogliamo, volete, vogliono
PAST DEFINITE volli, volesti, volle, volemmo, voleste, vollero
FUTURE vorrò, vorrai, vorrà, vorremo, vorrete, vorranno
CONDITIONAL vorrei, vorresti, vorrebbe, vorremmo, vorreste, vorrebbero
IMPERATIVE (rarely used) vogli, voglia, vogliamo, vogliate, vogliano
PRESENT SUBJUNCTIVE voglia, voglia, voglia, vogliamo, vogliate, vogliano